Central Peripheries

FRINGE

Series Editors
Alena Ledeneva and Peter Zusi, School of Slavonic and East European Studies, UCL

The FRINGE series explores the roles that complexity, ambivalence and immeasurability play in social and cultural phenomena. A cross-disciplinary initiative bringing together researchers from the humanities, social sciences and area studies, the series examines how seemingly opposed notions such as centrality and marginality, clarity and ambiguity, can shift and converge when embedded in everyday practices.

Alena Ledeneva is Professor of Politics and Society at the School of Slavonic and East European Studies of UCL.

Peter Zusi is Associate Professor at the School of Slavonic and East European Studies of UCL.

FRINGE

Central Peripheries

Nationhood in Central Asia

Marlene Laruelle

UCLPRESS

First published in 2021 by
UCL Press
University College London
Gower Street
London WC1E 6BT

Available to download free: www.uclpress.co.uk

A CIP catalogue record for this book is available from the British Library.

ISBN: 978-1-80008-015-7 (Hbk.)
ISBN: 978-1-80008-014-0 (Pbk.)
ISBN: 978-1-80008-013-3 (PDF)
ISBN: 978-1-80008-016-4 (epub)
ISBN: 978-1-80008-017-1 (mobi)
DOI: https://doi.org/10.14324/111.9781800080133

Contents

List of figures

Previous publication

Chapter 1 was previously published as Marlene Laruelle, 'The Concept of Ethnogenesis in Central Asia: Political Context and Institutional Mediators (1940–50)', *Kritika: Explorations in Russian and Eurasian History*, 9 (1) (2008): 169–88.

Chapter 2 was previously published as Marlene Laruelle, 'The Nation Narrated: Uzbekistan's Political and Cultural Nationalism', in *Constructing the Uzbek State: Narratives of the Post-Soviet Years*, ed. Marlene Laruelle, 261–82, Lanham, MD: Lexington, 2018.

An earlier version of Chapter 3 was published as Marlene Laruelle, 'The Return of the Aryan Myth: Tajikistan in Search of a Secularized National Ideology', *Nationalities Papers*, 35 (1) (2007): 51–70.

Chapter 4 was previously published as Marlene Laruelle, 'Kyrgyzstan's Nationhood: From a Monopoly of Production to a Plural Market', in *Kyrgyzstan beyond 'Democracy Island' and 'Failing State': Social *and Political Changes in a Post-Soviet Society*, ed. Marlene Laruelle and Johan Engvall, 165–84, Lanham, MD: Lexington, 2015.

Chapter 5 was previously published as Marlene Laruelle, 'Religious Revival, Nationalism and the "Invention of Tradition": Political Tengrism in Central Asia and Tatarstan', *Central Asian Survey*, 26 (2) (2007): 203–16.

Chapter 6 was previously published as Marlene Laruelle, 'The Three Discursive Paradigms of State Identity in Kazakhstan: Kazakhness, Kazakhstanness and Transnationalism', in *Nationalism and Identity Construction in Central Asia: Dimensions, Dynamics and Directions*, ed. Mariya Omelicheva, 1–20, Lanham, MD: Lexington, 2014.

Chapter 8 was previously published as Marlene Laruelle, 'In Search of Kazakhness: The Televisual Landscape and Screening of Nation in Kazakhstan', *Demokratizatsiya: The Journal of Post-Soviet Democratization*, 23 (3) (2015): 321–40.

Chapter 9 was previously published as Marlene Laruelle, 'Which Future for National-Patriots? The Landscape of Kazakh Nationalism', in *Kazakhstan in the Making: Legitimacy, Symbols and Social Changes*, ed. Marlene Laruelle, 155–80, Lanham, MD: Lexington, 2016.

Chapter 10 was previously published as Marlene Laruelle, 'The Nazarbayev Generation: A Sociological Portrait', in *The Nazarbayev Generation: Youth in Kazakhstan*, ed. Marlene Laruelle, 1–21, Lanham, MD: Lexington, 2019.

A note on web pages cited in this book

In some cases, web pages cited in previously published material are no longer available at the originally accessed URL. In such cases the information is retained for reference purposes. Readers may be able to locate archived versions by using the Internet Archive Wayback Machine, at https://archive.org/web, although this is not guaranteed.

Preface

The UCL Press FRINGE series presents work related to the themes of the UCL FRINGE Centre for the Study of Social and Cultural Complexity.

The FRINGE series is a platform for cross-disciplinary analysis and the development of 'area studies without borders'. FRINGE is an acronym standing for Fluidity, Resistance, Invisibility, Neutrality, Grey zones, and Elusiveness – categories fundamental to the themes that the Centre supports. The oxymoron in the notion of a 'FRINGE Centre' expresses our interest in both the tensions between 'area studies' and more traditional academic disciplines and the social, political, and cultural trajectories from 'centres to fringes' – and inversely from 'fringes to centres'.

The series pursues an innovative understanding of the significance of fringes: rather than taking 'fringe areas' to designate the world's peripheries or non-mainstream subject matters (as in 'fringe politics' or 'fringe theatre'), we are committed to exploring the patterns of social and cultural complexity characteristic of fringes and emerging from the areas we research. We aim to develop forms of analysis of those elements of complexity that are resistant to articulation, visualization, or measurement.

We are delighted to present this monograph by Marlene Laruelle, which focuses on a region of the world conventionally deemed peripheral, located as it is in a geopolitical space dominated by Russia, China and Iran. By engaging in a cross-country analysis of four Central Asian states – Kazakhstan, Kyrgyzstan, Tajikistan, and Uzbekistan – Laruelle examines themes of nationhood, ideology, and religion emerging in these post-imperial states.

The book questions the West-centric understanding of 'fringes' and promotes Central Asia as an experimental ground to explore notions of hybridity of political regimes, geopolitical positioning, and national construction. The region is revealed as simultaneously globalized and composed of sovereign nation-states. In a wider sense, Laruelle contributes to the growing literature on Huntington's idea of the 'rise of the rest'. This 'rising powers' perspective is fascinating because these

Central Asian regimes model themselves on both Putin's Russia and the Asian 'tigers' and 'dragons', experimenting with ideas of authoritarian modernization. At the same time, they rely on legitimacy mechanisms that have been given an Islamic framing, similar to those found in some Middle Eastern countries.

In the ethos of the FRINGE series, this study takes a multidisciplinary approach combining political science, intellectual history, sociology and cultural anthropology.

Alena Ledeneva and Peter Zusi,
School of Slavonic and East European Studies, UCL

Introduction: Central peripheries

Central peripheries. With that term, this book hopes to capture one of Central Asia's many paradoxes: its identity as both centre and periphery.

Geographically, of course, the region is central: it is one of the most landlocked spaces in the world, far from any ocean. Double-landlocked Uzbekistan is its most central state, while Urumqi, the capital of the Uyghur Xinjiang region in China, holds the record for the big city that is furthest from any ocean. Historically, too, Central Asia has been central: from centuries before the Common Era up until the sixteenth century, the region was a key venue for world products, ideas and people to be traded, exchanged and enriched. It pioneered irrigation techniques (the *qanat*, a network of underground canals that transport water from highland aquifers to the surface) and mastered metallurgical arts (the famous Scythian silver and gold craftmanship). During the Abbasid Caliphate, it became a key Islamic centre and, a few centuries later, one of the core pieces of the Mongol Empire. In recent years, the new Central Asian states have deployed the language of the international community to emphasize their centrality: they position themselves at the 'crossroads' of East and West; favour rhetorical tools such as 'Eurasianism' or 'New Silk Road'; promote transcontinental trade and newspeak about shared prosperity; and have worked hard to belong simultaneously to European, Asian and Islamic international cultural and financial institutions.

At the same time, however, Central Asia also has significant experience of being a periphery. It was a remote corner of the Persian-speaking world in the seventeenth and eighteenth centuries; a borderland of the Chinese, Russian and British empires in the nineteenth century; and a *cul-de-sac* of the Soviet Union during the Cold War decades. Today, it is often described in Western media as the backyard of both Putin's Russia and Xi's China, sandwiched between two neighbours with global aspirations.

Central Asia's ambivalent status as both a centre and a periphery is paralleled by two contradictory conventional narratives about the region's place on the international scene: Central Asia as the centre of the geopolitical tensions of the post-Cold War world, where Washington, Moscow and Beijing compete for influence and display their muscles against each other, versus Central Asia as the epigone of our world, a remote region that is the least connected to global transportation infrastructure and has almost no agency over its own destiny. This binary reflects a Western-centric view of the world that magnifies the great powers, articulates normative ideas about where countries 'fit' on ladders of development, and seeks to rank states' governance.[1]

Central Asia's post-postmodernism

To cope with these ambivalences, Western analysts and scholars have been exploring the notion of hybridity. Central Asian political regimes are indeed hybrid in the sense that they combine features of authoritarianism, patronalism and nepotism, on one hand, with a belief in democratic representation and a technocratic, rational elite, on the other. Central Asia's state-building takes a similarly diverse, 'all-you-can-eat buffet' approach: it combines concepts from Soviet-era Marxist-Leninist theories, the admiration for Europe as the continent of the nation-state *par excellence*, borrowings from Asian 'tigers' and 'dragons' that promote authoritarian modernization, and legitimacy mechanisms shaped by an Islamic repertoire. Yet the notion of hybridity remains normative: it frames situations that do not fit the conventional typologies by defining them as 'in-between' without challenging the existence of conceptual binaries themselves.[2]

Here, I prefer to see Central Asia as a typical example of post-postmodernism. Post-postmodernism rejects postmodernism's relativist paradigm, instead assuming a neo-realist view of the world and of human interactions.[3] At the level of nationhood and international affairs, post-postmodernism questions postmodernism's cosmopolitanism, as well as its belief in the abolition of boundaries and the 'death of the nation'.

Although relative latecomers on the international scene, the Central Asian states see themselves as globalized: they engage with as many multilateral institutions as possible; their internationalized elites use their skills and knowledge of the world to travel and study abroad, and to offshore national wealth; and millions of their citizens work abroad as migrants, creating remittances-to-GDP ratios that are among the highest in the world as well as transforming religious belonging and inaugurating new trans-spatial practices – what Rustamjon Urinboyev has nicely coined 'smartphone transnationalism'.[4]

And yet in spite of – or perhaps precisely *because* of – this, the Central Asian states still hold a very classical vision of the nation-state, one that is founded on the archetypal elements (constructed and reconstructed) of national language, national heroes and dynasties, and 'ethnic' cultural products or folklore that are honoured as having survived centuries of oppression or the erasure of the nation. Their unabashed celebration of very classical nationhoods built on postmodern premises challenges the Western view of nationalism as a dying ideology that ought to have been transcended by post-national cosmopolitanism.[5]

Inspired by an Herderian vision of nationalism emanating from Central and Eastern Europe, Central Asian nation-makers believe that nationalism – in the sense of the construction of the state and the promotion of a national identity – is the path to universalism and, today, integration into and recognition by the international community. They read the term 'concert of nations' literally. The choice is not between a backward-looking national identification and a postmodern globalism: the two coexist, on their own terms. Central Asia's nationhood trajectory thus shows the ability of peripheral states and latecomer nations to re-appropriate and question Western ideological productions. It encapsulates the tension inherent in a large part of today's world, in which countries seek to be both postmodern in their eclecticism and traditional in their values. Central Asian elite thus feel at ease with the current rise of illiberal movements across the globe and the latter's insistence on recreating political, economic and cultural boundaries; they consider nationalism to be a tool for gaining agency in the world.

How can a post-postmodern nationhood be built in light of such contrasts? How can Central Asia's peripherality be diluted (at least rhetorically) and its centrality insisted upon? How can a usable past be scripted and taught to the population? As with any other nationhood, the answer is to highlight some historical moments; obscure or silence others; and compress time, almost glossing over some centuries while engaging with others in detail and at length. As Ernest Renan famously declared, to exist, a nation has to remember together, but also forget together.[6]

In the crafting of Central Asian nationhoods, many other paradoxes also have to be taken into account. First, nationhood must promote the nation's ethnic continuity and its autochthonism on its contemporary territory by essentializing ethnic features, rediscovering a golden age and reinventing national heroes. But in the process, it must confront a long tradition of mobility – from nomadism and transhumance to more recent population displacements and labour migrations – that is difficult to integrate into a linear and uniform narrative of history.

Second, nationhood must combine ethnic and civic senses of belonging, managing to promote inclusivity while simultaneously deploying exclusion mechanisms that favour the titular group.[7] That is, it must create a civic nation whose cultural features are heavily borrowed from the ethnic majority. All the Central Asian states have maintained the Soviet distinction between nationality and citizenship – a dichotomy that was not problematic in the Soviet era, when the ethnic nation was a *local* nation, but now makes it difficult to determine who is a legitimate part of the polity.

Last but not least, nationhood must insist on historical continuity in the face of innumerable political and cultural ruptures that have disrupted collective memory, particularly in the twentieth century. The old elites, associated with the colonial *Ancien Régime*, were largely destroyed by the violence of the Russian civil war and the arrival of the Soviet regime. The new generations, who were educated in the early twentieth century and largely rallied around the Bolshevik regime – the Jadids, national-communists, and so on – were purged at the end of the 1930s. Nomadic societies were the most fundamentally transformed by the Soviet policy of violent sedentarization and collectivization. In this process, one-third of the Kazakh population died and another third fled abroad – meaning that the new Kazakh nation that emerged in the 1940s and 1950s was built on only one-third of the original population. The Second World War killed about 1.5 million Central Asians and heavily impacted the social fabric. It was not until the second half of the twentieth century that more stable intergenerational transmission began to take place, helping to steady the collective memory process. To a lesser extent, the 1990s inaugurated another loss of memory: millions of people left the region, especially ethnic minorities with higher-than-average skills and knowledge; millions of people changed jobs and left Soviet public service for the private sector; and in Turkmenistan and Uzbekistan, the alphabet shift and the obliteration of Soviet-era national literature created new impediments to knowledge transmission.

As everywhere in the world, crafting a coherent narrative that can be learned and internalized requires taking some liberties with the historical truth, as the past is often resistant to efforts to compress it into simplifying teleological frames.[8] But perhaps more importantly, Central Asian nation-makers found themselves in an ambivalent post-imperial situation. Should they interpret Soviet rule as a form of colonialism? The discursive line taken on this sensitive topic directly affects whether the nation is presented as an agent of its own past or as the disempowered object of victimization. What Talal Asad calls the 'irrevocable transmutations'[9] caused by Western colonial rule have been especially transformative in Central Asia, as the Soviet Union invested a huge amount of both state violence and human capital into dramatically reshaping the social fabric of Soviet nations.

Finding the right equilibrium between agency and victimhood is challenging. Unlike Ukraine or the Baltic states, the Central Asian countries cannot refer to numerous, clearly identifiable figures and groups that fought for independence, nor to the existence of a modern independent state that was temporarily incorporated into the Soviet Union.[10] A victimhood narrative increases the danger of 'Orientalizing' Central Asia as a backward region whose populations were unable to stand up for themselves and to take advantage of the opportunities of the Soviet regime while coping with its limits. How can today's Central Asian states acknowledge that their Soviet-era citizens had agency, felt empowered by Soviet modernizing projects, and embraced many aspects of Soviet culture and behavioural norms, yet avoid disavowing the independence that these states received – without fighting for it – in 1991? How can they refrain from framing the Soviet decades as a foreign imposition and instead recognize this era as an internalized transformation that gave agency to local societies and can be re-appropriated today with a critical perspective?

Nationhood as a commonsensical mythmaking process

Theories about the creation of nations have long been divided between two main schools: primordialism, which sees nations as enduring entities with essentialist features, and constructivism, which sees the nation as a top-down modern social construct process initiated by state elites. A third school, ethno-symbolism, has tried to move away from this dichotomy by arguing that although nations are indeed a modern construct, they are built upon pre-existing cultural and ethnic roots that are then reinterpreted in this new context.[11]

Central Asia offers a fascinating case study of this multi-layered construction, in which ancient roots and contemporary statecraft merge to advance what authorities hope is a consensual narrative.[12] National history is apprehended as a teleological process whose natural and only output is today's statehood: nationhood requires a 'usable' past that can be deployed to respond to contemporary political and cultural challenges.

Yet a *longue durée* perspective should not be ruled out merely because nationhood is constructed: although obviously transformed by the massive socioeconomic and cultural changes of the Soviet era and reinterpreted through a new set of values, some roots have persisted, including in societal structures, family genealogies, spatial representations and individuals' relationship to the natural environment.[13]

Here, I interpret nationhood as a symbolic construction that not only requires political and social preconditions, as explored by Eric Hobsbawm, Rogers Brubaker and Ernest Gellner,[14] but that also engages cultural, religious, historical and geographical myth-making, as proposed by Benedict Anderson, Anthony Smith and Michael Billig.[15] I follow, for instance, Anthony Smith's definition of nationhood as 'an amalgam of selective historical truth and idealization, with varying degrees of documented fact and political myth'.[16] Nationhood should be understood as offering a grid of intelligibility that makes it possible to navigate the complexity of social relations, promoting a reified past and making it commonsensical through schooling, museification, mass communication, changes in urban space, sport celebrations, and so on.[17]

Nationhood aims to define cultural normality, which helps individuals in their search for answers to the 'big questions'. It is not only, as mordantly formulated by Karl Deutsch, 'a group of persons united by a common error about their ancestry and a common dislike of their neighbors',[18] but a necessary in-group logic to decide who belongs to the citizenry and who is excluded, and on which grounds individuals will be willing to share with and sometimes sacrifice themselves for the collective. It is, in essence, a boundary-making enterprise that defines who is 'us' and who is outside the group. Thus, even in so-called well-established democracies, nation is always a space of conflict:[19] it advances compelling visions of identity, history and the place of religion, and it shapes everyday practices through which citizens adapt the national metanarrative to their individual realities.

As a scholarly object, nationhood in Central Asia has been framed through Rogers Brubaker's seminal concept of 'nationalizing states': the state projects itself as an ethnocultural entity in which symbolic production identifies with the titular majority.[20] This feature is far from a specificity of Eastern Europe and Eurasia: all states, including established democracies with a strong civic identity like France, are based on an ethnic core that is supposed to accommodate, assimilate and acculturate other groups.[21] In the Central Asian case, the five states claim, to different degrees, an intrinsic relationship with the titular ethnic group, and even in those which emphasize supranational civic belonging such as

Kazakhstan, the pre-eminence of the ethnic core is openly expressed. A process of self-ethnicization, as well as an obsession with 'counting' who belongs to the in-group, therefore accompanies nationhood.[22]

While this ethnic core nation dominates, some other components of the national toolkit, such as religion, are more challenging to articulate. Inherited Soviet atheism, an authoritarian definition of secularism, and the fear of ideological competition from Islam(ism) has made Central Asian nation-makers suspicious of Islam: while celebrated as a national heritage and a moral grounding, it remains repressed or at least marginalized as an identity marker.[23] In many respects, Islam is treated as the main 'internal other' of Central Asia's nationhood, the main unspoken subtext.[24]

Although attempts have been made to adapt national biographies to post-independence conditions, nationhood remains deeply moulded by the Soviet legacy. Today's Central Asia nationhoods have exchanged one ideological constraint – the Marxist-Leninist reading of history – for another – the mandatory celebration of independence as the natural development and final stage in the history of a titular ethnic group. The new nationhood has preserved the former's teleological understanding of history, treating the nation's history as a linear progression across centuries and even millennia, but whereas this progression used to be toward communism, it is now toward independence.

Another constraint on Central Asian nationhoods, the paucity of local sources able to articulate local perspectives on some of the key moments of national history,[25] has even deeper roots. This problem is especially acute in the case of countries with a nomadic past, such as Kazakhstan, Kyrgyzstan and Turkmenistan, where knowledge and memory were oral and are therefore partly – though not yet entirely – lost to us. Kazakhstan's state-sponsored 'Cultural Heritage' programme (2004–11), which focused on collecting external sources related to the country's history from around the world,[26] epitomized the desire of the authorities to reclaim the nation's narrative and insert local voices into the mostly externally-framed narratives that have prevailed to date.

The notion that one can access post-Soviet modernity through the revival of traditions is a prevalent frame of thinking in the region, with the result that reinventing traditions is perceived as a sign of modernization. This overlap between modernization and re-traditionalization explains the fascination of many Central Asian political and intellectual circles with Japan, South Korea or Singapore: seen as having succeeded in modernizing without westernizing or Europeanizing, these countries are considered by many to be a model to follow. But the Central Asian countries' efforts to achieve the lauded balance between modernization or globalization, on the one hand, and 'rootedness' or cultural preservation, on the other, remain fragile, nurturing resentment and disillusionment and providing fertile soil, fed by conspiracy theories, for feelings of a nationhood under attack.

Nationalism as a technology of power

Nationhood also serves to legitimate or naturalize a given configuration of political authority. In Central Asia, national biographies are closely interlinked with state-building. The interaction between nationhood and statehood, and therefore between the ideology of the nation, on one side, and power relations and the nature of the political regime, on the other, is intense.[27] Each nationhood project is essentially statist: it believes in the state as the quintessence of the nation. With the partial exception of Kyrgyzstan, nationhood narratives are produced under authoritarian state structures, which see themselves as having a duty to be involved in crafting the national narrative in order to secure the state, the nation and the political status quo – though as synonyms.

As Soviet authorities, the national elites of independent Central Asia think of themselves as nation-makers: they have devoted an impressive amount of resources – human, administrative and financial – to elaborating and popularizing a new nationhood. As Asel Murzakulova and John Schoeberlein explain, 'political authorities, large segments of intellectual circles, and the population share the assumption that a national ideology is a critical element of statehood that contributes to guaranteeing social order.'[28] While the national construction starts as a top-down project, it aims to secure the governmentality of the regime, in the Foucauldian sense: the authorities can reign only if the population internalizes power relations. To justify their domination, the authorities need popular consent to domination, even in an authoritarian context.

Nationalism thus serves as a technology of power. The authorities attempt to mitigate their authoritarianism and limit the use of repressive tools by being the agenda-setter and preventing ideological contestation.[29] Regime security now hinges on nationhood, which drives consensus and makes it possible to surmount political divisions: the authorities rely on performative non-democratic mechanisms that not only saturate the public space with imaginaries of nation/statehood, but also involve citizens, individually and collectively, in joint performances.

Too often, studies of Central Asian regimes look only at their authoritarian features, neglecting their nationhood strategies. Yet the latter show a more consensual form of governance, one that has succeeded in developing co-creational mechanisms that help make the current political order appear natural. In that sense, the Central Asian regimes are national-populist: they think the national collective is a direct subject of history and they use and abuse references to the nation and its supposed unified will to circumvent representative mechanisms such as elections or institutionalized political pluralism.[30]

As the proverb goes, the past tells us, above all, about the present. Jan Assmann explains that memory is important not for its factuality but for its actuality.[31] The regimes' use of the national past is a way to exit politics and artificially boost popular unity: today's political path cannot be questioned, as it results from the objective trajectory of the nation along a unique path on which there are no possible alternative routes. This obsession with the past goes hand-in-hand with a strong aspirational identity: with Kazakhstan initiating the trend, the region's states project a modern, globalized statehood based on a developmentalist ideology.[32] With this dual focus – national/ethnic when looking backward, developmentalist when looking forward – the authorities hope to promote a depoliticized narrative that is not open to contestation. This ideology can be policed to a greater or lesser degree – loosely in Kyrgyzstan, tightly in Turkmenistan – depending on the regime's degree of authoritarianism.

Often described through a normative Western lens as stagnant, rigid or even immobile, the Central Asian states have in fact made inventive use of the largest possible array of tools for performing the nation. They did not stop at rewriting official historiography, school textbooks and museology, all of which serve as the state's representatives in educational affairs. Instead, they invested in innumerable other ways to convey the new national message to the population as a whole. Chief among these have been changes to the urban landscape, from modifying toponymy and creating new statuary to erecting new buildings and even creating new cities. In sum, the Central Asian states have used an impressive range of ideological materials to represent the nation publicly and to craft a new ideological script. They have excelled in symbolic politics.[33]

The book

With all this in mind, the present book aims to offer the reader a comprehensive look at nation-building in post-Soviet Central Asia (with the exception of Turkmenistan), taking into consideration the ways in which the Soviet past has influenced the construction of national storylines, as well as the diversity of each state's narratives and use of symbolic politics.

The book is based on the principle that only multidisciplinarity can help us to untangle the puzzle of nationhood. It therefore uses mixed methods, combining political science, intellectual history, sociology and cultural anthropology. Even if the book focuses on official production of nationhood, it tries not to leave out the imaginational registers that are advanced by non-state actors.[34] It has been inspired by more than two decades of fieldwork in the region and a deep knowledge of the state of local academia and the political environment. Based in Uzbekistan at the French Institute for Central Asian Studies (IFEAC) for five years in the late 1990s and early 2000s, I was able to travel to almost every remote corner of the five republics. Since 2005, I have been returning to the region every year, mostly to Kazakhstan, Kyrgyzstan and Tajikistan, and have come to focus on Kazakhstan. This book compiles a series of articles published over the course of the 15 years between 2004 and 2019, updating them and giving them internal coherence. I am grateful to the journals and publishers concerned for authorizing the republication of these chapters.

My knowledge of Russian allows me to read a large number of academic publications and to interact with the intellectual elites of each country. That being said, I lack access to publications in national languages, which limits my capacity to capture that part of the academic debate and, more importantly, to engage with folk literature and discussions on some segments of social media. To partially compensate for this shortcoming, I have worked closely with the new generation of Central Asian scholars at the George Washington University's Central Asia Program and oriented the Program to promote research based on national-language sources.

The first part of the book offers a broad overview of state-sponsored nation-building narratives in the Central Asian region. It first reminds the reader that each state's post-Soviet nationhood is deeply rooted in its Soviet past. The conceptual framing of the nation was elaborated in the 1940s and 1950s and developed gradually in the academic circles of each republic, thus providing the new independent countries with a ready-made national teleology. All that remained to be done in the independence era was to make an ideological shift that entailed reinterpreting the nineteenth and twentieth centuries. The key element inherited from Soviet times is the concept of ethnogenesis, which justifies the supposed uninterrupted ethnic continuity of the nation over the centuries (Chapter 1).

Moving to the post-Soviet period, the first part of the book looks at three case studies – Uzbekistan, Tajikistan and Kyrgyzstan – and explores their different trajectories for writing the biography of the nation. Uzbekistan under Islam Karimov succeeded in developing a nationhood intimately articulated with regime securitization and centred on the historical continuity of the nation since ancient times and its centrality in Central Asia (Chapter 2). Tajikistan, too, attempted to develop a unifying narrative that would overcome the deep divisions of the civil war, in its case by exalting its Aryan identity. Such an identity allows Tajikistan to set itself apart from its Turkic neighbours and avoid giving Islam too prominent a place in the national construction (Chapter 3).

Reflecting its plural and decentralized political life, nationhood in Kyrgyzstan has remained quite uncertain and chaotic, advancing a multitude of competing narratives. Even if the state has tried to put forward a unifying discursive line, the more universal narrative is increasingly that of a nation whose sovereignty is under threat from multiple enemies. A multiplicity of competing narratives on the nation have challenged the state's and academia's traditional legitimacy as nation-makers (Chapter 4). The final chapter of the first part of the book turns to alternative conceptions of the nation, looking at the example of Tengrism, a revivalist religious movement that combines ethno-nationalism, pan-Turkism and the rejection of Islam. While agreeing with the authorities on the need for more centralized and authoritarian forms of power, Tengrism positions itself somewhat in opposition to the official line (Chapter 5).

The second part of the book focuses exclusively on Kazakhstan. It takes a more comprehensive look at different components of Kazakhstan's nation-building process, seeing the nation-building arena as a contested space where different agents seek to promote their own visions of the nation. It first addresses the three paradigms elaborated by state authorities about the country's identity: Kazakhness, Kazakhstanness, and what I call transnationalism (Chapter 6). It then delves more deeply into Kazakhstani authorities' Eurasian profession of faith, exploring a vast array of narratives that include everything from Olzhas Suleimenov's new philosophy of language to elites' pragmatic, foreign policy-oriented strategies to brand Kazakhstan's place in Eurasia and Asia more globally (Chapter 7).

The book then moves from state narratives to more diverse spaces where the nation is discussed. It does this first by looking at television – a nation-building tool that is curiously understudied in the Central Asian context. On Kazakhstani TV, documentary films using state-backed discourses of the nation compete with more innovative discourses crafted by private actors who aim to perform the nation in a way that I define as patriotic entertainment (Chapter 8). Second, the book turns to look at the crucial and growing role of the nationalist landscape, which, although marginalized for two decades by the Nazarbayev regime, has seen an impressively rapid renaissance in recent years. A new generation of nationalist publicists in the social media world now promote anticolonial discourses targeting Russia (Chapter 9). Last but not least, the book explores the identity patterns of what I call the Nazarbayev Generation – the millennials and members of Generation Z born under the first president. They display the features that will characterize Kazakh identity in the coming decades: a vivid debate between a cosmopolitan identity and an inward-looking vision of Kazakhness, as well as over the definition of national authenticity, re-traditionalizing gender roles and the place of Islam in the national pantheon (Chapter 10).

The conclusion explores other forms of national biography: non-textual biographies sponsored by the state and biographies promoted outside of any forms of state control (such as collective and family memory, popular history developed by non-professional historians and alternative history brandished by the political opposition). It concludes by stating that we are now witnessing a gradual shift toward a new historiographical landscape in Central Asia – a more plural, less consensual, less state-centric one that features increased co-creational mechanisms.

Notes

1 Cooley and Snyder (eds), *Ranking the World*.
2 Bogaards, 'How to Classify Hybrid Regimes?'.
3 See Kirby, 'The Death of Postmodernism and Beyond' and, also, Kirby, *Digimodernism: How New Technologies Dismantle the Postmodern*.
4 On globalized elites, see Cooley and Heathershaw, *Dictators without Borders*. On the transformative role of social media in the lives of migrants, see Urinboyev, 'Smartphone Transnationalism in Non-Western Migration Regimes'.
5 Breen and O'Neill (eds), *After the Nation?*
6 Renan, 'What is a Nation?'.
7 Ferrando, 'Policies and Practices of Language Education'.
8 Ilkhamov, 'National Ideologies'.
9 Asad, 'Afterword: From the History of Colonial Anthropology to the Anthropology of Western Hegemony'.
10 For a comparative perspective between Central Asia and the United States, see Kudaibergenova, *Toward Nationalizing Regimes*.
11 See the classic work of Anthony Smith, *National Identity*.
12 Isaacs and Polese, *Nation Building in Post-Soviet Spaces*; Kolstø, *Political Construction Sites*. On challenging Western scholarship on nationhood, see Weller, *Rethinking Kazakh and Central Asian Nationhood*.

13 The place of 'clans' in today's Central Asian identity and politics has been one of the most debated scholarly topics. For early views on this subject, see Collins, *Clan Politics and Regime Transition in Central Asia*; Schatz, *Modern Clan Politics and Beyond*. More sophisticated and nuanced perceptions have since developed, for instance, Gullette, *The Genealogical Construction of the Kyrgyz Republic*; Finke, *Variations on Uzbek Identity*.

14 Hobsbawm, *Nations and Nationalism since 1780*; Brubaker, *Nationalism Reframed*; Gellner, *Nations and Nationalism*.

15 Anderson, *Imagined Communities*; Smith, *Nations and Nationalism*.

16 Smith, *Nations and Nationalism*, 63.

17 De Cillia, Reisigl and Wodak, 'The Discursive Construction of National Identities', 153.

18 Deutsch, *Nationalism and Its Alternatives*, 3.

19 Hutchinson, *Nations as Zones of Conflict*.

20 Brubaker, *Nationalism Reframed*. See also Bohr, 'The Central Asian States as Nationalising Regimes'; Kudaibergenova, 'The Archaeology of Nationalizing Regimes': Kudaibergenova, 'Nationalizing Elites and Regimes'.

21 Kuzio, '"Nationalising States" or Nation-Building?'.

22 Balibar, *Race, Nation, Class*; Dave, 'Entitlement through Numbers'; Kudaibergenova, 'National Identity Formation in Post-Soviet Central Asia'. On the counting aspect, see Ferrando, 'Manipulating the Census'.

23 Khalid, *Islam after Communism*.

24 Blakkisrud and Nozimova, 'History Writing and Nation Building'.

25 Morrison, *Russian Rule in Samarkand 1868–1910*.

26 Karamanova, 'State Program "Cultural Heritage" of Kazakhstan'.

27 Kudaibergenova, 'Compartmentalized Ideology'.

28 Murzakulova and Schoeberlein, 'The Invention of Legitimacy'. See also Oka, 'Nationalities Policy in Kazakhstan'.

29 Schatz, 'The Soft Authoritarian Tool Kit'.

30 Ó Beacháin and Kevlihan, '"Imagined Democracy"?'.

31 Assmann and Czaplicka, 'Collective Memory and Cultural Identity'.

32 Kudaibergenova, 'The Ideology of Development and Legitimation'.

33 Cummings (ed.), *Symbolism and Power in Central Asia*; Matveeva, 'Legitimising Central Asian Authoritarianism'; Marat, 'Nation Branding in Central Asia'; Fierman, 'Identity, Symbolism and the Politics of Identity in Central Asia'.

34 On that central question, see Isaacs and Polese, 'Between "Imagined" and "Real" Nation-Building'.

Part 1
Writing the national biography

1

The *longue durée* of national storytelling: Soviet roots and the quest for ethnogenesis

The Soviet period both continued and discontinued the late tsarist regime's nationalities policy and its definition of ethnicity.[1] Though some elements of the prior regime were maintained – in particular, a public policy of assigning national identity to individuals and the confounding of social class and ethnic hierarchies – techniques of population control in the name of scientific knowledge took on unprecedented scope with the officialization of Marxist-Leninist science. The Soviet regime elaborated a new nationality paradigm that combined territorial anchorage (rights were attributed to a group on its historical territory) with historicism (the nation had to have existed since ancient times to be legitimate).[2] National assignment was not only collective but also individual: it affected the legal rights of each citizen by partially determining his or her course through society. Citizens identified as members of 'punished peoples' (Chechens, Crimean Tatars, Volga Germans and so on) or as Jews faced a more complex – and more frequently tragic – trajectory through the Soviet system. This stratification has had a long-term impact on society: thirty years after its disappearance, the Soviet system of territorial and collective identification continues to shape many ethnic claims and territorial tensions.

Hierarchized pluralism and the assignment of identities

For Marxism, the national question was secondary to the class one, as nation was a product of the bourgeoisie and therefore destined to disappear with it. That being said, some intellectual currents, such as

Austro-Marxism, which germinated in a Habsburg Empire in which the national question was highly sensitive, insisted on the idea of institutionalizing individual cultural autonomy.[3] As early as the start of the 1920s, however, Stalin rejected the Austro-Marxist principle of extra-territorial individual cultural autonomy advocated by Otto Bauer and Karl Renner, condemning it for its petit-bourgeois individualism.[4] He gave preference instead to a territorial definition of identities that was closer to the tsarist vision of ethnic groups. This approach necessitated not only objectivizing historical, cultural and administrative markers, but also collectivizing rights: the individual was endowed with rights only because he was a member of a larger group.

Stalin defined the nation as 'a stable, historically constituted community of language, of territory, of economic life and of psychic formation, which translates into a community of culture'.[5] Territory thus became the guarantee of the indigeneity of the people, with language and 'psychic formation' enabling an essentialist and naturalist reading of the community. The expression 'historically constituted' emphasized that the Marxist timeline was the sole possible mode of interpreting national identity through time.

In order to rally the minorities of the tsarist empire behind the revolutionary cause, Lenin transformed Russia into the Russian Soviet Federative Socialist Republic (RSFSR) and promised a large degree of autonomy to all national groups. On 30 December 1922, the Soviet Union, which then encompassed four republics – the RSFSR, Ukraine, Byelorussia and Transcaucasia – was born. The Twelfth Congress of the Bolshevik Party, held in 1923, hierarchized nationalities based on territory as the primary marker of identity: some nationalities were endowed with a federated republic, while others were given an autonomous republic or an autonomous district, or merely the right to schooling in their national language in regions where they enjoyed high population density.

The Soviet federal system was structured in stages. In 1924, Moscow granted Uzbekistan and Turkmenistan, then part of the Autonomous Republic of Turkestan, the status of federated republic. In 1929, it promoted Tajikistan from the status of an autonomous republic within Uzbekistan to that of a federal republic. Then, in 1936, it separated Kazakhia and Kirgizia from the RSFSR; both then acceded to the coveted federal status.[6] With that, the five republics of Central Asia were born, and since then they have faced only very minor adjustments to the delimitation of their borders: a few small territories were exchanged in the 1950s, while the most recent external border delimitations, which were more polemical, were signed with China in the 1990s–2000s.

In contrast to the South Caucasus, which remains mired in territorial conflicts that threaten state sovereignty, national identity-related issues in Central Asia are rarely linked to territorial status.

Officially, the borders of the republics were drawn according to ethnic identity. In practice, this was often hardly pertinent. Many populations did not claim any externally assigned identity, tending instead to describe themselves as being 'from here' or as 'peasants' when they wanted to distinguish themselves from townspeople or as 'Muslims' when they sought to distinguish themselves from the Russian colonists. Seeking to rationalize the use of land, the authorities introduced economic rationales into their administrative divisions. As Juliette Cadiot rightly remarks, 'this topographical conception of nationality was linked to a project of land settlement'.[7] Two scientific rationales, ethnographical and economic, thus confronted each other. These rationales were put forward by two sets of institutions. On one side was the People's Commissariat of Nationalities and the Commission for the Study of the Ethnic Composition of Russia's Population, which both sought to foster the small peoples against the Russians and to put an end to the tsarist-era processes of assimilation, in particular Russian agricultural colonization. On the other side stood the Regionalization Commission of Gosplan (the State Planning Committee), which promoted a model of modernization-by-colonization and saw economics as a way to bring civilization to 'backward' peoples.[8]

The distribution of arable lands, waterways, factories and extant industries – but also of sites of memory – made border division a rather delicate task. But contrary to the widespread idea that Stalin himself drew borders in order to better 'divide and rule', indigenous elites in each republic were closely associated with territorial division. Their multiple conflicts found echoes in the Bolshevik leadership structures: border delimitations were in large part decided on the basis of local power relations between political groups, nationalities and regions – and indeed the personal interests of local leaders. The Tajik elites, for example, clamoured for Bukhara, Samarkand and part of Surkhandaria to be given to the Tajik republic, while the Tashkent elites maintained the 'Uzbekness' of these regions and organized a lobby in Moscow to advocate for the Uzbek republic to keep them.[9] Some Uzbek leaders from the Fergana Valley wanted their natal villages to be attached to Uzbekistan and not to Kirgizia – something they achieved by creating territorial exclaves that continue to cause tensions in the bilateral relationships between Uzbekistan and Kyrgyzstan and between Kyrgyzstan and Tajikistan to this day.[10]

Nor did the populations stand passively by and watch the carving-up of their territories. The communities organized themselves to make their issues heard over sections of land, valley slopes, waterways and transhumance territories. Some villages made collective requests to change their identity so that they could be incorporated into a neighbouring republic or obtain certain advantages: nationalities regarded as sedentary, for instance, had a right to arable lands at the expense of those that were not. After the 1924 Commission of National Delimitation for Central Asia, several villages of the Uzbek republic declared themselves Kazakhs and denounced the repression of their identity by the centre; the countervailing phenomenon emerged in the Kazakh republic.[11] The claim that border zoning was a matter of Stalin's personal choice is thus an historical oversimplification that denies individual and collective agency within the system.

In parallel with the territorial delimitation of the republics, the Soviet regime established a nationality policy based on assigning an ethnic identification to every citizen and typologizing rights in accordance with that identification. Immediately after the end of the civil war, the Bolshevik authorities commissioned large ethnological surveys across the entire country, even though the economic situation was extremely challenging and some territories were still facing sporadic revolts. The objective was to map national diversity with the utmost precision. In counting the number of existing ethnic groups, the political authorities and the ethnologists associated with the task took multiple criteria into account. Chief among these was language, but given that this was imprecise, it was complemented by a study of dialectical differences, the consideration of clan differences wherever they existed, and recognition of variations in farming culture, folklore and sometimes physical anthropological features.

The number of recognized 'nationalities' underwent significant fluctuations. In the 1920s, when the autonomy of the republics was particularly extensive, fragmentation was intense, since the nationalities were able to organize themselves at the micro level. With the first Soviet census of 1926, the Commission for the Study of the Ethnic Composition of Russia's Population accepted 600 terms of ethnic identification, which it classified into 196 recognized nationalities, each endowed with specific rights.[12] Terminological debates were tense as well: nineteenth-century Russian ethnology employed two terms translatable as 'nationality', namely *narodnost'* – a common designation for the Slavic peasantry – for the so-called 'evolved' peoples and *natsional'nost'* for the supposed 'backward' peoples. In the 1920s, this usage reversed when the national republics requested to be classified as *natsional'nost'*, seeing it as a sign of greater cultural and economic evolution. The polemics over terminology were particularly virulent in Ukraine and in Byelorussia, where to be classified as *narodnost'* commonly meant that a people would be considered a branch of the Russian populace rather than a distinct nation.[13]

The allocation of identities was not solely a question of territorial distribution or hierarchization of national groups, but rather affected the individual rights of each citizen. The authorities forced citizens into an identity assignment. In the 1920s, the first civil state questionnaire forms had included the question of nationality and accepted self-definitions. However, the regime stipulated that forthwith, an individual's nationality would depend upon the nationalities of his or her parents and not on his or her place of birth, a measure intended to prevent so-called 'suspicious' nationalities from disappearing, particularly Jews and Ukrainians, who could identify themselves as Russians if they were born on the territory of the RSFSR.[14] When passports were introduced in 1932, the choice of nationality was still left to the citizen, but from 1938 people had to prove their nationality via documents stipulating the nationalities of their parents, and once decided, their designation could not be altered.

The coding of identities followed the political fits and starts of the regime.[15] The famous 1937 census, which was supposed to corroborate the transformations of Soviet society in the space of a decade, was cancelled by Stalin when it failed to meet his expectations. The data provide a glimpse of the impact of collectivization and the famines, in particular in Ukraine and Kazakhstan, as well as demonstrating that more than 40 per cent of the population continued to declare themselves believers in the 'homeland of atheism'. The 1939 census, carried out after the brutal reorganization – through purges – of Soviet statistical circles,[16] was based on a strong evolutionist logic: small ethnic groups were ordered to assimilate with a majority nationality as a sign of their transition to socialist modernity. Many ethnonyms with religious connotations disappeared (including the Kryashens, who were Orthodox Tatars), while the Cossacks lost their right to a distinct nationality. Meanwhile, priority was given to territorial entities. Thus, the Iranophone populations of the Pamirs were considered Tajik, since they lived within the Tajik republic; the Sarts, a term which served to define the city dwellers of Turkestan, were encouraged to declare themselves Uzbeks; and terms with clannish connotations, such as Kipchak, were eliminated in favour of Uzbek. Though the Commission still admitted 800 terms of possible identification, only 106 official nationalities were eventually accepted and endowed with rights.[17]

After many debates between ethnologists and statisticians, between republican and federal bodies, between the administrative commissions and the party's decision-making circles, the decision was made to hierarchize national identities into three main groups: *natsional'nost'*, *narodnost'* and ethnic groups (*etnicheskie gruppy*). The categorization of a given national identity depended largely on its territorial status: the first group included those with a federated or autonomous republic; the second those with a region or an autonomous district (although some densely populated groups without administrative recognition were also included in this category); and the third what Moscow referred to as national minorities – that is, populations that had a kinstate outside Soviet borders and whose loyalty to the Soviet state was viewed with suspicion.[18]

In the 1920s, Soviet rationales privileged a diversity of identifications, in particular among small groups, in order to challenge traditional collective identities, especially those that were refractory to the Bolshevik ideological project. As of the 1930s, identity assignment became more restrictive and closely connected to a territorial administrative entity. The hierarchization of national groups, the obligatory and exclusive allotment of an identity, and the obsession with classification all remained crucial drivers of the nationalities policy of the Soviet regime until its collapse. As Yuri Slezkine puts it, from the 1930s, 'all Soviet children inherited their nationality at birth, and their individual ethnicities became biological categories that were impermeable to cultural, linguistic, or geographical change'.[19]

The science of ethnos or the paradoxes of Soviet ethnology

Reprising the imperial tradition, Soviet ethnology was ascribed the mission of academically legitimating Soviet nationalities policy.[20] This occurred through the Institute for the Study of Nationalities of the Soviet Union, led by Nikolay Marr (1865–1934), and later the Miklukho-Maklay Ethnology Institute, led by Yulian Bromley (1921–90).

Long in search of its object of study, Soviet ethnology had to maintain its submission to history, one of the key sciences for Marxism, which required that the study of the characteristics of peoples be rooted in a temporal reading of their existence.[21] The national collectivities were thus studied in time, as an evolutionary process that was spread along a common scale divided into very precise stages of development (*stadial'nost'*): tribe (*plemia*), nationality (*narodnost'* or *natsional'nost'*), people (*narod*) and nation (*natsiia*). Each corresponded to a historical stage of the development of humanity as proposed by Marxist-Leninist science: primitive communism, feudalism, capitalism, socialism and communism. At the end of the 1930s, the influence of Marr's theory of stages of development, and its claim that migrations have no direct impact on the evolution of language,[22] contributed to the birth of ethnogenetics (*etnogenetika*), the science of the (historical) genesis of ethnic groups.[23] Ethnogenetics hailed itself as a discipline that could only 'reach its authentic scientific realization in the Soviet Union, on the basis of the theories of Marxism-Leninism and with the aid of progressist teachings in the domain of linguistics such as those of Nikolay Marr'.[24]

Ethnogenesis emerged as Soviet ethnology's main research object in a second context: the ideological confrontation with Nazism. Since the eighteenth century, Russian science had sought both to emulate German science and, simultaneously, to compete with it. Many Soviet–German scientific collaborations were undertaken in the 1920s, but the country's closure under Stalin and Hitler's rise to power in Germany severed these historic links. Whatever the relationship between the two countries, however, Soviet scholars had always violently rejected Germanic (German as well as Austrian) discourses that considered the peoples of the Russian Empire to be too backward on the evolutionary scale to be able to develop. They posited instead that humanity is determined by socioeconomic conditions, not by innate biological characteristics.[25]

Soviet science also sought to demonstrate the possibility of a non-racist science of race (*rasovedenie*), a science that would study peoples' physiological features and their relationship with nature but without making any socio-biological presuppositions: no people would be placed on a scale of intrinsic value. One of the most famous Soviet scholars in physical anthropology, Georgii F. Debets (1905–69), propounded such a view: according to him, bourgeois Western anthropology either developed racist theories or denied the links between race and language. Soviet science, by contrast, had accurately demonstrated 'the correspondence between anthropological types and linguistic, cultural, and ethnic groups', the study of which correspondence had proved to be 'the principal means for a multifaceted analysis of the processes of ethnogenesis'.[26]

Interpreting any migrationist theory as denying Soviet peoples' legitimacy, Soviet scholars stood strongly in favour of autochthonous theories. They rejected the Germanic discourse on the non-Europeanness of the Slavs, a discourse that placed their cradle in Asia, and claimed the East-European plain as the origin of Slavs from the Bronze Age. Aleksandr Bernshtam (1910–56), a famous historian of the Kyrgyz, asserted that migrationist theories were 'reactionary' and derived from bourgeois science whose goal was to diminish the Soviet peoples' place in world history.[27] Soviet discourse likewise criticized the Western tradition of political history for not adequately taking into account the economic elements highlighted by Marxism: 'ethnic history ... cannot be reduced chiefly to migrations provoked by political events and military confrontations. Such an approach could hardly be deemed scientifically correct'.[28] What was applicable to the Slavs, the main targets of Germanic discourses, was then replicated for all the Soviet Union's nationalities: each nationality's historiography was invited to focus on autochthonism and reject migrationist theories.

Physical anthropology accompanied the all-encompassing search for ethnogenesis – here, too, following a tsarist tradition.[29] According to Georgii Debets, Soviet science had accurately demonstrated 'the correspondence of anthropological types with linguistic and ethnographical groups'.[30] In the late 1950s and throughout the decade that followed, the Khrushchevian Thaw had a substantial impact on ethnological debates, as it encouraged Soviet scholars to introduce more biological references into their definitions of ethnic groups. This evolution was supported by the new Director of the Ethnology Institute, Yulian Bromley, who held his position from 1967 until perestroika. His publications on the ethnos as the primary object of Soviet ethnology, based on a pre-revolutionary tradition centred on nationality, were in part inspired by the works of Sergei Shirokogoroff (1887–1939).[31] An ethnologist who emigrated to China to flee the 1917 Revolution, Shirokogoroff elaborated a general classificatory model of ethnos based on studies conducted on a Siberian people, the Tunguz. In his view, ethnos had to serve as a global explanatory framework into which both the history of peoples and their cultural specificities were integrated. For humankind, the ethnos was thus held to be the equivalent of the species.[32]

Bromley applied the norms of a Marxist reading of history to this postulate: the ethnos is a socio-historical phenomenon explicable by the forces of production and the social relations that result from it. This stance was politically correct for Soviet science; beyond it, however, the Bromleyan ethnos was conceived in essentialist terms.[33] For even if the birth of the ethnos was a historical and not a biological phenomenon, once present, ethnic identity became absolute: it passed from one generation to the next, imposing itself on individuals who were unable to rebuke it, and it was unable to be combined with other ethnic categories or to evolve over time. For example, although the medieval Kievan Rus', the Muscovy principality under the domination of the Mongol Horde and the Romanov empire, all belonged to different 'ethno-social organisms', there allegedly existed a single temporally invariant entity, the 'Russian ethnos'.[34] This concept thus made it possible to reconcile the evolutionism of Marxist theories with a primordialist conception of national identities.

In the 1970s–80s, Soviet ethnology specialized in the study of so-called ethnic processes. If some controversial scholars like Lev Gumilev (1912–92) were condemned for publicly defending the biological character of the ethnos,[35] most official works, whether published by the publishing house of the Academy of Sciences (Nauka) or by academic journals such as *Sovetskaia etnografiia*, maintained similar discourses. Whereas Soviet propaganda advocated friendship between peoples and their possible merging into a single Soviet nation, ethnologists were investigating the modes of preservation of the supposedly specific 'genetic pool' (*genofond*) of each Soviet people. A plethora of works polemicized over the divisions in *subethnos*, set out to investigate whether diasporic communities belonged to the *ethnikos* (for instance, do the Tatars of Moscow form a different ethnos to the Tatars of Tatarstan?) and discussed the formation of *superethnos'* or *megaethnos'* (such as, for example, the *superethnos* of Turkic-speaking peoples or Arctic peoples).

Endogamous postulates also broadly dominated Soviet ethnographical scholarship. Researchers who specialized in studying the peoples of the Far North were concerned, for example, with the consequences of miscegenation between Siberian peoples and Slavic populations, since this was supposed to weaken the genetic capacities of young generations born of mixed marriages to withstand the cold.[36] Believing in the existence of 'degenerate behaviours', Soviet science largely referred to medical works from the early twentieth century and the first Bolshevik years, which were marked by eugenics, even though the term was subsequently prohibited as bourgeois. A biological representation of heredity made it possible for ethnology to slip from the medical register (notably using the salience of the question of alcoholism) toward the political and the cultural repertoires.[37] In this context, physical anthropology could easily carve out space for itself. The existence of the nation as a physical unity was thus affirmed by producing an amalgam of craniological, serological, odontological and dermatological data, as well as by using diverse ethnonyms given to the ancient races and to contemporary populations interchangeably.

As Élisabeth Gessat-Anstett has noted, Soviet ethnography 'developed a complex theoretical discourse while dispensing with an epistemology of its own practice'.[38] Founded on solid empirical fieldwork research, it combined theories of ethnos and extremely descriptive studies of the cultural mosaic of the country. The desire to classify cultural differences, in particular in the field of material culture – the *byt*, or everyday life: habitats, customs, handicraft, folklore, rituals – contributed to the conceptualization of ethnic groups as reified entities.[39] Material culture was studied as the expression *par excellence* of the 'ethnic specificity' of each people and of its 'genetic fund'. The naturalness of the ethnos could thus be formulated in cultural terms conceived as apolitical but whose bedrock was the rejection of the multiplicity of human identities. Soviet ethnology therefore ontologized human communities by giving ethnos a meaning almost comparable to that of race.

Competing for antiquity: crafting Central Asians' ethnogeneses

Pushing back against Germanic theories about the Asian origins of Slavs, Soviet ethnology emphasized the antiquity of Soviet peoples and of their ethnogenesis. In 1936, an *Ancient History of the Peoples of the USSR* (*Drevniaia istoriia narodov SSSR*) was published on the initiative of academician Iurii Got'e. The Academy of Sciences decided to pursue this initiative further, and, under the leadership of Aleksandr D. Udal'tsov, it organized four conferences on ethnogenesis: one on the peoples of the Far North in 1940, another on those of Central Asia in 1942, another on the Slavs in 1943, and a final one in 1944 that was more specifically devoted to the Indo-European question. The conference on Central Asia was held in August 1942 in Tashkent and involved some 15 researchers, mostly Russians, whose papers were published in summary form in a 1947 volume of *Sovetskaia etnografiia*.[40] This foundational conference established the principles of ethnogenesis for Central Asia: each eponymous people was to establish a dynasty of reference and identify a chronologically well-defined historical period in which the process of the nation's formation was completed. For maximum prestige value, the period should be as ancient as possible.

Reading the papers from the 1942 conference, one cannot help but be struck by the insistence of all participants on the issue of inter-ethnic miscegenation, on one hand, and on a people's degree of 'purity', on the other. Although no value judgment was rendered on the latter question – a more hybrid people was not deemed inferior – the logic of autochthonization went beyond territoriality and was associated with the notion of ethnic or even racial continuity. As several papers from the August 1942 session imply, reconciling the findings from linguistics, archaeology and physical anthropology can solve the question of a people's ethnogenesis, as it allows scholars to know whether it the 'same' people that is being discussed across time. Several conference papers pondered the 'racial type of the natives' (*rasovyi tip aborigenov*) in order to determine whether the type had been preserved in this or that republic. The Soviet authorities' explicit rejection of Nazi theories and lack of a racial policy thus does not mean that racial criteria were absent from the academic debates of the time: race was seen as one among many legitimate components involved in the crafting of national identities.[41]

The development of an ethnogenesis theory for each eponymous people of Central Asia paralleled the institutionalization of each republic's Academy of Sciences. From the 1920s onward, each capital city had opened subsidiaries of the Soviet Academy of Sciences, but a national academy would not be established in each republic until the Second World War or later – as late as 1954 for Kirgizia. Although the Tashkent conference of 1942 marked the official introduction of the ethnogenetic topic into the national historiographies of Central Asia, the concept was already being used a year earlier in Uzbekistan. The quincentennial celebration of the birth of the poet Alisher Navoy (1441–1501), considered the greatest figure of Uzbek literature but also claimed by the Tajiks for their national pantheon, helped the new Uzbek elites, massively purged during the 1937–8 purges, to express a national feeling that was compatible with Stalinist ideology.

The Uzbek Communist Party's Alisher Navoy Jubilee Committee commissioned the historian and Orientalist Aleksandr Iu. Iakubovskii (1886–1953), an expert on the Golden Horde, to compose a small brochure on the ethnogenesis of the Uzbek people, published as *On the Question of the Uzbek People's Ethnogenesis (K voprosu ob etnogeneze uzbekskogo naroda)*. The brochure challenged the historiography elaborated in the 1920s–30s that traced the origin of the Uzbeks to the arrival of the Shaybanid dynasty, a nomadic group that moved from the eastern part of the Golden Horde to today's Uzbek territory at the beginning of the sixteenth century. While the Shaybanids were considered the Uzbeks' national symbol in the interwar period, the rewriting of history in 1941 refuted this too-recent crystallization of Uzbek national consciousness and offered instead a genealogy that was more ancient – and therefore more prestigious. To build its refutation, Iakubovskii criticized the idea that the Uzbeks could have appeared as a people on the world stage only with the advent of their ethnonym. From the first sentence of his book, he enunciated the fundamental postulate of future ethnogenetic research: 'We must distinguish the conditions under which this or that people was formed from the history of its name'.[42]

As soon as an Uzbek Academy of Sciences was created in 1943, local historians undertook to publish a two-volume *History of the Peoples of Uzbekistan* (*Istoriia narodov Uzbekistana*). Paradoxically, it was volume II, covering the period from the Shaybanids to the 1917 Revolution, that, in 1947, was the first to appear, a decision rooted in local historians' desire to challenge Iakubovskii's vision of national history. This first volume continued to identify the Shaybanid dynasty as the key element that signalled the birth of the Uzbek nation. But by the time that the second volume was published in 1950, Iakubovskii's theories had gained control over the ethnogenetic discourse: in the volume's preface, the Russian historian reiterated the claim that the Uzbek people's existence predated its ethnonym.[43]

Iakubovskii's approach was continued by the historian Sergei P. Tolstov (1907–76), one of the great figures of Stalin-era Soviet scholarship. From 1939 to 1951, Tolstov held the chair of ethnology at Moscow State University, and from 1942 to 1965 he chaired the Soviet Academy of Sciences' Institute of Ethnography and its prestigious journal *Sovetskaia etnografiia*. His public career declined after Stalin's death; under pressure from his opponents, he was even forced to resign as scientific secretary of the Academy of Sciences in 1954. Tolstov was nonetheless named honorary academician when he retired in 1965, and he continued to lead prestigious multidisciplinary expeditions to Khorezm until 1969. Tolstov's famous book, *Ancient Khorezm* (*Drevnii Khorezm*), won the highest Soviet award, the Stalin Prize, in 1949.[44] This distinction reflected the interest of the country's top leader in the Central Asian region, in particular in the gigantic project of the Great Turkmen Canal, which was supposed to give desertic Khorezm access to the Caspian Sea by water. The awarding of the prestigious prize did not occur without some twists and turns: it was supposed to go to Boris Rybakov, a historian of early Russia but, at the last minute, Stalin decided to give the prize to both Rybakov and Tolstov.[45]

Tolstov was also one of the main editors of the second major historical anthology on Uzbekistan, *The History of the Uzbek Soviet Socialist Republic* (*Istoriia uzbekskoi SSR*), published in five volumes between 1955 and 1958. In the preface to the first volume, the authorial collective made no secret of the revisions to which the nation's history had been subjected between the publication of the 1947–50 *History of the Peoples of Uzbekistan* and the present edition. The authors specifically noted that 'the division between volumes one and two does not correspond to Marxist historical periodization, thereby giving the reader the impression that the authorial collective regards the era following the Shaybanid conquest as a new period'.[46] The scene was set for decades of ethnogenetic research seeking the most ancient possible antiquity.

The quest to locate the moment of the nation's crystallization in antiquity threw the Central Asian nations into competition with each other. In Tajikistan, the key Stalin-era figure, Bobodzhan Gafurov (1909–77), affirmed that the Tajik nation had formed as early as the Samanid dynasty in the tenth century (see Chapter 3), thereby leaving Uzbek scholars with no choice but to look for an even more ancient origin. The Shaybanid dynasty was decidedly too late. Kazakhstan likewise found itself in an ambivalent situation to Uzbekistan. In tsarist historiography and up until the 1930s, the prevailing approach was to date the ethnogenesis of the Kazakhs back to the development of the Kazakh Khanate from the wreckage of the Golden Horde. The mid-fifteenth-century departure of two nomadic chieftains, Janibek and Girey, was said to symbolize the separation of the future Uzbeks and Kazakhs and mark the creation of the first Kazakh Khanate. However, since this theory had the flaw of deriving from migrationist principles and insisting on the common past of two ethnic groups, it was challenged by the emerging ethnogenetic discourse in the 1940s.

In 1950, Viktor F. Shakhmatov denounced the *History of the Kazakh SSR* (*Istoriia kazakhskoi SSR*), published in 1943, as too subservient to bourgeois migrationist theories. He advocated instead that Kazakhstan follow the lead of the *History of the Peoples of Uzbekistan,* which asserted the soundness of autochthonist theories. Although the post-1941 historiography of Uzbekistan was recognized as setting the standard for the other republics, the competition between republics for their share of history remained intense. Indeed, while praising the ground-breaking vision of Uzbek historiography, Shakhmatov also criticized it: claiming the Sogdians as the original inhabitants of Uzbekistan implied that the Kazakhs were latecomers to the area.[47] On the contrary, according to Shakhmatov, one could speak of a Kazakh nationality as early as the pre-feudal stage – that is, before the Uzbek ethnogenesis. Capturing the Sogdians and more generally the Scythians as the first embodiment of a Kazakh nation enabled Kazakhstan to rival its Uzbek neighbour in terms of antiquity. On this view, Kazakhs' nomadic way of life in no way signified non-autochthonism.

In Turkmenistan, the founder of ethnogenetic discourse was none other than Iakubovskii himself. Following his brochure on Uzbek ethnogenesis, the Russian researcher turned his attention to Turkmenistan, publishing an article in *Sovetskaia etnografiia* entitled 'Questions of Turkmen Ethnogenesis in the Eighth to Tenth Centuries'. The title clearly indicates the historiographic issue at stake – to situate the birth of the Turkmen as a nation as far back in time as possible. Until then, the conventional discourse had the Turkmen arriving on the territory of present-day Turkmenistan in the eleventh century, during the Seljuk migrations toward Anatolia. Yet according to Iakubovskii, Arab sources attested to the presence of Oghuz Turks near the Ustyurt plateau as early as the ninth century, with the term 'Turkmen' designating those who had converted to Islam. For Iakubovskii, the encounter of these Oghuz with the other Turkic populations that had been present in southern Turkmenistan since the sixth century represented the origin of the Turkmens as such.[48] Here again, the goal of the ethnogenetic discourse was to anchor in ancient times the titular nation's presence on the republic's territory.

By the late 1940s, all the Central Asian republics had at least one book that established the principle of their ethnogenesis – all, that is, except for Kirgizia, which stood out for the trouble it experienced in constructing an ethnogenetic orthodoxy as quickly as its neighbours. Reconciling the different historical sources that mention the term 'Kirgiz' proved difficult and required a choice between two different approaches: either do without authoritative historical sources and make the undocumented autochthonist claim that the Kirgiz were the original inhabitants of the Tian-Shan, or else glorify the Kirgiz as having constituted a state since ancient times but in various places located outside the borders of the present-day republic.

In 1952, the Kirgiz branch of the Soviet Academy of Sciences expressly asked the Presidium to organize a series of ethnological expeditions able to deliver convincing results for one theory or the other. A special session of the Academy of Sciences, held in Frunze in 1956, was devoted exclusively to the question of the ethnogenesis of the Kirgiz, followed by three anthologies of Kirgiz history combining approaches from ethnology, linguistics, folklore and physical anthropology to provide a consensual answer that would be, it was hoped, definitive.[49] Bernshtam's opinion, reflecting the dominant view, was officially reproduced in 1956 in the first *History of the Kirgiz SSR* (*Istoriia kirgizskoi SSR*): the ethnogenesis of the Kirgiz happened in multiple historic stages and locations, from Siberia to the Tian-Shan.[50] Kirgizia thus failed to produce a well-oiled ethnogenetic myth, causing the little republic to stand out from its neighbours.

Subsequent nationalist rewritings and reinterpretations

The implementation of ethnogenesis theories in each of the USSR's union republics suggested a process of translation and adaptation to local contexts. For Central Asia, two important shifts in meaning shaped the development of ethnogenetic discourses in the second half of the twentieth century: first, the confusion of ethnic and racial discourses within the concept of ethnogenesis, and second, the desire to use ethnogenetic theories to deny the importance of clan divisions. These shifts in meaning were particularly visible in Kazakhstan and Turkmenistan.

In the 1920s–30s, physical anthropology attempted to retrace the great phenotypes present in Central Asia, a project that was almost systematically dissociated from historical and ethnological research. The main physical anthropology scholars, such as Debets and Lev V. Oshanin (1884–1962), came from the medical or biological disciplines, not the human sciences. They saw no direct link between the major original races and contemporary peoples: on the contrary, Soviet doctrine insisted on the common racial origin of Tajiks and Uzbeks, even though they had distinct histories and therefore dissociated ethnogeneses. With the arrival of ethnogenetic research, the linkages between the concepts of ethnicity and race grew more complex, with some researchers tending to treat the two terms as synonyms and hoping to prove the continuity of a people's physiological traits across time. Beginning in the 1940s, several texts conflated the somatic data collected by archaeology and anthropological investigations among contemporary peoples and employed interchangeably the various names given to ancient races and the ethnonyms of today.

In Turkmenistan from the 1950s on, the question of ethnogenesis was closely tied to research in physical anthropology. This research supposedly confirmed the preponderance of the Iranian substratum in 'Turkmen physiognomy', thereby validating both the people's antiquity and its ethno-racial continuity.[51] In the 1960s, at the Turkmen Institute of History, Ata Dzhikiev (1933–2013) argued that the continuity between the contemporary Turkmen and ancient peoples could be proven thanks to Oshanin's research, which linked contemporary Turkmen to the ancient dolichocephalic Caspian race. Hence, 'from the anthropological point of view, the Turkmen are the direct descendants of the Scythians'.[52] Dzhikiev likewise asserted that the Turkic languages were native to Central Asia and that the region had always been characterized by Persian–Turkic bilingualism. He thus transposed a desire for ethnic/racial autochthonism into a linguistic autochthonism. In 1967, at a special conference of the Academy of Sciences of Turkmenistan on the ethnogenetic question, the speakers insisted on the importance of Turkmen racial features that were said to validate the ethnogenetic theory of their Scythian dolichocephalic autochthonism.[53]

In Kazakhstan, the same racializing of ethnogenetic discourse became apparent in the 1960s and was formally theorized in the following decade. The Laboratory for Ethnic Anthropology at the Institute of History and Ethnology of the Kazakh Academy of Sciences, led by Orazak Ismagulov (b. 1930), has, since the 1970s, continuously published studies in physical anthropology to demonstrate the racial unity of the Kazakhs. According to Ismagulov, there not only exists a specific Kazakh race that is uniform throughout the entire republic but this race also occupies a central position among Turkic peoples and exceeds them in the harmonious way in which it combines various somatic criteria.[54] Ismagulov's 1977 work, *The Ethnic Genogeography of the Kazakhs* (*Etnicheskaia genogeografiia kazakhov*), in which he defends the idea of 'man's biosocial nature', came under direct attack from the Communist Party of the Soviet Union, which belatedly labelled it as nationalist. Yet milder discourses on the unity and antiquity of a supposed 'Kazakh race' were allowed within the local academic system.

These racial references were employed in an ambiguous manner with respect to the ethnic question: the dolichocephaly of the Turkmen was, as Oshanin suggested, a 'persistent racial feature' (*stoikii rasovyi priznak*) that made it possible to differentiate the Turkmen from the other peoples of Central Asia.[55] Orazmukhammed Babakov, a specialist in physical anthropology, analysed the place of the Turkmen 'in the racial system' (*v rasovoi sistematike*) of the region and affirmed the Turkmen people's anthropological unity despite their tribal diversity.[56] As in Kazakhstan, the persistence of tribal and/or clan divisions posed a problem for scholars defending ethno-racial unity: omnipresent in oral literature through genealogies and often invoked in emic definitions given by a part of the population, especially rural, the reference to tribe disrupted the idea of unity that underpinned the modern socialist nation.

Physical anthropology was thus instrumentalized to prove the physical unity of the nation using data from craniology, serology, odontology and dermatology. The internal divisions represented by tribes, clans or regionalisms were considered to be matters of history or culture, 'vestiges' (*perezhitki*) that were doomed and scarcely relevant to understanding the reality of contemporary societies. While ethnogenetic discourses anchored each nation in the most ancient past possible, physical anthropology asserted the ethnic/racial unity of Soviet Central Asian societies and therefore their socialist modernity.

Soviet ethnological science institutionalized ethnogenesis as one of its core research objects in Central Asia for the brief period between 1941 and 1956. This quest for ethnogenesis remained part of the ethnological orthodoxy throughout the entire Soviet period. All its main theoreticians for Central Asia – Iakubovskii, Tolstov, Gafurov and Shakhmatov – had brilliant academic trajectories. Although trained in Moscow in a specific intellectual and political context, that of Stalinism, their legacy was never repudiated, even in a new, post-Soviet context; instead, they remain celebrated founding fathers of local academia to this day.

The arrival of political independence in 1991 has not challenged but instead reinforced the quest for the most ancient ethnogenesis: national historiography still aims to demonstrate the permanent presence of the nation on its eponymous territory dating back to ancient times and to refute the idea that the Turkic population arrived from the Eastern Siberian steppes. In Kazakhstan, the disciples of Ismagulov continue to assert that 'the Kazakhs' genetic stock is biologically indivisible and unified, and a division into clans, tribes, or hordes is not justified'.[57] The Museum of National History in Almaty maintains a physical anthropology department that displays tableaux on Kazakh ethnogenesis based on the physical appearance criteria worked out by Ismagulov.

The republic-level tradition of 'archaeological patriotism' – looking as far back in the past as possible to trace the nation's origins – is still seen as a unifying thread for national historiography to this day. Although Soviet historiography was certainly not aiming to achieve the independence of the republics, it indirectly elaborated a repertoire of scholarly arguments in support of the nation-state. It offered a 'ready-to-think' checklist for nationhood that did not require major methodological transformations: minor adjustments were needed with regard to the most recent historical periods, those which have involved interactions with Russians, but the *longue durée* vision of the nation could easily be transferred from Soviet times to the post-Soviet context of political independence.

Notes

1 Tolz, *Russia's Own Orient*.
2 Martin, *The Affirmative Action Empire*.
3 Haupt et al., *Les Marxistes et la question nationale, 1848–1914*.
4 Carrère d'Encausse, *Le Grand défi*, 51.
5 Stalin, *Le Marxisme et la question nationale et colonial*, 15.
6 Haugen, *The Establishment of National Republics*. See also Sabol, 'The Creation of Central Asia'.
7 Cadiot, *Le Laboratoire imperial*, 117.
8 Hirsch, *Empire of Nations*.
9 Bergne, *The Birth of Tajikistan*.
10 Gabdulhakov, 'The Highly Securitized Insecurities of State Borders in the Fergana Valley'.
11 See more in Hirsch, *Empire of Nations*.
12 Cadiot, *Le Laboratoire impérial*, 133; Hirsch, *Empire of Nations,* 148–65.
13 Hirsch, *Empire of Nations,* 156.
14 Moine, 'Passeportisation, statistique des migrations et contrôle de l'identité sociale'.
15 Suny and Martin (eds), *A State of Nations*.
16 Blum and Mespoulet, *L'Anarchie bureaucratique*.
17 Cadiot, *Le Laboratoire impérial*, 192.
18 Cadiot, *Le Laboratoire impérial*, 202–4.
19 Slezkine, 'The USSR as a Communal Apartment'.
20 Suny, *Intellectuals and the Articulation of the Nation*.
21 Bertrand, 'Une science sans objet?'.
22 Seriot (ed.), 'Un paradigme perdu'.
23 Shnirelman, 'Zlokliucheniia odnoi nauki: etnogeneticheskie issledovaniia i stalinskaia natsional'naia politika'.
24 'Sessiia po etnogenezu Srednei Azii', 301.
25 Hirsch, *Empire of Nations*, 231–72.
26 Debets et al., 'Antropologicheskii material kak istochnik izucheniia voprosov etnogeneza', 24, 28.
27 Shakhmatov, 'K voprosu ob etnogeneze kazakhskogo naroda', 81.
28 Abramzon, *Kirgizy i ikh etnogeneticheskiie i istoriko-kul'turnye sviazi*, 28.
29 Mogilner, *Homo Imperii*; Rainbow (ed.), *Ideologies of Race*.
30 Debets (ed.), *Trudy kirgizskij arkheologo-etnograficheskoi ekspeditsii*, 24.
31 Chirokogoroff, 'La théorie de l'ethnos'.
32 Skalnik, 'N. Ia. Marr and the National Origins of Soviet Ethnogenetics'; Skalnik, 'Towards an Understanding of Soviet Etnos Theory'.
33 Bromley, *Soviet Ethnology and Anthropology Today*.
34 Banks, *Ethnicity: Anthropological Constructions*, 17–24.
35 On Lev Gumilev, see Bassin, *The Gumilev Mystique* and Laruelle, *Russian Eurasianism*.
36 Bromlei, 'Etnos i endogamiia'.
37 I thank Élisabeth Gessat-Anstett for her thoughts on this topic. On eugenics in Russia, see Adams (ed.), *The Wellborn Science*; Solomon, *Health and Society in Revolutionary Russia*.
38 Gessat-Anstett, 'Les mots/maux de l'etnografiâ', 70.
39 Tishkov, 'The Phenomenon of Ethnicity in Russian Context'.
40 'Sessiia po etnogenezu Srednei Azii'.
41 See, in particular, Hirsch's article, 'Race without the Practice of Racial Politics'.
42 Iakubovskii, *K voprosu ob etnogeneze uzbekskogo naroda*, 1.
43 Iakubovskii, *Istoriia narodov Uzbekistana*, 1–8.
44 Tolstov, *Drevnii Khorezm*.
45 Germanov, 'S. P. Tolstov: maître, docteur, commandeur'.
46 Tolstov et al. (eds), *Istoriia uzbekskoi SSR*, vi.
47 See Shakhmatov, 'K voprosu ob etnogeneze kazakhskogo naroda', 87.
48 Iakubovskii, 'Voprosy etnogeneza turkmen v VIII–X vv'.
49 Debets, *Trudy kirgizskoi arkheologo-etnograficheskoi ekspeditsii*, 234.
50 Abramzon, *Kyrgyzy i ikh etnogeneticheskie i istoriko-kul'turnye sviazi*. In an article in *Sovetskaia Kirgiziia* (28 February 1973), the First Secretary of the Kyrgyz Communist Party, T.U. Usunbaliev, criticized the book for undervaluing the Russian contributions in the region and

the changes experienced by the Kyrgyz in the Soviet period. If Abramzon's study was insufficiently conciliatory on the question of the Russian 'older brother' or the analysis of the nineteenth and twentieth centuries, the text did end up representing orthodoxy in ethnogenetic matters and is still considered a reference work today.

51 See, for example, Vasil'eva, *Etnograficheskie dannye o proiskhozhdenii turkmenskogo naroda*.

52 Dzhikiev, *Ocherk etnicheskoi istorii i formirovaniia naseleniia iuzhnogo Turkmenistana*, 28.

53 See *Vsesoiuznoe soveshchanie po etnogenezu turkmenskogo naroda*.

54 Ismagulov, *Etnicheskaia antropologiia Kazakhstana*, 9.

55 Ismagulov, *Etnicheskaia antropologiia Kazakhstana*, 8.

56 See Babakov, *Antropologicheskii sostav turkmenskogo naroda v sviazi s problemoi etnogeneza*, 18. This 'racial system' comprised a europoid dolichocephalic Transcaspian race (the Turkmen), a europoid brachycephalic race situated between the Amu Darya and Syr Darya (the Uzbeks, the Tajiks and a portion of the Karakalpaks), a europoid dolichocephalic Caspian race (the Azeris) and a Siberian race from the south of Semirechie (the Kazakhs and Kirgiz).

57 Isliamieva, 'Gosudarstvennaia teoriia etnogeneza kazakhov v istorigrafii XX veka', 149.

2
Centrality and autochthonism: Uzbekistan's nationhood

Since independence, Uzbekistan's strategy has been to promote two forms of state nationalism. The first was a political nationalism that reflected the authoritarian nature of the Karimov regime, which regarded the political order as natural and uncontroversial and the state as the ultimate embodiment of the nation. The second was a cultural nationalism that gave preference to the titular ethnic group in everything symbolic. To this day, even after Karimov's death and the arrival in power of Shavkat Mirziyoyev, the ideological premise of the Uzbek state, inspired by German Romanticism, rests on the idea that each people has a spirit that endures across time and expresses its essence under different ethnic labels. The ideology of national independence as a political project is, therefore, closely interrelated with the sublimation of the Uzbek nation in its supposed essence, manifested through a linear historical trajectory with the independent nation-state as its most evident achievement.

Under President Islam Karimov, the Uzbek regime successfully crafted a historical grand narrative as well as a wide array of national symbols whose meaning is largely understood by the population – a strategy nicely described by Laura Adams as the 'spectacular state'.[1] Thus, the new Uzbek state is displayed through a political architecture style that could be named 'dubaio-timurid', a reinterpretation of the classic Timurid style with a modernity inspired by the Emirates.[2] What Michael Billig defines as *banal nationalism* also constitutes an integral part of the Uzbek nationhood process. This is the case, for instance, for Uzbek pop music, which combines a Russian-Soviet legacy with Oriental flavours (Arabic or Persian in style, with some borrowings from Bollywood) and offers a pantheon of modern idols and their 'people' stories.[3] It is also the case for Uzbekistan's vibrant film industry: Uzbekkino is the only cinema production agency in Central Asia able to produce commercially viable films that attract a large domestic audience.[4] Uzbek cuisine has also became a brand that works both domestically, where its rich symbolic background (family, community, hospitality)[5] means that it is easily celebrated, and internationally, with chains of Uzbek restaurants all over Russia, for instance.

The literature on post-Soviet Uzbek nationhood is rich, with masterful studies by Laura Adams and Peter Finke joining older works on late Soviet Uzbekistan such as those by William Fierman. In addition, articles by Andrew F. March, Nick Megoran, Timur Dadabaev, Shahram Akbarzadeh, Charles Kurzman, Reuel Hanks, Johan Rasanayagam, Sarah Kendzior, Nancy Rosenberger and others examine various aspects of the nationhood process.[6] In this chapter, I focus on the intersection of the political and cultural aspects of the official Uzbek ideology of nationhood, especially the ways in which its authors have rewritten the nation's historical trajectory.

Pillars of post-Soviet Uzbekistan: stability as a brand

After Turkmenistan, Uzbekistan under Islam Karimov (1938–2016) was long the most stable and repressive regime in Central Asia. It avoided Tajikistan's path to civil war and the political upheavals of Kyrgyzstan, as well as the appearance of opposition coalitions at regular intervals as occurred in Kazakhstan. Though the rise and fall of the president's eldest daughter, Gulnara Karimova, and other squabbles over property rights suggested the existence of scores to be settled among the elite, these remained mostly behind closed doors. After pushing oppositional nationalist figures – such as Muhammad Salih of the Erk movement and Abdurakhim Polatov of Birlik – into exile in 1992–3, authorities faced minimal externalized intra-elite tensions. There were, of course, some exceptions, such as vocal regime-critic Rustam Usmanov, a businessman who founded Uzbekistan's first private bank – Rustambank – in 1990. The regime also succeeded in hunting dissidents abroad by using mechanisms of extraterritoriality shared with neighbouring countries.[7]

Uzbekistan's wealth derives mainly from a few major industries and resources, principally cotton, gold, uranium and hydrocarbons; the country has a limited private sector. This wealth structure has helped to consolidate elites around a few rent-seeking opportunities. The Karimov family monopolized the most profitable sectors, especially the national mineral industries and Gazprom's gas sales, as well as such niches as construction, cement production, trade with China, and communications and entertainment – at least until Gulnara Karimova's commercial empire was dismantled in 2013–14.[8]

Closely linked to the president's family but nonetheless autonomous, the security services (known as the SNB), the successor organization to the KGB, became one of the main actors in the Uzbek economy. From their early days selling off Soviet-era military spare parts, the SNB's main figures, especially Rustam Inoyatov, built a veritable commercial empire. Over time, a faction at the SNB took control of fiscal sectors, the Customs Committee, the Ministry of Foreign Economic Relations, the Border Guards and the National Migration Agency, as well as cotton export state holdings, the banking system and wholesale markets. The regional elites, although they had been powerful in the 1990s, were gradually pushed to the margins of decision-making processes in Tashkent, then relegated to managing day-to-day affairs in their own regions and focusing on their primary assets, cotton and agriculture.[9] The luckier and better-connected among them controlled part of the industrial production and communication sectors.

In this context, the grand national narrative rapidly positioned Uzbekistan as a fortress of stability in the face of unstable neighbours. The authorities branded Tajikistan and, to an even greater extent, Kyrgyzstan as counter-models of statehood, states that were failing due to civil war and colour revolutions, respectively. They also released propaganda against Islamist – or allegedly Islamist – attempts to challenge Karimov's legitimacy, painting them as an existential threat to state sovereignty and to national survival. The authorities crushed the Islamist opposition in the Fergana Valley, led by Tohir Yuldashev (1967–99) and Juma Namangani (1968–2001), as early as 1991–2; accused Islamists of organizing the Tashkent terrorist attacks of February 1999; fought against incursions of the Islamic Movement of Uzbekistan coming from the Tajik and Kyrgyz sides of the Fergana Valley in the summers of 1999 and 2000; and abruptly repressed the Andijon riots of May 2005. With the exception of minor skirmishes at the Uzbek–Kyrgyz border,[10] the regime then enjoyed a decade of stability without any visible fomented instability until the natural death of Islam Karimov in September 2016.

Under the first president, the authorities not only skilfully liquidated any potential opposition, but also used coercive tools on a large scale in order to maintain stability. Restrictions on the freedoms of speech, press and association – as well as an isolationist policy aimed at limiting external influences of all sorts – secured the political status quo for two decades.[11] Yet it would be a mistake to think that this popular support was obtained through coercion alone. The regime also succeeded in articulating several political, economic and nationhood-related narratives that consolidated its legitimacy. It branded itself as the only secular force able to resist the supposed Islamist threat,[12] an approach that won the regime the support of many citizens who had been traumatized by the neighbouring Tajik civil war and were fearful of any risk of destabilization. The regime also articulated a paternalistic vision of the relationship between leader and people that gained the support of the large part of the population that was concerned by the collapse of the Soviet welfare state and wanted the state to continue to provide public goods. Lastly, the regime structured widespread patronal practices that integrated each citizen into a clientelist pyramid based on the exchange of several types of duties (extended family, neighbourhood community, regional kinship, professional community and so on).[13]

Closely interrelated to this patronal politics was Uzbekistan's economic policy. In the 1990s, the choice of gradualism – that is, moving slowly towards a market economy and avoiding the shock therapy promoted by Western donors or international financial institutions – proved decently successful, protecting the Uzbek population against upheavals in their standards of living.[14] This success gave rise to the so-called Five Principles of Uzbek economics, which the country officially followed for almost three decades.[15] However, the model stopped working as early as the 2000s: Uzbekistan lost many of its foreign investors in the mineral and energy industry; could not reform the agricultural sector (which still employs half the population); failed to rapidly develop new, tertiary, service-based economic domains; and began to face massive labour migration (at least 3 million Uzbek citizens were working in Russia just before the economic crisis of 2014, with hundreds of thousands more employed in South Korea, Turkey and the United Arab Emirates) and brain drain due to the departure of its younger, highly skilled generations.[16]

This economic devolution was reflected in Uzbekistan's regional policy. At the beginning of the 1990s, Tashkent was hoping to become the new regional leader of Central Asia, a claim based on its historical pre-eminence and demographic domination (half the Central Asian population is Uzbek, or about 30 million of the region's 60 million people). However, unsatisfied with its reluctant neighbours, and then rapidly surpassed by a rising Kazakhstan boosted by oil prices, Uzbekistan withdrew into an isolationist policy.[17] This strategy had two main goals: first, to avoid any disruptive external influences from world powers such as Russia and the United States (as well as from international institutions pushing for regional cooperation and integration); and second, to secure the regime in the face of regional instabilities that threatened to spill over into Uzbekistan, from the wars in Tajikistan and Afghanistan to inter-ethnic tensions in Southern Kyrgyzstan.[18] This isolationist policy dramatically hampered regional cooperation, fuelling tensions with Tajikistan and Kyrgyzstan over cross-border hydroelectric management, limiting the country's natural role as the region's trade power, and weakening the regime's narrative of Uzbekistan as the crossroads between East and West, Europe and Asia.

The ideology of national independence

In parallel, the Karimov regime rapidly and effectively built a state-sponsored discourse to replace the previous, discredited Marxist-Leninist ideology, with the goal of preventing a potential ideological 'vacuum'. This discourse aimed to neutralize any external influences that could divide the country, whether Islamic, ethnonationalist or inspired by Western liberal values. The regime continued to subscribe to the Soviet epistemological view that ideology is not only above politics, but also objective and neutral when based on uncontestable realities. In Karimov's own words, 'It is natural that the state system, its operation and accompanying policies should above all be constructed on the basis of a concretely formulated ideology'.[19]

In the first years after the collapse of the Soviet Union, Karimov tried to revive the historical name of Turkestan and promoted a regional identity based on Turkic and Muslim values, an identity that he dubbed Turanism.[20] He thus positioned himself in direct ideological competition with Kazakhstan's president Nursultan Nazarbayev, who put forward the rival concept of Eurasia (see Chapter 7). While the notion of Turkestan as the new Central Asia, with Uzbekistan at its heart, did not resonate regionally, it had long been embraced domestically by the Uzbek opposition. Both Muhammad Salih and Abdurakhim Polatov, for instance, belonged to a semi-dissident literary tradition, formed in the 1960s and 1970s, that called for a more Islamo-nationalist orientation and the revival of Turkestani unity.[21] Regardless, the reference to Turkestan was rapidly replaced by a more Uzbekistan-centric narrative that posited the existence of unique national pathways to development.

The so-called Uzbek path aimed to anchor the country in a *longue durée* perspective, as the result of centuries – even millennia – of history, and called for the president himself to personalize the historical trajectory of the nation-state. However, Karimov's cult of personality was less extreme than that of Saparmurat Niyazov in neighbouring Turkmenistan.[22] Unlike Niyazov, Karimov was not exalted for any personal (and almost supernatural) powers, but for embodying the state and the nation – for being, according to Andrew F. March, 'the Great Uzbek Statebuilder'.[23] In the 1990s, in particular, the urban landscape was covered with billboards of Karimov in the role of the 'father of the nation', with slogans celebrating the homeland (*vatan*), which he personified.

The ideology of national independence that Karimov embodied took form through a meticulous process of crafting a consistent corpus of texts. As Sarah Kendzior notes, some of these texts were published immediately, while others were held in reserve to respond to events in the country when the time was right. The president himself supposedly wrote several books promoting a vision that Uzbekistan was on a unique path: *Uzbekistan: National Independence, Economic Policy and Ideology* (*O'zbekiston: milliy istiqlol, iqtisodiy siyosat va mafkura*, 1993); *Our Highest Goal: Independence and Blossoming of the Nation, Freedom and Prosperity of the People* (*Ozod va obod Vatan, erkin va farovon hayot – pirovard maqsadimiz*, 2000); and *The Idea of National Independence: Main Aspects and Criteria (Milliy istiqlol g'oyasi: asosiy tushuncha va tamoyillar*, 2003). All these works, made mandatory reading on school and university curricula, celebrate the nation as a *fait accompli* of Uzbek history. As Karimov stated, 'The ideology must first reflect the spiritual particularity and uniqueness of the sacred traditions and aspirations of our nation, formulated over many centuries and millennia'.[24]

A long list of clichéd values was presented as comprising the core of the Uzbek national consciousness: respect for family, elders and traditional values; friendship; peace and tolerance; openness to other civilizations; patience; hospitality; and industriousness.[25] Nevertheless, it took several ideologists or court writers to shape this grand narrative, including Karimov advisers Rustam Zhumaev[26] and Habibullah Tadzhiev,[27] as well as, more importantly, the academic Ozod Sharafidinov (1929–2005), a former secretary for ideological issues of the Uzbek Communist Party. The first two men mainly advanced the discourse of the millennia-long struggle of Uzbekistan for its independence and national identity, while Sharafidinov became the official ideologist of *Ma'naviyat,* the Uzbek term for spirituality or morality (meaning, in Islamic tradition, the acceptance of God's word).

Obsessed with 'alien' influences – particularly liberal values, Western consumerism, ethnonationalism and Islamism – the Uzbek state aimed to develop 'ideological immunity' (*mafkuraviy immunitet*), embodied by *Ma'naviyat*. The Karimov regime began to use the term

Ma'naviyat in 1994, ultimately launching a television channel and publishing house with the same name. Following it, classes on *Ma'naviyat va Ma'rifat* (Spirituality and Enlightenment) were introduced to school and university curricula. In 2004, *Ma'naviyat* was further institutionalized through the creation of a Republic Centre for Spiritual Propaganda (*Respublika Ma'naviyat va Ma'rifat Kengashi*), a kind of Ministry of Ideology. Among its responsibilities, the Centre oversaw the hiring of a vice-dean of *Ma'naviyat* in each higher educational institution. This vice-dean not only supervised the teaching of the discipline, but also inspected the clothing worn by young men and women at the university to be sure that this attire reflected the norms of morality and 'humble' behaviour.[28] In 2008, Karimov published *High Spirituality: An Invisible Force* (*Yuksak ma'naviyat – yengilmas kuch*), which encapsulated the quintessence of *Ma'naviyat*. The volume touts high morality as an intrinsic quality of the Uzbek people, a virtue that, Karimov claims, has been under threat from potential external interference for centuries. The text also defends state paternalism, patriotism and respect for traditional hierarchy and elders; celebrates *mahalla* (the neighbourhood community) as the Uzbek version of civil society;[29] advances conservative social mores, especially male superiority;[30] advocates for protecting younger generations from Western values and mass culture; and integrates Islamic references into the *Ma'naviyat* doctrinal corpus.[31]

Through the structured doctrine of *Ma'naviyat*, the Uzbek regime positioned itself as the bearer of moral authority for the whole society. Ideology has, therefore, become closely associated with social and cultural control. It has allowed for the delegitimization of the political opposition, which has been accused of colluding with the enemies of the nation and of not respecting the principles of Uzbekness; the Andijon violence of May 2005, for instance, was framed as having been orchestrated by people who were not authentically Uzbek.[32] The regime's ideology also justified the establishment of a censorship code based on the morality narrative: the state agency for arts, Uzbeknavo, for instance, took performance licences away from pop singers such as Lola Yuldasheva and film directors such as Zulfikar Musakov on the grounds that they did not respect the principles of *Ma'naviyat*.[33] In the early 2000s, the official youth movement, Kamalot, which was modelled on the Soviet-era Komsomol (Communist Youth), embraced *Ma'naviyat* by performing symbolic collective actions and demonstrating loyalty toward the regime.[34]

For over a quarter of a century, the Uzbek regime succeeded in building a supposed consensus on the essence of Uzbekness. Reminiscent of Soviet ideological language, this Uzbekness was presented as a positive force that valued world peace, advanced a unique national development path, and was able to resist decadent liberal values, destructive Islamism and ethnonationalist principles. The Karimov regime also pioneered the narrative on the need to 'de-Westernize' the nation's social and cultural values, a discourse that became mainstream across the post-Soviet region in the 2010s.

A straightforward nationhood process?

Compared to its neighbours, Karimov's Uzbekistan has enjoyed a relatively painless and straightforward nation-building process. Several structural reasons account for this fortunate situation. The first of these is Uzbekistan's rich history. Since the early 1920s, when the Soviet regime constructed the first national entities, the country has always presented itself – and been seen by Moscow – as the heart of Central Asia. Created in 1924, the Uzbek Soviet Socialist Republic took precedence over its neighbours, including all the regions populated by sedentary peoples and almost all the ancient cities of Transoxiana. Uzbek elites successfully lobbied Moscow to include Bukhara and Samarkand in the republic over the opposition of Tajik elites.[35]

Tashkent became the obvious capital city of the region thanks to its status as the capital of the tsarist governorate of Turkestan, and it maintained this prominence until the collapse of the Soviet Union. The city hosted prestigious institutions, particularly in academia and higher education, as well as the Spiritual Board of Muslims of Central Asia (SADUM). The Soviet regime also lauded Uzbekistan as embodying the alliance between socialism and the Orient, instrumentalizing this narrative as a foreign policy tool when Moscow reached out to the Islamic world.[36] Moreover, Uzbekistan is home to much of the region's celebrated architectural heritage, which has been interpreted as a sign of the state's historical centrality and continuity. Even though local communist elites never actively sought independence, it was easy for them to construct an independent Uzbek nation-state on these premises.

The second reason is demographic. Unlike in Kazakhstan or Kyrgyzstan, the ethnic make-up of the population did not lead to identity-related insecurities. Ethnic Uzbeks constituted 71 per cent of the population in the final Soviet census (1989), a figure that has reportedly increased to about 85 per cent (there has not been an official census in the past three decades). The authorities have been accused of forcing citizens to self-identify as part of the titular ethnic group in order to reinforce the country's ethnic homogeneity,[37] but even without coercion, Uzbekistan is undoubtedly the nation-state of Uzbeks. The only noticeable tensions have occurred with the Tajik-speaking segment of the population, mostly located in Bukhara and Samarkand, which was forced to Uzbekify – that is, to identify themselves as ethnically Uzbek in their passports and not to claim the right to speak Tajik in public spaces, administrations and educational institutions. Officially, Tajiks now account for less than 5 per cent of the population, but this number is not relevant, as many families in Bukhara and Samarkand are bilingual and could identify ethnically with either group.[38]

Other ethnic groups are not considered to pose any risks to the country's ethnic homogeneity. The Russian minority has significantly decreased – from 1.6 million in 1989 to about 500,000 (again, there is no official data) today – and is concentrated in Tashkent and the city of Navoiy, which hosts the country's main extractive industries.[39] Unlike in Kazakhstan, Uzbekistan's Russian minority has never claimed any specific rights and has not been associated with any secessionist risks. The Karakalpak minority (about half a million people), located in the north western part of the country, still formally holds autonomous status, but this autonomy is almost nonexistent except in some very limited cultural respects.[40] The city of Nukus and the whole Karakalpakstan Autonomous Region are among the poorest and most remote areas of the country. Many Karakalpaks have emigrated to nearby Kazakhstan, which offers more economic opportunity and greater linguistic and cultural affinity.

Third, Uzbekistan rapidly built (and has maintained) a straightforward nationality and citizenship policy. It declared Uzbek the only state language – with Russian losing any official status – and shifted to the Latin alphabet as early as 1993 in order to further cut symbolic ties with its Russian past.[41] It seems that many official documents, especially those that use legal and technical language, are still written in Russian before being translated and officially published in Uzbek.[42] However, Uzbek is, without a doubt, the language used most frequently in public spaces, the media and academic institutions, while Russian is increasingly marginalized.

Contrary to its language policy, which was implemented to break away from the country's Soviet past, Uzbekistan's citizenship policy was built on its Soviet legacy: the difference between citizenship and nationality/ethnic group has been maintained in passports and administrative documents. All persons born in the republic or residing on its territory as of 1991 are considered Uzbek citizens, while people who identify as Uzbeks but reside beyond the national borders fall outside the purview of Tashkent.[43]

Political stronghold over academia

Establishing the ideology of national independence required the academic world to support the new ideational regime. The Academy of Sciences, for instance, was asked to publish a 'popular-scientific dictionary of independence' that would lend academic legitimacy to the new vocabulary of nationalism and serve as an encyclopaedia of Uzbekistan's post-Soviet ideology.[44] More importantly, the disciplines considered essential to justifying the new national grand narrative – namely, history, archaeology and ethnology – were placed under tight supervision.

The authorities visibly strengthened their control over the historical narrative in 1998. That year, apparently dissatisfied with the Institute of History's lack of output, President Karimov convened a conference of Uzbek historians, after which the Cabinet of Ministers issued a decree 'On the Improvement of the Activity of the Institute of History of the Academy of Sciences of Uzbekistan'. The influence of political authorities on the discipline of history is affirmed in the first point of this statement: 'The Cabinet of Ministers decrees that the main purpose of the activity of the Institute of History is the study of the authentic history of the Uzbek people and their state'.[45] Every semester, the institute was required to organize a seminar on the history of Uzbek statehood; to collect information on the history of the Uzbek people, its governance and its ethnogenesis; and to advance archaeological knowledge and research on local written sources (manuscripts). The decree also guaranteed new financial resources to promote national history, including the creation of the journal *O'zbekiston Tarihi*.

Dilorom Alimova was appointed deputy director and then director of the Institute of History, a position she held until 2010. A former specialist on women's liberation in the Soviet era, Alimova shifted to the study of Muslim modernist movements of the early twentieth century, a particularly sensitive issue for the authorities (see below). Under her leadership, the Institute became more dynamic: Alimova developed contacts with foreign colleagues; had researchers participate in international conferences; attempted to revive publications; and recruited specialists and PhD candidates in medieval and ancient history, disciplines that require the mastery of manuscripts.[46] As during Soviet times, contemporary history remains the most sensitive topic, as it is entirely subordinate to the official state narrative.[47] Historians who wish to distance themselves from these schemes must take refuge in more ancient history, though even this is not entirely free of political overtones.

Archaeology, too, has become highly strategic, as it holds the power to either confirm or deny the presence of ancient Uzbek people on their current territory and to attribute to them or not the brilliant sedentary civilizations that developed in Bactria and Sogdiana. Required to discover physical evidence of the ancient presence of an Uzbek nation on contemporary Uzbekistani soil, the field of archaeology has been subordinated to the autochthonist ideology sponsored by the authorities.

Ethnology remains one of the premier sciences of Uzbek nationhood. Where historical sources are lacking, only ethnology can establish a foundation for the pre-eminence of the Uzbek people over other national groups in their titular state and prove their ethnic continuity since time immemorial. Often based on solid empirical research, ethnology focuses on material culture: housing, clothing, crafts, folklore, rituals and ceremonies. Notwithstanding the discourse on disciplinary renewal and its distancing from Soviet-Russian perspectives, which are denounced as colonial, the vast majority of Uzbek ethnological work continues to be based on Russian sources from the second half of the nineteenth century and into the Soviet period.

Political science and sociology, already scarce in the Soviet academic tradition, have been further marginalized. While Tashkent's National University had had a chair of sociology (within the philosophy faculty), other universities offered very few, if any, courses in the field. Studies of new social practices, such as migration – both internal and international – were considered too sensitive, as they revealed the failure of the Uzbek economic model. Political science was officially banned from Uzbek universities in 2015, accused of being a 'Western pseudo-science' conceptualized by external powers to interfere in Uzbekistan's domestic affairs.[48] Some topics deemed neutral – for instance, Uzbekistan's membership in international organizations – were, however, still permitted to be studied under the guise of international relations.

The nation's grand narrative

Independent Uzbekistan rapidly constructed a grand historical narrative that insisted on the nation's ancient history and its continuity regardless of the attendant state structure.[49] It made extensive use of historical commemorations: 660 years since the birth of Tamerlane

(1996), 2,500 years since the foundation of Bukhara and Khiva (1997), 2,500 years since the foundation of Tashkent (2009), and so on. Any political or scientific work must begin by commenting on the unique ancient lineage of the country. For instance, as mentioned in UNESCO's *History of Uzbekistan*, 'Uzbekistan is a country of ancient and original history, whose peoples have contributed much to world history. The territory of Uzbekistan is one of the sources of development of the original man'.[50] Based on these premises, the country's historical grand narrative can be schematically divided into three core periods: Antiquity, classical Transoxiana and Soviet-Russian domination.

Antiquity: the older the better

The first direction is to secure the indigeneity of Uzbeks as far back in history as possible, with a triple aim: to deny Iran and Tajikistan the legitimacy of the Indo-European legacy; to monopolize the prestigious Scythian heritage; and to refute the Western and Russian perception of Turkic peoples as nomads who moved from eastern Siberia to Central Asia. As seminally discussed by Peter Finke, the conception of the Uzbek people as sedentary Turkic-speakers requires striking a balance between the legacy of the Iranian oases-dwellers and that of the pastoralists in the Steppe[51] – that is, to decide which of these two cultural realms should receive symbolic pre-eminence, both in time (who can claim indigeneity?) and in associated values (which culture is seen as superior?). It also forces Uzbek scholars to address the mismatch between the ethnonym of Uzbeks (who emerged with the Shaybanid dynasty in the sixteenth century) and the earlier presence of a Turkic population in Transoxiana, the Dasht-i Qipchaq (who came from the Steppe).

As discussed in the previous chapter, advocacy of autochthonism is rooted in the Soviet academic tradition, but it was conspicuously magnified by independence. Epitomizing this continuity between the Soviet and post-Soviet eras were Karim Shaniazov's (1924–2000) intellectual *oeuvre* and his institutional status. Shaniazov received his candidate's degree in 1960 and his doctorate in 1975. In 1967, just after the arrival of Yulian Bromley at the Miklukho-Maklay Institute of Ethnography in Moscow, Shaniazov was elected as head of the Ethnology Department of the Uzbek Institute of History. His 1974 book, *For an Ethnic History of the Uzbek People* (*K etnicheskoi istorii uzbekskogo naroda*) focused on Kipchaks, who, along with the Karluks and Oghuz, are traditionally apprehended as ethnic ancestors of the Uzbeks. The value of the Kipchaks lies in the fact that they are mentioned in Arabic sources from the eighth and ninth centuries. By cross-referencing data sources and ancient philological, etymological and geographical information, Shaniazov thus positions the Kipchaks as part of what he called the 'indigenous people' (*korennyi narod*) of South Siberia.[52] He argues that although medieval sources date the arrival of the western Kipchaks on the present-day territory of Uzbekistan only back to the fifteenth century, these sources neglected to mention the existence of *eastern* Kipchaks, who had been present since the tenth century. For him, the 'main features of the ethnic Uzbek nationality' thus date back to the tenth century.[53]

After 1990, Shaniazov led a scientific group studying the ethnic and ethnogenetic processes of the Uzbeks and supervised all the Institute's theses in ethnology. The only ethnologist who was also a member of the Academy of Sciences of Uzbekistan, he continued to publish on the question of national ethnogenesis until his death in 2000, pursuing the theories enunciated by Iakubovskii and Tolstov half a century earlier.[54] The ideological continuity of his Soviet and post-Soviet works reveals the extent to which Uzbek research on ethnogenesis has never called into question the founding assumptions developed under Stalin, namely that ethnology should search for the oldest possible existence of a national consciousness and affirm its continuity on the territory over time.

Already obsessed with demonstrating the existence of a first substrate of Turkic people before the arrival of Indo-Europeans during the Soviet period, Shaniazov's search for the most convincing historical argument accelerated with independence. In *The Kang State and People* (*Kanf davlati va kanglilar*),[55] published in Uzbek in 1990, Shaniazov denied that the Turkic khaganat (around 552 to 744 CE) announced the arrival of Turkic peoples in the region. According to him, the first wave of Turkic population arrived earlier – in the fourth millennium BCE – from southern Siberia and Dzhungaria and founded the Kang dynasty in Central Asia in the second and first millennia BCE. Thus, he argued, Central Asian populations mentioned in ancient sources, like the Scythians, should retrospectively be equated with the Turks, not with Indo-Europeans.

In a 1998 article, 'Some Theoretical Questions about the Ethnogenesis of the Uzbek People', Shaniazov returned to the question of a founding dynasty for the Uzbeks. For him, Uzbek nationhood can in no way be associated with the emergence of the 'Uzbek' ethnonym during the Shaybanid dynasty in the sixteenth century. Instead, it has to be found in the Kang state, dating Uzbeks' origin back to the second millennium BCE. If this earlier dating is accurate, then one of the peculiarities of the Uzbek ethnogenesis would be its immutability: Uzbek ethnic identity, as defined by language and territory, would show a continuity undisrupted over millennia.[56]

To emphasize the superiority of the Uzbek sedentary culture over its Turkic neighbours, Shaniazov accused nomadic peoples of not being able to bypass the tribal stage, a move that allowed him to disparage at a stroke the neighbouring Kazakhs, Karakalpaks and Turkmens. The supposed territorial continuity between Kang, Karluks, Kara-Khanids and Uzbeks was intended to confirm the existence of a sedentary Turkicness that both denies Persian-speaking populations their indigenous status and rejects the symbolic legitimacy of the Seljuks, the Ottomans and then the Turkmens, as well as of the Kazakhs.[57]

In this article, Shaniazov also developed arguments that are much more about a nation-building ideology than about historical knowledge per se. He, for instance, expressed the idea that 'everyone has the right to know the ethnogenesis and ethnic history of his people'.[58] He plainly rejected the Soviet legacy, affirming the sole right of Uzbeks to write their own ethnogenesis and criticizing scholars 'from the centre [Moscow]'[59] who would have preserved a colonial approach. But despite this apparent denial, Shaniazov never genuinely challenged Soviet concepts. He took up Bromley's definition of *ethnos*, which insists on the unity of language, territory, culture and historical destiny. He also affirmed the positioning of all peoples on a single timeline, on which evolution proceeds from tribe, to nationality, to the nation (Uzbek: *kablia*, *èlat* and *millat*). He began his chronology of the Uzbek *ethnos* with exactly the same historical stages as Soviet science: slavery, feudalism, capitalism and socialism.[60]

Shaniazov built on this reading of national ethnogenesis in a book published posthumously in 2001, *The Processes of Formation of the Uzbek Nation* (*O'zbek xalqining shakllanish jarayoni*).[61] This book is regarded in some segments of the Uzbek scholarly community as a seminal reference work. Shaniazov's profile and the fact that he finished this work on his deathbed explain the emotion surrounding the piece, the desire to disseminate it widely and the Institute of History's decision to translate it into Russian. In an introduction dedicated to President Karimov, the author stressed the need to return to Uzbekistan's national roots in order to build the future of the new state: by not fairly assessing the significance of the past, he argued, one risks debasing Uzbek culture and underestimating its age.[62]

The book includes a historical outline that Shaniazov – who sought seeking to put forward a final period in the discussion of national history – developed throughout his career, with chapters ranging chronologically from ancient times to the nineteenth century. In this outline, the historian-ethnologist first reaffirmed the presence of Turkic peoples in Central Asia before the arrival of the first Indo-Europeans and interpreted the state of Kang in the second millennium BCE as 'the first Turkic population in the region'.[63] He praised the state of Kang's early culture and its sedentary nature, endowing it with borders stretching from the Urals to the Syr Darya and a political centre in the present-day region of Shymkent. The Kang *ethnos* formed at that time was born of the assimilation by the Turkic peoples – who are always presented as 'absorbing' and never as 'being absorbed' – of other peoples present on the same territory, such as the Bactrians and Sogdians, whose potential Indo-European origin is pointedly overlooked.[64]

Thanks to this primordialist reading of history, Shaniazov was able to claim not only a very early ethnogenesis for the Uzbek nation but also uninterrupted ethnic continuity stretching from the first century BCE until the arrival of Russians in Central Asia. Based on his intellectual legacy, Sakae and Massagetae are now presented as Uzbek ancestors in national history textbooks.[65]

Reclaiming classical Transoxiana

A second core period for Uzbekistan's national construction is the classical heritage of sedentary Transoxiana (*Ma wara an-nahr* in the Islamic tradition), studied with the aim of demonstrating Uzbeks' pre-eminence among Central Asian peoples.[66] Immediately after the collapse of the Soviet Union, Uzbekistan proclaimed itself the direct heir of Central Asia's 'Golden Age' (*oltin asr*, which fell between the ninth and fifteenth centuries CE) and claimed all philosophers, scientists, writers and Islamic thinkers who lived on the territory of present-day Uzbekistan. These thinkers are celebrated with eponymous metro stations in Tashkent and their images appear on banknotes.[67]

The iconic embodiment of this Golden Age, however, remains Tamerlane (Amir Timur, 1336–1405), who ruled over the region from 1370 to 1405. His likeness replaced the Lenin statue on Tashkent's main square as early as 1992, and Karimov openly identified with him. In reality, this choice is quite paradoxical: Tamerlane was Mongol in origin (but not from the Chingiskhanid bloodline) and struggled to be recognized as a legitimate leader in parts of the Islamic world. Nonetheless, he offered a valuable symbol for a regime in need of a usable past: he was born in the heart of Transoxiana, in Shakhrisabz near Samarkand, and therefore 'belongs', territorially speaking, to Uzbekistan. He ruled over a large part of Eurasia and Asia, as far as India (the founder of the Mughal Empire, Babur, was a Chaghatay Turk nobleman hailing from Andijon), helping to justify Uzbekistan's claim to regional influence today; the Timurid museum in Tashkent, for instance, displays a scale model of the Taj Mahal to showcase the export of Uzbek cultural heritage to South Asia. Timur also embodied the political authority of the *khan*, the kind of paternalistic ruler Karimov aspired to be.[68] Finally, Timur acted as a patron of the arts; the artistic and architectural achievements realized under his rule and those of his heirs continue to stoke Uzbekistan's aspiration to be at the forefront of Central Asian culture and to strengthen its brand abroad.

The Soviet regime took an ambivalent view of Tamerlane that varied depending on the sinuous Soviet nationalities policy. Some scholars denounced him as a representative of the culture of the Golden Horde, which was distinguished by supposed Asian cruelty and repression. Others celebrated his military achievements and centralization of power, rehabilitated the era's architectural legacy, and highlighted the role of his grandson, Ulugh Bek (1394–1449), the founder of modern astronomy. In the 1970s and 1980s, even if Tamerlane as an individual was not integrated into the official pantheon of the Uzbek Soviet Socialist Republic, the Timurid dynasty was already seen as a period of high cultural achievements. Post-Soviet Uzbekistan, therefore, had relatively little to add before confirming Tamerlane's status as a father of the Uzbek state.[69]

Other key figures of the nation's pantheon belong to the theological or literary realm – for instance, the fifteenth-century literary icon Alisher Navoy (1441–1501), also known as Nizām-al-Din *Alisher* Herawī. Navoy is the greatest poet and prose writer in classical Chaghatay, the Turkic language that served for centuries as a *lingua franca* in Central Asia, with a strong infusion of Arabic and Persian words. The basis of Navoy's legitimacy is different from that of Tamerlane – it is not territorial, as he was born in Herat (today's Afghanistan), but instead derives from the authority of Chaghatay as a precursor of the modern Uzbek language (a combination of Karakhanid and Khorezmian). Here, too, the independent Uzbek state did not craft this new hero from scratch; Navoy was already celebrated in the 1920s as 'announcing' the Uzbek language and culture and became a key figure of the Uzbek Soviet pantheon in the post-war period.[70]

If Tamerlane, Ulugh-Bek and Alisher Navoy comprise the first tier of national heroes, another group ranks just below them. It includes scientists such as Al-Fergani (800/805–870), one of the most famous astronomers of his time; Al-Khorezmi (d. 850), a mathematician, astronomer and geographer during the Abbasid Caliphate; Al-Biruni (973–1048), a scholar and polymath from Khorezm; and Ibn Sina (known in the west as Avicenna) (980–1037), an Islamic neo-Platonic philosopher famous for his works on medicine. To this scientific lineage should be added two key figures in Islamic culture who epitomize the influence of Bukhara over the whole Ummah at that time: Imam al-Bukhari (801–70), who authored the hadith collection known as *Sahih al-Bukhari*, which is regarded by Sunni Muslims as one of the most authentic hadith collections; and Bahouddin Naqshband (1318–89), the founder of the main Sufi order, the Naqshbandiyya, and a revered mystical poet. In fact, the restoration of Naqshband's shrine was celebrated by Karimov with great pomp in 1993 as a symbol of the nation's reconnection with its Islamic past, while the main street in Bukhara, formerly named for Lenin, is dedicated to him.[71]

There are some glaring omissions in this Uzbek pantheon, however. The most obvious one is the Shaybanid dynasty and its founder Muhammad Shaybani (1451–1510), who occupies a relatively minor position in today's narrative. Indeed, the Shaybanids arrived too late in the nation's history to be considered founding fathers, and they have been shut out of the competition for antiquity that drives Uzbek historiography. Moreover, they are too explicitly linked to the Golden Horde, competed with the Timurids and shared the same origin as those who would later become Kazakhs, all elements that made them unsuitable for the nativist claim of the Uzbek grand narrative. The later periods of the seventeenth and eighteenth centuries, too, are largely painted over, as they show Uzbek Khanates and a Bukhara Emirate that no longer appear at the centre of continental empires or the cultural vanguard of the Persian-Turkic world, but rather as backward provinces progressively marginalized from new trade routes and relegated to the peripheries of new empires.[72]

Uzbekistan's symbolic takeover of the classic Transoxiana-Turkestani Golden Age has created tensions with neighbouring republics. This is true particularly of relations with Tajikistan (see Chapter 3) but also with the other Turkic republics, whose leaders want their legitimate share of the same cultural Turkestani tree: Kyrgyz and Kazakh historiographies are sometimes forced to define themselves against Uzbekness as Central Asia's cultural benchmark.

A difficult balance: Russian and Soviet domination

The third core period is the most ambivalent, as it deals with the recent past – namely, that of Russian colonization and the Soviet experience.

This is the only part of Uzbekistan's grand narrative that has dramatically evolved since the collapse of the Soviet Union, for the obvious reason that such transformation was necessary to justify the nation's independence.[73] In line with Tashkent's geopolitical stance of rejecting any regional alliance under Russian leadership and an early policy of moving away from the Russian-Soviet cultural legacy, the historiographical narrative on the nineteenth and twentieth centuries focuses on the negative and destructive. The whole period from the early nineteenth century (that is, even before the Uzbek Khanates and the Bukhara Emirate became tsarist protectorates) to independence in 1991 is labelled an era of 'Russian colonial domination'. As noted by Sergey Abashin, this discourse more or less reproduces all the anticolonial truisms of Marxist historiography in the 1920s and 1930s.[74] History textbooks spread this narrative and it is also illustrated in the Museum of Political Repressions, established in 2001 in a Tashkent neighbourhood where many graves from Stalin's purges were exhumed.

However, while Uzbekistan associates the Soviet regime with tsarist domination, it has struggled to find a way to critique the repressive aspects of the Soviet system while simultaneously embracing the modernization efforts that were part of the Soviet experience and remain highly valued by today's regime: mass urbanization, industrialization and a robust literary scene. It also faces difficulties in defining the role that Uzbek elites played in the Soviet system and in naming national heroes who could be celebrated for their fight against this alleged colonialism. Indeed, the dilemma of the Uzbek grand narrative is that those who were repressed by the Soviet regime represent a counter-narrative that is not in tune with modern Uzbekistan's ideological principles, while the Uzbek communist elites, whose existence challenges the notion of the Soviet Union as a simple colonial power, are ideologically closer to the values of today's regime.

The history of the popular revolts against the tsarist regime (Andijon in 1898 and *Urkun*, the regional uprising of 1916) and then that of the Basmachi against the Soviet regime in the 1920s is troublesome for today's regime due to these events' open references to Islamic values, and even sometimes to Shari'a. For a Karimov regime whose secular authoritarianism was legitimated by the struggle against religious fundamentalism, references to Islam as an ideology of national liberation cannot be publicly stated.[75] Consequently, the Basmachi movement, presented in the early 1990s as a movement of national liberation, was progressively downgraded to a simple 'armed movement' (*vooruzhennoe dvizhenie*) to avoid associating Islam too openly with the idea of national liberation.

A relatively similar pattern has been observed with the Jadids and the national-communists of the 1920s and 1930s who sought to reconcile socialism and nationalism and were later liquidated by Stalin during the Great Purges. Academic historiography does not deny them: Dilorom Alimova wrote a book praising Jadidism,[76] and its main figures, such as Abdurrauf Fitrat (1886–1938), are revered by many Uzbek intellectuals today. However, the Jadids remain largely absent from the state-sponsored pantheon offered for broad public consumption. Indeed, the Jadids and national-communists mostly arouse suspicion among today's elites on account of their clearly pan-Turkic commitments. Their calls for all Central Asian peoples to unite displeased an Uzbek state protective of its own sovereignty and, in the early post-independence years, hardly inclined to regional integration.

Moreover, as in Russia, Uzbekistan has found it easier to denounce the victims of the Soviet regime than to identify their tormenters, as the latter approach would entail pointing the finger at Soviet Uzbek elites. The rulers of today are, indeed, unquestionably the heirs of their Soviet predecessors, a continuity that is problematic for the regime's ideological claims. That is why the Khrushchev and Brezhnev eras seldom appear in Uzbek official historiography and museums, with the single – but crucial – exception of First Secretary of the Uzbek Communist Party Sharaf Rashidov (1917–83), who reigned over the republic for more than two decades, from 1959 to 1983. Rashidov is regarded as a national hero who defended the interests of his people against the interests of Moscow – even if this celebration partly contradicts the narrative of the Soviet Union as a colonial dominator.

Politics and ethnology: the case study of *The Ethnic Atlas of Uzbekistan*

The polemics around *The Ethnic Atlas of Uzbekistan* are an exemplary illustration of how sensitive the Uzbek narrative on nationhood has been. Published by the local Open Society Foundation in 2002 and edited by Alisher Ilkhamov (a sociologist and executive director of the Open Society Institute Assistance Foundation), the *Atlas* sought to import a constructivist view on the question of nationhood, directly confronting the prevailing nationalities policy's official line on the topic. Contrary to what the title suggests, the book was not an atlas per se, as it featured few maps, but rather a dictionary of the 'nationalities' of Uzbekistan.[77] The first part, written by a large team of local and foreign scholars, provided an alphabetical list of about seventy 'nationalities' living in the country, while the second part – which was more polemical and was written entirely by Ilkhamov – was devoted to Uzbek nation-building.

After the scandal surrounding the *Atlas*, the Soros Foundation failed to renew its registration at the Ministry of Justice and was forced to close in 2004. (It had not reopened at the time this book was being prepared for publication in early 2021.) The political dimension of the controversy only becomes intelligible if placed into the wider political context of the 'colour revolutions' in Georgia and Ukraine and the support given by Open Society Foundations to these street movements. In a speech broadcast on the main Uzbek television channel, Karimov justified the closure of the Foundation by accusing it of having engaged in illegal activities and also made discreet mention of the controversy surrounding the *Atlas*:

> There have been very serious attempts [by Soros] to mobilize splinter elements of the population. For example, on the issue of interethnic relations, they began to distribute publications and translations on the issue of interethnic relations. Where are the Uzbeks derived from, where do the Tajiks come from, etc. These editions, books, newspapers have no basis and cannot withstand basic criticism. Our historians have spoken and said that. But their main objective … was to choose representatives of the Uzbek intelligentsia who could support them tomorrow and … go up against the constitutional order.[78]

The allegations against the *Atlas* were organized by the Institute of History of Uzbekistan. In the autumn of 2003, an article debunking the *Atlas* was published in the electronic journal *Etno-Zhurnal*. Its author was Ch. Kamoliddin, an Arabist by training and programme manager at the History Institute. A long article in the very official *Pravda Vostoka* followed on 14–15 January 2004, signed by Alimova, Kamoliddin and Zoia Arifkhanova, head of the Ethnology Department. In April of the same year, the three authors republished the same article (with slight changes) in the leading history journal of Uzbekistan, *O'zbekiston Tarihi*. While Alisher Ilkhamov attempted to address these various criticisms, *Pravda Vostoka* refused to publish his response.[79] He then defended his cause in two papers published online in *Etno-Zhurnal* and on the website of the Open Society Foundation in Uzbekistan before its closure.

In 'Objcctivity and Accountability: That Which Should Not Be the *Ethnic Atlas of Uzbekistan*', Alimova, Arifkhanova and Kamoliddin organized an ordered refutation of the work. They began by criticizing the nationality entries and the ambiguity of certain terms, such as the use of 'ethnic minorities', considered in the Soviet tradition to be a derogatory term. They denounced what they considered the failure of the rules governing ethnographic research, which required the systematic description of the ethno-demographic characteristics, specific culture, lifestyle, material culture and rituals – in that order – of each ethnic group mentioned. The arguments, however, quickly became more political. Alimova asserted, for instance, in accordance with official discourse, that the Tajiks are not forced to Uzbekify but that there is a natural process of symbiosis between Tajik and Turkic peoples, who had existed for centuries. Once past these criticisms, all modest and some well-founded, the core subject of the controversy appeared: what is permitted to be said on Uzbek nationhood.

In the second part of the *Atlas*, Ilkhamov openly questioned the official narrative. Criticizing the theories of ethnogenesis that have been *de rigueur* in Uzbek science for over half a century, he referred to constructivist theories developed in the West, to the idea that the nation is a political, intellectual, and state construct, to Benedict Anderson's 'imagined communities', and posited that it would be 'naïve to depict the formation of Uzbek nation as a natural and objective historical process'.[80] Ilkhamov accused the Soviet classics of contributing to the 'canonization of Uzbek national history'[81] and turning the story into the teleology of the nation. He insisted that one of the fundamental ambiguities of Soviet ethnology, the confusion between *ethnos* and nation, caused many epistemological errors in ethnogenetic science. When publishing the *Atlas* online, Ilkhamov restated his conviction:

> The notion of ethnogenesis seems not to fully reflect [reality] as it draws from the arsenal of the biological sciences, representing social processes such as natural historical phenomena, where the will of individuals, institutions, authorities, groups, and especially the elites, in short, social issues remain outside the framework of analysis.[82]

Ilkhamov also tried to rehabilitate the role of the Shaybanid dynasty in national history and devoted an entire chapter to the construction of national identity during the Soviet period, placing special emphasis on the territorial division and establishment of the Uzbek Soviet Socialist Republic in 1924. He insisted on the edification of a codified literary language based on only one Uzbek dialect and mentioned three major political forces that had an interest in developing an Uzbek national consciousness: the Jadids, the national-communists and the party apparatus.

This iconoclastic reading of national identity raised an outcry from official academic circles. In the Soviet tradition, they accused Ilkhamov's points of being 'unscientific',[83] a term that crops up regularly throughout the articles published in response to the *Atlas*. The many references made by Ilkhamov to Western anthropology, which implied its theoretical superiority, shocked the Uzbek academic realm, which had limited access to the Western texts in question. As Alimova and her colleagues stated:

> [Ilkhamov's] design is based on the theory, widely distributed in Western anthropology, of constructivism, which is far from being recognized as sound by the ethnological community, since constructivism denies the existence of ethnic communities as objective realities and recognizes only ethnic characteristics constructed by men as a function of circumstances. As such, the formation of the Uzbek nation is understood not as a natural historical process, but as the result of political construction.[84]

The Institute of History held an explicitly negative position not only toward the constructivist school of thought, but also toward Ilkhamov's attempts to renew with the pre-Iakubovskii's vision of the Shaybanid dynasty as the rupture moment in the history of nationhood. Ilkhamov's insistence on the sixteenth century as a time of Uzbek ethnogenesis was seen as an insult to the nation, whose national consciousness – according to prevailing narratives – could not be so recent. The main accusation reveals the inherent affective and symbolic character of the attack against the *Atlas*:

> By their anti-scientific views and preconceptions, these people [Western scholars and people close to them, like Ilkhamov] try to depict the Uzbeks and other Turkic peoples of Central Asia as uncultured nomads, pastoralists, immigrants and conquerors without any cultural traditions in the region ... It is therefore necessary (for carrying out scientific research) to reject certain stereotypes rooted in historical science and misrepresentations of the role of the Turkic peoples in history.[85]

Other key components of the dispute relate to the Uzbek nation's autochthonism and antiquity. Kamoliddin indicted Ilkhamov for implying that the Turkic peoples have always been inherently nomadic, while Uzbek historiography is based crucially on the assumption of a prestigious sedentary past. Kamoliddin insists that 'ancient Turks were the first inhabitants of Central Asia and constitute a part of the indigenous people of the region'.[86] According to him, archaeology has proven the existence of a large sedentary culture in this area from as early as the second millennium BCE, even before the arrival of Indo-Europeans. Following the tradition of Shaniazov, Kamoliddin obviously wants to attribute this first civilization to Turks, claiming: 'The latest toponymic and linguistic studies allow one to suppose that in the second millennium BCE, the Dravidian-speaking peoples lived in close proximity and interaction with the proto-Turkic peoples, and these ties were broken by the flood of Indo-European arrivals'.[87] To him, therefore, it is legitimate to state that 'proto-Turks were the first inhabitants of this region and constituted a part of its ancient pre-Indo-European population'.[88]

The controversy around the *Atlas* can also be interpreted as a disciplinary struggle. The Institute of History refused to see the ethnological field escape its jurisdiction and be gradually taken over by researchers from sociology, much less sociology funded by Western advocacy institutions. Kamoliddin, for instance, stated that ethnogenesis 'cannot be understood through popular sociological theories, but primarily by the principle of historicism'.[89] To him, only the historian would have the adequate institutional competence to consider ethnic processes. Sociology could indeed 'be useful for communities recently formed or being constituted on the territory of other nations, but it cannot explain the history of peoples whose national formation occurred on the basis of an autochthonous population'.[90] Sociology thus encroaches on territory considered, in the Soviet tradition, to be the very object of the ethnological discipline.

Alimova confirmed this reading, declaring that 'it is the Institute of History that should have published this *Atlas*'[91] and that it was unacceptable for the Open Society Foundation not to have consulted with the Institute ('no recognized ethnologists of Uzbekistan were aware of the preparation of this publication'[92]). The book was, indeed, not overseen by local academics licensed on ethnic issues and the Institute of History not associated with its publication, although several *Atlas* authors were members of the Institute. A unique combination of political tensions around 'colour revolutions' and scholarly debates on the constructivist versus primordialist vision of nationhood, the *Atlas* dispute encapsulates the heavy symbolism of everything related to Uzbek ethnogenesis. That a Western advocacy foundation dared to encroach on such a symbolically significant field was judged unacceptable by both the political authorities and the local academic community.

Compared to several of its Central Asian neighbours, Uzbekistan's nation-building efforts have been less hesitant. It has faced fewer issues in terms of interpreting the past and dealing with the questions of cultural continuity, territorial unity and ethnic homogeneity. Many aspects of today's nationhood were already identifiable in the claims of Jadids or Uzbek national-communists: the centrality of Uzbekistan, its status as a benchmark of Turkestani identity, its historic continuity with the Transoxiana legacy, its blend of sedentary and nomad, Persian and Turkic features. Soviet institutions in charge of history, ethnography and folklore consolidated several segments of Uzbek nationhood in the post-war decades. Uzbek history was thus already largely nationalized even before the collapse of the Soviet Union. Independent authorities just had to add a new layer reinterpreting the Russian-Soviet past and go even further back into ancient history to completely nativize the nation in its ties to its territory.

However, Uzbekistan also encountered challenges in the nation-building process, mostly regarding the articulations between what is seen as national and what is considered foreign. As with every origin story, Uzbekistan's nationhood obscured some inconvenient elements in order to create the impression of linear development and to avoid disturbing paradoxes. Many implicit and ambivalent moments of national history have thus been discreetly put to the side. The relationship to the Soviet past, officially denounced as colonial – although many citizens display strong Soviet nostalgia[93] – is probably the most difficult contradiction to manage. The place of Tajiks in Uzbek society and the existence of a shared identity between the two nations is another theme that remains undiscussed because it does not correspond to the strict boundary project required by the nation-state. More globally, the role of other Central Asian nations in building a Transoxiani and Turkestani culture is obscured. Uzbek nationhood does not seem ready to share a common pantheon of cultural heroes and continues to capture this common legacy for itself. Last but not least, the arrival of Islam in Central Asia is another of these silenced moments: for a regime keen to denounce any foreign interference and afraid of Islamism, it has proved tricky to admit that Uzbekistan's national religion arrived through foreign influence (Arab conquest).

Like any other country in the world, Uzbekistan can live with a nationhood narrative full of ambivalences and unspoken elements. However, two challenges that have the potential to dramatically reshape the social and cultural landscape will need to be addressed by the post-Karimov regime. The first is the articulation of Islam with national identity. The previous regime's posture was, in a sense, schizophrenic. Islam was glorified as a national religion in all official speeches, local pilgrimage sites were valorised and the great national figures linked to Sufism were celebrated. Simultaneously, however, religious practices were strictly monitored, sermons controlled, religious education highly restricted, and interactions with the rest of the Ummah looked upon with suspicion.[94]

'Uzbekness' remains intimately articulated with 'Muslimness' (*musulmonchilik*), but the latter is acceptable only when Uzbekified – that is, when it is seen as a national tradition, a cultural and folkloric heritage, or an architectural legacy. The space left for Islam in terms of practices and norms for behaviours and attitudes, much less in terms of invoking Islam to legitimize political claims, has been heavily restricted.[95] As encapsulated by Charles Kurzman, Islam was 'politically neutered by the regime'.[96] This contradictory policy will likely become increasingly challenging to maintain, as Islamic practices are increasing among the younger generations, which see it as part of their individual and collective identity. The state secularism inherited from the Soviet regime is thus progressively eroding in the face of the population's development of various ways to display 'Muslimness'. A new Uzbek official narrative will have to take these deep societal evolutions into account.[97]

The second critical element was the role of labour migration, the existence of which was virulently denied by Uzbek authorities under Karimov. The President's declaration that migrants were 'lazy' and that only the most disgraced go to Russia to work[98] exemplified the negative connotations of labour migration and the government's denial of the socioeconomic reality that pushed several million citizens to look for work abroad. Migration has become a rite of passage for many young men and their families in all rural regions of Uzbekistan, helping to structure both individual identities and collective mechanisms of solidarity and economic strategy.[99] Migration also seems to have affected the population's relationship to Islam, as many young migrants are introduced to Islamic practices during their time abroad. One way or another, the identity-shaping power of migration will have to be recognized and integrated into the nation's narrative, developing it into a narrative that is less isolationist and more willing to celebrate Uzbek citizens as globalized actors.

The *longue durée* of the nation's grand narrative does not preclude the existence of changes and evolutions, both abrupt and slow. The death of the 'father of the nation' in 2016 reopened windows of opportunity for the Uzbek regime to evolve and reformulate its nation-building project. Shavkat Mirziyoyev rapidly made several noticeable changes: he criticized the *Ma 'naviyat va Ma 'rifat* as 'jingo patriotism' (*ura urachilik*)[100] that is not fit for purpose at a time when greater economic efficiency should be the driving ideology of the country; recognized (eventually) the importance of labour migration as a unique perspective for many young Uzbeks; and relaxed legislation on religion to allow more flexibility in everyday expressions of Islamic identity. The disappearance of the 'father of the nation' figure from Uzbekistan's politics certainly signified the end of an era and the opening of a new one, with profound adjustments to the country's construction of nationhood. The new atmosphere of increased academic freedom and the reshaping of the higher education system have likewise opened new paths by which the nationhood narrative may be rethought and reframed, even if its main features and symbolic benchmarks are unlikely to evolve.

Notes

1 Adams, *The Spectacular State*.
2 Paskaleva, 'Ideology in Brick and Tile'.
3 Merchant, 'Popping Tradition'.
4 Abikeeva, 'Uzbekistan: "Chopping Board" or Serious Cinema?'.
5 Rosenberger, 'Patriotic Appetites and Gnawing Hungers'.
6 Analysis of the main benchmarks of Uzbek historical discourses has been conducted by Akbarzadeh, 'Nation-Building in Uzbekistan'; Kurzman, 'Uzbekistan: The Invention of Nationalism in an Invented Nation'; and March, 'The Use and Abuse of History'.
7 Lewis, 'Illiberal Spaces'.
8 Lillis, 'Uzbekistan's First Daughter Gulnara Karimova'.
9 Markowitz, *State Erosion*.
10 Megoran, *Nationalism in Central Asia*.
11 Markowitz, 'Explaining Political Order in Uzbekistan'.
12 Khalid, *Islam after Communism*; Rasanayagam, 'The Politics of Culture and the Space for Islam'.
13 Ilkhamov, 'Neopatrimonialism, Patronage and Factionalism in Post-Soviet Uzbekistan'; Kılavuz, 'Political and Social Networks in Tajikistan and Uzbekistan'.
14 Spechler, *The Political Economy of Reform in Central Asia*.
15 The 'Five Principles' are: (1) Economics has priority over politics; (2) The state is the main reformer; (3) All reform must occur under the rule of law; (4) The state underlines the importance of strong social protection; and (5) The transformation to a market economy must be thought-out and gradual. See Spechler, *The Political Economy of Reform*; Sattarov, 'Is the Uzbek Development Model a Path towards True Modernization?'.
16 Kayumova, 'Emigration of the "Crème de la Crème" in Uzbekistan'.
17 Spechler and Spechler, 'The Foreign Policy of Uzbekistan'; Tolipov, 'Flexibility or Strategic Confusion?'; Weitz, 'Uzbekistan's National Security Strategy'.
18 Fumagalli, 'Ethnicity, State Formation and Foreign Policy'.
19 Karimov, 'Natsional'naia ideologiia', 451.
20 Karimov, *Turkistan, nash obshchii dom*.
21 Fierman, 'Cultural Nationalism in Soviet Uzbekistan'; Critchlow, *Nationalism in Uzbekistan*.
22 Denison, 'The Art of the Impossible'; Polese and Horák, 'A Tale of Two Presidents'.

23 March, 'State Ideology and the Legitimation of Authoritarianism'.
24 Karimov, 'Natsional'naia deologia', 89.
25 National Society of Philosophers of Uzbekistan, *Ideia natsional'noi nezavisimosti*.
26 Zhumaev, *Politicheskaia sistema Respubliki Uzbekistan*, 148.
27 Tadzhiev, *Teoreticheskie i metodologicheskie voprosy natsional'noi ideologii*, 4.
28 Sattarov, 'Spirituality and Enlightenment'.
29 Masaru, 'The Politics of Civil Society'; Urinboyev, 'Law, Social Norms and Welfare as Means of Public Administration', 33.
30 Megoran, 'Framing Andijon, Narrating the Nation'; Reeves, 'Migration, Masculinity, and Transformations of Social Space in the Sokh Valley'.
31 Kendzior, 'Reclaiming *Ma'naviyat*'.
32 Megoran, 'Framing Andijon, Narrating the Nation'.
33 The Echo of Central Asia, 'The Naked Truth about Censorship in Uzbekistan'.
34 McGlinchey, 'Searching for *Kamalot*'.
35 Khalid, *Making Uzbekistan*.
36 Cucciolla, 'Sharaf Rashidov and the International Dimensions of Soviet Uzbekistan'.
37 Ferrando, 'Manipulating the Census'.
38 Foltz, 'The Tajiks of Uzbekistan'.
39 Tsyryapkina, 'Evolution of the Russian Language'; Kosmarskaya, 'Russians in Post-Soviet Central Asia'.
40 Jacquesson (ed.), 'Karakalpaks et autres gens de l'Aral'.
41 Landau and Kellner-Heinkele, *Politics of Language in the Ex-Soviet Muslim States*.
42 Author's interviews with anonymous Uzbek lawyers based in the US. See also Schweitzer, 'Alphabet Transition in Uzbekistan'.
43 Fumagalli, 'Ethnicity, State Formation and Foreign Policy'; Fumagalli, 'Framing Ethnic Minority Mobilisation in Central Asia'. See more in Fumagalli, *Ethnic Conflict in Post-Soviet Central Asia*. See also Hierman, 'Central Asian Ethnicity Compared', 521.
44 Jalolov and Qo'chqor, *Mustaqillik: Izoxli Ilmiy-Ommabop Lug'at* (Tashkent: Sharq, 2000), quoted in Megoran, 'Framing Andijon, Narrating the Nation'.
45 Decret no. 315 'O sovershenstvovanii deyatel'nosti Instituta istorii ANRU'.
46 Dilorom Alimova, Institute of History, interviewed by the author, Tashkent, 19 February 2004.
47 Rakhimov, 'Post-Soviet Transformations'.
48 Luhn, 'Uzbek President Bans Teaching of Political Science'.
49 March, 'From Leninism to Karimovism'; Ilkhamov, 'The Archaeology of Uzbek Identity'; Akbarzadeh, 'Nation-Building in Uzbekistan'.
50 Shirinov et al., 'Arkheologicheskie issledovaniia v ANRU'; Keller, 'Story, Time, and Dependent Nationhood in the Uzbek History Curriculum'.
51 Finke, *Variations on Uzbek Identity*.
52 Finke, *Variations on Uzbek Identity*, 32.
53 Finke, *Variations on Uzbek Identity*, 10.
54 For a short biographical notice, see *Obshchestvennye nauki v Uzbekistane*, 6 (2000): 69–70.
55 Shaniiazov, *Kanf davlati va kanglilar*.
56 Shaniiazov, *Kanf davlati va kanglilar*, 40.
57 Shaniiazov, *Kanf davlati va kanglilar*, 37.
58 Shaniiazov, 'Üzbek halkining etnogeseziga', 31. I am grateful to Khudaikul Ibragimov and Ulughbek S. Mansurov for translating this text from Uzbek into Russian.
59 Shaniiazov, 'Üzbek halkining etnogeseziga'.
60 Shaniiazov, 'Üzbek halkining etnogeseziga', 32.
61 Shaniiazov, *Üzbek halkining šakllaniš žaraëni*.
62 Shaniiazov, *Üzbek halkining šakllaniš žaraëni*, 9.
63 Shaniiazov, *Üzbek halkining šakllaniš žaraëni*, 10.
64 Shaniiazov, *Üzbek halkining šakllaniš žaraëni*, 235–382.
65 Shnirelman, 'Aryans or Proto-Turks?'; Horak, 'In Search of the History of Tajikistan'.
66 Ilkhamov, 'National Ideologies'.
67 Dunn, 'The Paper Nation'.
68 Liu, *Under Solomon's Throne*.
69 Forbes Manz, 'Tamerlane's Career and Its Uses'.
70 Shin, 'Inventing a National Writer'.
71 Louw, *Everyday Islam*.

72 Clarke, 'The "Centrality" of Central Asia in World History'.
73 Rakhimov, 'Post-Soviet Transformations'.
74 Abashin, '*Mustakillik* i pamiat' ob imperskom proshlom'.
75 Dudoignon, 'Changements politiques et historiographiques'.
76 Alimova, *Dzhadidizm v Srednei Azii.*
77 'Nationalities' recognized in the Soviet census benefited from cultural and linguistic rights via their administrative status, which the central government bestowed on them. The post-Soviet Central Asian states have continued this tradition of officially developing national diversity, proudly boasting of 'more than a hundred nationalities'.
78 Islam Karimov, speech on *Channel One*, 30 April 2004.
79 Anonymous informant, interviewed by the author, Tashkent, 19 February 2004.
80 Ilkhamov (ed.), *Etnicheskii atlas Uzbekistana*, 288.
81 Ilkhamov (ed.), *Etnicheskii atlas Uzbekistana,* 295.
82 Ilkhamov, 'Arkheologiia uzbekskoi identichnosti'.
83 Alimova et al., 'Ob"ektivnost' i otvetstvennost''.
84 Alimova et al., 'Ob"ektivnost' i otvetstvennost'', 78.
85 Alimova et al., 'Ob"ektivnost' i otvetstvennost''.
86 Kamoliddin, 'Neskol'ko zamechanii'.
87 Kamoliddin, 'Neskol'ko zamechanii'.
88 Kamoliddin, 'Neskol'ko zamechanii'.
89 Kamoliddin, 'Eshche raz ob *Etnicheskom Atlase*'.
90 Kamoliddin, 'Eshche raz ob *Etnicheskom Atlase*'.
91 Dilorom Alimova, Institute of History, interviewed by the author, Tashkent, 19 February 2004.
92 Alimova et al., 'Ob"ektivnost' i otvetstvennost''.
93 Dadabaev, *Identity and Memory*. See also Dadabaev, 'Recollections of Emerging Hybrid Ethnic Identities'.
94 Khalid, *Islam after Communism*.
95 Rasanayagam, 'The Politics of Culture and the Space for Islam'.
96 Kurzman, 'Uzbekistan: The Invention of Nationalism in an Invented Nation'.
97 Jones, *Islam, Society, and Politics in Central Asia*; Laruelle, *Being Muslim*.
98 Sidikov and Kjuka, 'Karimov: Uzbek Migrants Are "Lazy"'.
99 More in Laruelle (ed.), *Migration and Social Upheaval*.
100 'Prezident Uzbekistana raskritikoval televizionnyi "ura-patriotizm"'.

3
Aryan mythology and ethnicism: Tajikistan's nationhood

In contrast to Uzbekistan, which has constructed itself as the most central state in Central Asia, Tajikistan has found its nationhood quite endangered. The southernmost and poorest state in Eurasia, the country has faced several symbolic handicaps. First, Tajikistan collapsed immediately upon the fall of the Soviet Union and plunged into a bloody five-year civil war (1992–7) that left over 50,000 people dead and more than half a million displaced.[1] The memory of this watershed moment makes references to the Islamic past of Tajik culture a sensitive topic that the authorities cautiously attempt to manipulate. Second, its cultural capitals of Samarkand and Bukhara were allocated to Uzbekistan during the Soviet delimitation of national territories in the 1920s. The fact that the Tajik republic was first created as an autonomous entity inside the Uzbek republic before achieving full nationhood status in 1929 contributes to Tajikistan's feeling of victimhood and resentment toward Tashkent.[2] As Tajik President Emomali Rahmon declared in 2013, 'Anyway, Samarkand and Bukhara will be ours again one day!'[3] Third, being the only Persian-speaking nation of the five Central Asian countries (the rest are Turkic-speaking) offers Tajikistan an easy way to differentiate itself, yet this language difference also contributes to an obsession with encirclement, creating tensions with neighbouring Iran and rousing fears of being subsumed into a far larger sphere already dominated by Tehran.

Despite these challenges,[4] Tajikistan's nationhood has been able to build on the solid foundation left by the founding father of Tajik Soviet historiography, Bobodzhan Gafurov. It has developed a narrative that, like Uzbekistan's, stresses autochthonism, precedence over neighbours and the nation's contribution to world culture. A key element of the reconstruction of this historical nationhood has been the rehabilitation of an Aryan identity, officialized to the point that Rahmon declared 2006 the

'Year of Aryan Civilization', albeit, as we will see, without any assessment of the heavily loaded heritage of the term and its role in the Holocaust. Aryanism contributes myriad useful identity references to Tajikistan's nationhood toolkit: it is a sign of uncontested antiquity, it is associated with some forms of cultural superiority inspired by nineteenth-century Western academic standards, and it allows Tajikistan to bypass an unfriendly Turkic environment to symbolically connect with Europe and Russia. That being said, Aryanism relies heavily on old-fashioned and contestable confusion between ethnic identity and the ideology of race.

Fragile nation-building and the presidential rewriting of history

After the 1997 Peace Agreements, Tajikistan stood out as the only post-Soviet country to recognize an Islamic party: the Islamic Renaissance Party of Tajikistan (IRPT), which was a key actor in the civil war but also in postwar reconstruction and democratization.[5] The IRPT was unique in the region in that it was a democratic Islamic party that accepted the secular nature of the state and parliamentary representation. However, this recognition was short-lived: in 2015, the authorities accelerated their authoritarian drift by banning the Islamic Party on the (false) pretext of its links with the Islamic State in Syria and Iraq.[6]

Since the civil war, the relationship between the centre and the regions has always been precarious. In the restive Rasht Valley and the autonomous region of Gorno-Badakhshan (situated in the Pamirs), tensions have regularly flared between local elites and Dushanbe. Labelled 'Islamist' by the authorities so as to strengthen the government's domestic legitimacy and make Tajikistan eligible for international support, these insurgencies have involved several conflicts of interest within the shadow economy as well as the rebalancing of influences from former warlords and central elites.[7] As such, scholars continue to debate whether these events suggest state weakness or, on the contrary, state success insofar as they have recentralized the polity around Rahmon, who has since removed presidential term limits and looks set to establish a multi-generational dynasty by promoting his son Rustam as his successor.[8]

Declared 'Founder of Peace and National Unity – Leader of the Nation' (a title later enshrined in the Constitution and which grants its bearer a number of privileges, including the right to run for president for life), Rahmon has succeeded in making himself and his family the focal point of political power in Tajikistan. Jesse Driscoll advances the notion of *Hobbesian Neopatrimonialism* to illuminate the roots of the broad-based social legitimacy Rahmon enjoys. Warlords – both rebel militia and pro-regime paramilitary commanders – have progressively built a 'warlord state' based on patronal mechanisms (the only pathway to economic security) that relies on kinship and regional rural identities.[9]

The Tajik regime continues to work hard to control the national narrative and has developed a complex process of oblivion and erasure around the perestroika years and the civil war. This struggle to control the nation's memory focuses on the relevance of political Islamic activism that took shape against the Soviet regime as early as the 1970s and, therefore, the significance of Sunni Islam in defining morality and collective identity.[10] After the 1997 Peace Agreements, the authorities attempted to pave the way for the consolidation of the nation-state and had to avoid tackling not only the place of Islam in nationhood, but also the nation's difficult relationship with Iran, which is simultaneously a brother in Tajikistan's struggle against Turkic peoples and a potential competitor for the country's 'Persianness'. As a result, for several years, world-famous Persian literary figures who had been re-emphasized shortly after independence – such as the poets Rudaki (860–941), known as the 'Adam of Poets', and Ferdowsi (940–1020), author of the famous *Shahnameh*, one of the world's longest epics – were somewhat marginalized in favour of an identity system that stressed neither the Islamic component of these works nor their Persian language.[11]

Academic circles were asked to contribute to this project through the development of a state-backed science of the nation, a science that was deeply enmeshed with authoritarian practices and a growing cult of personality. The journal of the Institute of History of the Academy of Sciences, *Merosi niëgon – Nasledie predkov*, for example, was regularly compelled to devote its first page to the president. The director of the Institute of History from perestroika to 2015, Rakhim Masov (1939–2018), had to praise the head of state for his decisive role in nation-building and, in 2003, called for people to vote in favour of Rahmon's extension of presidential mandates as the only meaningful choice to secure the country's stability.[12]

After hesitating for several years about the historical symbols that should be given to the new state, the Tajik presidential apparatus decided in favour of the rehabilitation of the Samanid dynasty (875–999) that ruled over Transoxiana. By selecting state-builders and not cultural figures as their national symbols, the authorities hoped for an easy consensus around secular statehood. In 1999, the presidential apparatus organized – with great pomp – the 1,100th jubilee of the foundation of the Samanid state, and the dynasty has remained the embodiment of the Tajik nation ever since – even if the grave of the dynasty's founding father, Ismail Somoni (849–907), is located in Bukhara. The official newspeak asserts a direct link between the Samanids and the newly independent state; after more than a millennium of what Rahmon considered to be the 'genocide' of the Tajiks,[13] the nation was finally reborn from its ashes as 'it is historical law' (*zakonomernost'*) for ancient nations to be reborn.[14]

In order to promote this reading of history, Rahmon published a large, multi-volume historical book, *The Tajiks in the Mirror of History (Tadzhiki v zerkale istorii,* 1999), under his own name. The first and most essential volume of this book, *From the Aryans to the Samanids*, illustrates the two core components of Tajikistan's nation-building narrative: while the Samanids are erected as state-builders, they need to be accompanied by an older, more ancient reference to prove the unique antiquity of the Tajik nation and its precedence over the Turkic peoples. For that purpose, Rahmon underlined the Zoroastrian era and an Aryan/Indo-European identity as core to the Tajik ethnogenesis. In a Muslim country whose intellectual and artistic history is inherently connected to Islam, it may seem paradoxical to hear the president claim that Zarathustra was 'the first Prophet of the Tajiks' and hope that he 'will be the spiritual leader and guide of the Tajik people'.[15] According to Rahmon, however, in spite of the gap between Zoroastrianism and Islam, there is a close link between these two great periods in the history of the Tajik people. Consequently, despite being Muslim, he explained, 'Ismail Somoni remained unfailingly faithful ... to the elements of Aryan statehood', and even allowed 'the wise implementation, through the state apparatus, of the spiritual standards of Islam and their fusion with the Aryan heritage'.[16]

Tajik Aryanism: a discourse anchored in Soviet science

This official emphasis on Aryan identity was not born suddenly and solely from the mind of the Tajik president, but rather magnifies the research carried out by nineteenth-century tsarist science and adapted by Soviet ethnology to the ideological conditions of Marxism-Leninism.

In the second half of the nineteenth century, the imperial advances of European countries into Asia and Africa contributed to the development of a body of literature surrounding white civilization's so-called mission to bring Enlightenment to the rest of the world. The topic of Aryan identity, originally developed in a linguistic framework that emphasized the existence of an Indo-European language family, became a tool of a heavily politicized agenda – in Europe, to justify anti-Semitism and the hierarchy of European nations, and abroad, to legitimize European colonialism as a product of the white race's superiority.[17] In the 1850s, for instance, the British authorities were instrumental in propagating the notion that colonization was just a reunification between one of the young branches of the Aryan family, which had emigrated to Europe, and the oldest branch, which had stayed in the original cradle.[18]

St. Petersburg's expansionist desires – aimed at gaining control of Central Asia, Manchuria, Xinjiang, Mongolia and Tibet – also yielded a romantic imperialism founded on the Aryan myth. Such an Aryan reading of the Russian colonization was promoted by the Turkestan Circle of Lovers of Archaeology (*Turkestanskii kruzhok liubitelei arkheologii*), created in 1895 in Tashkent, then-capital of the Turkestan Governorate. It presented Russians as the new Aryans, suggesting that they alone could bring to light and revive Central Asia's forgotten past, re-establish its Aryan identity and erase its supposedly backward and temporary Turkic element. Turkestan Governor General Aleksandr Vrevskii (1834–1910), honorary president of the Circle, solemnly declared: 'Presently, destiny has led us, the Aryans, to these very places that our ancestors once left. That is why we have the sacred duty to reunite and preserve the historical monuments of these lands where an Aryan culture once blossomed that we are called upon to restore'.[19] A key figure of Russian and then Soviet Turkology, Vassili Barthold (1869–1930) denounced the prevalent Turkophobia of tsarist circles in Tashkent:

> An over-idealized representation of the cultural capacities of the Aryans and of the barbarity of the Turks did not fail to influence the understanding of Russia's scientific missions in Turkestan. Thus, in 1895, during the opening of a local archaeological circle under the direction of the Russian authorities in the area, the suggestion was made to study the region's ancient Aryan culture, which had been destroyed by the Turkic barbarians and was experiencing a renewal under the domination of other Aryans – that is, the Russians.[20]

This Aryan reading of the Tajiks was continued within Soviet scholarly circles in the 1920s and 1930s, especially by Aleksandr A. Semenov (1873–1958), whose work bridge the tsarist and Soviet period. Semenov played a major role in presenting mountainous Tajikistan, in particular the Pamirs and Karategin, as the Aryan brethren, and Tajiks are obvious heirs of Aryans.[21] The first generation of Tajik researchers, many of whom emerged after the Second World War, re-appropriated the theme. Such is the case of the founding father of the Tajik nationhood narrative, Bobodzhan Gafurov, who focused extensively on the importance of the Indo-European origin in all his works in order to assert the autochthonous status of the Tajiks. It is also worth mentioning that Aryanism was a key ideological feature of neighbouring Iran under the Pahlavis as well. Since the late nineteenth century and in the 1930s as an official ideology, the Aryanness of Iranians was praised by Tehran as a sign of cultural and racial superiority, as providing an intimate connection with Europe and as a means of othering the main enemy – in its case, not the Jews but the Arabs.[22] In a historical irony, Soviet doctrine and the ideology of the Shah thus shared the same myth of Aryan roots.

After completing his studies at the Moscow Communist Institute of Journalism and commencing a PhD at the Institute of History in Moscow, Gafurov was appointed Secretary of the Central Committee of the Tajik Communist Party to produce propaganda. Then, in 1946, he was promoted to First Secretary of the Tajik Communist Party. His most famous book, *The History of the Tajik People in a Short Version* (*Istoriia tadzhikskogo naroda v kratkom izlozhenii*), was published in Tajik in 1947 and in Russian in 1949.[23] The book was a huge success and was re-edited in Russian in 1952 and 1955. Gafurov held the position of First Secretary until 1956, when de-Stalinization compelled him to leave office and continue to devote his life to historical research. He was appointed head of the Moscow Institute of Oriental Studies and ran the magazine *Aziia i Afrika segodnia*. After the 20th Congress of the Communist Party of the Soviet Union, he reorganized the Institute to adapt it to the conception of the East promoted by Nikita Khrushchev.[24] He continued to work on Tajik history, initiating a seminal *History of the Tajik People* (*Istoriia tadzhikskogo naroda*) with Semenov, published in three volumes in 1963–5, before ultimately joining the Academy of Science of Tajikistan in 1968.

Gafurov insisted on the necessity of the nationalization of the past, going against a historiographic trend of the 1920s in which authors wrote regional (that is, not national) histories of Central Asia. According to him, this regionalization distorted history and did not allow each nation to be represented fairly.[25] He also challenged the historical norms formulated by Vassili Barthold in his book, *Tajikistan: An Anthology of Articles* (*Tadzhikistan: sbornik statei*), which likened the Tajiks to central Persian – read: Iranian – culture.[26] Gafurov inverted the comparison by alleging that the Tajiks were at least as ancient as the Iranians and that they had been the mouthpiece of Persian culture. He rejected the idea that Iran should be considered the only inheritor of the prestigious ancient period, instead giving historical primacy to the future Soviet territory by positioning Tajikistan as the original cradle of Persian culture. Gafurov was also the first Tajik scholar to venture out of the geographic framework of the Soviet republic – which he deemed too narrow and which did not correspond to the reality of the historical Tajik population – to claim that the Tajik legacy was visible across the whole of Central Asia. This led him into a direct conflict with Uzbek historiography, which sought to appropriate the same antiquity.

In his 1947 book, which spans from the origins of the Tajiks to the Bolshevik Revolution of 1917, Gafurov aimed to negate the crystallizing role of the Samanid dynasty, which he considered too late to embody the Tajik ethnogenesis. He reminded his readers that the statehood (*gosudarstvennost'*) of Iranian-speaking tribes dates back to the first millennium BCE. Ancient Chinese sources, as well as the Avesta,[27] confirmed that the first state in the region was Iranian-speaking and located on the easternmost bounds of the Iranian world, putting it within the territory of current-day Tajikistan. To support this account, Gafurov quoted Nikolai Marr several times; he also asserted that, in the first millennium BCE, 'on the ethno-linguistic level, the population in Central Asia was Japhetic (*iafeticheskii*)'.[28] If he supported the notion of the superiority of the Indo-European peoples, however, he did not – like Marr – believe in the massive migration of Indo-Europeans across the continent. Instead, Gafurov insisted on the autochthonism of these first Iranians/Tajiks:

> Iranian nationalities and tribes have never presented a 'pure race,' they were not 'pure blood Aryan', victorious newcomers, as *bourgeois* historians have groundlessly asserted. It is well known that the theory of a 'pure blood race' is a reactionary lie, a myth. The Iranian eastern populations did not come to Central Asia out of nowhere but constituted themselves there, on the ground.[29]

By the logic of this ethnogenesis, cultural supremacy is understood as being proportional to the antiquity of the people settled within its national territory. Thus, 'Bactria, Sogdiana and Khorezm turn out to be the most ancient centres of the Central Asian peoples and their statehood was constituted before that of western Iran',[30] even playing a key role in the Achaemenid Empire.[31] This claim allowed Gafurov to then kill three birds with one stone, claiming that the ethnogenesis of Tajiks is older than that of Iranians *and* that of Turkic peoples, but that it ends – not begins – with the Samanid dynasty. On his view, Samanid rulers brought to completion a 'tendency of a number of sedentary Central Asian peoples toward unification and fusion into one – the Tajiks'.[32]

Gafurov continued his research on the most ancient possible Tajik ethnogenesis in his last book, *The Tajiks: Antique, Ancient and Medieval History* (*Tadzhiki: Drevneishaia, drevniaia i srednevekovaia istoriia*), published in 1972. If one compares this new version to the 1947 one, one may notice two key differences: the complete disappearance of any reference to Marr and the Japhetids (who had fallen into disgrace in the 1950s) and an increase in criticism of Turkic peoples, especially the Uzbeks.

Indeed, during the 1970s, Gafurov was much more willing to distinguish between the Tajiks and the Uzbeks. For instance, in a sub-chapter specifically devoted to the 'issue of the ethnogenesis of the Uzbek people' (which, according to the Soviet scholarly division, is a provocation in itself in a book dedicated to the Tajiks), Gafurov asserts in no roundabout way that 'the Uzbek people have taken shape on the basis of a sedentary Iranian-speaking population'.[33] Not only did the Uzbeks arrive there tardily, he argues, but they are autochthonous in Central Asia only because of their Iranian/Tajik substratum, while their Turkic features make them foreigners, invaders from the East. Gafurov also questioned the cultural contribution of Turkic peoples: according to him, many figures considered Uzbek by Uzbek academia spoke Khorezmi or Farsi (that is to say, oriental Iranian) and should therefore be claimed by Tajikistan – and even when Chaghatay reached its full development in the sixteenth century, half its lexicon remained Arab or Persian.

Such statements obviously sparked indignation in the Uzbek republic. As early as the 1930s, Uzbek scientists insisted that Tajik history should be limited to the borders of the federal republic and could not overflow into neighbouring entities. In 1972, the Academy of Science of Uzbekistan complained officially to the Central Committee of the Communist Party of the Soviet Union about figures considered Uzbek, such as Al-Khorezmi, Al-Farabi and Al-Biruni, being presented in a book about the Tajiks. Uzbek researchers criticized the fact that the supervisor of the book was Boris A. Litvinskii, a Russian whom they believed should have been impartial in matters of competition between the Soviet peoples.[34] Hoping to have these claims validated, Tashkent even attempted to get Leningrad Orientalists to make critical revisions to the book. Yet despite these actions, Tajik–Uzbek controversies continued unabated. At a conference in 1976, for example, Gafurov and Litvinskii once again aroused controversy when they claimed that the conclusion of the Tajik ethnogenesis was particularly precocious in comparison with that of the Turkic peoples.[35]

The frantic quest for an Aryan identity in post-Soviet Tajik science

President Rahmon's decision to emphasize the Aryanness of Tajiks thus appears as an obvious continuation and even reinforcement of the Soviet narrative: Gafurov was declared a 'hero of Tajikistan' and his works still serve as introductory textbooks for the study of the nation's history. In the 1990s, some Tajik public personalities publicly converted to Zoroastrianism, proclaiming it to be the national religion of the Tajiks[36] – a phenomenon best understood in the context of the civil war, during which some people interpreted Islam as a destructive force. This conversion movement, however, limited as it was to a small, secular, nationalist group of elites, did not have a widespread impact.

The rehabilitation of Zoroastrianism has since moved to the academic world. In 2001, the political decision to celebrate the 2,700th anniversary of the Avesta prompted numerous publications on Zoroastrianism and Aryanism. Considered a reliable historical source by the majority of local experts, the Avesta has been read literally. Based on this text, some Tajik scholars declared the historicity of mythical dynasties such as the Pechdovids or the Kaenids, searching for evidence of the early ethnogenesis of the Tajik people as 'the ancient Aryan society'.[37] In this literature, Zoroastrianism is systematically presented as a modern faith that transformed the ancient Aryan polytheism into monotheism, helped to sedentarize nomads, and fostered a developed and urbanized social structure.[38] Aryan peoples would, they argued, have developed a high culture as early as the second millennium BCE, and as 'the new ethnic word "Tajik", used by all Iranians, turns out to be synonymous with the ancient word "Aryan"',[39] this prestigious posterity should reflect on the Tajiks. This stress on Zoroastrianism remains particularly visible in history textbooks, which present it as a native and constructive force – as opposed to an Islam that arrived from abroad, through Arab conquests, and brought devastation in its wake.[40] As in the rest of Central Asia, the Zoroastrian past is also indirectly celebrated every year during the spring equinox with the Nowruz festival, the Zoroastrian new year.[41]

The word 'Ariana' or 'Aryanland' (*Oriyozamin*) is literally interpreted as referring to the ancient country of the Aryans, whose territory would, of course, correspond to a contemporary 'Tajikland' (*Tojikzamin*). As the archaeologist Igor V. P'iankov summarized:

> In Antiquity, Ariana was the territory that corresponded more or less exactly to the territorial formation, at some later time, at the

> beginning of the Middle Ages, of the Tajik people. Ariana as well as the question of the existence and formation of an historical Aryan community are very closely linked to the prehistory of the Tajik people.[42]

The retroactive affirmation of identity links between Aryans and Tajiks also allowed Tajikistan to capture the prestige of the great empires of Asia Minor, the Achaemenids, Alexander the Great, the Sassanids and the Selevids as precursors of Tajiks, or at least as peoples to whom the Tajiks are indebted.[43] As Rahmon alleged, 'the glory and greatness of the Iliad and the Odyssey grow dim in front of the famous work of our ancestors'.[44]

This Aryan-centrism targets a key enemy: the Turkic world, particularly Tajikistan's powerful Uzbek neighbour. Tajik Aryan-centrism depicts Turks as foreigners who arrived late in history and should have no right to ownership of the region's ancient past. One can thus imagine the scandal that erupted in Tajikistan when Uzbekistan was able to organize the Year of Avesta in 2003 under UNESCO auspices. Speaking on this subject, Rakhim Masov declared that 'one could say, quite frankly, that once more we are witnessing an organized conspiracy against the history of the Tajik people – a conspiracy whose final aim is, as always, to belittle the great past of the people and the role of our Aryan ancestors in the history of world civilization'.[45]

However, the reference to Zoroastrianism and Aryanism also creates serious points of contention with Iran. As Rahmon stated, 'our historical product becomes often an object of theft'.[46] In this historiography, Khorassan, Bactria and Sogdiana should be seen not as remote provinces of Iran, but as the epicentre of the future Tajikistan, making the latter, and not the former, the only heir of this prestigious past. Several articles published in the *Vestnik Akademii Nauk Respubliki Tadzhikistana* attempted, for instance, to explain how only the Oriental part of the Iranian world, and not its better-known western part, has engendered such a developed religion: it is from this Eastern space that the holy scriptures of Avesta would have been spread to India, where they would have been transformed into Vedas.[47] But neighbouring Iran no longer really plays the Aryan card, since it considers Aryanism to be a symbol of the despised previous regime. Islamic revolutionary Iran has therefore advanced cautiously in terms of cultural diplomacy in Tajikistan, avoiding the Aryan topic but stressing Persian-speaking solidarity and promoting Islamic values in quite soft ways.[48]

Tajik Aryanism has occasionally been accompanied by radical remarks concerning the anthropological specificities – in the Soviet sense of physical anthropology – of Central Asian peoples. Many publications use, for instance, the adjectives 'racial' (*rasovyi*) and 'ethnic' (*etnicheskii*) synonymously, the aim being to demonstrate the absence of a shared subtract between the two peoples and the superiority of Tajiks over Uzbeks.

The famous nationalist Tajik historian Numan N. Negmatov (1927–2011) developed the terminology of 'racial genesis' (*rasogenez*) to explain how the 'racial formation' of the Tajiks was completed well before the arrival of the first Turkic peoples.[49] He claimed that: 'The racial type of the Tajiks is ancient, local, and has not suffered any fundamental change during the last two millennia, although there was a slight mongoloid crossbreeding on the main Europeoid type'.[50] Whereas race science has been disavowed by post-Second World War Western science, it has enjoyed a renewal in Tajikistan since the discovery of population genetics, which is interpreted in a very literal sense as providing genetic evidence of the historic existence of nations. According to F. Nasirova, for instance, molecular genetics will be able to 'help establish the different ages, historical formations, and paths of migration of the various peoples of Central Asia'.[51] The hope here is to demonstrate – no longer historically or linguistically, but rather genetically – that Europe's cradle is indeed in Tajikistan, which has already been 'proven to be not only the proto-motherland of Indo-European languages but the cradle of world civilization'.[52]

These narratives have been supported by Rakhim Masov in his fight against Uzbekistan. The late Director of the Institute of History was famous for his critique of the 1924–9 territorial delimitation that deprived Tajikistan of Bukhara and Samarkand – his book, *Tajiks: History Stamped 'Top Secret'* (*Tadzhiki: istoriia s grifom 'sovershenno sekretno'*) is one of the few bestsellers of the Tajik publishing market.[53] He contributed to posit the 1920s as a national tragedy for Tajikistan while simultaneously interpreting the Soviet experience as positive for the nation. Masov denied that the Soviet discourse, which claimed that Uzbeks and Tajiks shared a common racial background, had any legitimacy. For him, 'there cannot be any common roots, any ethnic community between peoples originating from entirely contrary races'.[54] He also insisted on the Tajik origin of many Uzbek national communist leaders, who, in the 1920s, accepted the loss of Samarkand and Bukhara; being 'ethnogenetically Tajiks',[55] they must be considered traitors to the motherland.

His condescension toward Turkic peoples expressed itself in many of his works. For him, the whole history of the country – from the arrival of the Turkic peoples in the first millennium CE until the rebirth of the

Tajik independent state in 1991 – should be read as a history of submission, humiliation and genocide of the Tajiks at the hands of the culturally inferior Uzbeks. 'The period of the formation of the Uzbeks as an autonomous ethnos dates, in historical terms, from yesterday. In such a short historical period, it is impossible to create important cultural values like those created by the Tajiks over millennia'.[56]

On the other side of this judgemental statement stands Russia. Masov, a member of the International Eurasianist Movement led by Alexander Dugin and an advocate for a strong reintegration process, regularly and vocally praised the friendship between Tajikistan and Russia, whose geopolitical proximity he considered to be based on the racial and linguistic closeness between the two supposed Aryan nations.[57] Here, too, Masov's view has become mainstream: as nicely formulated by Helge Blakkisrud and Shahnoza Nozimova, Tajik history textbooks present the Russians – both Aryan brothers and Soviet modernizers – as the Tajiks' 'external self'.[58]

One can see from Tajik academia's position on Aryanism that it has entirely adopted classic stereotypes of nineteenth-century Western science on the superiority of Indo-European/urban cultures and the backwardness of Turkic/nomad civilizations. Interestingly, Tajik texts are devoid of any reference to more recent Western scholarly production, which, over several decades, has questioned the relevance of the Aryan reference, the idea of a primary cradle and, crucially, the notion of racial supremacy. Local Tajik researchers seem only to have access to nineteenth-century texts and to Soviet historiography devoted to archaeology or Indo-European linguistics. They do not engage with the refutation of racial and cultural unity between Indo-European peoples – and even of linguistic unity built on a genealogical principle – by contemporary science.[59]

The 'Year of Aryan Civilization': a polemical performance of the nation

The officialization of Aryanism in Tajikistan picked up steam in September 2003, when Rahmon ordered that the fifteenth year of independence, 2006, would be the 'Year of Aryan Civilization' – probably in response to Uzbekistan's 'stealing' of the Avesta through UNESCO. The presidential decree presented the jubilee as aiming 'to study and make known the contribution and the role of the Aryans in the history of world civilization, to educate generations in the spirit of national consciousness and self-determination, to develop connections between peoples and cultures'.[60] However, the appearance of propagandistic billboards featuring swastikas announcing the jubilee sparked internal discussions with international repercussions. And indeed, Tajik publications on Aryanism stand out for their lack of discussion of the German Aryan myth and its role in Nazi ideology and the Holocaust.

Several associations of Second World War veterans, in Tajikistan and Russia alike, complained about the use of the swastika, forcing the authorities to react. Abdukhakim Sharipov, head of the ideological section of the administration for the Sughd region, regretted that veteran associations who had fought Nazism in Europe had made a false (in his opinion) analysis of the swastika and did not understand that it only represents the 'eternal movement of the sun'.[61] Nurman Negmatov criticized Hitler and German fascism for 'brazenly offending the good name of Ariana and the ancient, agricultural and talented people that the Aryans were'. Despite being conscious of the tendentious nature of the Aryan reference in the West, Negmatov defended the president's choice: 'Why deprive people of the possibility to specify their objective historical origin? Were our Aryan ancestors guilty? … Do we have the right reject our ethno-cultural heritage? … The Tajik people are the direct historical descendants of the proto-homeland Ariana'.[62]

This line of argumentation was also subsequently taken up by Masov, who called for the rehabilitation of Aryan culture and symbols and the restoration of their genuine meaning, for 'this [Aryan] idea has a humanist, cultural nature; it is an attempt to rehabilitate the historical reality'.[63] The same goes for the president of the Academy of Science, Mamadcho Ilolov, who regretted that 'the theme of the Aryans was terribly perverted in the nineteenth century and at the beginning of the twentieth century',[64] condemning the Nazi mystification of the subject. The Aryan symbol must, he claimed, be linked to democracy, peace and well-being, and 'the restoration of our ancestors' very rich heritage'.[65]

The officialization of Aryanism as a state-sponsored ideology for Tajikistan also intensified tensions with Uzbekistan. As soon as Rahmon announced the jubilee in 2003, the Uzbek historian A. Gershenzon denounced the Aryan reference as totally incoherent from a historical and linguistic perspective, as well as politically inacceptable.[66] The following year, a book published in Moscow and Tashkent by G. Khidojatov, *The Fall of the Samanids* (*Krushenie samanidov*), was perceived as a direct attack on the independence of Tajikistan, and as a belittlement of the political and cultural role of the Samanid dynasty. In 2005, one of the most famous Uzbek archaeologists, Ahmadali Askarov, published an article on the Aryan question entitled 'The Aryan Issue: New Approaches and New Thoughts', in which he sought to invalidate Tajik claims to an Aryan line of descent, denouncing the 'pan-Iranianism' of Western and Soviet sciences and attempting instead to appropriate the prestigious Aryan heritage for the Uzbek people.[67] To make his claims convincing, Askarov affirmed that Aryans should be differentiated from Indo-Europeans, with whom they had too long falsely been equated. According to him, the Aryans were Turkish-speaking peoples who lived a nomadic lifestyle from the Siberian steppes to the Danube; their cradle was not the Altay, he claimed, but ancient Bactria and Sogdiana – a narrative that makes Uzbeks the obvious heirs of the Aryans, even though they do not speak an Indo-European language.

The text sparked a virulent controversy between Uzbek and Tajik scholars on the website CentrAsia. This was one of the first uses of an online platform to host such debates, which were impossible in more traditional printed formats. During the first academic semester of 2006, the website published a dozen articles on the topic, and the polemics continued through 2007. Masov was, of course, the first to answer Askarov's offensive. According to him, the sole aim of Askarov's article was to credit the Uzbeks as the heirs of the first inhabitants of Central Asia, making the article a work of politics rather than of scholarship.[68] Anvar Akhmedov from the Institute of Oriental Studies in Tashkent defended Askarov and denounced 'the creative intelligentsia of Tajikistan, [which] has been living for a long time, at least since Gafurov's *The Tajiks* was published in 1972, with a chauvinistic and national spirit', even referring to the Nazi tradition and accusing Masov of advocating Nietzschean principles.[69] Masov replied, criticizing the lack of scientific evidence marshalled in favour of the Aryanity of Turkic peoples.[70] He asserted that the Uzbeks' somatic features made it impossible for them to be Aryan: 'they are in no way similar in terms of their physical appearance and their racial origin: … the Aryans had blond hair and blue eyes and were tall, while the Turks have large faces, small eyes, squashed noses, little beards and a mongoloid physical appearance'.[71] Having been widely disseminated on the internet, Masov's answers were collected into a volume by the Tajik Institute of History.[72] This was accompanied by a special issue of *Merosi niëgon – Nasledie predkov* devoted to Aryanism, including an introduction from Masov that refuted both Uzbek and Western critiques of the use and abuse of Aryan motives.[73]

The officialization of an Aryan myth reflects the need for the Tajik post-Soviet state apparatus to come up with a unifying ideology not based on

Islam, as well as the continuation of the Soviet historiographical tradition by local academic elites. This Aryan myth enables an isolated and peripheral Tajikistan to feel connected to Russia and Europe, which are seen as bearer of a form of cultural superiority, and to diminish the historical and geographical centrality of its Uzbek neighbour. Although Iran is simultaneously apprehended as both a brother and a competitor, Tajikistan's 'jealousy' toward Iran appears more easily manageable than the heavy grievances it feels against its Turkic neighbours.

Not only is Aryanness a mythical construction – indeed, even theories of Indo-European linguistic genealogy are now questioned – but the refusal of Tajik elites to comment on what it means, in light of Aryanism's use by the Nazi regime, to treat Aryanism as the nation's key to primacy in the region is problematic. It can be interpreted as a form of provincialism in Tajik academia, disconnected from contemporary social sciences, or, on the contrary, as a form of post-colonial resistance to reading everything through the European prism. However, the latter viewpoint does not stand up, as Tajik academia has itself pursued a very colonial and Orientalized vision of the region's history. Indeed, it shares the old Russian perspective that the whites/Aryans/Indo-Europeans were engaged in a so-called civilizing mission against the backward Turkic nomads, believes that phenotypical features reveal civilizational characteristics, and upholds forms of cultural superiority borrowed from nineteenth-century science.

The Tajik nationhood narrative is also problematic at several other levels. First, its victimhood posture does not help the construction of a patriotic feeling in the country: a nation cannot be based only on grievances, it needs something to be proud of. Second, the Uzbek minority (around 15 per cent of the population) obviously does not recognize itself in the existing narrative. Third, a usable past alone is not enough; it needs to be articulated alongside some vision of the future. The Tajik regime has taken that turn of late by investing in symbolic architecture on the model already developed by Azerbaijan and Kazakhstan. It inaugurated the Qasri Millat, or Palace of Nations – the president's residence, which boasted a flagpole that was once the tallest in the world – in 2008; the Parchan (or Independence Monument) in 2011; and the National Museum in 2013.[74] But it is the construction of the Rogun Dam that works best as a forward-looking mobilization theme announcing the supposed bright future of the nation and its long-awaited prosperity.[75]

Fourth, and most importantly, the avoidance of Islam – and, even more, the indirect critique of Islam hidden within the praise of Zoroastrianism – appears to be the central issue of this national construction.[76] The excessive rejection of everything Muslim began to be readjusted in the late 2000s, which saw the decision to make 2009 the Year of Imomi Azam and new centrality given to Rudaki and Ferdowsi in the national pantheon. In the 2010s, the Tajik authorities began crafting a language of conservative values on the need to respect 'national traditions', accompanied by repressive policies that primarily entailed controlling women's clothes and body – as always, a symbol of power relations.[77] The gradual marginalization and then ban of the Islamic Renaissance Party, bearer of the Islamic flag, may push the reconciliation of symbols even further: the state apparatus can now more easily claim Islam without giving the floor to its Islamic/Islamist opponents, even if this may lead to the secular nature of the state being challenged in the future. Yet just as Uzbekistan's emphasis on its ancient indigeneity and its status as the heir to Transoxiana have remained prominent parts of its national narrative even in the post-Karimov era, it is likely that the Indo-European roots/Aryan myth theme will remain prevalent in Tajikistan even once Islam becomes better integrated into its nationhood narrative.

Notes

1 Scarborough, 'From February to February'; Scarborough, '(Over)Determining Social Disorder'; Heathershaw, *Post-Conflict Tajikistan*.
2 Bergne, *The Birth of Tajikistan*.
3 Kucera, 'Tajikistan's Dream'.
4 Akbarzadeh, 'Why Did Nationalism Fail in Tajikistan?'.
5 Epkenhans, *The Origins of the Civil War in Tajikistan*'.
6 Zuijderduijn, '"Traitors of the Tajik Nation"'.
7 Heathershaw and Mullojonov, 'Rebels Without a Cause'.
8 Driscoll, 'Hobbesian Neopatrimonialism'.
9 Driscoll, 'Hobbesian Neopatrimonialism'.
10 Epkenhans, 'Oblivion, Ambivalence and Historical Erasure'.
11 Shozimov, *Tadzhikskaia identichnost' i gosudarstvennoe stroitel'stvo v Tadzhikistane*.
12 Masov, 'Nash obshchii dom v Sodruzhestve Nezavisimykh Gosudarstv', 2.
13 Rakhmonov, 'Tysiacha let v odnu zhizn", 2.
14 Rakhmonov, 'Opening Speech', 1.
15 Rakhmonov, in *Zoroastrizm i ego znachenie v razvitii tsivilizatsii narodov Blizhnego i Srednego Vostoka*, 28.
16 Rakhmonov, 'Tadzhikskaia gosudarstvennost", 1.
17 Poliakov, *The Aryan Myth*; Goodrick-Clarke, *Hitler's Priestess*.
18 Figueira, *Aryans, Jews, Brahmins*.
19 Baron Vrevskii, speech delivered at the Circle's inauguration on 11 December 1895, *Protokoly TKLA* (1895): 2.
20 Barthold, *Zadachi russkogo vostokovedenija v Turkestane*, 529.
21 Battis, 'The Aryan Myth and Tajikistan'.
22 Motadel, 'Iran and the Aryan Myth'.
23 Judging from the commentaries of those who have been able to compare the Russian and Tajik editions, it seems that the text is different in the two versions, but nobody has compiled a comprehensive list of the differences between the two texts.
24 Laqueur, *The Struggle for the Middle East*.

25 See Mukhtarov and Sharipov, *Akademik Bobodzhan Gafurov*.
26 See *B. G. Gafurov*.
27 The Avesta is a collection of the sacred texts of the Zoroastrian religion (Mazdeism). Although some of the texts are very old, the term *Avesta* itself only dates to the second century CE. The most important portion is the hymns, which are thought to have been composed by Zarathushtra himself around 1000 BCE.
28 Gafurov, *Istoriia tadzhikskogo naroda*, 23.
29 Gafurov, *Istoriia tadzhikskogo naroda*, 26.
30 Gafurov, *Istoriia tadzhikskogo naroda*, 50.
31 Tolstov et al. (eds), *Istoriia uzbekskoi SSR*, vi.
32 Tolstov et al. (eds), *Istoriia uzbekskoi SSR*, 173.
33 Gafurov, *Tadzhiki: Drevneishaia, drevniaia i srednevekovaia istoriia*, 294.
34 See Ashurov, 'Ideinaia bor'ba vokrug knigi Akademika B. G. Gafurova *Tadzhiki*'.
35 See Gafurov and Litvinskii, *Uzlovye problemy etnogeneza*, 7.
36 This information was provided by Nargiz Khodzhaeva, junior scholar at the Institute of History, and confirmed by Rakhim Masov, Dushanbe, June 2004.
37 *Avesta i mirovaia tsivilizatsiia*, 153.
38 *Drevniaia tsivilizatsiia*.
39 *Vklad iranskikh narodov v razvitie mirovoi tsivilizatsii*, 15.
40 Hojiev, 'Nation-Building and Nation-State Formation'.
41 Nourzhanov, 'Nation-Building and Political Islam'.
42 P'iankov, 'Ariana po svidetel'stvam antichnykh avtorov', 39.
43 Negmatov, *Tadzhiki: Istoricheskii Tadzhikistan*, 16.
44 Rakhmonov, *Tadzhiki v zerkale istorii*.
45 Masov, 'Turan – eto ne Turkestan', 21.
46 Masov, 'Turan – eto ne Turkestan', 129.
47 Mumidzhanov, 'Avesta ob etnogeneze tadzhikov'.
48 Anderson, 'Iran's New Cultural Nationalism'.
49 Negmatov, *Tadzhikskii fenomen*, 97–104.
50 Negmatov, *Gosudarstvo samanidov*, 231.
51 Nasirova, 'Chtrikhi k prarodine ariev', 187.
52 Nasirova, 'Chtrikhi k prarodine ariev', 199.
53 Masov, *Tadzhiki: istoriia s grifom 'sovershenno sekretno'*.
54 Masov, *Tadzhiki: istoriia s grifom 'sovershenno sekretno'*, 20.
55 Masov, *Tadzhiki: istoriia s grifom 'sovershenno sekretno'*, 87.
56 Masov, *Tadzhiki: istoriia s grifom 'sovershenno sekretno'*, 29.
57 Masov, 'Rol' Rossii v istoricheskikh'.
58 Blakkisrud and Nozimova, 'History Writing and Nation Building'.
59 Renfrew, *L'énigme indo-européenne*.
60 Rakhmonov, 'O gode ariiskoi tsivilizatsii', 1.
61 'Rakhmonov velel tadzhikam vspomnit' a svoem ariiskom proiskhozhdenii'.
62 Negmatov, 'Istoki etnogeneza', 4.
63 Volkov et al., 'Storony "ariiskoi" medali'.
64 Ilolov, 'Nasledie nashikh predkov'.
65 Ilolov, 'Nasledie nashikh predkov'.
66 Gershenzon, 'Ariiskaia mifologiia i Tsentral'naia Aziia'.
67 Askarov, 'Ariiskaya problema'.
68 Masov, 'Tiurkizatsiia ariitsev'.
69 Akhmedov, 'Vozvrachshaias' k istorii "ariitsev"'. See also another article opposed to the Tajik point of view: Arslonzoda, 'Istina rozhdaetsya v spore'.
70 Akhmedov, 'Echshe raz ob ariiskoi'.
71 Masov, 'Fal'sifitsirovat' i prisvaivat' chuzhuiu'.
72 *Arii: istoriia i sovremennost'*.
73 *Nasledie predkov*, 9 (September 2006).
74 Blakkisrud and Nozimova, 'History Writing and Nation Building'.
75 Féaux de la Croix and Suyarkulova, 'The Rogun Complex'; Menga, 'Building a Nation'.
76 Blakkisrud and Kuziev, 'Museums, Memory and Meaning Creation'.
77 Thibault, *Transforming Tajikistan*.

4
National unity versus pluralism: Kyrgyzstan's nationhood

Works devoted to nation-building in Kyrgyzstan typically explore the ambivalence of the civic versus ethnic models of national identity construction and leaders' failed attempts to integrate minorities and symbolically secure the titular nation,[1] especially since the 2010 Osh riots.[2] The civic/ethnic dichotomy has been questioned by many works and quite rightly cast as an 'ideal-type', unobservable in any reality. Studies by ethnologists such as David Gullette and Svetlana Jacquesson have shown how insufficient this framework is for grasping the current search for a national and state identity in Kyrgyzstan. Past analyses of 'clan politics' have also misconstrued the complexity and modernity of political life in the country.[3] In this chapter, I argue that what we usually see as Kyrgyzstan's struggle to choose between ethnic and civic identity is a misinterpretation: the authorities' goal is certainly to make ethnic Kyrgyz attributes – language and cultural symbols – the bonding element around which a civic identity can emerge. The titular group is thus urged to merge its ethnic and civic identities, while minorities are compelled to embrace a civic identity, many elements of which are constituted by 'Kyrgyzness'.

At stake for Kyrgyzstan, I argue, is not the *choice* between two opposing policies, civic and ethnic, but the *evolution* from a monopoly over the construction of nationhood to an open market shaped by multiple actors and narratives. This plurality is perceived by the authorities as a threat to sovereignty and a means to weaken attempts at nation-building by fragmenting what is traditionally perceived as unified and above division. In Soviet times and in the 1990s, the state apparatus and academia had a stranglehold over the definition of nationhood. This narrative could sometimes be challenged, but it was possible for people to differentiate between orthodox and heterodox points of view. Since the

2000s, however, it has become more difficult to provide this symbolic security, as the discourse on nationhood has been deeply decentralized. It is this decentralization, and the accompanying contest for hegemony, that is perceived as chaotic, directionless and therefore endangering the nation.

This chapter follows the post-independence framework through which the Soviet tradition of ethnogenesis was reformulated as a search for Kyrgyzstan statehood, with Manasology as the *primus inter pares* argument in favour of the nation-state, and new genealogies developed as a legacy of the Soviet-era study of 'ethnic processes'. It then focuses on two layers of decentralization: a plural political environment that questions the legitimacy of state-backed nationhood, and a plural editorial market that tests academia's monopoly over the contents of nationhood.

From ethnogenesis to statehood: *Manas* and *Kyrgyzchilik*

The ethnogenesis doctrine posits – implicitly during Soviet times and explicitly after 1991 – that the nation-state emerges as the legitimate result of centuries of ethnic development. Formulated in a post-Soviet framework, this means postulating statehood (*gosudarstvennost'*) as the final goal of the nation. Nationhood and statehood are thought of as intimately linked: the supposed presence of an ancient people on its contemporary equivalent's present territory offers political legitimacy to that people by implying that the nation's titular group intersects with the state both territorially and culturally.[4] Post-Soviet Kyrgyz historiography, like that of Kyrgyzstan's neighbours, is thus built on a teleological logic: the history of the nation can only be that of marching toward its independence. The idea that futures are multiple and that linearity is a retroactive construction is not considered.[5] Historical moments that are inconsistent with this linearity are conceptualized as transgressions standing in the nation's path toward its destiny and put it into hibernation.

History is also ethnicized. Peasants and nomads are exaggeratedly foregrounded as the repository of national authenticity, whereas urban cultures, in which minorities are dominant, receive more discreet mentions. The nation is seen as an *ethnos* that possesses a genetic pool (*genofond*) to be preserved, often expressed in the form of cultural and linguistic purism, sometimes with a biological note about the supposed need for ethnic purity. National history is, therefore, simultaneously populist and statist, as was Stalinist National Bolshevism:[6] statist because only the state represents the completed form of national consciousness in this narrative and populist because the ethnicized people form the centre of attention, as evidenced by the incessant references to a national mentality (*mentalitet*) or psyche.[7]

To pursue the Soviet tradition of patriotic archaeology, the first president of independent Kyrgyzstan, Askar Akayev, who reigned over the country's destiny from 1991 to 2005, organized several jubilees, most notably the 3,000th anniversary of the city of Osh. However, the jubilee also had a clear political aim: curbing the popularity of the former secretary of the Kyrgyz Communist Party, Absamat Masaliev (1993–2004), who received 80 per cent of votes in the 1995 presidential election in his native Osh region.[8] In 2003, Akayev celebrated '2,200 years of Kyrgyz statehood' in the hope of reviving his popularity (which had begun to decline following several protests against the cession of territories to China) and improving public support ahead of the 2005 presidential elections.[9] On this occasion, the Academy of Sciences published a new history textbook, *History of the Kyrgyz of Kyrgyzstan*, that was uniquely centred on the titular ethnic group.[10]

However, compared with the history textbooks of neighbouring republics, those edited in Kyrgyzstan are more nuanced. As in Soviet times, the idea that the Kyrgyz went through a unique ethnogenesis at a precise time and place remains contested, with most textbooks giving priority to the notion that there were multiple phases of 'ethnic crystallization' for the Kyrgyz people. The textbooks also recognize that the territory of the Kyrgyz has varied enormously, stretching from Altay to present-day Kyrgyzstan, whereas their neighbours lay claim to their autochthonism or nativism.[11] Kyrgyzstan's historiographic vacillations, inherited from the 1950s, have thus been imported into the contemporary corpus and accepted as the dominant framework.

Again unlike its neighbours, Kyrgyzstan cannot celebrate a founding dynasty whose reign can be commemorated as the golden age of the nation, a glory to be reached again in the future. To compensate for the absence of any historically proven dynasties or founders, the authorities have focused their attention on the hero of the Kyrgyz national epic, *Manas*. The *Manas* epic, celebrated for being longer than Homer's *Iliad* and *Odyssey*, was recorded in written form for the first time by the Kazakh ethnologist and historian Chokan Valikhanov (1835–65) in the Issyk-Kul region in 1856, then completed by Vasilii Radlov (1837–1918), who, between 1862 and 1869, noted down further episodes from the Bugu in the Tekes Valley, the Sary-Bagysh of Issyk-Kul and the Soltu of the Tokmak region. During the Soviet period, the great bards Sayakbay Karalayev (1894–1971) and Sagynbay Orozbakov (1868–1930) gave the epic poem its definitive form. The details related in the epic are, however, vague enough to facilitate today's attempts at ideological appropriation.

In the first years of the USSR, the *Manas* epic was well received. In 1925, the poet Kasym Tynystanov (1901–38), first minister of education of Kirgizia, supported the publication of *Manas*, but the rise of Stalinism and its suspicion toward anything identified as part of the ethnic republics' nationalism blocked the project. Not until 1946 would it be possible to see an extract of the epic poem published in Moscow, when the Kirgiz lobby nominated the *Manas Opera* for the Stalin Prize. But *Manas* fell victim to the ideological hardening in the arts and culture symbolized by Andrei Zhdanov (1896–1948), who accused it of 'bourgeois cosmopolitanism'. In 1951–2, the ideological struggle over *Manas* raged between the Kirgiz republic's two official dailies – *Kyzyl Kyrgyzstan*, which was in favour of the epic, and *Sovetskaia Kirgiziia*, which echoed Moscow's official line – as well as between the sections of the Communist Party in Frunze (today Bishkek) and in Moscow. The major figures of the Kirgiz cultural world – such as Aali Tokombaev (1904–88), who was member of the Party and a deputy in the Supreme Soviet of the Republic; Kasymaly Bayalinov (1902–79), then-president of the Writers' Union; and writer Tugelbay Sydykbekov (1912–97) – took a stance in favour of the epic poem.[12] In 1952, official discourse shifted, criticizing the epic for being anti-Russian, anti-Chinese – a serious political accusation at the time, given the Sino-Soviet honeymoon – and pan-Islamic. Celebrated writer Chingiz Aitmatov (1928–2008) re-opened the discussion in the 1980s, and the first statue to Manas, the hero of the epic, was eventually erected in 1985, during the first months of perestroika.

With independence, *Manas* received acclaim as the embodiment of Kyrgyzstan's nationhood. Manas is now considered to be a historical figure who lived in the ninth century, the man who gathered the scattered Kyrgyz clans together and launched the great campaign of 840–2, which laid the foundation for the first Kyrgyz state. With the support of UNESCO, President Akayev organized a jubilee marking the millennium of Manas in 1995. The authorities built a historical park, Manas Ordo, in Manas' supposed birthplace, Talas, where a Karakhanid mausoleum thought to be his final resting place is situated. Between 120,000 and 150,000 people visit Manas Ordo every year,[13] confirming its status as one of Kyrgyzstan's main tourist spots.

For the celebration of 2,200 years of Kyrgyz statehood, Akayev invoked Manas as the embodiment of this statehood with a book supposedly authored by the president himself, *Kyrgyz Statehood and National Epos Manas* (*Kyrgyzskaia gosudarstvennost' i narodnyi epos Manas*). In this work, the president did not hesitate to draw religious parallels: 'For the Kyrgyz people, *Manas* is more than an epic ... It is what the Bible is to Christians'; 'My thoughts lead me to draw a parallel between Manas and the biblical figure of Moses, who took his people back to their native country, leading them out of captivity'.[14]

During the festivities, the Kyrgyz president also delivered a political speech in which he extrapolated 'seven commandments' from the epic, which he declared the core of his programme of action for independent Kyrgyzstan: (1) unity and cohesion of the nation; (2) international concord, friendship, and cooperation; (3) national honour and patriotism, prosperity through hard work and knowledge; (4) humanism; (5) generosity and tolerance; (6) harmony with nature; and (7) consolidation and protection of Kyrgyz statehood. The list reads as wishful thinking that lacks any precise political programme beyond that of maintaining a collegial relationship between the Kyrgyz majority and the Uzbek and Russian minorities. But the goal of this speech was not to provide concrete policies but to lay the foundations for a new national ideology. As Akayev wrote:

> By seeking to evaluate the *Manas* epic from the viewpoint of the idea of the state that it contains, it is easy to see that for the ancient Kyrgyz people and its constituents, the epic was a prototype for the national constitution, a code of laws and decrees, a code of honour and morals, a testament for the Kyrgyz generations to come.[15]

This elevation of Manas to a form of national ideology has since taken off. The discipline of Manasology (*manasovedenie*) has, for instance, become mandatory in many university curricula. It follows a syllabus focused on both knowledge of the epic poem itself, its main characters and events, the values it defends, and its role in national identity construction.[16] The Academy of Sciences launched the National Centre for Manasology, exclusively devoted to studying the epic, and a group of literature and folklore specialists led by the centre's director, Sagymbai Orozbakov, worked from 1994 to 2014 to compile and publish a monumental nine-volume edition of *Manas*.[17]

To Bishkek's chagrin, China in 2003 launched the first campaign to include *Manas* on UNESCO's National List of Intangible Cultural Heritage. Beijing claimed to be acting on behalf of its Kyrgyz minority in Xinjiang, and under China's lobbying, UNESCO approved Beijing's application in

2009. If the Kyrgyz political authorities are proud of this international recognition, they nevertheless had to live down the humiliation of China's having usurped the paternity of the epic.[18] Despite this Chinese appropriation, Manas remains a hero who embodies the values publicly cherished by the Kyrgyz state: a warrior defender of the motherland, a representative of the incessant struggle for independence waged by the Kyrgyz and their need for self-reliance (although the multi-ethnic nature of Manas' entourage is also emphasized).[19] However, the epic's applicability for nationhood purposes is not simple, and it may raise more questions than it can answer. For instance, the epos insists on the division of the Kyrgyz tribes, depicting them as unable to unify except when fighting an external enemy. It does not specify Manas' tribe either, only that he was born in today's Talas region.[20]

Aside from Manas, the Kyrgyz have few historical figures with whom to construct a national pantheon. Among the oldest is Yusuf Khass Hajib, also known as Yusuf Balasagun (d. 1070), an eleventh-century Turkic poet based in Balasagun, the capital of the Karakhanid Empire, located on the territory of today's Kyrgyzstan. However, the Uyghurs contest this heritage and see Balasagun as theirs. In more modern periods, the country can celebrate Atake Baatyr (1738–1854), who initiated contacts with the Russian Empire of Catherine the Great at the end of the eighteenth century. More recently, the authorities have emphasized 'The Queen of Altay', Kurmanjan Datka (1811–1907), a female tribal leader who initiated annexation to Russia and fought against the Uzbek-led Bukhara emirate and Kokand Khanate, and her adviser Shabdan Baatyr (1839–1912). That these are pro-Russian figures presents no difficulties for Kyrgyzstan: Kyrgyz nationalist groups are more guided by historical rivalries with Uzbekistan and Kazakhstan, as well as strong Sinophobia, than by anti-Russian feelings.

To make up for the lack of historical continuity in their national narrative, the political authorities have turned to campaigns to 'raise national awareness', making efforts to establish Kyrgyzness as a brand or some unique 'Kyrgyz path' (*kirgizchilik*), and to revive Kyrgyz traditional genealogies (*sanjyras*). The celebrated *kirgizchilik* implies respect for ancestral customs (*ata babadan kalgan salt*), duties stemming from kinship (*tuuganchilïk)* and genealogical belonging (*uruuchuluk*), and, in particular, knowledge of one's local history (*jurchuluk*) and lines of descent for several generations.[21] Parliament is one of the main sounding boards for this discourse, as Members of Parliament (MPs) must cultivate their constituencies, often of rural origin. As Svetlana Jacquesson notes, MPs make use of a simple formulation with significant political consequences – namely, that 'the best leaders are those with whom we share a common ancestor'.[22] The political authorities' interest in genealogy was confirmed in 1996 with the publication of the genealogy of President Akayev, which claimed to belong to the Sarybagysh clan, which has a long tradition of holding power.[23]

The Soviet prism has thus been at once maintained and transformed within the new framework of Kyrgyzstan's independence. The principle of ethnogenesis remains the theoretical foundation of attempts to authenticate the nation: the quest to find the overlap between ethnicity and state is thus reformulated under the umbrella of an atemporal statehood. This linearity materialized in the official appropriation of the *Manas* epic, which, once forbidden, is now sanctified not only as the historical origin of the nation but as a living encyclopaedia of the cultural and moral values of the Kyrgyz nation. The ethnic obsession of Soviet ethnography has been carried over into *kirgizchilik*, a symbol of the quintessence of the Kyrgyz ethnic group, and into the *sanjyras*, which, with official state sanction, make it possible to chart the substructures that comprise the modern nation.

Nationhood decentralized? A plural market for narratives of the nation

While the nationhood narrative in Kyrgyzstan remains quite in line with its Soviet predecessor, it is probably in the production of discourses that the change is most abrupt. This change had its full effect not with the immediate collapse of the Soviet Union, but rather a decade later, once the political and social fabric of Kyrgyzstan had been altered. In Soviet times, the state and academia were the sole authorized bearers of discourse on collective identity, requiring academics to achieve the political objectives of the state apparatus – a model obviously challenged by independence.

The centralized process of stating – and staging – the nation has been increasingly tested by the pluralistic nature of Kyrgyzstan's public space. Diversity has emerged both among politicians and within society: at both levels, competing agendas use the language of nationhood to advance new societal projects. The first plurality pertains to the political elites, many of whom raise the issue of nationhood to secure their political legitimacy and capture constituencies. The second space of pluralism is academia, which is increasingly fragmented due to the emergence of competing institutions and, more importantly, of new, popularly produced interpretations of nationhood.

Pluralism and the state

In the 2000s, some segments of the political elites, often originating from the southern provinces of Osh, Jalal-Abad and Batken, developed a narrative on nationhood that challenged the state-produced discourse. From their perspective, state-backed nationhood has several disadvantages. First, it is too oriented toward creating a civic nation that offers preferential rights to ethnic minorities – both Russians/Russophones and Uzbeks.[24] According to these elites, the ideology of a civic nation, which is sponsored by Western funders, threatens the revival and reassertion of the Kyrgyz titular group, its language and its traditions, and pushes Kyrgyzstan toward a failing nationhood where the titular ethnicity does not control the country's future.

Second, they denounce the state-backed narrative as being produced mostly by northern elites. They criticize the rewriting of history as northern-centric (Manas himself is seen as a symbol of the North), focused on the relationship with Russia and Kazakhstan, favouring a positive reading of Russian colonization and the Soviet era, and offering no room for southern elites to express their regional identity and their Fergana-centred sensitivities.

This more assertive Kyrgyz nationalism, which emerged as a reaction to the civic vision of Kyrgyzstan promoted by the Akayev regime, was embraced as a tool by southern political figures – and even supported by some northern politicians. For instance, Kurmanbek Bakiyev, Kyrgyzstan's president from the 2005 Tulip Revolution until his overthrow in 2010, relied on a different style of political mobilization than his predecessor: his legitimacy, both symbolically (through crafting new discourses) and pragmatically (by creating consensus among elites), was based on a more Kyrgyz-affirming nationalism.[25] Two other figures have promoted a similar muscular discourse about Kyrgyz identity: parliamentary deputy Adakhan Madumarov, who did not hide his ethnonationalist convictions when he declared that the 'Kyrgyz in the country are masters of their own house, the others are only renters';[26] and, to a lesser extent, Omurbek Tekebayev, a former presidential candidate and leader of the opposition group Ata-Meken ('Fatherland').

With the 2005 Tulip Revolution and the partial turn-over of elites, the state narrative lost the uniformity it had had under Akayev. The new ruling elites shared their predecessors' assumption that the state should generate a unifying ideology, but the contents of this ideology became more difficult to define once Akayev's regime was removed. The Bakiyev era was marked by a long succession of (failed) attempts to build a new state narrative, with several commissions charged with determining the appropriate components. In late 2005, for instance, Bakiyev signed a decree establishing a Commission intended to elaborate 'guidelines (*kontseptsiia*) for the state and national ideology of Kyrgyzstan'. The commission was first chaired by Dastan Sarygulov, a former secretary of the local Communist Party known for advocating an anti-Muslim, ethno-religious revival called Tengrism (see Chapter 5). The Sarygulov Commission reported interviewing several thousand people and asking them to answer questions about national ideology. Pupils in the last classes of secondary school were also required to hand in an essay on the question: 'What should be the ideology of the State of Kyrgyzstan?'[27] Although Sarygulov was quickly forced to resign, calls for a more assertive Kyrgyz voice continued. In 2006–7, State Secretary Adakhan Madumarov was appointed head of the commission in charge of developing 'guidelines for a pan-national ideology'.[28] As the Madumarov Commission proved unable to forge a consensus, no guidelines were ever published, and it was disbanded as part of the 2009 government reorganization.

State elites were not the only ones trying to formulate a new nationhood narrative with a more ethnonationalist colour. Between 2005 and 2010, the number of political groups using the Kyrgyz ethnic nation as their central point of reference multiplied. In 2005, a new nationalist party, Uluu Biridik ('Great Unity'), was created. The party was led by the former vice governor of the Issyk-Kul region, Emilbek Kaptagaev, a member of the united opposition against Bakiyev. The party's main mission was declared to be the preservation (*sberezhenie*) of the Kyrgyz people, and it called for Kyrgyzstan to be defined as the ethnic state of the Kyrgyz.[29] Kaptagaev made regular calls to strip Russian of its official-language status, arguing that such recognition damaged the development of Kyrgyz national consciousness.

Then, in 2007, the first *kurultai* (a traditional assembly or council in Turkic and Mongol cultures) of self-described national-patriotic forces convened in Osh. This *kurultai* brought together several dozen small, scattered political groups.[30] Sarygulov, who was in attendance, accused the authorities of having 'lost their sense of the holiness of the homeland',[31] and Nazarbek Nyshanov, leader of the small Patriotic Party of Kyrgyzstan, made similar remarks. After the overthrow of Bakiyev and the introduction of a parliamentary system in 2010, the new political diversity allowed ethnic nationalism to be heralded as a legitimate political agenda by parties such as Ata-Zhurt, but also by political figures such as the former ombudsman Tursunbai Bakir Uulu of the Ar-Namys party, famous for his advocacy of political Islam.

For the past decade, Kyrgyzstan has also witnessed the rise of ethnonationalist street movements that act as vigilantes. Such is the case of Kyrgyz-Chororu (or Kyrk-Chororu, the 'Forty Knights', a reference to the Manas Epic), which claims to unite several vigilante groups of up to 5,000 members,[32] although this number is likely inflated. Famous for filming their raids and posting them online, the 'Knights', who use the traditional Kyrgyz hat (*kalpak*) as their symbol, have organized violent raids against foreign businesses, targeting Uyghurs working at the Madina market and allegedly illegal Chinese migrants. They also target nightclubs and saunas, where they beat sex workers, whom they accuse of not respecting Kyrgyz national values and of polluting the genetic pool of the nation.[33] They likely have patrons within the political establishment and law-enforcement agencies – in 2015, their leader, Zamir Kochorbaev, claimed to have signed Memoranda of Understanding with several state institutions, such as the GKBN (Kyrgyzstan's security services, the successor of the KGB), the Ministry of the Interior, the Ministry of Emergency Situations, the Procurator, and even the Ministry of Youth.[34] Another group, the 'Patriots', has been targeting Kyrgyz women dating non-Kyrgyz men, especially Russians and Westerners.[35] These vigilante groups contribute to the spread of narratives – and violent practices – based on the rightfulness of 'Kyrgyzness' and the need to protect it from so-called liberal corrupt moral values, echoing a rising trend in Kyrgyz society in favour of social and moral conservatism.

Pluralism and academia

Pluralism has also emerged within Kyrgyzstan's academic realm. Kyrgyz higher education has been deeply transformed and weakened by three decades of painful economic transformations. The Academy of Sciences and its institutes have lost a significant proportion of their funding, human capital and scientific legitimacy. Intellectual circles have become more diverse and, due to the country's openness to foreign initiatives, Kyrgyzstan has become a particularly competitive environment for higher education.[36] Many private universities – including the Slavic-Russian University, the American University of Central Asia, the OSCE Academy and Turkish universities such as the Turkish-Kyrgyz Manas University – have attracted young professionals and the best scholars away from state-run institutions by providing a more dynamic environment with higher salaries for faculty and better international career prospects for students. These institutions tend to produce plural narratives that do not necessarily follow the state storyline, and they offer a more diversified market for textbook publishers.

Compared with the Soviet era, contemporary Kyrgyz academia has also shed its unidirectional approach. If the most conventional academic elites still largely share the idea that the mission of intellectuals is to substantiate a national ideology, it has become more difficult to identify such a unifying ideology. Polemics around reinterpreting the Soviet legacy of ethnogenesis among Russian scholars have likewise impacted Kyrgyzstan. Long-time Director of the Moscow Institute for Ethnology and Anthropology Valerii Tishkov, for instance, was a passionate supporter of the constructivist approach,[37] and the debates in Russia's main ethnological journal, *Etnograficheskoe obozrenie*, reverberated in Kyrgyz publications such as *Izvestiia Natsional'noi Akademii Nauk*. Physical anthropology, considered a legitimate discipline during the Soviet decades, has fallen into obscurity, while the simultaneous rise of population genetics has created a new smokescreen for the same work by seeming to validate biology-based approaches to nationhood.

Finally, alternative history has become an important component of the popular production of narratives on nationhood. The combination of freedom of speech and the effect of the market economy on the publishing world has created a boom in alternative histories across the former Soviet Union and especially in Kyrgyzstan. This genre blurs the boundaries between legitimate science and popular knowledge and enables numerous autonomous actors to invade public space with their own, sometimes highly imaginative, narratives. While some authors label these alternative histories as fiction, others position themselves in direct competition with what they denounce as 'official scholarship'. The decline of the Marxist meta-narrative has generated new interpretative frames, including the notion that no single explanation can be legitimate and that 'hidden hands' have shaped history, giving rise to myriad popular conspiracy theories.[38]

As in Kazakhstan, alternative history in Kyrgyzstan has taken the form of pan-Turkic nationalism with the country's titular ethnic group at its centre. The historian Lev Gumilev (1912–92), who advocated for a Turkic-centred historical metanarrative, enjoyed unique posthumous prestige in Kyrgyzstan. President Akayev quoted him several times, repeatedly acknowledging him as a source of inspiration for his own analysis of the peoples of the Steppe.[39] Gumilev embodies a specific version of Eurasianism that gives prominence to Turkic peoples, particularly nomads, and projects a magnified history dating back from the mass migration of the Huns to the Mongol Empire.[40] Gumilev straddles the worlds of academia and pseudoscience, and his scientific output has produced heated debates between those who consider him one of the greatest historians of the Turkic world and those who see him as a marginal figure. His biology-based definition of *ethnos* and valorization of the nomadic past have also made him a key reference for many Kyrgyz scholars with nationalist sensibilities.

More clearly identified as promoting alternative histories, Murad Adzhi (1944–2018) helped spread an epic vision of the Turkic past and its role in world history. Adzhi's work can be considered the Turkic equivalent of the New Chronology movement advanced by Anatoly Fomenko in Russia, which states that Russia was the cradle of major ancient civilizations but had its legacy stolen by German historiographers in the service of European powers fighting against Russia.[41] An economist by training, Adzhi specialized in the early 1990s in an alternate history of the Turkic world, claiming that a huge historiographical plot had been orchestrated by the Russians to erase from the eyes of the world the unity of the Turkic world and its state, *Dasht-i Qipchaq*.[42] Silently borrowing from the 'sun theories' of Ottoman Turkey,[43] Adzhi proclaimed that Turks are the origin of all the great ancient and modern civilizations, that they brought Christianity to the European barbarians, and that Turkic languages were the *lingua franca* of Europe and Eurasia until the Renaissance. His best-known book, *Europe, Turks, and the Great Steppe* (*Evropa, Tiurki, velikaia step'*), published in 1998, was widely available in Kyrgyzstan – and in Kazakhstan – and inspired many local writers to produce similar storylines for popular consumption. His success declined in the 2000s, however, with the emergence of more relevant historiographical production of genealogies.

Indeed, the public space devoted to debating nationhood has been deeply transformed by the growing mass production and mass consumption of genealogies and local history, which have emerged as their own field. As insightfully explored by Svetlana Jacquesson, the popular 1990s mass media accounts of Kyrgyz customs and traditions accelerated in the 2000s and 2010s into a frenzy of genealogical searches (*uruu/uruk*), narratives and family trees, with an impressive level of popular involvement. Fluid oral traditions progressively consolidated into fixed narratives that are now presented as reflecting the 'true' and 'authentic' roots of the Kyrgyz nation.[44] These genealogies have recently invaded the educational system, with textbooks that mention the clan-based origins of the main national heroes,[45] and are widely discussed on social media and television. As Svetlana Jacquesson explains, 'The relocation of history production from the academy to the realm of mass media and the internet acts as a powerful spur for producing more and more history-related "truths"'.[46]

This process has challenged the conventional state-backed nationhood project, largely inherited from Soviet academia, which dismissed genealogies as shameful and conflated political clans with lines of descent. On the contrary, genealogy is now regarded as the embodiment of an authentic Kyrgyz democracy, providing a written form to a collective identity and memory in which morality and behaviours play an important role.[47] The construction of this popular knowledge about nationhood has been facilitated by the internet and social media, where numerous sites offer genealogical reconstructions or discuss them. Once again, academic knowledge seems dispossessed of its right to speak at the expense of a nationhood narrative presented as the advent of the people.[48] Amateurs or connoisseurs of local history have reached such levels of notoriety that, from now on, it will be difficult for official historiographers to avoid integrating their narratives into the official nation-building project.[49]

What is at stake for Kyrgyzstan is thus not the binary choice between a civic or ethnic nation, but the *evolution* from a monopoly over the production of nationhood to an open market shaped by multiple actors and narratives. David Gullette and John Heathershaw have correctly insisted on the importance of collective emotions to the definition of sovereignty, as well as the need for scholars to explore the field of affectivity in order to understand the current – diffuse, but sustained – feeling among the population that the fundamentals of Kyrgyz sovereignty are under threat.[50] Cai Wilkinson has shown the degree to which difficult interactions with the international community and disagreements over what Kyrgyzstan *should* be have played a traumatic role in reshaping nationhood.[51] An additional component could be added to their argument, namely that present-day Kyrgyzstan lacks a hegemonic voice that could achieve a consensus on staging the nation.

The state, in Kyrgyzstan, no longer speaks with one voice: elites in power, the presidential apparatus, the parliament and the political parties all project multiple, sometimes conflicting, narratives on nationhood.[52] The state itself has become an object of competition among different groups, leaving nationhood's symbols and meanings open to negotiation and competition. This decentralization has also hit the traditional places of narrative production with full force: academia has lost its uniformity but also its legitimacy – among its last exclusive rights is the publication of history textbooks for school pupils – and many alternative actors are advancing their own agendas, claiming a right to participate in defining the nation.

Exploring the efforts to produce a narrative on nationhood in Kyrgyzstan thus opens the door to several broader theoretical debates, especially concerning the growing overlap between consumers and producers of nationhood. Similar to the world of social media, each person can alternate between the roles of consumer and producer. This inherent, emerging plurality makes it possible to blur the boundary between orthodox and heterodox narratives, between science and para-science, and between the global and the local. The frenzy for genealogical knowledge and local history, often mixed with broad statements about globalization and the need to know one's own roots, highlights the 'glocalism' of Kyrgyz public space. This decentralized, competitive production of rival discourses on nationhood gives many actors the impression of chaos, echoing fears related to endangered sovereignty.

Two components should be added to this discussion. First, this plurality of narratives is increasingly a Kyrgyz-speaking one. The gap between the rigidity of the Russian-speaking market on nationhood – mostly produced by the state, academia and official institutions – and the lively and multifaceted Kyrgyz-speaking public space is growing. Second, a new actor has entered this race to produce a narrative on the nation, and it is Islam-related. The success of neo-fundamentalist piety movements such as Tablighi Jamaat and other proselytizing groups is making Islamic proponents fashionable and respectable and, in producing new individual and collective identities, adds a supplementary, and probably decisive, element to Kyrgyzstan's decentralized – and democratic – nationhood.

Notes

1 See Marat, '"We Disputed Every Word"'; Gullette and Heathershaw, 'The Affective Politics of Sovereignty'.
2 Liu, *Under Solomon's Throne*; Megoran, 'Shared Space, Divided Space'; Bond and Koch, 'Interethnic Tensions in Kyrgyzstan'.
3 Gullette, *The Genealogical Construction of the Kyrgyz Republic*.
4 Ismailova, 'Curriculum Reform in Post-Soviet Kyrgyzstan'; Tchoroev, 'Historiography of Post-Soviet Kyrgyzstan'.
5 Suny, 'Constructing Primordialism'.
6 Brandenberger, *National Bolshevism*.
7 Suny, 'Provisional Stabilities'.
8 Marat, 'National Ideology and Statebuilding', 38.
9 The 2,200 figure is based on ancient Chinese sources that refer to the existence of a Kyrgyz state in 200 BCE.
10 Kakeyev and Ploskikh, *Istoriia Kyrgyzov Kyrgyzstana*.

11 Umetbayeva, 'Official Rhetoric and Individual Perceptions'. See also Ismailova, 'Curriculum Reform in Post-Soviet Kyrgyzstan'; Tchoroev, 'Historiography of Post-Soviet Kyrgyzstan'.
12 Dor, 'L'épopée centrasiatique'.
13 '147 Thousand Pilgrims'.
14 Akayev, *Kyrgyzskaia gosudarstvennost'*.
15 Akayev, *Kyrgyzskaia gosudarstvennost'*, 282.
16 Van der Nienke, *Spirited Performance*.
17 'V Kyrgyzstane zavershili rabotu'.
18 Jacquesson, 'Claiming Heritage'.
19 Gullette, *The Genealogical Construction of the Kyrgyz Republic*.
20 Umetbayeva, 'Official Rhetoric and Individual Perceptions'.
21 Jacquesson, 'Power Play Among the Kyrgyz'.
22 Jacquesson, 'Power Play Among the Kyrgyz'.
23 Jacquesson, 'Power Play Among the Kyrgyz'.
24 See more in Marat, '"We Disputed Every Word"', and Laruelle, 'The Paradigm of Nationalism in Kyrgyzstan'.
25 Matveeva, 'Legitimising Central Asian Authoritarianism'.
26 'Kto v Kirgizii khoziain'.
27 On that issue, see 'Gossekretar' KP D. Sarygulov'.
28 *Kontseptsiia obshchenatsional'noi ideologii.* Madumarov was appointed secretary of the Security Council in 2008–9.
29 Katargin, 'Kirgizia dlia kirgizov?'.
30 'V Oshe namechaetsia provedenie respublikanskogo'; Khamidov, 'Propishetsiia li kurultai "patriotov"'.
31 'D. Sarygulov perechislil prichiny'.
32 Niyazova, '"Kyrk choro."'.
33 Orospakova, '"Kyrgyz chororolu" – eshche odna peshka v politicheskikh igrakh'; Dzhumakadyrov, '"Kyrk-choro" – provlastnyi proekt?'.
34 Niyazova, '"Kyrk choro"'.
35 Ermatov, 'Understanding Illiberal Sentiments'.
36 DeYoung (ed.) *Lost in Transition*; Akçali and Engin-Demir (eds), *Politics, Identity, and Education in Central Asia*.
37 Tishkov, *Rekviem po etnosu*.
38 See Radnitz, 'Paranoia with a Purpose'.
39 Akayev, *Kyrgyzskaia gosudarstvennost'*, 15–16.
40 More in Bassin, *The Gumilev Mystique,* and Laruelle, *Russian Eurasianism,* 50–81.
41 See more on Fomenko in Sheiko and Brown, *Nationalist Imaginings on the Russian Past* and in Laruelle, 'Conspiracy and Alternate History in Russia'.
42 Adzhi, *My – iz roda Polovetskogo*; Adzhi, *Polyn' polovetskogo polia*; Adzhi, *Evropa: Turki.*
43 Aydingün and Aydingün, 'The Role of Language'; Aytürk, 'Turkish Linguists against the West'.
44 Jacquesson, 'From Clan Narratives to Clan Politics'.
45 Umetbayeva, 'Official Rhetoric and Individual Perceptions'.
46 Jacquesson, 'Genealogies as a Craft', 117.
47 Hardenberg, 'Collective, Communicative, and Cultural Memories'.
48 More in Jacquesson, 'Genealogies as a Craft'.
49 On the role of amateurs, see Light, 'History, Experience, and Narration'.
50 Gullette and Heathershaw, 'The Affective Politics of Sovereignty'.
51 Wilkinson, 'Imagining Kyrgyzstan's Nationhood and Statehood'.
52 See Juraev, 'The Evolving Role of Political Parties'.

5

Reborn nation, born-again religion? The case of Tengrism

Within the new political context of Central Asia's independence, and at a time of large social transformations, the relationships to meaning and to believing have been significantly re-articulated. The reshaping of nationhood has impacted all religions, from the already institutionalized ones like Islam and Christianity to the more diffuse movements based on a form of 'traditional spiritualism'. Of the latter, Tengrism likely represents the most telling of the interactions between a supposed national rebirth and a born-again phenomenon around ethnic faiths. The Tengrist revivalist ideology is based upon a so-called return to the allegedly ancient religion of Turkic peoples. It epitomizes the famous 'invention of tradition'[1], studied by Eric Hobsbawm and Terence Ranger, that accompanies every crafting of nationhood. It illustrates the tensions between politics and religion: contrary to the widespread idea of secularization as the obvious way forward, we live in a world in which new forms of religiosity and beliefs – from proselytizing movements to New Age and conspiracy theories – shape worldviews and influence politics and national construction. This religiosity is nurtured by a decentralization of historical production and consumption in which individuals look for their own agency in world history through the creation of popular historical narratives devoted to the hidden greatness of their nation's spirituality.

From Tengri to Tengrism: an interrupted trajectory

The word *tengr* or *tergir* (*tänri* in old Turkic) means 'sky' in the Turkic–Mongol languages. The worship of the sky or its deities is confirmed by many written and archaeological sources dating back to the Turkic kingdoms of Siberia in the sixth through eighth centuries. According to these sources, 'Sky' became at that time a political institution connected with the Emperor, and it was used as such to unify the Turkic empires until their conversion to Buddhism, Manichaeism or Islam.[2] Certain ancient Islamic texts written in the Turkic language associate *tänri* with Allah, endorsing its use as a synonym for God.[3]

The term was introduced into the Russian language in the nineteenth century to designate the religious system of the ancient Turks, as, for instance, in the works of Kazakh ethnographer Chokan Valikhanov (1835–65). Danish historian Vilhelm Thomsen (1842–1927) gave it new life when he deciphered runic writing of the Orkhon steles in the upper Yenisei basin at the end of the century. In the Soviet era, the Kazakh writer Olzhas Suleimenov (see Chapter 7) introduced the word *tengrianstvo* in his famous book *Az i Ia*, presenting it as 'the most ancient religion in the world, elaborated as a philosophical teaching four thousand years ago'.[4]

Although contemporary Tengrism asserts historical connections to an ancient cult of the sky, it has been unable to demonstrate that any Tengrist practices have in fact been maintained throughout the centuries. Functioning primarily as an intellectual trend for cultured urban elites, it is intended to be a religion of the reborn nation. Since the 1990s, the neologism *tengrizm* has increasingly competed with the word *tengrianstvo*, or 'practices linked to the Sky', whose final suffix signals not only its conceptual nature but also a possible practical implementation. All the contemporary followers of Tengrism present their faith as monotheistic, as the existence of a pantheon of divinities does not contradict their belief in a superior abstract force. Some Tengrist ideologists, such as the Kazakh Nigmet Ayupov, denounce a Eurocentric vision of Tengrism that makes it nothing more than a form of paganism. On the contrary, Ayupov argues, Tengrism offers a complete cosmogony of the world and gives its disciples a system that is at once religious, philosophical, mystical and practical.[5]

Places and actors of Tengrism

Tengrism is promoted by small intellectual circles in Kazakhstan and Kyrgyzstan, as well as in several national republics of the Russian Federation, including Tatarstan and Buryatia. In Buryatia, the hero of the national epic, Geser, was set up as the nation's symbol as soon as the Soviet Union collapsed. The republic's authorities as well as academic circles have institutionalized this mythic figure and organized official celebrations that combine shamanist and Buddhist referents with allusions to Tengri.[6] In Mongolia, the expression *Höh Mönh Tenger*, 'Eternal Blue Sky', which has been associated with the foundation of the empire by Chingis Khan in the thirteenth century, is now a major symbol of statehood. But whereas revivalist movements in historically Buddhist or shamanist Siberia can easily add Tengrism to the national pantheon without creating tensions, in the Muslim republics, Tengrism positions itself in direct confrontation with Islam.

Tatarstan hosts the main Tengrist newspaper, *Beznen-Yul* (Our Path), published since 1997 in the town of Naberezhnye Chelny, known for its Tatar nationalist scene and its active Salafi underground. The monthly newspaper was long edited by Damir Shaikhetdin and Zinnur Agliullin, the latter of whom was one of the former leaders of the Public Pan-Tatar Center (*Vsetatarskii obshchestvennyi tsentr* or VTOTs), a key institution promoting the renewal of Tatar identity in the first half of the 1990s. Since losing the support of a segment of public opinion in the second half of the decade, the Tatar nationalist movement has shifted to a more explicit Islamic identity as the only force able to preserve national identity.[7] Agliullin has moved in the other direction, calling for an anti-Muslim Tatar nationalism based on the rehabilitation of Tengrism. The journal accordingly tried, though without success, to influence the local presidential administration under Mintimer Shaymiev (1991–2010), who preferred to institutionalize a narrative on the harmony between Islam and Orthodoxy at the republic level.

In Bashkortostan, Talgat Tadzhuddin, the Chief Mufti of the Central Muslim Spiritual Directorate of Russia (of Tatar origin), drew attention to himself several times by speaking out in favour of Tengrism. He presented it as the first monotheistic religion and asserted that the Tatars prayed to Allah under the name of Tengri well before the birth of the Prophet. He claimed that popular Islam is based on a syncretism between Tengrism and classical Islam made possible by the maintenance of some proto-Islamic rituals and traditions. He also defended the idea of local pilgrimages to places such as Bulgary and Biliar, a practice heavily condemned by the muftiyat of Kazan, which refuses to acknowledge their status as a small *hajj*.[8] Tadzhuddin's positive assessment of Tengrism is rooted in his vision of a Eurasian syncretic unity of religions. He has, for instance, showcased his friendship with late Moscow Patriarch Alexey II, whom he considered the country's supreme spiritual leader, and he has used the expression 'Holy Russia' on several occasions.[9] Tadzhuddin's view remains a minority one: the main Islamic institutions and leaders are much more critical of Tengrism, which they see as a pre-Islamic paganism that should be eradicated.

There is also a small Tengrist movement among the Krymchaks, a community of Rabbinic Jews of Turkic origin living in Crimea, close to the Karaites – a Jewish community which does not recognize the Talmud but only the Torah. Some Krymchak intellectuals insist on their Turkic identity rather than on their Jewishness: since they are Turkic-speaking, their 'true' religion could not be Judaism but must be Tengrism.[10]

In Kazakhstan, as in Tatarstan, the Muslim Spiritual Directorate has refused any syncretic bringing-together of Islam and Tengrism, an attempt apparently initiated by some Sufi movements that hoped for the assertion of a specific 'Kazakh Islam'.[11] Published in Almaty, *Rukh-Miras*, a quarterly journal launched in 2004, offered several articles praising Tengrism. Edited by the writer Murat Auezov (b. 1943), the almanac advocates for a civilizationist approach, based on the idea that the world is divided into cultures or civilizations, which are conceptualized in an essentialist religious mode; the uniqueness of Kazakh civilization would be found in its Tengrist conception of the world.[12]

Yet it is in Kyrgyzstan that the Tengrist movement has achieved the highest visibility. It went through a first phase of institutionalization at the start of the 2000s, with the founding of the Tengir-Ordo Association for the Preservation of the National Heritage (*Fond sokhraneniia natsional'nogo naslediia Tengir Ordo*). The association's deputy is Dastan Sarygulov (b. 1947), a former secretary of the regional Communist Party, who, after Kyrgyzstan's independence, continued his political career as governor of the Talas region. Sarygulov is best known for (corruptly) running Kyrgyzaltyn, the state-owned company in charge of exploiting the country's gold reserves. Dismissed from office in 1999 by President Askar Akayev, whom he accused of ruining him, Sarygulov then defected to the opposition. Despite their political disagreements, Akayev has on several occasions mentioned Tengrism as the original religion of the Kyrgyz. During his 2002 trip to Khakassia, he even made a visit to the runic steles on the banks of Yenisei, declaring that they constitute a pilgrimage to a holy place for the Kyrgyz just like the pilgrimage to Mecca.[13]

Sarygulov is not the only Tengrist ideologue in Kyrgyzstan. He maintains close relations with less politicized personalities who operate in informal networks without any affiliation with academic institutions. Among them are individuals such as the philologist and journalist Shoyun Omuraliev, his publisher Tailak Abdydabekov, the historian and journalist Abdrahman Alymbaev (who goes by the pseudonym of Bayas Tural) and the writer Assan Yakchylykov. The Tulip Revolution of March 2005, which overthrew Akayev, has enabled Tengrist actors to gain greater visibility in the public space. Omuraliev, Alymbaev and

Yakchylykov helped former presidential candidate Urmat Barktabasov to create his own political movement, known as 'Mekenim Kyrgyzstan' (My homeland, Kyrgyzstan).[14] Their hope was to transform the movement into a political party based on Tengrist ideas and, ultimately, to gain parliamentary representation.[15]

A close associate of the next president, Kurmanbek Bakiyev, Sarygulov succeeded in getting himself appointed to the prestigious office of State Secretary and quickly set about denouncing the absence of any national ideology capable of putting the country back on its feet. His leadership of the Commission in charge of elaborating the country's national identity provoked virulent criticism from all those worried that Tengrism was about to become officially sanctioned. Their fears were allayed in May 2006, when Sarygulov was dismissed both from his post as State Secretary and from the Commission. Since Bakiyev's overthrow in 2010, Sarygulov has continued a political career close to the so-called national-patriotic opposition, but he has done so without again reaching his former level of influence.

Tengrism as a New Age movement: ecocentrism and natural democracy

Tengrism can be interpreted as one of the Eurasian versions of the worldwide New Age movement. A movement that appeared in the 1960s, New Age has no structured doctrine: its followers believe in an eclectic and personalized combination of different religious inspirations based on the idea that there are different levels of reality. This loose religious conglomeration usually consists of three main poles: alternative spiritualities interested in Oriental religions, esotericism, occultism, astrology and UFO research; alternative therapies advocating holistic medicine and wellbeing; and alternative political or social organizations.[16]

The followers of Tengrism claim that their faith offers a comprehensive cosmology adapted to the contemporary world, a natural religion for humankind.[17] The absence of a personification of God would confirm that Tengrism represents a forward-looking vision of religion adapted to postmodernity and globalization. It indeed combines eclectic references inspired by different religious traditions: it questions rational knowledge, alludes to the theosophy movement of Elena Blavatsky (1831–91), and displays an affinity for some Buddhist and Hindu principles. *Beznen-Yul* referred regularly to Western-style occultism, while *Rukh-Miras* puts forward the notion of traditionalism or perennialism, as founded by René Guénon (1886–1951),[18] even mentioning Frithjof Schuon (1907–98), one of the main traditionalist thinkers who converted to Sufism.

Proponents of Tengrism like to mix their cultural references. Several of them praise Shintoism as the only religion that has managed to preserve its so-called 'ethnic feature' over the centuries. Among the admirers of Shintoism is the Tatar thinker Rafael Bezertinov, author of *Tengrism: The Religion of the Turks and Mongols* (*Tengrianstvo – religiia tiurkov i mongolov*), published in Kazan but distributed widely among Tengrist circles in Kazakhstan and Kyrgyzstan. Bezertinov celebrates the supposed religious proximity between Shintoism and Tengrism, claiming that this can be explained by the common ethnic origin of the Turkic peoples and the Japanese – several centuries before our era, he argues, a Hunnic tribe crossed the Sea of Japan to settle on the Japanese islands.[19]

Although they admire Asian people for their rejection of cultural Westernization, the proponents of Tengrism were all raised with late Soviet culture. They therefore refer regularly to Russian traditions such as Cosmism, especially Vladimir Vernadsky's (1863–1945) theories on the bioenergy of the peoples, and even the neo-Eurasianist ideology of the infamous Alexander Dugin (b. 1962).[20] Cosmism is a non-conventional spiritual tradition that combines strong allusions to Christianity (redemption via resurrection), a pan-psychic reading of the universe, and belief in still-unknown cosmic forces and an extra-terrestrial future for humanity. Its complexity resides in its twofold scientific aspect. It is both a science of spatial conquest – construed as conventional, legitimate science and endorsed by the Soviet regime as the embodiment of progress – and a science of modifying current material realities using the force of the spirit, which our societies perceive as illegitimate or irrational.[21]

One of the central arguments advanced by adherents of Tengrism relates to the movement's environmentally friendly posture: it would promote a religious ecocentrism.[22] According to Sarygulov, the rapid development of technological knowledge has given men the illusory idea that they control nature. The West has started down a dead-end path that leads the whole of humankind to its downfall; indeed, the Soviet experience confirmed the failure of human domination over the natural world. This denunciation of industrial modernity is a recurring theme of all Tengrist narratives, which rehabilitate the spiritual to the detriment of the material.[23] They blame Abrahamic religions for humankind's technological madness. Sarygulov, for instance, condemns Christianity and Islam as anthropomorphic religions: by asserting that man was created in the likeness of God, and by suggesting that the latter could have been incarnated as a man (Christianity) or could have transmitted his message through a man (Islam), these two religions have distorted the place of humankind within nature. Only nature should be considered as the representative of the divine on earth, with humans occupying a modest position in this hierarchy.[24]

Proponents of Tengrism thus position themselves in favour of a political and economic deglobalization that would refuse to export Western values or neoliberal practices to the rest of the world. They call for a return to national traditions, ethnic faiths, nation-states, and a doctrine of world peace and non-interference. This postmodernist position goes hand-in-hand with the supposed democratic essence of Tengrism. According to Sarygulov, Tengrism represents the natural religion of the nomads: unlike sedentary people, the nomads would have never become slaves to material wellbeing and would have experienced neither feudalism, monarchy nor despotism. The Kyrgyz state would have differentiated itself from its neighbours by its democratic nature. Power would always have been elective and not dynastic; the country would not have experienced revolution, uprising nor civil war, and it would have been marked by the absence of any institutionalized coercive force. The original Kyrgyz people was thus economically and spiritually free until the coming of the Russians brought the 'decline of the national spirit, the loss of the national pride'.[25]

Tengrist followers insist on a direct, unmediated link between humans and the divine: Tengrism is a faith without a prophet, without a holy text, without any institutionalized place of worship, without a clergy, without dogma or interdicts, without rites and prayers. Raphael Bezertinov further contends that Tengrism is a religion devoid of any social exploitation, without power relations, without any financial or institutional reality, whereas Abrahamic religions have always promoted the cultural domination of one group over the others and served the interests of foreign powers.[26]

Racialized nationalism as Tengrism's ideological matrix

Rooted in a post-colonial narrative, Tengrism strikes a balance between adhering to postmodern values and anchoring itself into the ethnic past of the nation. The latter trend seems to dominate, with heavily ethnicized and racialized language largely similar to the Russian neopagan movements. As in Western Europe, many 'new religious movements' have developed in Russia over the past three decades. Alternative spiritualities,

Eastern religions, esotericism, occultism, astrology and research on aliens first became fashionable among Soviet urban elites in the 1970s.[27] Among these, the *Rodnoverie* (ethnic faith or Mother Faith) movement, which seeks to restore the pre-Christian religion of the Slavs, has benefited from the simultaneous search for spirituality and the paranormal and the rediscovery of ancient Russian traditions and folklore: it calls on followers to interact with Mother Earth and her gods, but also to find their place among the ancestors and thus preserve a supposedly pure Russian ethnic identity. The same goes for Tengrism.

For instance, Sarygulov writes that if the Kyrgyz were able to survive waves of invasions, whether by Arabs, Mongols, Dzhungars, Chinese or Russians, it is precisely because 'the Tengrist vision of the world was the ideological, spiritual, and moral basis of the people and supported the state in all stages of its existence'.[28] In Tatarstan, Tengrist proponents cannot celebrate political independence and thus prefer to insist on the antiquity of ancient Steppic peoples and their role in building the first Eurasian states. Tengrism can thus ally with pan-Turkic claims. Rafael Bezertinov and *Beznen-Yul* focus on praising 'the traditional vision of the Turkic world', referring to the Scythians, the Huns, the Bulgars of the Volga, and the empire of Chingis Khan, which would all have had Tengrism as their main religion. The journal even insisted, in several articles, on the links between the Finno–Ugric and Turkic–Mongol peoples, as well as rehabilitating the Volga Bulgars as genuine natives of the Volga region before the arrival of Mongols.[29]

All Tengrist ideologists are obsessed with Sumer, seen as the older prototype of a developed civilization and ancient stateness (*gosudarstvennost'*) that Turkic people need to reconquer.[30] This comparison of the Turkic–Mongol languages with Sumerian and Etruscan languages, as well as the assertion of close cultural links between them, originated in nineteenth-century European linguistics but is still vivid in some post-Soviet intellectual circles. *Beznen-Yul* claimed that Sumerians spoke a Turkic language and that their writing would have been close to the runic alphabet discovered in Siberia. Nigmet Ayupov also thinks that Tengrism was the ancient religion of Sumer.[31] According to Sarygulov, the kings of Sumer were called *Tengir* and all the great ethical teachings of humankind were born in the Orient because Tengrism was dominant there for several millennia.[32]

Believing in the need for an ethnic faith, defenders of Tengrism have taken vocal public positions on what they consider the still-colonial situation of their respective countries. Fixated on the dangers threatening the survival of the nation, they blend all enemies into one: Russia, the

United States, Israel and Arab countries are all accused of 'ideological expansion'[33] as well as 'neocolonialism and the distorting process of globalization'.[34] In Kyrgyzstan, Sarygulov favours a 'cleansing' of the country from any foreign influence, whether from Russia, China, the Middle East or the United States. In Tatarstan, *Beznen-Yul* received a warning from the Russian Ministry of Justice for incitement to inter-ethnic hatred. An article published in 2006, titled 'Catechism for the Non-Russians' and signed by the 'Movement against the Russification of Tatarstan', denounced the colonial culture of Moscow and the risk of the disappearance of the Tatar nation.[35] The journal called for a return to runic writing, claiming that 'writing ... carries the genetic code of the nation'.[36] The loss of the 'national' alphabet would signal the loss of identity: as long as the Tatars continue to use the Cyrillic alphabet or go back to the Arabic script, national rebirth cannot be secured.

Proponents of Tengrism do not hide their deeply biological definition of the nation and their racial credo. In Kazakhstan, the musicologist Assiya Mukhambetova spoke about the existence of a 'Tengrist superethnos', mixing religious belonging with ethnicist theories inspired by Lev Gumilev.[37] Biological metaphors are also a recurring theme in Sarygulov's remarks: with the disappearance of national traditions, he says, Kyrgyz would lose their 'genetic code'.[38] As for *Beznen-Yul*, it has on several occasions asserted an opposition to mixed marriages, claiming that they would cause hazardous genetic combinations.[39] Bezertinov, too, has contended that 'the spirit of a nation is defined along three main lines: the unity of blood, language, and religion'.[40] He condemns the Westernization of Tatar society, which he describes as coming in the form of alcohol, tobacco, homosexuality, monogamy and the elevated status given to women, and calls for the return to a patriarchal and polygamist conception of the family. He even denounced the existence of an Institute of Blood Transfusion in the USSR, claiming that the Institute aimed to weaken the patriotism of each people by decreasing its biological defences.

For Tengrist ideologists, Islam should be publicly decried as a faith foreign to Turkic peoples and imported by Arab conquerors. The hidden narrative here is that Islam, as an Abrahamic religion, has a Jewish background and therefore indirectly defends the interests of the alleged world Jewish domination: classical anti-Semitism, inspired by the infamous *Protocols of the Elders of Zion* and the conspiracy theory of the so-called Zionist Occupation Government (ZOG), has been integrated into the ideological portfolio of Tengrism.[41] Bezertinov's biological determinism, for instance, is inspired by a virulent anti-Semitism that sees the Abrahamic faiths as a coalition united in favour of Jews: 'On the face of it, all the Semitic religions – Judaism, Christianity and Islam – are opposed to each other. But in fact, their representatives in high places live peacefully with one another'.[42]

A famous Kazakh nationalist writer, Aron Atabek (see Chapter 9), writing for *Beznen-Yul*, theorized the link between Tengrist theories and racialist doctrines. For him, the Creator is a neutral cosmic force that receives prayers from human beings: 'A man, finding himself in his ethnos and in his ethnic religion, prays in his ethnic language to his ethnic, natural, and genetic god'.[43] He claims that the Jews therefore founded three religions – Judaism, Christianity and Islam – in order to receive the force of the peoples praying to these gods. By praying to a Semitic god, his theory goes, the Turkic peoples thus give their energy to the Jews and not to themselves. As we can see, the revival of ethnic faith remains deeply anchored into racist and anti-Semitic clichés, with an ideological genealogy sometimes descended directly from the Nazi *Rassenkunde*.

Competing with Islam for the status of national religion

In Kyrgyzstan, where Tengrism is the most developed, the movement's main struggle has been to compete with Islam for the status of national religion. The 'invented tradition' of *tengrichilik* (the Tengri way) remains a top-down ideological creation with little popular appeal. Some references to *Tengri*[44] do exist, notably in rural areas, but there are gaps between the emic perception of *Tengri* in a traditional system of representation and its ideological and political reinvestment by theoreticians. As for the possibility of implementing the mode of 'believing' specific to Tengrism, Shoyun Omuraliev states:

> There are some people who practise *tengrichilik*, but they are very few. They form small groups that pray on their own. But they don't know all the rites of *tengrichilik*, they know only some fragments. We must set up a system to unify all the rites. We must reunite all that is scattered. Praying five times a day comes from Zoroastrianism, but this practice was spread by Semitic peoples. When the Arabs pray, they do not do it by praying to the whole universe. But we *do* pray to the whole universe: the Sun, the Moon, etc. For each rite, there is a corresponding text. For the moment, all this remains scattered, but it exists. We have to revive everything that exists.

> All the rites have to be written in Kyrgyz, our national language. We have to systematize and unify all that refers to Manas, to shamanism, everything that appears in the *bata* [invocations], and the hopes expressed by the youth.[45]

Tengrists' political aims, which include securing for Tengrism the status of national religion, have of course elicited resistance from representatives of institutionalized Hanafi Sunni Islam. Yet following the example of Tengrist theoreticians, some of these Islamic institutions' representatives have also become involved in promoting Islam as a form of ethnic faith specific to the Kyrgyz and devoid of any transnational or universalist dimension, save for attention to potential dangers of radicalization and politicization. If a certain Islam is held to be specific to the Kyrgyz, it is precisely because of the presence within it of Tengrist elements that are interpreted by certain Islamic officials as belonging to a 'national tradition' and not to a theological corpus *per se*. Kyrgyzstan's former supreme mufti Murataly Zhumanov declared, for instance:

> The *tengrichilik* is not a religion but an organization created in order to bolster the nation. To my mind, this does not contradict Islam. But we have received complaints on behalf of certain citizens who say the persons organizing the *tengrichilik* do not have good relations with Islam. They say that these persons do not like Islam. There are many rumours such as these, I don't know if it is the truth. In the *Shari'a*, there exists a single religion, and that is Islam … The word Tengri signifies Kuday [God]. In Arab, it is Allah. In the Turkic languages, one says Tengri. In Farsi, one says Kuday. The Kyrgyz use expressions like *Tengirim koldosun* ('May the Tengri protect us') or *Tengirim zharatkan* ('It is Tengri who created us'). The word Tengri ought not be confounded with *tengrichilik*. At the same time, during the era when Islam did not exist, when people had no education, it was to Tengri that they prayed.[46]

Omurzak Mamaiusupov, former director of the State Agency for Religious Affairs of Kyrgyzstan, even more explicitly asserted the existence of a specifically Kyrgyz Islam:

> A lot of specialists confuse the Kyrgyz with Arabs, Turks, Uzbeks, Tajiks, etc. But it is crucial to know the Kyrgyz way of being Muslim. The Kyrgyz are a people which has never abandoned its traditions. They have never renounced their *kalpak* [a traditional Kyrgyz hat

> worn by men]. They have not changed their highland character … We call ourselves Muslims, but we are Muslims with distinctive features. Even if they are Muslim, the Kyrgyz do not follow the nuances of Islam … We, we have such distinctive features. Religion, Islam, has been understood as a tradition. We conceived of Islam according to the *kirgizchilik*. The Islam of the Turks, the Tajiks, the Uzbeks, and the Turkmen is clearly different from ours.[47]

But Mamaiusupov expressed caution about creating stronger ties between this local version of Islam, alleged to be 'specifically Kyrgyz', and *tengrichilik*:

> There are attempts being made today to make certain traditions to which we have adhered comply with the principle of *tengrichilik*. But we call Allah either Tengri or Kuday. That is the particularity of our *mazhab* (one of the four juridical schools of Islamic law). The Tatars in Russia also call it Tengri. It is therefore quite improbable that *tengrichilik* could ever be accepted here as a religion. One thousand years ago, Islam entered into our genes and our blood. We have maintained the principle of *tengrichilik* within us as a tradition. It would require a thousand years to make all Kirghiz into *tengrichi* … Nobody can prove whether the fact of tethering pieces of fabrics to the *mazar*, for example, stems from *tengrichilik*, Sufism or tradition.[48]

Rakhat Achylova, a scholar working on women's issues who was a member of the Presidential Commission for National Ideology in 2006, presents *tengrichilik* as a 'philosophical outlook' that cannot be considered a religion. She states in a very expressive way the specificity of Kyrgyz Islam, which she describes as being mixed with *tengrichilik*: '*Tengrichilik* came into Islam along with its traditions. In our Islam, one can see traditions which come from *tengrichilik*. By accepting Islam, our ancestors used *tengrichilik* to adapt to what we were'.[49]

As we can see from this brief overview, two ethnic-national ideologies, each articulated around a religious reference, Islam or Tengrism, have come to compete with one another to define Kyrgyzness. With the passage of time, both now find themselves challenged by more universalist readings of Islam, which are becoming mainstream. By reducing the space for a specifically 'Kyrgyz Islam', more universalistic readings of Islam have also accelerated the marginalization of Tengrism in Kyrgyzstan's public space.

Tengrism can be read as an attempt to ethnicize the divine: according to it, true religion is not universal but instead rooted in an exclusive belonging to a collective, in an ethnic or racial definition of humanity. This is one of the key paradoxes of this movement, which in some respects – including its rejection of institutionalized doctrine and clergy, as well as its ecocentrism – positions itself as a postmodern faith. Tengrism is not unique in that contradiction: many ethnic faith revivals, especially Europe's neopagan movements, share a lot with the New Age atmosphere, yet rise in a different ideological ecosystem in which ethnicity, if not race, is interpreted as a major element of collective identity. *Beznen-Yul* even published the declaration of the Estonian neo-pagans at the World Congress of Ethnic Religions and has been supporting efforts to launch an 'International of Natural Religions'.[50]

Even if Tengrism positions itself as highly critical of the Soviet Union, which is seen as a form of Russian colonial domination, it remains deeply anchored in several aspects of Soviet ideology. Its argumentation against Abrahamic religions, for instance the claim that Islam and Christianity justified the exploitation of the lower classes and the wars between nations, are borrowed from Soviet anti-religious propaganda.[51] Its proponents belong to cultivated urban middle classes that were pauperized by the Soviet collapse and changes in habits, as discussed by Serguei Oushakine in his seminal *Patriotism of Despair*.[52] They find themselves more at ease with a religion that demands no regular ritual observance nor theological background and which is limited to the praising of Mother Earth.

Tengrists use Tengrism as an allegory to speak about the reborn nation, whether centred on the acquisition of independence or integrated into pan-Turkic claims. In Kazakhstan and Kyrgyzstan, Tengrism stresses the competition with Islam for the title of national religion – a lost cause – while in the Russian republics, it is used with more pan-Turkic tones to denounce Moscow as a colonial power. In both cases, the central notion put forward is that Turkic statehood cannot be completed and secured without the officialization of its own ethnic faith. Freeing the nation from a foreign religion and reviving ethnic faith is thus advocated as the last step toward full, sovereign nationhood.

Notes

1 Hobsbawm and Ranger, *The Invention of Tradition*.

2 I thank Roberte Hamayon for sharing this information with me.

3 See the headword 'tänri' in Houtsma et al. (eds) *Encyclopédie de l'Islam*, 685.

4 Suleimenov, *Az i Ia*.

5 Ayupov, *Tengrianstvo kak religioznaya sistema drevnikh tiurkov*.

6 See Hamayon, 'Construction of a National Emblem'; Hamayon, 'Shamanism, Buddhism and Epic Heroism'.

7 See Mukhametchin, 'Les composants islamiques de la politique confessionnelle'.

8 See Laruelle, 'L'appartenance à l'islam comme critère politique?'.

9 'Talgat Tadzhuddin: "Russian Muslims already have their Caliphate: It's called Holy Russia"'.

10 Moroz, 'Ot iudaizma k tengrianstvu'.

11 Atabek, 'Tengrianstvo – osnova natsional'nogo samosoznaniya kazakhov'.

12 Mukanov, 'Svetlaia vera rodiny tiurkov'.

13 Akayev, *Kyrgyzskaya gosudarstvennost'*, 83.

14 The demonstrators who stormed and briefly held the main government building in Bishkek on 17 June 2005 identified themselves as supporters of the businessman Urmat Barktabasov, whom the Central Election Commission had refused to register for the 10 July presidential election on the pretext that he holds dual Kazakh–Kyrgyz citizenship. Police later succeeded in driving the demonstrators out of the building.

15 Šoyun Omuraliev, interviewed by Aurélie Biard (in Kyrgyz), Bishkek, 15 June 2006.

16 Introvigne, *Le New Age des origines à nos jours*.

17 Ayupov, 'Naturfilosofiia tengrianstva'.

18 Sedgwick, *Against the Modern World*. René Guénon (1886–1951) formalized the main concepts of Traditionalism in the 1920s. Traditionalism believes in the Tradition, that is, in the existence of a world that was steady in its religious, philosophical and social principles and started disappearing with the advent of modernity in the sixteenth century. For Guénon, all religions and esoteric traditions – regardless of their concrete practice – reveal the existence of a now-extinct original sacred Tradition. He urges the modern world to regain an awareness of this unity in the face of desacralization and secularization. This appeal has influenced numerous Gnostic and Masonic currents, as well as several Sufi orders.

19 Bezertinov, *Tengrianstvo – religiia tiurkov i mongolov*, 10.

20 On Dugin, see Laruelle, *Russian Nationalism*, 95–133.

21 Laruelle, *Russian Nationalism*, 19–36.

22 Sarygulov, *Tengrianstvo i global'nye problemy sovremennosti*, 35.

23 Sarygulov. *XXI vek v sud'be kochevnikov*.

24 Sarygulov, *XXI vek: chelovek i obshchestvo*, 48.

25 Sarygulov, *Kyrgyzy: proshloe, nastoashchee i budushchee*, 24.

26 Raphaël Bezertinov, interviewed by the author, Almaty, 25 February 2005.

27 For Russia, see Stephens, 'The occult in Russia today'.

28 Sarygulov, *Kyrgyzy: proshloe, nastoyashchee i budushchee*, 31.

29 See Shnirelman, *Who Gets the Past?*, 40–5; Shnirelman, 'Ot konfessional'nogo k etnicheskomu'. Bolgars represented the ancient Turkic population of the Volga-Kama region, which was subjected to the Mongol Empire and then assimilated, little by little, under the ethnonym of Tatar. The contemporary Bolgarist movement seeks to bring back this historical and ethnic reference in order to assert Tatar autochthonism and to reject any assimilation by the Mongols.

30 Bezertinov, *Tengrianstvo – religiia tiurkov i mongolov*, 14.

31 Ayupov, 'Tengrianstvo', 86.

32 Ayupov, 'Tengrianstvo', 92.

33 Sarygulov, *Kyrgyzy: proshloe, nastoiashchee i budushchee*, 54.

34 Sarygulov, *Kyrgyzy: proshloe, nastoiashchee i budushchee*, 8.

35 'Katekhizis dlia nerusskikh'.

36 Birdib, 'Globalizm – politika kolonizatorov'.

37 Mukhambetova, 'Tengrianskii kalendar' i vremia kazakhskoi kul'tury', 13.

38 Sarygulov, *Kyrgyzy: proshloe, nastoyashchee i budushchee*, 27.

39 'O smeshannikh brakakh'.

40 Bezertinov, *Tengrianstvo – religiia tiurkov i mongolov*, 34.

41 The party's website has been banned since 2016. On Demushkin, see Verkhovskii et al. (eds), *Radikal'nyi russkii natsionalizm: struktury, idei, litsa*.

42 Bezertinov, *Tengrianstvo – religiia tiurkov i mongolov*, 337.

43 Atabek, 'Liudi i bogi ili kak vybirat' religiiu', 2.

44 For instance, references such as *Kökö Tengir koldosun, tengirim koldosun* ('May the Tengri

protect us'), which, most of the time, are combined with invocations to *Umay-ene*, which itself is apprehended, according to emic representations, both as a foster mother, land and midwife protector of family and children, as in the following phrase: *menin kolym emes Umay enemin kolu* ('it is not my hand [that heals] but *Umay-ene*'s').

45 Šoyun Omuraliev, interviewed by Aurélie Biard (in Kyrgyz), Bishkek, 15 June 2006. All are taken from a joint article by Laruelle and Biard, '"Tengrism" in Kyrgyzstan'.
46 Murataly Zhumanov, interviewed by Aurélie Biard (in Kyrgyz), Bishkek, 23 May 2006.
47 O. Mamaiusupov, interviewed by Aurélie Biard (in Kyrgyz), Bishkek, 24 May 2006.
48 O. Mamaiusupov, interviewed by Aurélie Biard (in Kyrgyz), Bishkek, 24 May 2006.
49 R. Achylova, interviewed by Aurélie Biard (in Kyrgyz), Bishkek, 22 May 2006.
50 'Privyz k priverzhentsam etnicheskikh religii ural'skikh narodov'.
51 Shnirelman, 'Nazad k iazychestvu?'.
52 Oushakine, *The Patriotism of Despair*.

Part 2
Politics and the Nazarbayev order

6
Hybridity in nation-building: the case of Kazakhstan

All the states that emerged from the former Soviet Union have been studied for their state- and nation-building, as well as for the ways in which they have transformed the Soviet-era nationality policies. These transformations, although featuring some shared elements, have been specific to each case.[1]

In the post-Soviet patchwork of nation-building strategies, Kazakhstan constitutes a unique case for several reasons. First, upon the fall of the Soviet Union, the Kazakh republic was in the singular position of having a titular nationality that comprised a minority of the population (only 39.7 per cent of Kazakhstan's population identified itself as Kazakh).[2] It was home to the largest Russian minority after Ukraine (6.2 million)[3] and its territory was settled in segregated fashion, with the so-called European minorities residing in the north, north-west and east of the country, Uzbeks largely in the south, and ethnic Kazakhs in the central regions, albeit with very low population density. Second, Kazakhstan developed the most sophisticated version of the post-Soviet 'friendship of peoples', stressing the notion of a civic Kazakhstani nation as well as Eurasianist ideology, which was promptly turned into a domestic and an international brand in a more consistent way than it had been in Russia. Third, Kazakhstan represents the post-Soviet state that best internalized the criteria of a 'globalized' nation, adeptly raising its transnational potential and displaying unabashed architectural modernity largely modelled on the Gulf countries.

Kazakhstan is, therefore, a textbook case for the construction of a hybrid state identity.[4] It presents several identities, some of which were already established in the Soviet period[5] and each of which is designed for a specific audience. In this chapter, I look at the three identity paradigms promoted by the authorities: Kazakhness, Kazakhstanness and transnationalism. Indeed, Kazakhstan defines itself simultaneously as a political entity of the Kazakh people, a multi-ethnic Kazakhstani nation at the crossroads of the Eurasian continent, and a transnational country integrated into world trends. While nodes of competition exist between these three paradigms, they also overlap on some occasions and are articulated not in opposition to each other but as a hierarchical pyramid. Kazakhness has always been seen as the fundament, the cornerstone of Kazakhstan's state identity and the centre around which to develop Kazakhstanness. Transnationalism, meanwhile, is seen as a path of development that could potentially be emulated by other countries.

The paradigm of Kazakhness

The first discursive paradigm deployed by Kazakhstan is that of Kazakhness, which has been operationalized through state-run narratives about the country's identity and two key public policies: ethnic repatriation and the promotion of the Kazakh language.

Kazakhness as a narrative of the state about itself

The Kazakhness paradigm was the first to be expressed during the perestroika years of state-building and preparation for full sovereignty. As early as October 1990, in the 'Declaration of Sovereignty of the Kazakh Soviet Socialist Republic', the reference to Kazakhness began to be flaunted: the Declaration states that the republic 'bears the responsibility for the Kazakh nation' and that the 'rebirth and development of a specific culture, traditions, the language, and the reinforcing of national pride of the Kazakh nation and the other nationalities living in Kazakhstan constitutes one of the main missions of the statehood of the republic of Kazakhstan'.[6] The new constitution, adopted in 1995, takes up this call by stipulating that the creation of the state is being carried out on indigenous Kazakh land: 'We, the people of Kazakhstan, united by a common historic fate, creating a state on the indigenous Kazakh land'.[7] The symbolic identification of Kazakhstan with Kazakhness is thus unambiguously stated in the highest legal text.

Kazakhness is equally cultivated in presidential speeches. Former President Nursultan Nazarbayev's work *V potoke istorii* (In the Flows of History, 1999), for example, is an ode to Kazakh identity. In it, Nazarbayev insists on the Kazakhness of Kazakhstan as a historic legal accomplishment recognized by the international community: 'A legal, constitutional and international foundation has been given to the fact that all Kazakhstan is the historic-genetic territory of the Kazakh nation'.[8] The central argument of legitimacy used in such presidential narratives is that of historical precedence: Kazakhs were present on the territory of present-day Kazakhstan before the Russians came to settle there. Any historiography based on the idea that there was a free space available for settlement, as proclaimed in Russian conceptions, thus pertains to colonial untruths.[9] This line of argumentation was affirmed in the 1996 Concept for the Formation of a State Identity of the Republic of Kazakhstan, which proclaimed that, as Kazakhs do not possess statehood anywhere else in the world, Kazakhstan must be a national, Kazakh state.[10]

Kazakhs' pre-eminence is not supposed to reduce the rights of non-Kazakhs but to urge them to internalize values identified as specifically Kazakh. 'The culture of the Kazakhs must be seriously assimilated by the representatives of the other ethnic groups, just as the Kazakhs, in their own time, earnestly studied Russian culture'.[11] Kazakhness is thus promoted as a driving force behind building Kazakhstanness: 'The formation of Kazakhstani citizenry (*grazhdanstvennost'*) ... is impossible without the transition to a higher level of spiritual development of the Kazakh nation'[12] since 'Kazakh culture has to be objectively the kernel around which will grow ... the cultural community of all the Kazakhstani people'.[13] This ambivalence between Kazakhness and Kazakhstanness is a direct legacy of the paradoxical Soviet nationalities policy, in which the Russian people constituted the backbone of Soviet integration and the link connecting all other identities to each other.[14] In this context, Kazakhness would also constitute a factor of horizontal integration (between all ethnic groups) and vertical integration (between the state and its citizens), such that it allegedly does not stand in contradiction to Kazakhstanness.

Kazakhness is proudly displayed at all levels of Kazakhstan state symbolism. The state emblem includes a *shanyrak* (the round aperture at the top of a yurt), and many features inspired by the Kazakhs' nomadic heritage (for instance, the eagle) are used in official iconography as well as semantics. The Golden Man – a Scythian warrior discovered in a *kurgan* (a tumulus constructed over a grave) at Issyk – became the symbol of the country's independence and nomadic past and is one of the most reproduced artefacts in Kazakhstan. Renaming streets in honour of Kazakh historical figures has made it possible to build a distinctly ethnicized national pantheon. Kazakhifiying city names (either by giving them back their original Kazakh names or by creating such names from scratch) has helped to territorialize the nation and thereby legitimize its contemporary borders. The Kazakh Khanate has increasingly been considered the main political entity confirming the Kazakhness of the contemporary state since the fifteenth century. State-sponsored cinema from the film company Kazakhfilm has also contributed to elaborating an ethnocentric narrative of the national history. Films such as *Nomad* (*Kochevnik*, 2005), *Mustafai Shokai* (2008), *The Sky of My Childhood* (*Nebo moego detstva*, 2011), *Warriors of the Steppe* (*Myn Bala*, 2012), *Kazakh Khanate: Diamond Sword* (2016) and *Tomiris* (2019) aim to instil pride in Kazakh heroism throughout the centuries by staging the national epic on screen.[15]

Kazakhness also appears in the architecture of the new capital city, Astana (now Nur-Sultan). Although Astana was originally a Russian and Soviet city, its anointment as capital city was legitimized by archaeological digs that unearthed the existence of an ancient nomad settlement there, demonstrating the Kazakhness of the city's territory.[16] References to Islamic motives and to Central Asian blue ceramics are part of the general design of the new capital's architecture. The masterpiece of the city's left bank, Baiterek, which symbolizes the country's independence, is inspired by Kazakh folklore and features a tree with a golden orb at its top. The Khan Shatyr building, a giant and very elite-oriented entertainment centre, serves an architectural metaphor for the traditional Kazakh yurt.[17]

Nor was the narrative of the Kazakhness of Kazakhstan deployed only during the first years of post-Soviet state-building.[18] On the contrary, it is continually updated, occupying a growing share of public debates. Between 2008 and 2010, preparations for a Doctrine of National Unity revived the question of the pre-eminence of Kazakhness over Kazakhstanness. In launching this doctrinal project, the regime surely did not think it was opening a Pandora's box. Nevertheless, the first draft released by the presidential administration aroused very strong reactions among nationalist groups and Kazakh-speaking intellectual milieus, with some threatened to go on a hunger strike, and rapidly published an alternative document.[19]

After several months of debate, President Nazarbayev approved a new National Unity Doctrine. This version, radically different from the original draft, integrated over 500 proposals from nationalist leaders, political parties and academics. Although the draft of the text contained the term 'Kazakhstani' no less than 17 times, this word was entirely absent from the final text, which used the term 'Kazakh' to refer to both the ethnic and civic nation.[20] This evolution is not unique to Kazakhstan: it can also be found in Russia, where the term *russkii* (a person who is ethnically and culturally Russian) increasingly replaces the term *rossiiskii* (a person with Russian citizenship) and is now open to being interpreted in both a civic and an ethnic way.

In the new doctrine, the Kazakhs are referred to using the term 'people' (*narod*), whereas the 'political nation' (*natsiia*) is implicitly understood as being Kazakhstani. The final text proclaims that 'in new historical conditions, the Kazakh people, having given its proud name to the country, has the responsibility of a historical mission to become the consolidating centre of the unity of the Nation (*konsolidiruiushchii tsentr ob"edineniia Natsii*)'.[21] The text also proclaims that one of the state's missions is the 'promotion, preservation and development of the ethnic, cultural and linguistic identity of Kazakh ethnic groups'.[22] The use of the plural 'groups' raises questions: Does it refer to different Kazakh ethnic groups (tribes, *juz* or hordes) or to all the ethnic groups that make up Kazakhstan? As in Russia, muddying terminology is an integral part of the state strategy to keep things related to national identification malleable in their interpretation.

Kazakhness and the regime issue

Kazakhstan's foundational ambivalence in deploying narratives about Kazakhness can largely be explained by reference to the founding years of perestroika and the birth conditions of the republic. Early in the perestroika years, the Soviet order and Moscow's legitimacy in supervising local affairs were undermined on the basis of national motifs. The December 1986 riots symbolized this seamlessly: the Zheltoksan (Kazakh: 'December') Riots occurred as a response to Gorbachev's dismissal of Dinmukhamed Kunayev (1912–93), then-First Secretary of the Communist Party of Kazakhstan and an ethnic Kazakh, and subsequent appointment of Gennady Kolbin, an outsider to the republic and an ethnic Russian. The student crowds protested against the nomination of a Russian for a position that had been traditionally given to a Kazakh, seeing this as an unacceptable act of humiliation on Moscow's part.[23]

The Zheltoksan events deeply marked the political culture of the independence decades in Kazakhstan. Nursultan Nazarbayev, Prime Minister under Kunayev since 1984, came to power in this context; he was obliged to take a stand against the riots because they challenged the policy that Moscow had implemented, but ultimately came out as the winner by being named party leader in 1989 and then Chairman of the Supreme Soviet in 1990. From the outset, then, Nazarbayev had to manage the contradiction of being both an opponent of and a product of Zheltoksan. As president of independent Kazakhstan, he had to celebrate the event as the rebirth of the humiliated nation against the Soviet colonial centre, while, as a politician, he could not base himself on the legitimacy of having personally participated in the revolt. In Almaty in 2006, for the twentieth anniversary of the events, he inaugurated a Dawn of Liberty monument, pointing to Zheltoksan as the epitome of Kazakhstan's struggle for independence.[24]

This ambivalence toward the national question continued in the first years of independence. The three main nationalist parties that formed in 1989–90 – Zheltoksan, Alash and Azat – positioned themselves as the rivals of the local communist elites.[25] From the outset, therefore, Nazarbayev conflated political opposition and nationalism: with the exception of the Russian associations,[26] the Kazakh nationalists were his most fervent opponents. On several occasions throughout the 1990s, they tried to form opposition coalitions and defy the increasingly authoritarian regime. This situation was reproduced in the 2010s: anti-Nazarbayev narratives are no longer crafted by Russian minorities or by pro-Western liberal advocacy groups, but are borne by young generations of Kazakh political activists who use social media and wield increasingly nationalistic themes, particularly directed against a Russia-backed Eurasian Economic Union (see Chapter 9).[27]

The Kazakhness paradigm therefore finds itself in a permanently ambivalent status: it is promoted, especially toward the Kazakh-speaking part of the population, as the fundament of state identity – and ethnic Kazakhs do display the highest rate of identification with the state[28] – but it is also looked at with suspicion by the authorities, which see in it a potential competitor proffering a rival ideology. Another element explaining the ambivalence of Kazakhstan's authorities toward the Kazakhness paradigm is linked to the latter's relationship to Islam. The authorities are very cautious not to conflate Islam and national identity. As analysed by Mariya Omelicheva, 'President Nazarbayev opted for the superordinate concepts of "religion" and "faith" as the substitutes for Islam',[29] stressing the role of religious values in general, instead of Islam, as a source of unity of the nation. Growing debate over the place of Islam in the public space and the collective identity of Kazakhs is interpreted as a threat to the secularist state ideology. The mobilization potential of an ethnic nationalism partnered with Islam could indeed challenge the political status quo built over three decades.

Kazakhness as public policy

The ideology of Kazakhness rarely shapes the country's public policies, with two main exceptions: the policies of repatriating ethnic Kazakhs from abroad and prioritizing Kazakh as the state language.

About five million persons who identify as Kazakh live abroad: 1.5 million in Uzbekistan, 1.5 million in China, 1 million in Russia, 100,000 in Turkmenistan, 80,000 in Mongolia and several tens of thousands in other neighbouring countries.[30] In two decades, a total of about one million *Oralmans* (repatriates) have been repatriated, mostly from Uzbekistan and Mongolia, or have emigrated to Kazakhstan on their own.[31]

The repatriation policy was initiated in November 1991, just before the collapse of the Soviet Union. The Law on Immigration, adopted in 1992, stated that all ethnic Kazakhs abroad are potential volunteers to 'return to their historical homeland (*vozvrashchaiushchiesia na istoricheskuiu rodinu*)'.[32] Here, the term homeland is above all symbolic, since the majority of these potential repatriates have always lived outside of Kazakhstan's contemporary borders, even though a number of them are the descendants of Kazakhs who fled Soviet persecutions in the 1920s and 1930s.[33] In the same year, this policy was complemented by a document on internal migration designed to encourage ethnic Kazakhs already residing within the republic to move to regions dominated by non-Kazakhs,[34] a text published with the unconcealed aim of avoiding the division of the country along ethnic lines, a Russified north versus a Kazakhified/Uzbekified south.

Contrary to the compatriot policy launched by Russia, which makes anyone who considers Russia to be his or her homeland eligible for repatriation without ethnic distinction, Kazakh law defines *Oralman* on exclusively ethnic grounds. Some texts specify that an *Oralman* is 'a person of indigenous nationality' (*litso korennoi natsional' nosti*)[35] or 'any foreigner or stateless person with Kazakh ethnicity who resided outside the boundaries of Kazakhstan on the day of independence and who entered Kazakhstan in order to settle on a permanent basis'.[36] Russians, Uzbeks or Uyghurs who might like to benefit from this policy or can prove they had ancestors who lived in the territory of current-day Kazakhstan are unable to take advantage of it.[37] For a time, the *Oralmans* even enjoyed an exemption that allowed them to retain dual citizenship, but the authorities abolished this in 1995 to avoid being accused of ethnic discrimination.

The repatriation policy has a double purpose: first, to overcome the disadvantageous demographic position of ethnic Kazakhs within Kazakhstan, and second, to rebalance the geographical distribution of Kazakhs within the national territory. While it was relatively successful in reaching its first goal, it has largely failed to achieve the second. *Oralmans* were invited to settle in the northern regions in order to counter Slavic domination, but the majority settled and continue to settle in the south of the country or the already rather Kazakh-dominated western regions (particularly Mangystau).[38] Moreover, this state-run process of ethnic Kazakhization of Kazakhstan has failed to address several social problems experienced by *Oralmans*: high levels of unemployment, difficulties in educating their children, a lack of integration mechanisms, and – for those who came from outside the former Soviet realm – a lack of familiarity with Soviet cultural codes and the Russian language.[39] Much though the authorities might try to downplay it, the level of xenophobia toward *Oralmans* among the Kazakh/Kazakhstani population reveals the difficulties inherent in trying to artificially strengthen the Kazakhness of Kazakhstan.

The second Kazakhifiying policy implemented by the state relates to language policy. During perestroika, the Kazakh language was established as a symbol of the nation under threat and was at the heart of demands made by nationalist circles for the protection of Kazakh culture.[40] Declaring Kazakh the state language was one of the first symbolic measures taken to express the sovereignty of what was then still the Kazakh Autonomous Soviet Republic. Throughout the three decades of Kazakhstan's independence, the laws and decrees that attempt to enshrine the state status of the Kazakh language (with Russian retaining its status as a language of communication) have multiplied,[41] but it has been difficult to enforce them, since linguistic habits do not change via top-down decisions. The state has made knowledge of Kazakh a mandatory requirement for entering the state administration, as well as for students to receive public funding and grants. It has increased the proportion of Kazakh-language broadcasting and funds the development of Internet sites that use the state language.[42] However, the quality of Kazakh-speaking schools is still considered lower than that of Russian-speaking ones, minorities continue to be (self-)excluded from the Kazakh-speaking environment, and many members of the elite (albeit fewer than before) still have trouble navigating their careers and everyday lives in Kazakh.[43]

The Kazakhification of Kazakhstan's public space is indeed well underway.[44] Minorities have largely internalized the idea that not knowing Kazakh curbs their potential for professional advancement in certain sectors.[45] Russian-speaking Kazakh elites feel guilty about their lack of fluency in Kazakh and tend to apologize for this situation, a sign that they have internalized the idea that mastering the official language is expected of them not only by the state but also by their fellow citizens. According to the 2009 census, the share of Kazakhstani people who fluently write, read and understand Kazakh has risen sharply with the younger generations (see Figure 6.1). In the educational system, Russian is progressively being displaced by Kazakh. In 2003, 55 per cent of Kazakhstani students were studying in Kazakh and 41 per cent in Russian.[46] 10 years later, in 2013, 66 per cent were studying in Kazakh and just 31 per cent in Russian.

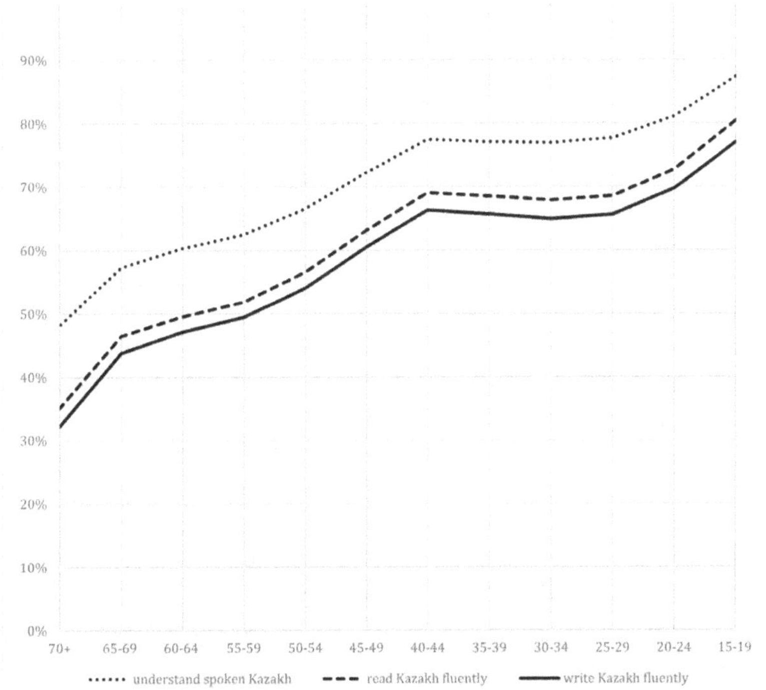

Figure 6.1 Proportion of Kazakhstan's age groups with various levels of command of the Kazakh language. Source: Statistical Agency of the Republic of Kazakhstan, 'Natsional'nyi sostav, veroispovedanie i vladeniia iazykami v Respublike Kazakhstan—itogi Natsional'noi perepisi naseleniia 2009 goda v Respubliki Kazakhstan', 2010. Calculated from command of Russian by age group (p. 269) and total size of age groups (p. 4).

Added to this is the difficult question of Kazakhness being a discriminatory selection tool in the job market. Minorities in Kazakhstan claim that they are excluded based on unofficial ethnic criteria, and indeed, the statistics seem to bear this out: whereas Kazakhs represent about 60 per cent of the country's population, more than 90 per cent of state administration positions are occupied by ethnic Kazakhs.[47] However, there are other elements that are difficult to measure statistically that come into play here: minority individuals may self-select into the private sector, which allows for a greater degree of transnational interaction and makes it possible for them to prepare for emigration if necessary. Moreover, many jobs are gained through clientelist networks: selection on the basis of kinship ties unintentionally favours ethnic Kazakhs over minorities.

The Kazakhstanness paradigm

Kazakhstanness, as a civic definition of national identity, constitutes the second paradigm deployed by Kazakhstan's authorities. It relies on the Soviet dissociation between citizenship and nationality/ethnic identification, which is still recorded in Kazakhstan's passports (the famous fifth point after family name, first name and patronymic, date, and place of birth). The Soviet-style celebration of multi-nationalism has indeed been kept alive more by Kazakhstan than by any other former Soviet state. Official discourse vaunts the harmony in which its more than 130 nationalities live thanks to the frequently-mentioned 'hospitality' (*gostepriimnost'*) of the native Kazakh people. This multi-nationality is alleged to have engendered a supra-ethnic civic identity. The articulation between multi-nationality and civic identity is not, however, a given: citizens can feel free to display their ethnic culture without identifying with a supra-ethnic identity.[48]

The Assembly of the People (previously the plural Assembly of Peoples, hereinafter 'the Assembly'), created by presidential decree on 1 March 1995, posits itself as the institutional embodiment of Kazakhstan's multi-nationality. The birth of this new institution, led by the president himself, can be explained by the political context of its time: to compete with the Parliament, which was considered too rebellious against the regime, Nazarbayev wanted to institutionalize a civil society that was more supportive of his policies. The authorities' strategy was thus to replace formal representative democracy with the expression of a civil society in which the structuring element would not be social class or political orientation, but national belonging.[49] Although it is merely a consultative body, the Assembly has initiated two referenda, one about extending the presidential term of office and another about the new Constitution. Its 350 members are not elected but appointed by the president. In 2007, the Assembly gained the right to elect nine deputies to the *Mazhilis* (Parliament).

Using terminology that is still very Soviet, the Assembly is presented as the 'laboratory of the friendship of the peoples'[50] and functions according to the principle of co-option.[51] It represents all minority cultural centres, from the smallest (Assyrians) to the most numerous (Russians), overseeing about 800 associations that represent almost 50 ethnic groups. It also finances about 170 weekend schools teaching about 20 native languages, several minority-language newspapers, and the Kazakh, Russian, German, Korean, Uzbek and Uyghur national theatres.[52] Debates on politicized issues, such as minority representation in political life and in the higher echelons of the economy, are absent from the preoccupations of the Assembly, which is devoted to folkloric activities, such as days of Slavic culture, Armenian music, Tatar chorale, Korean cuisine and so on.[53]

Propaganda related to the nationalities policy remains characterized by a hierarchy of ethnic identities. The place of each nationality largely depends on what it brings to the country's international branding. The authorities tend to celebrate national minorities that represent countries with which Kazakhstan has developed close economic and diplomatic ties. In this framework, Germans and Koreans are at the top of the symbolic pyramid thanks to their active involvement in the development of Kazakhstan as well as the country's close relationship with Germany and South Korea.[54] Poles, Armenians and Greeks are also viewed positively, although Kazakhstan has fewer economic links with their kin states. Russians, meanwhile, have been prevented from becoming intermediaries in the relationship with Russia, which remains controlled by Kazakhstani elites.[55] For other minorities, symbolic integration is more complicated. This is the case, for example, for the Uyghurs, Chechens and Uzbeks, who face greater discrimination, are often suspected of being hidden Islamists and are associated with the difficult political situations in their kin state.

The Assembly thus fulfils several missions: it celebrates the country's national diversity for both international and domestic audiences; supports small and depoliticized minorities that are satisfied with the cultural rights they are given; and marginalizes minorities with the potential for political mobilization, like Russians, Uyghurs or Uzbeks.

A similar, albeit less elaborate, strategy has been developed to present Kazakhstan as a harmonious place for religions, symbolized by the Congress of World and Traditional Religions (hereinafter 'the Congress'). Launched in 2003, the Congress takes place every three years. It is hosted in Astana at the Palace of Peace and Accord, a Norman Foster construction built in the form of a pyramid, the four sides of which are supposed to symbolize openness to the world's four cardinal points.[56] The Congress sessions offer an occasion to brand Kazakhstan internationally by inviting foreign heads of state and high-level diplomats and religious figures, as well as to regulate religious issues around a consensual narrative of the 'dialogue of civilizations' or 'dialogue of religions'. The Congress promotes so-called traditional religions over non-traditional 'sects' and radical groups: it recognizes Islam (Sunni), Christianity (above all Orthodoxy, but also Catholicism and Lutheranism), Buddhism, Judaism, Daoism, Shintoism and Hinduism, and excludes both proselytizing Protestant groups and Islamic movements that do not recognize the authority of national religious institutions.[57]

The Kazakhstanness paradigm has thus succeeded in combining the old Soviet trope of the 'friendship of people' with a more fashionable narrative on the 'dialogue of civilization'. It speaks to the older generations as a continuation of Soviet memory and to some of the younger ones as a fashionable multiculturalism.

The transnationalism paradigm

A third paradigm emerged as early as the mid-1990s. Boosted by the financial manna flowing from oil redistribution, it would become Kazakhstan's main discursive currency by the second half of the first decade of the 2000s. This paradigm can be described as transnationalism – the idea that interconnectivity and globalization alter the nation-state and its integration into the world community. For both domestic and international audiences, this paradigm is intrinsically linked to the regime's legitimacy and purposely conflates the Kazakhstani state and the Nazarbayev regime. It is endowed with certain characteristics of the cult of personality: the president is supposed to embody not only the unity of the nation beyond ethnic and political differences, but also its different temporalities (past, present and future).

The transnational narrative of the nation

The physical embodiment of this third paradigm is the new capital city, Astana/Nur-Sultan. The change of capital, announced in 1994 and accomplished in 1997, has often been interpreted as a gesture in favour of the country's Kazakhness: the Soviet-era capital, Almaty, was seen as a linguistically and culturally Russified city (as well as being the home of the majority of human rights activists and Russian-speaking political opponents) at a time when fears of the secession of the northern regions made it imperative that the country's capital be more centrally located.[58] However, Nazarbayev's project went much further: the point of building a new capital was to position Kazakhstan within the international community and to plot a bright future for it, a future materialized in the futuristic appearance of the city.

Soviet references are not totally absent from the city's storyline: Nazarbayev has often mentioned reprising the Virgin Lands campaign (Astana is built on the site of the small town of Akmola, centre of the Khrushchev-era Virgin Lands campaign) and was partly inspired by similar Soviet projects to build new towns from scratch in challenging climatic regions. However, Astana is, above all, a showcase of Kazakhstan's desired modernity, as well as a laboratory for its efforts to overcome the traditional dichotomies (north/south, urban/rural) and to metaphorically extend this new integration to the country as a whole. Astana's architecture, particularly the left bank, displays monumental avenues and buildings (the Presidential Palace, Baiterek, Atameken, the Pyramid, the Central Mosque, the National Museum and so on) that are meant to erase inequalities between social groups, display a globalized consumerism and project Kazakhstan as being on the 'path of progress'.[59] The city is largely forward-looking and the past ever less celebrated. Both the Memorial to the Victims of Political Repression and the Memorial to the Defenders of the Homeland were, for instance, placed in peripheral neighbourhoods at the time of their construction. As the city developed, these areas became more central, leading to decisions to change the fate of both sites. The former was transformed into a host for the world's fourth-largest national flag,[60] inaugurated by Nazarbayev in 2009: any mourning of the past has been replaced by a Guinness-Book-of-World-Records-style prestige.

Although building Astana was Nazarbayev's pet project (including for financial reasons: the construction of the city seems to have allowed him to offshore millions of dollars),[61] the transnationalism paradigm has been operationalized in many other ways. Some are discursive in essence, as with *Kazakhstan-2030*, a programmatic document released in 1997 that describes what the country will supposedly have achieved by 2030 and delineates the steps that must be taken to make these achievements a reality. Its strong utopian motives are 'directed at transforming the country into one of the safest, most stable ecologically sustainable states in the world, with a dynamically developing economy'.[62] The exercise was repeated a decade later with the *Strategy 2050* paper, which set the goal of Kazakhstan's becoming one of the 30 most advanced countries in the world by 2050.[63] The presidential address of 2014, entitled 'Kazakhstan's Way 2050: Common Aims, Common Interests, Common Future', was distinctly forward-looking, making little mention of the common past.[64]

The 2050 Strategy was commissioned as a commercial branding project, a kind of SWOT (Strengths, Weaknesses, Opportunities and Threats) analysis identifying the country's opportunities. Nation-branding has indeed been understood by the authorities as a central instrument of prestige and a symbol of globalization.[65] The government and its various ministerial branches, as well as its embassies, have been financing costly public relations actions in a bid to capture the attention of the world community and especially that of international business circles: these actions range from buying pages in major Western newspapers to vaunt the country's merits and attract foreign direct investment to trying to counter the negative images of the country that emerged with the blockbuster film *Borat* (2006).[66]

These actions can also resemble genuine electoral campaigns on the international stage. This was the case, for example, when Kazakhstan made a bid for the presidency of the Organization for Security and Cooperation in Europe in 2010 with a roadmap called the 'Path to Europe', the idea of which was to consolidate economic relations with major European companies. It reproduced a similar campaign, promoting its Islamic identity, to bid for the presidency of the Islamic Cooperation Organisation the following year, inviting Islamic financial institutions to invest in the country. This nation-branding was reactivated with Kazakhstan's application for UN Security Council non-permanent member status in 2016, a status that enabled the country to capitalize on its steady support for multilateralism at the UN since independence and its contribution to many UN regional frameworks.

Added to this is the authorities' very early cognizance that the country's status as a denuclearized power (since 1994) gave it untapped potential to engage in unique 'nuclear diplomacy'. In a context of growing tension between states that possess nuclear weapons, which promote non-proliferation, and states that do not, which emphasize disarmament, Kazakhstan is uniquely attuned to both non-proliferation and disarmament values thanks to its victimization by past Soviet nuclear experiments and its ambitious civilian nuclear programme (Kazakhstan is the world's largest uranium producer).[67] This nuclear diplomacy has been a central tool deployed to brand Kazakhstan on the international scene.

Lastly, Kazakhstan has implemented a third stage of nation-branding based on strategies of development with far longer-range consequences. Two examples demonstrate the diversity of these strategies. The first is the political decision to invest in sports – one example is the visibility gained by the Astana Team in cycling – in accordance with the idea that a great nation is a sporting nation. The Kazakhstani authorities learned from their socialist past that sports are a form of soft power that may allow a country to overcome international criticism concerning the nature of the regime.[68] The second is the selection of Kazakhstan as the host of Expo 2017 (the first time this event was held in a country from the former communist bloc), which gave Kazakhstan unprecedented visibility for a year. In this way, Kazakhstan hoped to obtain the recognition that it believes it deserves, as well as to get itself on the radar of new business circles so that it can transcend its current status as a producer of raw materials. The authorities also hoped to use the Expo to stimulate Kazakhstan's domestic innovation economies – in particular, green economies – by hosting companies that specialize in new technologies, launching technological parks and renewing state support for the hard and applied sciences.[69] One of the next stages of this nation-branding will likely involve proposing that Kazakhstan join the circle of MINT economies (Mexico, Indonesia, Nigeria and Turkey), an acronym that designates the booming economies that look set to follow in the footsteps of the BRICS countries (Brazil, Russia, India, China and South Africa).

Other projects embodying the transnationalism paradigm are based on the idea that the country needs to invest in its human resources. The Bolashak programme, established way back in 1993, was the first to enable the country to endow itself with a new elite workforce trained abroad. This was followed in 2000 by the establishment of the Foundation of the First President of Kazakhstan, which offers a broad range of cultural, educational and scholarly activities targeting youth and promoting patriotism – and hosts one of the country's main think tanks, the Institute for World Economy and Politics (IWEP).[70] At the end of the 2000s, the authorities embarked on a multiplicity of new initiatives in the human capital sector, mostly targeting an elite corps of technocrats and engineers. They created new educational institutions, often distinctly oriented toward the applied sciences and geared to industrial needs.

Nazarbayev University, established in Astana in 2009, is the flagship of Kazakhstan's educational reform, following an internationalized

Anglo-Saxon model that is also replicated in the Gulf countries.[71] It is accompanied by a Nazarbayev Endowment Fund financed by large Kazakhstani energy and mining firms. The University network is completed by the Nazarbayev Intellectual Schools, 20 primary and secondary schools that focus on the hard sciences and biology, with trilingual instruction in Kazakh, Russian and English. These new educational institutions have established a two-tier education system: the new schools, which are directly dependent on the presidential administration, are criticized for siphoning funding away from the Ministry of Education and the rest of the educational system.[72] Lastly, in 2012, the Nazarbayev Centre was launched as a 'multifunctional research and educational public institution dedicated to advancing research and broadening the information available on the history of statehood of Kazakhstan'.[73] All these initiatives aim to create a globalized elite that is able to promote Kazakhstan in the current world order and speak a globalized language of economic interconnectedness and prosperity.

Transnationalism or 'Nazarbayevism'?

It is striking that this transnationalism paradigm is intimately linked with the figure of Nazarbayev himself as a charismatic, almost magical, leader.[74] Is transnationalism, then, a synonym for a kind of 'Nazarbayevism'? All the initiatives related to improving Kazakhstan's human capital, from universities to schools, have been named after him. Astana Day, which celebrates the new capital, was placed on July 6, the date of the first president's birthday. The city also hosts a Museum of the First President of Kazakhstan, which describes Nazarbayev's early life in the Soviet Union as having laid the foundation for the country's independence and exhibits myriad awards, honours and gifts that the former president received from abroad. It is said that Nazarbayev himself rewrote the lyrics of the national anthem. In Baiterek, citizens place their hands in bronze casts of Nazarbayev's hands to make a wish, and his hand was even included for some time in the design of certain banknotes. Nazarbayev has become the subject of films, plays and even children's fairy tales, in accordance with a model that combines the Soviet tradition of youth upbringing via the life stories of their most famous men and locally based traditions of considering the sultan's personal destiny to encapsulate the destiny of the country.[75]

Last but not least, in 2010, both Houses of Parliament voted to endow Nazarbayev with the pompous title of 'leader of the nation' (Kazakh: *Elbasy*).[76] The attribution of this epithet can be interpreted as the growing megalomania of an aging leader. However, the stakes reside elsewhere: at issue were the preparations for the presidential succession. In a context in which the mechanisms of succession were not explicit, the title 'leader of the nation' made it possible for the authorities to grant Nazarbayev a privileged status during his lifetime. The bill guaranteed him this title for life and protected him, his family and their property from civic or criminal prosecution. The aim was thus to ensure immunity for his goods (following the model that Vladimir Putin set up for Boris Yeltsin in 1999), as well as the privilege of having the high ground.

How to interpret the meaning of this paradoxical personality cult? Obviously, Nazarbayev's personality is closely bound up with the three paradigms of state identity, but it is more noticeable in the third than in the first two. Despite being the 'leader of the nation', Nazarbayev's personality is largely absent from narratives of Kazakhness. As the latter was partly structured as an ideology of protest against Nazarbayev's regime, Kazakhness is, in a sense, in opposition to Nazarbayevism. This is not the case for Kazakhstanness, however: both the rhetoric of multi-nationality and the Eurasianist ideology were instrumental in Nazarbayev's crafting of both the state identity at home and abroad and his personal legitimacy as head of state.

Then why is it in this third paradigm that Nazarbayev's cult appears the most plainly? Several explanations can be put forward. The first is that the transnational paradigm is endowed with particular personal value for Nazarbayev, whose international ambition has often been noted by local and foreign observers. He thought of himself as Kazakhstan's best export brand, a status he acquired upon the country's independence thanks to his own role in the negotiations linked to denuclearization and his personal commitment to any and all regional and multilateral fora. The second is that the more 'denationalized' the paradigm is (transitioning from Kazakhness to Kazakhstanness and from thence to trans-nationalism), the more it needs to be embodied by a figure that metaphorically represents the nation. The state narrative about Kazakhstan as a transnationalized country should thus be seen not as going *against* nationhood but as an integral part of it, and the president's personality encapsulates this connection.

The third explanation is that Nazarbayev sought to bequeath a legacy to his country concerning its destiny in the twenty-first century. The fact that deputies from Nur Otan, the pro-presidential party that proposed the bill on the title of 'leader of the nation', compared Nazarbayev to George Washington, Mustafa Kemal Ataturk and Mahatma Gandhi[77] is not simply to be dismissed with a smile. It reveals seeing Nazarbayev as having given birth to a new nation-state (Washington), brought an old nation into modernity on the ruins of an empire, secularized state structures and the public space (Kemal) and having contributed to peace at home and abroad (Gandhi).

These three explanations are probably all true, and nor are they contradictory. But I argue here for a fourth. In my view, the difference between the first two paradigms and the third, which illuminates the over-investment in Nazarbayev's personality, is the following: Kazakhness and Kazakhstanness are self-referencing. Their only role is a kind of self-celebration of the nation's identity, regardless of how it is described (that is, as an ethnic or civic nation). The third paradigm, on the other hand, transcends the mere identity of the nation by offering content that decentres it from itself: it aims to demonstrate a path of development that can be adopted by other countries and which is not linked in essence to the Kazakh(stani) nation. It is likely that the aging Nazarbayev hoped to establish a state ideology and legacy that would not only sustain the country after he was gone, but also shape Kazakhstan's future in a way that transcended the nation, inspiring a path of development that could be called Nazarbayevism, much like Kemalism, Thatcherism, or Reaganism. He was probably also inspired by the mark left by Lee Kuan Yew on Singapore's development.[78]

Kazakhstan is a fascinating case of state-identity crafting, wherein at least three paradigms coexist. Each of the three targets a different audience: the first aims mostly at a Kazakh-speaking and, especially, rural audience; the second is directed at the Slavic minorities, the Russian neighbour, and other post-Soviet states; and the third is probably the most inclusive, as it targets a broader, internationalized audience as well as a domestic one that includes the new elites.[79] In speaking to Kazakhstan's domestic audience, the third paradigm hopes to transcend the Kazakhness/Kazakhstanness dichotomy by de-ethnicizing the national narrative and seeking to transform this old narrative into a 'civilizational' path of development. This ability to switch between different ideological codes is a sign of the regime's flexible pragmatism and the instrumental character of these official narratives.

One might wonder about the medium-term survival of these three paradigms: Will one discursively overwrite the others? It is likely that the Kazakhstanness paradigm will ultimately vanish. Demographically speaking, Slavic minorities are bound to make up an ever smaller part of the population: the Russian minority fell from 37 per cent of the population (6.2 million) in 1989 to 20 per cent (3.5 million) in 2018.[80] While minorities may see their rights preserved in a folkloric way in an increasingly Kazakh-centric and Kazakh-speaking state, the engine of consensus remains the country's economic success and its ability to deliver the improvements in living standards that it promises. The chances are low, therefore, that a movement contesting the Kazakhness of Kazakhstan will emerge in the years ahead. Instead, Kazakhstanness will probably be subsumed into the larger transnationalism paradigm, with the idea of Eurasian multi-nationality gradually becoming simply a historical legacy of Soviet times.

The most challenging articulation is still to be created between the first and the third paradigms, especially now that the country is gradually entering a post-Nazarbayev era. How will the transnationalism paradigm evolve without the figure of the 'leader of the nation'? Will the state identity narrative suddenly be decoupled from the regime's legitimacy? Can a post-Nazarbayev Nazarbayevism be built? This period may open the door to some new identity reconfigurations. One may also witness the birth of new paradigms – for instance, an Islamic paradigm, whose relationship with the Kazakhness paradigm could be either competitive or complementary.

Regardless, the core of these evolutions is probably contained in the Kazakhness issue alone. Kazakhness is the only one of the three narratives that is not monopolized by the regime and is instead crafted by political forces and social groups whose legitimacy challenges that of the regime. The coming rebalancing between Kazakhness as a contesting political force, transnationalism as a political project based on the country's economic achievements, and the 'Nazarbayevism' of the post-Nazarbayev regime will help to shape the future of the country's state identity.

Notes

1 I am very grateful to Peter Rollberg, Alexander Diener and Maria Omelicheva for their comments on the text.

2 *Natsional'nyi Sostav Naseleniia SSSR po Dannym Vsesoiuznoi Perepisi Naseleniia 1989 g.*

3 Peyrouse, 'Nationhood and the Minority Question in Central Asia'.

4 There is a massive literature on this topic, especially on the tensions between civic and ethnic identities. See, for instance, Kesici, 'The Dilemma in the Nation-Building Process'; Spehr and Kassenova, 'Kazakhstan: Constructing Identity in a Post-Soviet Society'; Sharipova et al., 'The Determinants of Civic and Ethnic Nationalisms in Kazakhstan'; Rees and Williams, 'Explaining Kazakhstani Identity'; Rees and Burkhanov, 'Constituting the Kazakhstani Nation'; Ó Beacháin and Kevlihan, 'Threading the Needle'; Burkhanov and Sharipova, 'Kazakhstan's Civic Identity'; Burkhanov, 'Kazakhstan's National Identity-Building Policy'.

5 Kudaibergenova, '"Imagining Community"'.

6 'O Deklaratsii o Gosudarstvennom Suverenitete Respubliki Kazakhstan'.

7 'Konstitutsiia Respubliki Kazakhstana'.

8 Nazarbayev, *V potoke istorii*, 195.

9 Nazarbayev, *V potoke istorii*, 124.

10 Anacker, 'Geographies of Power in Nazarbayev's Astana'.
11 Kølstø, 'Anticipating Demographic Superiority'.
12 Assembleia narodov Kazakhstana, *Ob osnovnykh napravleniiakj deiatel'nosti Assamblei*, 32.
13 Assembleia narodov Kazakhstana, *Dukhovno-kul'turnoe razvitie naroda*, 59.
14 Tillet, *The Great Friendship*.
15 Isaacs, 'Nomads, Warriors and Bureaucrats'.
16 See more in Anacker, 'Geographies of Power in Nazarbayev's Astana'.
17 Köppen, 'The Production of a New Eurasian Capital on the Kazakh Steppe', 599.
18 Esenova, 'Soviet Nationality, Identity, and Ethnicity in Central Asia'; Sarsembayev, 'Imagined Communities'.
19 Lillis, 'Astana Follows Thorny Path toward National Unity'.
20 Mentioned by Diener, 'Imagining Kazakhstani-stan'.
21 'Doktrina natsional'nogo edinstva Kazakhstana'.
22 'Doktrina natsional'nogo edinstva Kazakhstana'.
23 Kuzio, 'Nationalist Riots in Kazakhstan'. See also, for later events, Ro'i, 'Central Asian Riots and Disturbances, 1989–1990'.
24 'Kazakh Head of the State Unveiled a Monument in Almaty'. See also Sarsembayev, 'Imagined Communities'.
25 See Babak et al. (eds), *Political Organization in Central Asia and Azerbaijan*.
26 On the political activism of Russian minorities, see Laruelle and Peyrouse, *Les Russes du Kazakhstan*.
27 Lillis, 'Kazakhstan: Landmark Eurasian Union Treaty Signed Amid Protests and Arrests'.
28 Spehr and Kassenova, 'Kazakhstan: Constructing Identity in a Post-Soviet Society'.
29 Omelicheva, 'Islam in Kazakhstan'.
30 Diener, 'Kazakhstan's Kin-State Diaspora'.
31 Witte, 'Proposed Changes to Oralman Legislation to Relax Some Settlement Rules'.
32 UN Development Program, *Status of Oralmans in Kazakhstan: Overview*, 13.
33 Cummings, 'The Kazakhs: Demographics, Diasporas, and "Return"'.
34 Cummings, 'The Kazakhs: Demographics, Diasporas, and "Return"', 140–3.
35 Cummings, 'The Kazakhs: Demographics, Diasporas, and "Return"', 142.
36 *Law of the Republic of Kazakhstan 13 December 1997 No. 204–1 on Population Migration*.
37 Ferrando, 'The Central Asian states and their co-ethnics from abroad'.
38 UN Development Program, *Status of Oralmans in Kazakhstan*, 13.
39 On the case of Oralmans from Mongolia, see Diener, *One Homeland or Two* and, more specifically, Diener, 'Problematic integration of Mongolian Kazakh Return Migrants in Kazakhstan'.
40 On Kazakhstan's identity construction and the place of language therein, see Dave, *Kazakhstan: Ethnicity, Language and Power*.
41 Dave, 'National Revival in Kazakhstan'.
42 Fierman, 'Language and Identity in Kazakhstan'.
43 Fierman, 'Kazakh Language and Prospects'; Fierman, 'Language and Education in Post-Soviet Kazakhstan'.
44 Smagulova, 'Language Policies of Kazakhization'.
45 Jašina-Schäfer, 'Where Do I Belong?'.
46 Suleimenova, 'Iazykovaia politika i russkii iazyk v shkolakh Kazakhstana'.
47 Diener, 'National Territory and the Reconstruction of History in Kazakhstan'.
48 Diener, 'Imagining Kazakhstani-stan'.
49 Oka, 'Ethnicity and Elections under Authoritarianism'.
50 Dymov, *Teplo kazakhstanskoi zemli*.
51 See the official publications during the first years of its creation: *Istoricheskaia pamiat', Natsional'noe soglasie i demokraticheskie reformy*; Assembleia narodov Kazakhstana, *Natsional'noe soglasie*; Assembleia narodov Kazakhstana, *Dukhovno-kul'turnoe razvitie naroda*, etc.
52 See the website of the Assembly, https://assembly.kz/ru/struktury-ank/, for more detailed information.
53 Author's interviews with representatives of different national cultural centres in Almaty, June 2009.
54 Oka, 'The "Triadic Nexus" in Kazakhstan'.
55 Laruelle, 'Russia and Central Asia'.

56 See the Congress of World and Traditional Religions' website: http://www.religions-congress.org.
57 On the religious situation, see U.S. Commission on International Religious Freedom, 'Annual Report 2014'.
58 Wolfel, 'North to Astana'.
59 See Koch, 'The "Heart" of Eurasia?'; Koch, 'The Monumental and the Miniature'.
60 For a propaganda presentation, see 'A Summary of Cultural Objects of Astana'.
61 Koch, *The Geopolitics of Spectacle*.
62 'The Strategy for Development of the Republic of Kazakhstan until the Year 2030'.
63 See the website devoted to the Kazakhstan 2050 strategy at http://strategy2050.kz/en/.
64 Aitzhanova et al. (eds), *Kazakhstan 2050*. See also Weitz, 'Kazakhstan's National Development Strategies'.
65 Anholt, *Competitive Identity*. Applied to Central Asia, see Marat, 'Nation Branding in Central Asia'.
66 Saunders, 'In Defence of *Kazakshilik*'.
67 Kassenova, 'Kazakhstan and the Global Nuclear Order'.
68 Koch, 'Sport and Soft Authoritarian Nation-Building'.
69 Cull, 'Soft Power's Next Steppe'.
70 See the Foundation's website, http://www.presidentfoundation.kz.
71 See the University's website, http://nu.edu.kz.
72 See Kucera, 'Can a Homegrown University'.
73 See the Centre's website, http://www.nazarbayevcenter.kz/o-centre.
74 Isaacs, '"Papa"'.
75 See Laszczkowski, 'Shrek Meets the President'; Rollberg, 'Rascals, Misfits, Patriots'.
76 'Kazakh President Nazarbayev Granted "Leader of Nation" Title'.
77 Ma-Shan, 'Nursultan Nazarbayev, Kazakh "Leader of Nation"'.
78 Nazarov, *Kazakhstan posle…*
79 Kudaibergenova, 'Compartmentalized Ideology'.
80 Agenstvo Respubliki Kazakhstana po statistike, *Chislennost' naseleniia Respubliki Kazakhstan*.

7
Ideology of the 'crossroads': Eurasianism from Suleimenov to Nazarbayev

The Kazakhstanness paradigm goes hand-in-hand with the Kazakhstani authorities' officialization of Eurasianism as a state ideology. This is true to a greater degree than in neighbouring Russia, where Eurasianism has had to compete with other metanarratives, such as the 'Russian World'. As demonstrated in Luca Anceschi's seminal work on the topic, the Kazakhstani version of Eurasianism is a 'regime Eurasianism' that is fully integrated into the mechanisms of policymaking.[1]

Eurasianism emerged in the interwar period among Russian émigré intellectuals such as Nikolay Trubetzkoy (1890–1938) and Piotr Savitsky (1895–1968), who sought to demonstrate that Russia belonged more to the world of the Steppe than to European civilization.[2] Developed in the Soviet Union by Lev Gumilev, it has enjoyed an impressive Renaissance in Russia during the post-Soviet period, both as a revanchist ideology inspired by fascist traditions (as embodied by the infamous Alexander Dugin) and as a pragmatic project of regional integration under Russian leadership (as called for by Vladimir Putin and some of his advisers, including Sergey Glazyev).

Kazakhstan's Eurasianist profession of faith has remained steady over three decades. Admittedly, 2014 – the year of both the Russia-Ukraine war and the signing of the Eurasian Economic Union treaty – marked a geopolitical turning-point that made Eurasianism suddenly appear less attractive and overly dominated by Russia. But Kazakhstan's embrace of Eurasianism is far more than a short-term choice that can be overturned by current hesitations about using a narrative already monopolized by Moscow. Rather, it is rooted in a long intellectual history of interpreting the Steppic realm as the crucial link between the Slavic world (and European civilization more globally), on one side, and the rest of Central Asia (as well as, more globally, the Middle East and the Asia-Pacific), on the other.

Given Kazakhstan's geographical location, this Eurasian commitment makes sense as both a national positioning on the international scene and a commitment to a multilateral vision of the world. But much more than that, it also paints a picture of the nation as being centred on the notions of syncretism, crossroads and diversity. It advances a relatively positive view of Kazakhstan's interaction with Russia and the Soviet experiment yet suggests a path of development inspired not by Russia or Central Asia, but by distant Asian countries such as South Korea, Singapore, Malaysia and, closer to home, Mongolia. As an idealized spatial construct, Eurasia allows Kazakhstan to challenge its peripheral status by crafting a new centrality.

Eurasianism as a literary tradition: Olzhas Suleimenov

In Kazakhstan, Eurasianism is rooted in a long-standing intellectual tradition personified by Olzhas Suleimenov (b. 1936), a key representative of Kazakh culture since the 1960s. A Russian-language writer and poet impassioned by Eurasian history, during the Soviet times, Suleimenov expressed Kazakh national feeling within the framework then set by the 'friendship of peoples', which implied the superiority of the Russian 'older brother'. Since Kazakhstan's independence in 1991, one of his main aims has been to rehabilitate the Turkic cultures by proving their ancient status and their major role in Eurasian and world history.

A geologist by training, Suleimenov in April 1961 submitted to the editor-in-chief of *Kazakhstanskaia pravda* a poem honouring Yuri Gagarin, who had just undertaken the first inhabited space flight in human history. The poem enjoyed such success that it rapidly propelled its author to the status of the key representative of Kazakh Soviet literature. Suleimenov was employed by *Kazakhstanskaia pravda* the following year and sent to the famous Moscow Institute for Literature, where he associated with the great Soviet writers of the time, including Mikhail Sholokhov, Vsevolod Ivanov, Ilia Ehrenburg, Yevgeni Evtushenko, and more. The atmosphere of the *shestidesiatniki* – the liberals of the 1960s who, in the wake of de-Stalinization, challenged the Soviet ideological stranglehold on arts and letters – had a decisive influence on his intellectual and political development. Suleimenov went on to accumulate prestigious prizes, including the Komsomol Prize for

Kazakhstan, the State Prize of the Kazakh Autonomous Soviet Socialist Republic, the title of National Poet of Kazakhstan and so on.

But Suleimenov was not simply a writer; he has always also been a major figure in the public life of Kazakhstan. A member of the Communist Party, he joined his republic's Central Committee in the 1970s, served as Minister of Culture in the Kazakh SSR, and was named president of the Union of Writers of the Republic in 1983. In 1989, he was elected deputy of the Supreme Soviet of the USSR and started a political career as leader of the Nevada-Semipalatinsk ecological movement, which was instrumental in bringing about the closure of the country's nuclear test site, the Semipalatinsk polygon. After 1991, he took up the leadership of the party that he founded, the People's Congress of Kazakhstan, and was appointed Speaker of the Parliament, a position he held until 1994. He thus engaged in several political fights against Nazarbayev, which resulted in him being rapidly removed from positions of decision-making: he was appointed ambassador to Rome and then permanent representative to UNESCO in Paris. Despite this rapid political marginalization, Suleimenov has remained in the public eye as a 'cultural enlightener', enabling him to remain a popular figure without having to stand up against the regime.

Suleimenov is part of an old intellectual tradition that has, since the nineteenth century, promoted the cultural syncretism of the Kazakh people. This heritage includes, among others, Chokan Valikhanov (1835–65), a former student of the Omsk Cadet Corps who entered into the service of the tsarist Empire and participated in several ethnographic expeditions in Central Asia; Abay Kunanbayev (1845–1904), the son of one of the leaders of the Middle Horde, a great translator of Western works into Russian and the author of *The Book of Words* (*Kara Sozder*), a lyrical work that advocates for strengthening ties with Russian culture in a way that would not undermine Kazakh identity; and, lastly, Ibrahim Altynsarin (1841–89), one of the major figures of Kazakh pedagogy and founder of the first system of modern Russian-Kazakh schools. Suleimenov also owes much to Mukhtar Auezov (1897–1961), whose renowned *Path of Abay* (*Put' Abaia*), devoted to Abay, is considered to be a major text of Soviet Kazakh literature. Lastly, Suleimenov can be seen in parallel with his Kyrgyz alter ego, Chingiz Aitmatov (1928–2008), who also sought to write the history of his nation within the larger framework of Eurasia.

Suleimenov's manifesto on Eurasianism is his seminal work, *Az i Ia*, which was published in 1975 in a print run of 60,000 copies and unleashed a heated debate in the Soviet Union. The book brought about a profound change in his career and forced him into a semi-dissident position until perestroika. Immediately after its release, the book received vehement criticism from Russian nationalist journal *Molodaia gvardiia.* Leading the attack was Apollon Kuzmin, a historian who had also spoken out against Lev Gumilev's theories of a Eurasian common destiny based on a Slavic-Turkic cultural fusion and who accused Suleimenov of hostility toward Russians, of Turkic nationalism and of pro-Zionism. Following another attack in a different nationalist journal, *Russkaia literatura*, the debate reached the culture sub-department of the Central Committee's ideology department. In 1976, the latter forced Suleimenov to explain himself to the Academy of Sciences, which condemned his writings for national chauvinism and for glorifying feudal nomadic culture. The director of the publishing house was fired, and Suleimenov's publications as well as all books quoting him were withdrawn from bookstores and libraries. The writer received an instruction to write a self-critical letter; in the letter, published in *Kazakhstanskaia pravda* in 1977, Suleimenov acknowledged his errors and historical inaccuracies but refused to repudiate his conclusions. He was subsequently restricted to publishing poetry for many years. Only the intervention of the First Secretary of the Communist Party of Kazakhstan, Dinmukhamed Kunaev (1912–93), who took up the matter with Leonid Brezhnev, saved him from more serious legal problems.

Both supporters and opponents of Suleimenov's theory perceived the book as a work of historiography, even if its scholarly worth was questioned by his adversaries. The literary historian Harsha Ram has proposed another interpretation. Looking at *Az i Ia* as a work of literature, Ram suggests that the blending of genres – poetry, history and linguistics – was intentional: Suleimenov, Ram argues, needed the metaphor of *Az i Ia* to elaborate a new science of language.[3] In the title of the book, which may be read as the Russian term for Asia (*Aziia*), *Ia* stands for the first letter of the Old Slavonic alphabet and the last letter of the modern Russian alphabet, and also means 'I' in both languages. This pun introduces the book's two parts, the first of which is devoted to the Russian/Slavic world and the second of which is a critique of Indo-European linguistics. Thus, for Harsha Ram, the book's title signifies at once 'the Slavs and the Turks' and 'me and I', making it a subtle synonym for 'Eurasia'.

In this polemical book, Suleimenov attempted to rehabilitate the role of Turks in Eurasia's history. *Az i Ia* is a refutation of Soviet Orientalism and, more generally, of Russian historiography, much of which, Suleimenov argued, is based on a denial of the antiquity of Turkic peoples.[4] The book aimed to reconstruct the heretofore fragmented history of Turkic peoples and to demonstrate the Turkic acculturation of medieval Russia.[5] To that end, Suleimenov mounted a frontal attack on the famous *Lay of Igor's Host*, a monument of Russian literature. A medieval Russian text supposed to have been written in the twelfth century, it recounts the defeat of Prince Igor of Novgorod at the hands of the Polovtsians and appeals for the political unity of Russian principalities. The original manuscript, discovered at the end of the eighteenth century, perished in the burning of Moscow in 1812 and hence cannot be dated using modern techniques. Although corroborated by Soviet historiography, its authenticity remains highly contested; in fact, the document is probably a forgery, perhaps written in the fourteenth century.[6]

Though Suleimenov does believe in the manuscript's historical authenticity, he proposes an iconoclastic interpretation of it that stands in stark contrast to the Russian reading. He argues that the text's numerous stylistic and lexical borrowings from Turkic languages show that the political and economic elites of the time were bilingual – evidence of ethnic and cultural symbiosis between the Slavs and the Turkic peoples. The Turks, he argues, built the political and military structure of the first Russian state. According to him, the famous Polovtsian incursions into Kievan territory, described in the medieval Slavic chronicles as calamities sent from Heaven, were merely a response to a demand from the Russian princes, who were fighting amongst themselves.

Since the implosion of the Soviet Union, Suleimenov has not concealed his Eurasianist convictions: he states that though the communist regime was destined to disappear, the unity it brought between Eurasian peoples can only temporarily be destroyed and will re-emerge. The future, he asserts, belongs to a Eurasian Union, a belief that has led him to support all the various iterations of post-Soviet integration: the Russia-Belarus Union launched in 1996, the Eurasian Economic Community initiated by Nazarbayev in 2000, and Putin's Eurasian Economic Union in 2011. As he stated in 2005:

> We are destined to live together, by each other's side; there is no force that can move one of the countries to another continent. We are all Eurasian; our continents cannot be separated. Historically, geographically and in all other respects, we ought to be together. Our economies and our cultures form a united space.[7]

From this point of view, Suleimenov is in accord with the policies implemented by the Kazakhstani presidency.

The second part of *Az i Ia* is a more poetic reflection on the Turkic peoples' place in the world and their universality. Suleimenov criticizes Soviet linguistics, inspired by Western linguistics of the nineteenth century, for its Eurocentrism, which privileges Indo-European languages and consigns prestigious Turkic-language sagas to the dustbin of history. According to him, the rivalry between these two linguistic families reveals Europe's cultural colonialism. To show that the Turkic populations have a lineage that is just as ancient and as prestigious as that of the Europeans, Suleimenov draws on linguistics, specifically a nineteenth-century conception of etymology and philology. On the basis of this linguistic study, Suleimenov concludes that the Turks are the worthy heirs of the ancient Mediterranean civilizations, especially the prestigious Sumer. He claims that Sumerians spoke a Turkic language whose script is close to a Runic alphabet discovered in Siberia. He also emphasizes the cultural proximity of Turkic peoples to the Scythians, seen as the first state-builders of Eurasia.

Since Kazakhstan's independence, the writer has pursued the Sumerian and 'statist' line of argumentation that he first elaborated in the 1970s. In three books – *The Language of Writing* (*Iazyk pis'ma*, 1998), *The Turks in Prehistory* (*Tiurki v doistorii*, 2002) and *Intersecting Parallel Lines* (*Peresekaiushchie paralleli*, 2002) – he advances new etymological arguments in support of the claim that Sumerian and Etruscan are Turkic languages. What he thereby hopes to demonstrate is that Kazakhstan is not a recent state, born of a Russian and Soviet construction, but rather the last stage in a long Turkic history of statehood (*gosudarstvennost'*).

Though Suleimenov is part of Eurasianist thought, he also draws inspiration from cosmist postulates, as evident from his poem devoted to Gagarin. Cosmism, one of the main streams of Russian religious philosophy during the first half of the twentieth century, claims that humankind is intrinsically linked to the cosmos, that its historical and political development is governed by physical laws that apply to the totality of living beings, and that humanity is only ever on the right path when it moves with an awareness of this belonging to the cosmos.[8] Suleimenov also contributed to the rehabilitation of Tengrism; he was one of the first Soviet scholars to reintroduce the term into Russian, presenting it as 'the most ancient religion in the world, elaborated as a philosophical teaching 4,000 years ago'.[9] Once again, these philosophical and religious motives separate Suleimenov from the re-Islamization trend visible in some segments of the Kazakh intellectual world, placing him closer to the Russian ideational landscape.

Suleimenov's personal trajectory is revealing of Kazakhstan's experience as a multinational and multi-confessional polity. Soviet culture provided an extraordinary cultural incubator for intellectuals like him: after starting out in the hard sciences, Suleimenov was able to pursue a brilliant literary career, associate with the great names of Soviet literature, engage in perestroika-era politics on questions of ecology and peace, and then to promote Kazakhstan's brand by serving as its representative to large international organizations such as UNESCO. Suleimenov thus embodies a face of today's Kazakh culture that has been gradually ignored or held in contempt, a face that is Russophone and not Kazakhophone; nostalgic about the lost unity of Eurasian peoples; advances a postmodern and ecumenical vision of religions without giving any specific role to Islam; and convinced of the major historical role that the Kazakh Steppe played in ancient and contemporary world history. This is perhaps not all of his paradoxes: he also claims a Kazakhness that is unashamed of its Russification and Sovietization but is celebrated through the rehabilitation of the role of Turkic peoples in world history.

Eurasianism as Kazakhstan's state ideology

Far from being merely a Kazakh literary tradition elaborated during Soviet times, Eurasianism has been officialized as Kazakhstan's state ideology, functioning, as Luca Anceschi puts it, in 'quasi-symbiotic relationship [with] authoritarianism'.[10] Immediately after independence, in the first half of the 1990s, Kazakhstan began branding itself as 'the heart of Eurasia'. As Nazarbayev declared: 'Kazakhstan is a unique state in Asia where European and Asian roots are intertwined … The combination of different cultures and traditions allows us to absorb what is best in European and in Asian culture'.[11] This geographical centrality in Eurasia is captured by a sculpture in Zhastar Ayabagy Park in Astana through the explicit metaphor of a heart whose central red point suggests Kazakhstan.[12]

To compete with Uzbek President Islam Karimov, who advanced the notion of Turkestan, Nazarbayev referred to Eurasia in many of his texts. His 2005 book *In the Heart of Eurasia* (*V serdtse Evrazii*) encapsulates this Eurasianist commitment. He institutionalized this allegiance to Eurasianism by founding, in 1996, the Lev N. Gumilev Eurasian University in Astana on the foundations of the city's former pedagogical institute. During the celebrations of ten years of independence held at the university in 2001, the famous Kyrgyz writer Chingiz Aitmatov spoke favourably about Kazakhstan's Eurasianism and the decision to name the University after Gumilev, which he called a confirmation of Kazakhstan's status as the epicentre of Eurasia.[13]

Nazarbayev gave his personal blessing to this official reference to Gumilev: just as in Tatarstan, the Kazakhstani authorities subscribe to a positive view of Gumilev's legacy, both in Eurasian history and ethnic theories. Since then, the university has regularly organized conferences on Eurasianism as well as lectures on Gumilev's work. It even launched its own Eurasian Centre, which was charged 'to define a conception of Eurasianism that would respond to Kazakhstan's national interests; to develop a geopolitical methodology for the historical, socio-economic, and ideological interpretation of the development of contemporary civilization; and to advise state, educational, and academic organizations on Eurasianism'.[14] One of its former directors, Seit Kaskabasov, buttressed the president's vision of Kazakhstan's Eurasian mission with more elaborate historical arguments. He stated, for instance, that there exist three Eurasian states – Russia and Kazakhstan (both heirs to the Mongol Empire), and Turkey (with its Byzantine and Ottoman heritage) – that must jointly constitute a new trans-Eurasian axis. According to this logic, Kazakhstan holds the status of first among equals, as it finds itself geographically located between the other two powers.[15]

This state-backed Eurasianism results from the regime's need for securitization. At its independence, Kazakhstan had to deal with a massive Russian minority and the risk that northern regions might secede. A pragmatic way of ensuring stability was thus to promote the birth of a civic and supra-ethnic Kazakhstani identity, to offer an official status to the Russian language and to insist on Russia as the country's main partner. At the same time, Nazarbayev could not afford to lose his political clout to Kazakhstan's nationalist opposition: he had to appear to be defending the Kazakh nation. As he stated, 'The president is personally responsible for not letting the nation disappear in the coming century or two'.[16] Kazakhstani Eurasianism therefore had to find a way to reconcile the notion of being a bridge between cultures – a core Eurasianist principle – with that of the Kazakh nation as the quintessence of Eurasian cultures and/or the Turkic realm. Kazakhstani Eurasianism is thus Janus-faced, combining a multicultural profession of faith inspired by Soviet internationalism with more classical ethnonationalist rhetoric.

In the 1990s, the prolific field of Eurasianist publications exhibited a discursive line similar to that of Kazakh ethnonationalism, advancing the same historical arguments. A book by Bolebay Tashenov denounced Russia's presence as a 'colonial takeover'[17] that shattered Kazakh unity by reinforcing inter-*juz* struggles and thus destabilized the whole of Eurasia by obliterating its centrepiece, the Kazakh state. Tashenov also criticized the Russian peasants who settled in the steppes and are said to have learned everything from the nomads without offering anything in return except for the destruction of the nomads' traditional lifestyles. Another book, by K. A. Berdenova, insisted that Kazakhs' centuries-old struggle for independence began not in the eighteenth century but in 1585, with the clashes between the Cossack Ermak and the Khan of Siberia, Kuchum: 'With Kuchum begins the Kazakh people's struggle for liberation against Russian conquest'.[18]

In this Eurasianist literature, Kazakhs are celebrated as the quintessence not only of Eurasia but of the Turkic world: 'Contemporary Kazakhstan encapsulates the entire historical experience of the Turkic peoples, from the Yakuts to the Bolgars [the predecessors of Tatars], from the Seljuks to the Ottomans'.[19] This Kazakh-centric pan-Turkism stresses the supposed continuity of the Kazakh state from ancient times: from the Scythians and the Huns to the Turkic khaganate and the Dasht-i Qipchaq, the Steppic medieval realm. This Turkic legacy would come to definitive bloom in independent Kazakhstan: 'The Kazakh people may be seen as heir to the historic-cultural legacy of all the Eurasian spaces'.[20] The rationale for this is that 'the Kazakhs, known as a people under the name of Kipchaks, were the core of all the Turkic tribes'.[21] Similarly, one of the main official historiographers of the Kazakh republic from Soviet times, Manash E. Kozybaev (1931–2002), claimed there is a 'Eurasian racial type', which he presented as having all the features of Kazakhness.[22]

Kazakhstani Eurasianism has remained poorly conceptualized, with very few scholarly-based historical or philosophical works.[23] It has to take into account the existence of already well-formulated Russian versions of the same ideology and find a way to dissociate itself from its Russian competitors. It generally rejects the founding fathers of the interwar period and 'Soviet Eurasianism' – that is, Moscow's nationalities policy, which, Kazakhstani Eurasianists argue, was intended to erase national differences. For them, only Kazakhstan, not Russia, can demonstrate a continuous Eurasian destiny. Kazakhstan is, for instance, often presented as the heir of the Khazar khaganate of the ninth century, characterized by a spirit of tolerance and a rejection of extremism, as demonstrated by the conversion of the Khazar elites to Judaism and the presence of Nestorian Christians.[24] The Russified Kazakh elites of the nineteenth century – Chokan Valikhanov, Abai Kunanbaev and Ibrahim Altynsarin – would have formulated Eurasianist principles well before the Russian émigrés appropriated them in the 1920s. In the Soviet period, the Eurasianist idea would have survived in the works of Suleimenov and Murat Auezov (b. 1943), before being personified by Nazarbayev himself.

Kazakhstani publications also condemn the fascist tendencies of Russian neo-Eurasianists, such as Alexander Dugin, with several articles in academic periodicals criticizing the 'revival of Russian messianism and imperialism'.[25] However, in 2004, Dugin published a book glorifying President Nazarbayev, *The Eurasian Mission of Nursultan Nazarbayev* (*Evraziiskaia missiia Nursultana Nazarbayeva*),[26] commissioned by some official structures in Kazakhstan. The Russian thinker organized a tour to present his book in Almaty and Astana, at the Academy of Sciences and the Gumilev University, in the presence of several high-ranking officials (including Nazarbayev's oldest daughter, Dariga), and was invited to air his views in a show on the official Rakhat TV channel. His meeting with the Kazakhstani members of his International Eurasianist Movement, including Gani Kasymov, the leader of the small Party of Patriots of Kazakhstan, was widely publicized.[27]

Despite Dugin's short-term success, Kazakhstani political circles plainly state that Nursultan Nazarbayev's Eurasianism must be considered the third and final stage in the development of that ideology. After the founding fathers in the interwar period and Gumilev during Soviet times, the Kazakhstani president, they say, has established a definitive understanding of Eurasia, finally abandoning political philosophy to start implementing Eurasianist ideas in practice.[28] Indeed, Kazakhstan operationalizes Eurasianism not only as a state ideology targeting a domestic audience but as a fundament of its foreign policy. In this version of the ideology, Eurasianism appears as a pragmatic project of regional integration that is integral to the country's multi-vector policy.

Nazarbayev proposed a Union of Eurasian States as early as 1994. The organization was to have supra-national bodies and replace the ineffective CIS (Commonwealth of Independent States) with a new post-Soviet economic and political space that would be free of communist ideology. Nazarbayev's project spelled out the union's mode of functioning in detail: a referendum on membership in every candidate country; Russian as the working language; a consultative council for each sector of the economy; simplified procedures for changes of citizenship between member states; a rotating presidency; supra-national bodies, including a consultative parliament; a new common currency; a capital (Nazarbayev proposed Kazan or Samara) and so on.[29] The project was, of course, never implemented; at the time, it met with a rather disapproving response both in Yeltsin's Russia and in neighbouring countries, which were then busy moving away from their former Soviet brothers.

Throughout the 1990s, Kazakhstan and Nazarbayev himself constantly stood out on the post-Soviet scene for their commitment to regional cooperation between the Soviet-successor states. Several economic and customs treaties were signed, mainly between Russia, Belarus, Ukraine and Kazakhstan, but Nazarbayev's greatest victory was the creation, in 2000, of the Eurasian Economic Community (including Russia, Belarus, Kazakhstan, Kyrgyzstan and Tajikistan, later joined by Uzbekistan), even if it never stimulated genuine regional integration. It took until 2011, when Vladimir Putin launched his version of a Eurasian Union, for a regional institution to start affecting economic realities on the ground.

Kazakhstan at first enthusiastically supported Putin's idea, and Nazarbayev was probably personally pleased to see Putin recognize that the initial motivation for the Union came from Kazakhstan, not Russia.[30] However, this enthusiasm progressively transformed into reluctance with Russia's reassertion on the international scene, the war with Ukraine in 2014 and the subsequent US and European sanctions against Russia. At the highest levels of the Kazakhstani state, there is now therefore a quiet desire to slow down the process of integration.[31]

Indeed, Kazakhstan finds itself in a contradictory situation. In the long term, Astana sees itself not as a loyal second to Russia but as an equal partner. Nazarbayev formulated Kazakhstan's posture on the Eurasian Union project unambiguously and repeatedly. First, he claimed that those who would draw a parallel between Kazakhstan and the Soviet Union, either to denounce the current integration dynamic or in hopes of reviving the defunct Soviet structure, are in the wrong. He emphasized, 'There have been many rumours of Kazakhstan reportedly losing its independence, about the USSR allegedly being revived. Complete nonsense. Those willing to get the USSR revived are not in their right mind. We have gone a long way away from that'.[32]

Second, the Eurasian Union is an economic project, not a political one, and the Kazakhstani authorities have expressed strong reservations about any supranational institutions or parliament, as well as joint citizenship. On this point, Nazarbayev stated, 'Economic interest, rather than abstract geopolitical ideas and slogans, is the main engine of the integration processes'.[33] Third, Kazakhstan's membership in the Eurasian Union is the result of a choice that can be reversed if the country believes its interests are not being protected. Here, too, Nazarbayev has expressed his perspective plainly: 'If the rules which were previously established in the treaty are not fulfilled, then Kazakhstan has the complete right to end its membership in the Eurasian Economic Union. Astana will never be in an organization that represents a threat to the independence of Kazakhstan'.[34] He could not be clearer.

Regardless of this insistence, however, Nazarbayev's Eurasianist stance, which was supposed to ideologically justify the country's multi-vector foreign policy, now seems to have lost its meaning. The competing interpretation of Eurasia as a Russia-backed integration project has risen in influence with the Customs Union and the ratification of the Eurasian Economic Union.[35] These new integration projects create a serious imbalance in favour of Russia, sparking debate among Kazakhstan's elite and expert community. As a result, the Kazakhstani authorities now have to manage an unanticipated dilemma – that the Eurasian brand of their foreign policy, in which they have invested so much since their independence, has unexpectedly created an imbalance favouring Russia rather than guaranteeing the country's multi-vectoralism.

Looking for a third way? The Kazakh Eli solution

Since Kazakhstan has been partly dispossessed of its Eurasian terminology and could not avoid the centrality of Russia in the use of the term, could the country turn toward its Central Asian neighbours? Kazakhstani elites have always been ambivalent regarding the place of their country in the Central Asian historical and cultural space. Official discourse celebrates the region's cultural achievements dating back to ancient times and places Kazakhstan within Islamic tradition. At the same time, officials frequently emphasize the distinctiveness of the country compared to its southern neighbours, citing its late adoption of Islam and proud Steppic identity.[36] Indeed, Kazakhstani officials sometimes regard other Central Asian states with thinly veiled contempt, disparaging them for their perceived economic and cultural backwardness. Implicitly, being a part of the Central Asian region – including two other *-stans*, Afghanistan and Pakistan – is seen as a negative that allegedly carries with it the risk of Islamist spillovers. These threat perceptions have spurred strong criticism from some scholars, including Farkhad Tolipov of Uzbekistan, who as early as 2006 attacked Kazakhstan's choice of Eurasia as illusory due to Russia's overwhelming dominance; he invited Kazakhstan to remain a *-stan* and be proud of that.[37]

The change in direction of Uzbekistan's regional policy since the death of Islam Karimov in September 2016 has given some hope to those in Kazakhstan calling for more Central Asian integration: the new Uzbek president, Shavkat Mirziyoyev, has shown a strong commitment to re-establishing neighbourly relationships with Tajikistan and Kyrgyzstan, as well as to reintegrating the country into its regional environment. New economic perspectives and a transformed geopolitical context shaped by the overdominance of Russia and China have pushed Kazakhstani elites to look more favourably toward Central Asian cooperation. Yet to avoid having to choose between a Eurasian or Central Asian destiny for Kazakhstan, some look for a third way: one that would frame Kazakhstan as a specific, unique country following an Asian-leaning development path. In February 2014, during a visit to one of the new Nazarbayev Intellectual Schools in the Atyrau region, the president floated the idea that Kazakhstan could drop the suffix *-stan*:

> In the name of our country, as in many other countries of Central Asia, there is the suffix *-stan*. At the same time, foreigners show interest in Mongolia, with only 2 million inhabitants, and whose name has no suffix *-stan*. Maybe in the future we will have to address the question of changing the name of our country to Kazakh Eli [meaning 'the land of the Kazakhs' – ML], but before that it needs to be discussed with the people.[38]

Nazarbayev's allusion to the necessity of popular debate implied that this decision should be left for post-Nazarbayev generations. However, this was not the first time that the country's *-stan* had been identified as problematic. In 2013, Dariga Nazarbayeva herself stated that, 'Kazakhstan borders Central Asia geographically, but it is not a Central Asian country. We are a Eurasian state … We are not one more *–stan* for the media world and some politicians. Our historical orientations are not toward Saudi Arabia, but Norway, and countries such as South Korea and Singapore'.[39] The association of Central Asia with Saudi Arabia and of Kazakhstan with Norway, South Korea and Singapore is revealing of the identity projections of the Kazakhstani elites and their vision of the country as a developed European or South Asian one that unambiguously rejects everything associated with Islam.

One week after Nazarbayev's statement at the Intellectual School, the minister of foreign affairs denounced the name change proposal as a media trick, offering reassurance that the country did not intend to change its name.[40] Despite this immediate denial, public debate sprang up around the term Kazakh Eli on websites such as *Tengri News* and *Azattyq*. However, the domestic discussion did not revolve around

Kazakhstan's belonging to the Central Asian *–stans*, but around the multinationalism inherent in the term 'Kazakhstan'. The country's name not only refers to Central Asia through the shared suffix *-stan* but is also perceived as a legacy from the Soviet Union, since the word *Kazakh* comes from the Kazakh Soviet Socialist Republic, Kazakhstan's direct predecessor. Kazakh nationalist movements have therefore supported the idea of renaming the country Kazakh Eli (or, in some case, Qazaq Orda[41]) to reaffirm the preeminent role of ethnic Kazakhs. Some Kazakh nationalists of Tengrist persuasion have also argued for distancing the country from the *–stans,* which they see as overly Islamic.

It should also be noted that in the Russian-Soviet tradition, the Kazakh Steppe/Kazakhstan is indeed dissociated from the rest of Central Asia. In Russian, *Sredniaia Aziia* (Middle Asia) refers to the Turkestan Governorate, established in the final third of the nineteenth century – that is, at a time when the Kazakh Steppe was already part of the Siberian Governorate. The Soviet regime actively pursued this dual terminology. On several occasions, for example during the Khrushchev era, Moscow grouped Kazakhstan with Siberia, not Central Asia, in terms of its development trajectory. While Kazakhstan was still associated with Central Asia, the term *Sredniaia Aziia i Kazakhstan* stressed that it was not really part of Middle Asia.[42] It was not until the collapse of the Soviet Union that the Western term *Tsentral'naia Aziia* (Central Asia) came to be widely adopted in Russia and Central Asia, effectively erasing the historical distinction between the ancient Transoxiana (today's Uzbekistan and Tajikistan) and the Steppic world.

The fact that Nazarbayev evoked a possible name change in parallel with a reference to Mongolia invited the inclusion of foreign policy in the debate. The weakness of ties between Kazakhstan and Mongolia is striking, as only a 50-mile strip of Russian territory separates the two countries. Diplomatic relations between them are marked by the presence of a large Kazakh minority of about 160,000 people in western Mongolia, in the province of Bayan-Ölgii. Astana has 'repatriated' about 60,000 of these people as part of its compatriot programme. But beyond bilateral relations, Mongolia is paving the way for another kind of Eurasian identity that is attractive to Kazakhstan: neither a Russia-dominated Eurasia project nor a Central Asian '*stan*-ization' but a more Northeast Asian approach.

This Mongolian brand makes sense for Kazakhstan on a number of counts. Nazarbayev has always made positive references to what he considered an 'Asian model', lauding the economic dynamism of Asian countries as well as regimes that combine features of both liberalism and authoritarianism. At the end of the 1990s, Astana even translated the symbolism of the Asian Dragons (Hong Kong, Singapore, South Korea and Taiwan) and the Asian Tigers (Thailand, Malaysia, Indonesia, the Philippines and Vietnam) into a snow leopard symbol, insisting on Kazakhstan's prospects for a high-tech future and growing ties with Asia-Pacific nations.[43]

In this vein, Malaysia has quickly become the South-Eastern Asian country to which Kazakhstan looks as a potential model. A country with a Muslim majority that is also multi-ethnic and multi-religious, one of the best performing economies in Asia and the third-largest producer of computer components after the United States and Japan, the Malaysian model is one that Kazakhstan seeks to emulate. Kazakhstan's presidential party, Nur Otan, and the United Malays National Organization (UMNO) have established links between their parliamentarians and party structures, and the Malaysian strategy formulated in the Vision-2020 plan inspired Nazarbayev's Kazakhstan-2030 plan. The new administrative capital of Malaysia, Putrajaya (located twenty kilometres south of Kuala Lumpur and near the new city of Cyberjaya, which specializes in new technologies), was one of the models that the Kazakhstani authorities considered for Astana. The transformation of KLIA (the Kuala Lumpur International Airport) into a leading aviation hub for Southeast Asia also interested Kazakhstan, as did Malaysia's 'multimedia corridor', which overlaps with Kazakhstan's development objectives in innovative industries. Malaysia is further considered as a model for Kazakhstan in terms of its Islamic norms: Malaysian halal-food firms have been established in Kazakhstan since 2005 and Kazakhstani authorities have chosen to define their halal standards according to those of Malaysia.[44]

The 'Kazakh Eli' future that Nazarbayev mentioned is thus not only a response to pressure from increasingly nationalist public opinion. It also fits into a new potential foreign policy agenda. The proposed name change could both distance Kazakhstan from Central Asia should the region sink into economic crisis and state failure and offer an alternative to a Russia-dominated Eurasian identity and integration. Mongolia and Malaysia are seen as the archetypes for a possible third identity for Kazakhstan that would not deny the dominant role of Russia and China, but would draw up a more Asian future for the country.

For three decades, non-ethnic Russian intellectual circles have been criticizing the revival of Russian Eurasianism as a new form of imperialism. However, one can see from the Kazakh case that Eurasianist beliefs are intimately intertwined with nationalism. While Eurasianism always speaks of a large civilizational area spanning the centre of the Old Continent (with borders that may be more or less precise, and indeed often deliberately imprecise), it also celebrates one nation in particular (Russian or Kazakh) in much more conventional terms. The Eurasianist credo, once genuinely open to cultural influences from Russia and positive about Soviet internationalism with Suleimenov, has evolved into a Eurasianism that uses the same historical argumentation as Kazakh nationalism, denouncing Russia's domination as colonialism and celebrating the uniqueness of the Kazakh nation as the heart of the Turkic world. The state use of Eurasianism to express the country's domestic harmony around Kazakhstanness and its multi-vectoral policy on the international scene thus appear closer to Suleimenov's original vision, proposing a pragmatic path to its implementation. However, it also leaves room for a more nationalist, Kazakh-centric understanding of Eurasianism. This 'regime Eurasianism' thus appears as a post-colonial tool for pursuing, as Luca Anceschi states, 'Kazakhstan's continuous entanglement and its sudden disentanglement with the former centre of the Soviet Union'.[45]

Since its independence, Kazakhstan has preferred Eurasian integration under Russian leadership to Central Asian integration with a difficult Uzbek neighbour. However, the effects of the Eurasian Economic Union on Kazakhstan's economy do not seem to have lived up to their promises,[46] while post-Crimea Russia has partly jeopardized Astana's tradition of multi-vectoralism. In comparison, Central Asian emerging markets offer particularly easy expansion for Kazakh investors and could serve as a testing ground for Kazakhstan's private sector before reaching further afield. Additionally, post-Karimov Uzbekistan advances a more region-friendly agenda.

But perhaps more important than a choice in regional integration strategy is the challenge of self-representation. Historically, Kazakhstan was not fully a part of Middle Asia, even if its interaction with the Transoxiani/Turkestani world was intense. Another face of Kazakhstan, its Steppic identity as a state historically largely integrated in the Siberian world, serves as a 'push' factor to orient Kazakhstan more toward Russia. However, Russia is already such a dominant power on Kazakhstan's political, strategic, economic and cultural landscapes that an identity project oriented toward it would not make sense, and would in fact be more likely to reignite already vivid internal debates around the 'colonial' nature of the bilateral relationship between the two countries.

The prospect of renaming the country Kazakh Eli, therefore, offers a third approach that is neither Russian-Eurasian domination nor a difficult Central Asian integration. First, it allows Kazakhstan to position itself as a 'neither/nor', creating its own distinctive brand rather than being subsumed into a regional entity. Second, it highlights the ethnic Kazakh component of the country and the historic destiny of its Steppe culture, something that the younger generations increasingly support. Third, it takes Asian countries that are seen as successful in achieving economic modernity and globalization as its model while still preserving a strong national Kazakh identity. However, the Kazakh Eli idea sidelines the important issue of the role of Islam in the public sphere in Kazakhstan. Is Islam compatible with the mythology associated with the Kazakh Eli brand or would this element of the country's religious diversity prevent Kazakhstan from positioning itself as the next Mongolia? A growing Islamic identity could indeed help strengthen ties with the rest of Central Asia and encourage the progressive *stan*-ization of Kazakhstan.

Notes

1 Anceschi, *Analysing Kazakhstan's Foreign Policy*.
2 Laruelle, *Russian Eurasianism*, 16–49.
3 Ram, 'Imagining Eurasia'.
4 Diat, 'Olzhas Sulejmenov: *Az i Ya*'.
5 Baker, 'The Power and Significance of the Ethnic Past'.
6 Ingham, 'The Igor' Tale and the Origins of Conspiracy Theory'.
7 Aleksandr Shchuplov, 'Olzhas Suleimenov'.
8 On Cosmism, see Young, *The Russian Cosmists*.
9 Suleimenov, *Az i Ia*, 271.
10 Anceschi, *Analysing Kazakhstan's Foreign Policy*, 5.
11 Nazarbayev, *Evraziiskii soiuz*, 27.
12 Koch, 'The "Heart" of Eurasia?', 134–47.
13 Aitmatov, 'Drevnetiurkskaia tsivilizatsiia: pamiatniki pis'mennosti', 58.
14 See L.N. Gumilyov Eurasian National University, http://www.enu.kz/research/eurasia/mission.html.
15 Seit Kaskabasov, then-director of the Eurasianist Center at L.N. Gumilyov University, interviewed by the author, Astana, 16 February 2000.
16 Nazarbayev, *V potoke istorii*, 5.
17 Tashenov, *Evraziistvo v etnokul'turnoi istorii Kazakhstana*, 154.
18 Berdenova (ed.), *Evraziistvo v ekonomicheskoi i etnopoliticheskoi istorii Kazakhstana*.
19 Berdenova, *Evraziistvo v ekonomicheskoi i etnopoliticheskoi istorii Kazakhstana*, 81. See also Barbankulov, *Zolotaia baba*.
20 Akatai, 'Evraziistvo v kontekste kul'turnoi obshchnosti', 45.
21 Berdenova, *Evraziistvo v ekonomicheskoi i etnopoliticheskoi istorii Kazakhstana*, 105.
22 Kozybaev, 'Uroki otechestvennoi istorii i vozrozhdenie kazakhstanskogo obshchestva'.
23 With some exceptions such as Seliverstov, *Kazakhstan, Rossiia, Turtsiia*.
24 Eleukenov (ed.), *Evraziiskii talisman*.
25 Shaikhutdinov, 'A. Dugin i imperskaia modifikatsiia evraziiskoi idei'; Shaikhutdinov, 'Imperskie proekty geopoliticheskoi identichnosti Rossii'.
26 See Dugin, *Evraziiskaia missiia Nursultana Nazarbaeva*, 158.
27 However, not everyone falls for Dugin's stratagem. In September 2003, during a press conference-cum-debate between Dugin and the Kazakh nationalist scholar Azimbai Gali, the latter stated that Nazarbayev could not be considered a Eurasianist in Dugin's sense, since he

is neither anti-Atlanticist, anti-Semitic, nor anti-liberal – three features Gali considers to define Dugin's thought.

28 Bulekbaev and Unnarbaev, 'Evraziistvo kak ideologiia gosudarstvennosti'; Saudanbekova, 'Evraziistvo Gumileva i klassicheskoe russkoe evraziistvo'.

29 Nazarbayev, *Evraziiskii soiuz*, 38–50.

30 Putin has continued to recognize Nazarbayev's role in the Eurasian Union idea. See, for instance, 'Putin poblagodaril Nazarbaeva za vklad v integratsiiu is sozdanie EAES'.

31 Author's interviews with anonymous Kazakh experts in Almaty and Astana, June 2017.

32 'Economic Eurasian Union Bears No Resemblance to USSR'.

33 Ordabayev, 'Building Eurasian Economic Union on Consensus, Mutual Respect and Benefit'.

34 'Nazarbayev zaiavil o vozmozhnom vykhode Kazakhstana iz Evraziiskogo soiuza'.

35 See Kudaibergenova, 'Eurasian Economic Union Integration in Kazakhstan and Kyrgyzstan'.

36 On different aspects of Kazakhstan's national motives, see Diener, 'National Territory and the Reconstruction of History in Kazakhstan', 565–83; Isaacs, 'Nomads, Warriors and Bureaucrats'; Sarsembayev, 'Imagined Communities', 319–46; Omelicheva, 'Islam in Kazakhstan', 243–56; and Orange and Petersson, '"There Can Be No Other Sun in the Sky"'.

37 Tolipov, 'Tsentral'naia Azia – eto piat' "stanov"'.

38 'Poseshchenie Intellektual'noi shkoly goroda Atyrau i vstrecha s predstaviteliami obshchestvennosti oblasti'.

39 Nazarbayeva, 'Spetsifika i perspektivy politicheskogo razvitiia Kazakhstana'.

40 'Kazakhstan Will Not Change Its Name to Get Rid of the 'Stan' Ending'.

41 'Nazarbayev: Kazakhstan mozhet byt' pereimenovan v "Kazakh Eli"'.

42 More details on the history of these concepts can be found in Gorshenina, *L'invention de l'Asie centrale*.

43 Samubaldin, *Drakony i tigry Azii*.

44 More in Laruelle and Peyrouse, *Globalizing Central Asia*, 110–12.

45 Anceschi, *Analysing Kazakhstan's Foreign Policy*, 6.

46 Vinokurov, 'Eurasian Economic Union: Current State and Preliminary Results'.

8

Media and the nation: searching for Kazakhness in televisual production

Television is the most widely consumed form of media in Kazakhstan, as well as the most trusted,[1] even if competition from the internet is rising, especially among the younger generations. As in any other country in the world, television offers cheap entertainment and a mirror through which the nation can project itself as an 'imagined community'. It creates shared social touchstones among viewers, emphasizes common cultural denominators, minimizes socioeconomic gaps, sets family rhythms according to the schedules of news and primetime shows, and influences collective fashions and values. Television thus plays a critical role in building and shaping ideas of nationhood and citizenship. In Kazakhstan, the authorities waited a long time before investing in the small screen. The fact that the principal station, Channel One-Eurasia, aired mainly Russian programmes until around 2015 is a good example of this state disinterest. However, change has been underway since the Ukrainian crisis and the launching of the Eurasian Economic Union. Since then, Kazakhstani media and think tanks have been discussing the place and influence of Russian media and the lack of a state response.[2] The Kazakhstani authorities have come to understand the need to make better use of this powerful medium to advance their nationhood messaging, and private channels have also invested in national cultural productions that can strengthen patriotic feelings.

Profiling Kazakhstani television channels

In the late 2010s, Kazakhstan hosts 14 channels and more than 90 internet and cable television operators. Of this large diversity of channels, seven of the free channels receive the vast majority of viewership in about equal proportions.[3] The many satellite channels, which are available for a small fee, tend to target smaller segments of the audience with dedicated music, sports or regional programming.[4] Worth mentioning is Asyl Arna, an Islamic channel started in 2007 that broadcasts primarily in Kazakh but also in Russian in order to bring its programmes on Islamic values and the Quran to the Muslim communities of Kazakhstan (such as Chechens, Dagestanis, Tatars, Bashkirs, Uyghurs and so on).[5]

According to a 2014 study by J'son & Partners Consulting, 53 per cent of the available televisual content on the main channels available for free to every Kazakhstani viewer was domestically produced, while 47 per cent was internationally produced (mostly Russian).[6] However, this figure is not indicative of the audience share that each type of programming receives: Russian-produced content continues to attract the most viewers.

Similarly, domestic Kazakhstani productions filmed in Russian are more popular than those filmed in Kazakh. The debate over the place of language in the republic's media is anything but new. Until the early 1960s, Radio Kazakhstan aired more than half its programming in Kazakh, but that figure fell by one-third under Nikita Khrushchev, with another radio station, Shargar, partially offsetting the decline. The local television channels only broadcasted for three hours per day in Kazakh. As William Fierman has noted, in the Soviet era, Kazakh-language programmes were targeted at rural audiences, mostly covering topics related to agricultural life. In the case of both radio and television, material produced in Moscow and in Russian was more appealing and varied.[7]

Surprisingly, the situation evolved little between Kazakhstan's independence in 1991 and very recently. The domination of Kazakhstan's television market by Russian-language productions lasted well through the 1990s and 2000s. It took time for the authorities to interpret this lack of informational sovereignty as a danger to the national project and to try to counter the situation. The 1999 law on language in state media mandated that, at a minimum, Kazakh must be used at least as much as all other languages combined;[8] however, it was not possible to enforce this. In 2012, a new law on television and radio mandated that programming be at least 40 per cent nationally produced by 2016 and 50 per cent by 2018. In 2013, it was decided that each Kazakhstani channel should broadcast at least 35 per cent in Kazakh, rising to 50 per cent in 2015.[9] The majority of channels circumvented these laws by broadcasting in Kazakh at night so as not to lose their audience share during the day.

It also took time for the authorities to invest in supporting media; the state budget for media companies producing Kazakh-language programming jumped from 2.8 billion *tenge* in 2013 to 43 billion in 2013, reaching 53 billion in 2016, with a large share of that amount (30–40 per cent) devoted to television.[10]

Some channels, such as Channel One-Eurasia and Channel 7, draw a distinctly Russian-speaking audience. At least until recently, Channel One-Eurasia has mainly rebroadcasted programming from Russia's Channel One (called ORT and ORT-Kazakhstan before 2001). It is a joint project controlled 20 per cent by the Russian Channel One and 80 per cent by the Kazakhstani state – a rare case where a state channel is co-owned by another state. The small channel Mir (and its news channel Mir-24) constitutes a similar case, as its ownership is partly based in Russia. Mir began in 1992 under a mandate from the CIS and reaches most post-Soviet states as well as Central Europe and Germany, where its primary audience is made up of Russian-speaking diasporas. The channel broadcasts in Russian and targets audiences sympathetic to the Soviet past, airing programmes dedicated to the cultures of Eurasia and deploying a political discourse that supports regional integration.[11]

Some other channels are oriented more toward the Kazakh-speaking public. The most obvious example is the Kazakhstan state channel, which also airs in neighbouring countries with Kazakh minority populations (Uzbekistan, Kyrgyzstan, Russia, Mongolia, China) and, by government decision, became entirely Kazakh-language in 2011.[12] The effect of this decision is mostly symbolic, as the channel ranks only sixth in viewers, with less than 10 per cent of the Kazakhstani audience. Other examples include Khabar, which broadcasts in both languages but attracts few Russian-speakers, and two smaller channels, Astana and El Arna.[13]

The Kazakhstani television market reproduces many of the characteristics of its Russian neighbour. In 2014, 44 per cent of total broadcasting time was devoted to miniseries.[14] Private channels are primarily commercial and finance themselves through advertising. They thus specialize in profitable programmes, which are mostly entertainment – music, sports, films and series, reality TV shows, and talk shows – and tend to be clones of Russian productions.

The TV Media Advertising Agency study of the Kazakhstani television market provided precise figures for 2013.[15] On Channel One-Eurasia, the most-watched programmes were largely Russian: the *X-Factor* music competition and the main miniseries of the time (such as *Giulchatay*, *Rusalka*, *Znakharka*, and *Dom maliutki*). Among Kazakh-language programming, only a speech by Kazakhstan's president

Nursultan Nazarbayev attracted enough viewers to make it into the top six most-viewed programmes for the year. The first Kazakh-language miniseries, *Kasym*, which follows the adventures of a young Kazakh hero during the Second World War, came in seventh. On Khabar, a Turkish series about Suleyman the Great had the most viewers of any show for that year, followed by the Nazarbayev speech and several Russian miniseries. On Kazakhstan, the entirely Kazakh-language channel, *Kelin*, a Kazakh miniseries, came out on top, followed by Kazakhophone entertainment programmes, concerts and talk shows. The channel KTK set itself apart from the others, as all of its top shows are made in Kazakhstan and its programming includes local news broadcasts on various sensitive issues, such as corruption, as well as interviews with public figures.

The entertainment blockbusters from Russia continue to draw the largest audiences, and only a few local productions – news, concerts and, to a lesser extent, miniseries – can compete. The reason for this imbalance has been pointed out by many specialists: advertising revenue. As stated by Arman Shurayev, former director of KTK: 'To produce one hour of a good series, one can easily spend about 200,000 dollars in Russia … Here in Kazakhstan for the same hour I can spend maximum 10–15,000 dollars'.[16] The Kazakh-speaking advertising market will likely never be profitable enough to feed private advertising revenues back to Kazakh production companies; the latter will therefore have to continue to rely on state support. This is the paradox of Kazakhstani television: while it is largely regime-controlled and promotes official policy, the channels do not actually have a captive audience. The most enticing cultural products win, and in this race for viewers, Russian channels are much more competitive.

Concerns regarding this situation are regularly raised among state officials and the Kazakh-speaking part of the population. Accordingly, Kazakhstan has embarked on a more active state policy of producing Kazakh televisual products, efforts that have been particularly visible since the 2014 Ukrainian crisis. In early March of that year, the presidential administration reorganized the Ministry of Culture and Communications and upgraded its communications role into a State Agency for Communication and Information that was not attached to the government directly but functioned as a central executive organ.[17] Two months later, the government published a 'Strategic Plan of the State Agency for Communication and Information for 2014–2018' that calls for the modernization of internet infrastructure, as well as the reinforcement of national productions on television.[18]

The authorities also passed an explicit policy to avoid rebroadcasting Russian political talk shows. All the main channels now produce their own weekly prime-time analytical/political news shows. The popularity of these shows is rising: the programme *Analitika* on Channel One-Eurasia was among the top ten broadcasts in terms of viewership in 2019.[19] Notwithstanding some nuances (Khabar is more official, KTK more critical), they all remain inside the official line and do not criticize the government. While Kazakh-speaking production was once mainly confined to fiction and entertainment, since 2017 the authorities have also supported the growth of political and social talk shows in Kazakh. The first of these appeared on the Kazakhophone state channel Kazakhstan in 2017 and has been inviting an increasing number of nationalist-minded figures. In 2018, Channel One-Eurasia even launched the programme *Basty bagdarlama* as a Kazakh-language analogue to *Analitika*.

Raising patriotism: national history on the small screen

It remains difficult to identify the main decision-makers that oversee the production of televisual content, even if many of my local informants mentioned the name of then-State Secretary Marat Tazhin. Far easier to trace are those who push for the state to commission historical documentaries, a specific cultural production that has been on the rise in recent years.

The first figure in this group is former minister of culture and information Mukhtar Kul-Mukhammed, one of the members of the intergovernmental study group on national history (*Mezhvedomstvennaia gruppa po izucheniiu natsional'noi istorii*).[20] This intergovernmental group was created in 2013 under the leadership of Marat Tazhin to oversee all activities linked to the 'rebirth of national historical memory', including 'the study of the blank pages'.[21] Mukhtar Kul-Mukhammed is an influential politician close to Nazarbayev who has repeatedly held the posts of minister of culture and communications and state secretary. He was born in Xinjiang and was one of the Kazakhs of China repatriated to Kazakhstan in the 1960s. Many such *Oralmans* advocate for a more nationalist vision of Kazakhstan, driven by their memories of Stalinist repressions, forced collectivization and emigration to China. Mukhtar Kul-Mukhammed defended, for instance, a thesis on Alash Orda and ran several groups in charge of identity issues: a terminological and onomastic commission that oversaw the Kazakhization of place names and official terms; a commission on relations with co-ethnics abroad; and a commission supervising language policy.[22]

The second figure is film director Anvar Mamraimov, who also served as the director of the press-service of the Institute of Archaeology and is the author of several monographs popularizing the ancient history of the Steppe world and the Silk Roads. He began his career in the 1980s with a film about the mausoleum of Ahmed Yasavi in Turkestan, which was censored in Alma-Ata but finally found acceptance from central television in Moscow.[23] Since then, he has become the champion of Kazakh historical films, with more than 200 to his credit, of which 20 have been documentary films released by the state studio Kazakhfilm.[24]

The first historical documentary films commissioned by the Ministry of Education were part of the Cultural Heritage programme (*Kul'turnoe nasledie*), which President Nursultan Nazarbayev launched to collect thousands of archival documents about the history of the Steppic world from various world capitals. This state-sponsored programme kicked off new archaeological excavation campaigns, restored historical monuments, and republished significant works of Kazakh literature and classics of traditional Kazakh music to put them back in popular circulation.[25] Just before the closing of the programme, in 2010–11, Kazakhfilm studio was commissioned to produce 20 documentaries on national history. Although this number is mentioned in several documents, fewer than a dozen can be found online, and it is likely that the rest were not released.

An analysis of the documentaries that have been released illuminates which historical and cultural elements the state wished to emphasize in its national construction. They cover topics including *Korkut*, one of the most famous epics of the Turkic world; the mausoleum of the founder of the Sufi order, Ahmed Yasavi, in Turkestan; the Tamgaly petroglyphs, a huge collection of 5,000 rock carvings that testify to the rich prehistory of the region; and the Zharkent mosque, famous for its Chinese style. The only film to deal with more contemporary history looked at one of the few pre-revolutionary buildings, the tsarist officers' headquarters, which remains in place in the former capital, Almaty. These documentaries are filmed in a very conventional way that is boring for a non-specialist audience. They feature steppe landscapes and extras playing historical figures on parade (with voice-overs in Russian), regularly interspersed with interviews with museum curators, historians, archaeologists and so on. The narrative tone is emphatic, celebrating the wisdom of the Steppe world. The entertainment value is reinforced with a series of colourful New Age portraits of the figures being celebrated.

In 2013, the Kazakh-speaking channel Kazakhstan was chosen by the authorities to release three new historical films on the Sakhas, Huns and Usuns, the Steppe peoples who formed in the early Middle Ages the first state structures on the territory that would become Kazakhstan.[26] That year, it also premiered an eight-episode series commemorating the tricentennial of Abylay Khan (1711–81), who unified the three hordes and was recognized by Russia and China as the leader of a Kazakh-unified world. It is worth noting, however, that while selecting the only fully Kazakh-speaking channel to air these new documentary films was an important symbolic gesture to celebrate Kazakhness, it also reduced the ability of the stories to reach Kazakhstan's majority Russian-speaking viewers and educate them on that version of national history.

In choosing subjects for these state-sponsored historical documentaries, authorities gave priority to the region's ancient history. Kazakhstani television seems content to stage the less controversial aspects of national history that were celebrated during the Soviet period – namely ancient and medieval figures – and to avoid more sensitive subjects. It was not until the end of the 2000s that television finally reached for more contemporary issues, namely the integration of the Kazakh world into the Russian Empire in the nineteenth and early twentieth centuries. The channel Khabar inaugurated this bolder approach by commissioning and airing a film about Alash Orda, the modernist Kazakh elites from the early twentieth century who constituted a provisional Kazakh government from December 1917 until August 1920. Many Alash Orda members, among them their main leader Alikhan Bukeikhanov (1866–1937), rallied behind the Bolshevik regime and formed the first generation of national-communists, who were repressed progressively in the 1920s and then massively at the end of the 1930s.

On the whole, however, Kazakhstani television approaches the 'blank pages' of national history linked to Kazakhstan's interactions with the Russian world with a notable timidity. With the exception of the film on Alash, several short documentaries on its members, and a film about Mustafa Chokay (which is frequently replayed), Kazakhstani television has largely avoided discussing the difficult moments of Soviet history. Moreover, these films are often aired only in Kazakh and thus do not reach urban, educated Russophones. The Madeniet (Culture) Channel, launched in early 2014, screens many historical and cultural documentaries, but like its Russian counterpart Kul'tura,[27] it targets a cultured audience and its viewership is limited. That being said, the situation has evolved in recent years, with rising nationalist voices calling for a more open discussions of sensitive topics such as the repression of national elites and the famine of the 1930s (see Chapter 9).

More recently, the Kazakhstani authorities decided to prioritize the nationalization of the shared Soviet history and focus on the consensual period of this shared history: the Second World War or Great Patriotic War. In 2013, Khabar devoted a four-episode series to the only Kazakh general in the Soviet army, Bauyrzhan Momyshuly (1910–82), a series based on Alexander Bek's novel, *Volokolamsk Highway* (*Volokolamskoe shosse*, 1944). Momyshuly's career trajectory reveals the ambiguities of Soviet policy on promoting minorities. A platoon commander in the Central Asian Military District's 315th Regiment, he was sent to the front in 1941 and tasked with defending the highway passing through the city of Volokolamsk. Momyshuly gained recognition for his military exploits but was also known for his 'nationalist' views, about which he had been vocal since the 1930s and which prevented him from receiving the title of Hero of the Soviet Union during his life. The honour was bestowed on him posthumously in 1990, at the insistence of Nursultan Nazarbayev, who was then chairing the Kazakh Supreme Soviet. The series, however, pays greater attention to his Kazakh identity than to his loyalty to the Soviet regime.

In 2014, Talgat Bigeldinov, twice named a Hero of the Soviet Union and celebrated for his achievements in Soviet aviation, became the subject of another documentary, *To Rise in the Air!* (*Podniat'sia v vozdukh!*).[28] Then, in 2015, preparations for the 70th anniversary of the end of the Second World War led to the release of several films. These included a piece on the Panfilov division (which played a crucial role in the capture of Berlin and consisted mostly of soldiers from Kazakhstan and Kyrgyzstan), a film celebrating the role of Kazakh soldiers in the liberation of Kiev[29] and a series commemorating Kazakh hospitality in welcoming deported peoples and Russian soldiers during the war.[30]

Tensions around Ukraine in 2014 reinforced the Kazakh authorities' desire to invest in celebrating national history. At the Seliger youth camp in August 2014, Putin answered a question about the growth of nationalist feelings in Kazakhstan with an ambivalent statement. He celebrated Nazarbayev, who 'has performed a unique feat' because 'he has created a state on a territory where there has never been a state. The Kazakhs never had a state of their own, and he created it. In this sense, he is a unique person in the post-Soviet space and in Kazakhstan'.[31] The statement stirred Kazakh public debate, especially among young, nationalist-minded elites. In response, Nazarbayev announced that 2015 was the 550th anniversary of the birth of the Kazakh state, embodied by the Kazakh Khanate created by Kerey and Zhanibek in 1465. He posits: 'It may not have been a state in the modern understanding of this term, within the current borders … [But] it is important that the foundation was laid then, and we are the people continuing the great deeds of our ancestors'.[32]

Even more than previously, the festivities for the Day of Independence on 16 December 2014 were an occasion for muscular discourse on patriotism. There, Nazarbayev recalled: 'Independence was hard won by many generations of our ancestors, who defended our sacred land with blood and sweat … Independence is the unflinching resolution of each citizen to defend Kazakhstan, their own home, and the motherland to the last drop of blood, as our heroic ancestors have bequeathed us'.[33] A few days later, in his address to the nation, the President insisted on the need to develop patriotism among the younger generations, who no longer learn about history from books and should therefore have it delivered through public commemorations.

The authorities then allocated a significant budget to the festivities celebrating the half-millennium of Kazakh statehood: 3 billion *tenge*, or 16 million US dollars, are said to have been invested in exhibitions, video productions, conferences and archaeological expeditions, as well as a large historical re-enactment.[34] Television has been one of the premier tools deployed to impart this revived patriotic message. On Nazarbayev's order, a new series on the history of the Kazakh Khanate began production in January 2015.[35] Originally planned to be 20 episodes, it was reduced to 10 episodes, probably for planning reasons (it had to be written urgently for broadcast by the end of the year) but was then coupled with a series of documentary films and an animated movie.[36]

Rustem Abdrashev, known abroad for his movie *Gift to Stalin* (*Podarok Stalinu*, 2008) was chosen to direct the series, probably in recognition of his directorship of a film celebrating Nazarbayev's youth, *The Way of a Leader* (*Put' lidera*). The miniseries covers three centuries of history, beginning with the figures of Kerey and Zhanibek, who rejected the rule of Khan Abulkhair Sheibanid and moved to the Semirechie region, in the south-eastern part of present-day Kazakhstan, to create an independent khanate, and ending with Kenesary Kasymov (1802–47), the last khan, who tried to resist Russian advances in the steppes in the first half of the nineteenth century. Following the series, Abdrashev went on to direct the patriotic super-production *Kazakh Khanate: Diamond Sword*, also devoted to Kerey and Zhanibek, a TV show that many have dubbed the Kazakh *Game of Thrones*.[37]

Entertainment, religiosity and patriotism: the series *Signs: Legends of the Steppe*

The aforementioned documentary films are official productions commissioned by state authorities. Whatever their quality, they reach only a limited audience, which sees them as a state narrative that is often unattractive and unconvincing. Other, non-state-backed approaches allow viewers to familiarize themselves with national history in a more playful way, and to identify more directly and personally with their country. An in-depth analysis of Kazakhstani-produced miniseries and their role in staging the national 'us' is, however, still lacking from the scholarly landscape. For this chapter, I decided to focus on one series that, in my opinion, has renewed the genre: the 30-episode *Signs: Legends of the Steppe* (*Znaki: Stepnye legendy*), screened on Channel 7 since 2013.[38] During informal interviews I performed in Kazakhstan on the topic of the country's media landscape, many of my local informants mentioned Channel 7 as being the most innovative channel, indicating that it offered slightly different cultural products and was known for the dynamism of its team.

In *Signs: Legends of the Steppe*, Nuriddin Bidosov, one of the channel's most famous journalists, dressed in a relaxed way – jeans, T-shirt and cap – travels all over Kazakhstan to visit historic and religious sites. The staging is modern, inspired by reality shows such as *Survivor*. The series glorifies the adventure style; the narrative promotes technical feats, such as crossing more than 10,000 kilometres of the Kazakh Steppe in an SUV, often on unpaved roads in the desert, far from any urban centre. It also focuses on human exploits: the journalist and interviewees recount how they have reached 'their limits' in confrontations with supernatural, physical or spiritual risk. Indeed, the novelty of the series lies in its presentation of a trip that is simultaneously geographical, historical and spiritual. Distinctive landmarks provide structure for the trip: the journalist's route stops at every famous shrine (*mazar*, the tombs of saints, often spiritually elevated ascetics from Sufi mystical orders, but also mythical figures linked to the Prophet Mohammed's family) to which locals make pilgrimages.[39] This tradition was partly obscured during the Soviet era, but the regime never directly repressed it; it was seen as a national tradition and relic of the past (*perezhitki*), not as a religious practice that threatened the official atheism.

This practice of pilgrimage has taken on an unprecedented scale since Kazakhstan became independent.[40] The authorities have funded the rehabilitation of these shrines, not because of their religious value but in order to Kazakhify the national territory and showcase the national, Kazakh footprint thereon (with the indirect goal of avoiding any territorial confrontation with Kazakhstan's neighbours, especially Russia). Some of the chosen locations are natural landmarks – Charyn canyon, a cave with supposed magical springs, lakes with curative powers and so on – or mythical places from local legends. Others celebrate famous knights (*batyr*), as in the case of the cave of Konyr-Aulie, the supposed hidden tomb of Chingis Khan. The programme also visits the graves of great national figures (Bidosov calls them 'great men', or *velikie liudi*) such as the founder of the Sufi order Ahmed Yasavi,[41] the writer Abay Kunanbayev and the poets and *akyn* (folk singers) Suyunbay Aronuly and Zhambyl Zhabaev.

At each site, Nuriddin Bidosov recounts the associated local legends. The custodians of the shrines give colour to the lives of those buried there and explain different rituals linked to the sanctity of the place. They read verses from the Quran to visitors and introduce them to sacred lineages, promoting a discourse of rediscovery of authentic Kazakh values forgotten during the Soviet era.[42] They also sometimes act as fortune-tellers or blessing mediators.[43] Bidosov participates in these rituals and attends prayers. The 'evidence' of the holiness of a site is most often demonstrated by cases of miraculous healing – a young boy who had never spoken a word until entering the shrine of Suyunbay Aronuly, for example, or a paralyzed person who regained the use of his limbs by drawing water from the sacred spring of Charyn canyon. The revelation may also be of a more intimate nature, as in the case of a poet who found inspiration by visiting the shrine of Abay and an infertile woman who finally became pregnant after visiting the mausoleum of Aisha-bibi.

In each new place, the star reporter speaks to people who experienced dramatic changes in their lives' trajectories during their visits to that shrine. Many of them could be described as 'born-again', to borrow from the Christian vernacular: pilgrims often claim to have undergone spiritual regeneration following their visits to the shrine, enabling them to stop indulging bad habits and become respectable men or women. Shrines, healing and morality thus go hand-in-hand.[44] In most cases, deceased family members visited the interviewees in their dreams, inviting them to make the trip to the shrine. In the nomadic Central Asian tradition, ancestral spirits (*arbaks*) interact with humans and are worshipped in order to gain favour and benefit from their protection. Since ancestral spirits form the link to the world of the dead, they also symbolize the social and ethnic continuity of the nation.[45]

Bidosov emphasizes the eminently national character of these shrines. He recalls the historical context in which a saint or historical figure lived; mentions that ancient Turkic-Mongol peoples believed in heaven, *Tengri*; celebrates the popular devotion that surrounds these national figures; and recites verses or songs to commemorate their exploits on behalf of 'the good of the people' (*na blago naroda*). The programme is not content to rehabilitate Sufi spirituality or the *arbaks*. Rather, it links the places visited to extreme spiritual experiences. Many of the people Bidosov encounters describe having had extra-sensory experiences in their encounters/confrontations with the spirits of the place. Some say the spirits have physically challenged or injured them. For instance, the Ukash-ata shrine, which supposedly contains the tomb of a soldier of the Prophet Mohammed, is believed to 'punish' those who lack pure souls. Others have seen spirits in human form or via the unexplained movement of objects, or been saved from a mortally dangerous situation at the final moment through inexplicable coincidental circumstances. The production alternates between the narratives of the custodians and interview excerpts with dramatic reconstructions of these encounters with forms of higher consciousness. At the end of each episode, Bidosov leaves viewers with some concluding remarks about the need for spirituality, morality, national awareness and respect for ancestors.

The series represents a successful merging of genres. It borrows from the US genre of adventure and 'inexplicable phenomena' shows, employing the same set of staging techniques, lighting and special effects. It also borrows from similar shows on Russian channels, but offers a specifically Kazakh national take. The series combines the revival of Islamic piety with reflections on the growth of domestic religious tourism via pilgrimages to shrines. It also cultivates a fascination – present since the Brezhnev era throughout what was then the Soviet Union – with extrasensory phenomena, UFOs and vanished civilizations, as well as energetic healing, Asian medicine and East Asian-inspired philosophies.[46] In this, the programme is an accurate reflection of Kazakhstani citizens' contemporary spiritual quests, which blend elements of so-called traditional Islam with a New Age atmosphere.

The programme is also an innovative way to impart patriotic feelings to viewers. The audience discover new, often very remote, places in Kazakhstan and enjoys a fun *and* patriotic journey during which they get to know their own country and its forgotten corners. The programme sketches a new geography of Kazakhstan, focused mostly on the southern areas of the country (the region most famous for its shrines and historical monuments) as well as central Kazakhstan, around Kzyl-Orda, and eastern Kazakhstan, around Semey. In all the episodes available on YouTube, there is a noticeable absence of northern and western Kazakhstan, aptly reflecting the general symbolic marginalization of the latter in spatial representations of the country. The programme also plays on regionalist clichés. In Shymkent – the region known as the Texas of Kazakhstan[47] – for instance, Bidosov appears in a cowboy hat and Western film music plays in the background. However, he never mentions the different Kazakh hordes and clans, a sensitive issue in public opinion. Instead, in each episode, Bidosov stresses the country's unity by insisting on the fact that visitors from 'all regions of Kazakhstan' visit these holy sites.

The subtext of *Signs: Legends of the Steppe* also provides fascinating insight into Kazakh identity. The programme is aired entirely in Russian, and when interviewees speak Kazakh, their words are translated. Almost all participants in each episode are ethnic Kazakhs, although some Russians appear in secondary roles (only in one episode is a young Russian woman the main interviewee). All the places visited are linked to Kazakh identity; nothing in the landscape or discourse is reminiscent of Kazakhstan's Soviet past or current links to Russia. The programme celebrates rural life, a rarity in a Kazakh cultural arena that is more focused on the urban world. The show is a far cry from the Emirati-style buildings of the new capital, Astana, and its avant-garde architecture,[48] and equally distant from the opulent apartments of the upper-middle classes that are the setting of many Kazakh miniseries.[49] The everyday heroes of the series tend to be young people, but they often encounter members of the older generations – *arbaks* and shrine custodians – who are dressed in 'traditional' clothes and wear Muslim hats.

Paradoxically, the Steppe world is not actually celebrated in the series. Ancestral transhumance, adopted to graze cattle and symbolized by the yurt, is not a part of the displayed repertoire, even though this nomadic theme has become widespread in pop music.[50] On the contrary, because the programme focuses on pilgrimage sites, it insists on the sedentary heritage of the Kazakh nation – in accordance with the official Kazakhstani historiography since independence.[51]

In the show, Bidosov often emphasizes the importance of better knowing and understanding the 'Kazakh mentality'. The programme summarizes this supposed Kazakh mentality as being shaped by the spiritual legacy (*dukhovnoe nasledstvo*) of the ancestors, who could be Islamic religious figures, military heroes or carriers of Kazakh culture (such as folk singers, poets, or writers). This spiritual legacy has some religious motifs, but it cannot be understood as purely Islamic. Islam is present across the shrines, prayers and sacred lineages linked to the Prophet or Sufi saints, but it is also associated with beliefs that refer to the region's Tengrist and shamanic past, New Age trends that incorporate various healing practices and the supernatural as an integral element of the individual spiritual quest. Spiritual legacy, in the show's philosophy, also includes knowledge of one's own national past, respect for the pantheon of national heroes and awareness of oneself as a product of this past. Values that embody this Kazakhness include pride in the national past, generosity, sharing, responsibility and respect. In a sense, *Signs: Legends of the Steppe* offers a Kazakh version of the famous 'Russian soul', embodying the main human values, combined with a revalorization of so-called traditional Islam.

Television is both a window into public opinion and an incredibly powerful way to shape it. It operates in both directions, first by upholding political obligations in terms of official newspeak, forbidden and permissible topics and cultural values, and then by taking into account the tastes of an ever-less captive public that is increasingly able to turn to other media, including online sources and foreign satellite channels. Kazakhstan is a good example of the challenge of the dual role of television. Although the authorities see it as a core means of communicating with their constituencies, the channels also rely on ratings and advertisements, which form the basis of their commercial viability. The televisual landscape in Kazakhstan is thus plural in the sense that it retransmits official state discourse but also offers entertainment, most of which is produced outside the Kazakhstani state's control.

With the exception of the new cultural channel Madeniet and the cases discussed here, Kazakhstani television still offers few quality educational programmes on nationhood and has been relatively uninvested in such programmes. Efforts to represent the new nation have focused on advancing a forward-looking vision, as embodied by the symbolic architecture in Astana/Nur-Sultan, rather than improving citizens' understanding of their controversial past. The blank pages of Kazakh history, which relate to Russia in general and the Soviet Union in particular, remain difficult to assess in an unpolarizing way. The political will to avoid creating cultural gaps between the Russian minority, which still represents a quarter of the population, and the Kazakh majority – not to mention between the Russian-speaking, urban Kazakh population and the rural, Kazakh-speaking one – plays a critical role in the absence of these sensitive historical moments from television.

Even commemorations of the victims of the Soviet regime speak only to part of the population, explaining why Alash Orda was not commemorated at the founding historical moment of independent Kazakhstan. Having to determine the responsibility of the Soviet elites – whether federal ones based in Moscow or republican ones based in Alma-Ata – would intensify tensions and create new ideological divisions. Television productions have thus remained reluctant to address those troubled times and have long been resistant to the growing trend among young social activists and ethno-nationalist groups to campaign against the Soviet regime and the role of Russia in Kazakhstan's history.

Still, staging the nation may take many multiple forms, including less official, more popular and more innovative ways of branding the country than the rigid state-dominated narrative. In this context, television is a perfectly appropriate tool, hence the emergence of patriotic entertainment programmes like *Signs*, which succeeds in blending the revival of interest in the Kazakh past and in knowledge of the nation's vast territories with the rise in domestic tourism (especially healing pilgrimages), the fashionableness of the supernatural, and the celebration of the Kazakh 'mentality' and so-called traditional Islam. *Signs* thus sketches an alternative Kazakhness that is less official and more fluid, innovative, and in tune with global trends. This new genre of patriotic entertainment – already fully established in Russia – is probably destined to grow and mature. The authorities want to revive patriotic fervour in order to avoid pressure from Moscow, while the younger, increasingly Kazakh-speaking, post-Soviet generations display greater pride in the country's past and in the celebration of a reconstructed Kazakhness.

Notes

1 See Junisbai et al., 'Mass Media Consumption in Post-Soviet Kyrgyzstan and Kazakhstan' and Nikolayenko, 'Youth Media Consumption and Perceptions of Electoral Integrity in Kazakhstan and Kyrgyzstan'.
2 See, for instance, discussion of the Aspandau club in 'Informatsionnaia bezopasnost' Kazakhstana'.
3 The state-run Channel One Eurasia, which alone accounts for 25 per cent of the audience; KTK, launched in 1991 as the first private channel; NTK; Kazakhstan, which first broadcast in 1958 and was known in Soviet times as KazTV; Khabar, created in 1995 as the official channel of the information agency of the same name and famous for having been the centre of the late Rakhat Aliyev's media empire; Channel 31, a private channel started in 1992; and Channel 7, the newest channel, launched in 2009. Information from 'Televizionnyi rynok Kazakhstana'.
4 'Populiarnye onlain tv v kategorii "Kazakhstan"'.
5 See its website, http://www.asylarna.kz.
6 J'son & Partners Consulting, 'Obzor rynka televizionnogo kontenta v respublike Kazakhstan'.
7 Fierman, 'Reversing Language Shift in Kazakhstan'.
8 'Zakon Respubliki Kazakhstan ot 23ogo iulia 1999 goda no. 451–1'.

9 Ileulova (ed.) 'Obzor kazakhstanskogo rynka teleindustrii na primere sravnitel'nogo analiza videokontenta telekanalov KTK, 31 kanal, Khabar'.
10 *Public Foundation Pravovoi Media-Tsentr,* https://lmc.kz.
11 See its website, http://www.mirtv.ru/about.
12 'O telekanale'. See also James Kilner, 'Kazakh State TV Station Ditches Russian Language Broadcasts'. Yet I (ML) watched a Russian-speaking broadcast on that supposedly 100 per cent Kazakh-speaking channel in June 2015.
13 'Televizionnyi rynok Kazakhstana'.
14 J'son & Partners Consulting, 'Obzor rynka televizionnogo kontenta v respublike Kazakhstan'.
15 'Televizionnyi rynok Kazakhstana'.
16 Shuraev, '90 protsentov otechestvennykh serialov nel'zia pokazyvat", *meta.kz*, 2 March 2012, quoted in Ileulova, 'Obzor kazakhstanskogo rynka teleindustrii'.
17 'Ukaz "O dal'neishei sovershenstvovanii sistemy gosudarstvennogo upravleniia respubliki Kazakhstan"'.
18 'O strategicheskom plane Agenstva Respubliki Kazakhstan po sviazi i informatsii na 2014–2018'.
19 Kantar TNS, 'Survey of Kazakhstan TV Audience'.
20 'V Kazakhstane sniaty masshtabnye istoricheskie fil'my'.
21 'Sostoialos' III zasedanie Mezhvedomstvennoi rabochei gruppy po izucheniiu natsional'noi istorii'.
22 See the biographical page available at http://online.zakon.kz/Document/?doc_id=30105657.
23 'Anvar Mamraimo: Ia – mnogostanochnik'.
24 See his biography on his Facebook page, https://www.facebook.com/instarch/posts/774937529193301.
25 'Gosudarstvennaia programma "Kul'turnoe nasledie Kazakhstana"', http://www.madenimura.kz/ru/president-speech-madenimura.
26 'V Kazakhstane sniat ria istoricheskikh fil'mov'.
27 See Laruelle, 'The "Russian Idea" on the Small Screen'.
28 Mustafina, 'Voenno-patrioticheskie aktsii v den' rozhdeniia Talgata Begel'dinova stanut ezhegodnym'.
29 'Posol'stvo Kazakhstan Obzor kazakhstanskogo rynka a na Ukraine prezentovalo fil'm "V ogon' za rodinu"'.
30 Korchevskii, 'Seriia sotsial'nykh rolikov zapuskaetsia na kazakhstanskikh kanalakh'.
31 'Seliger 2014 National Youth Forum'.
32 'Kazakhskoi gosudarstvennosti v 2015 ispolnitsia 55 let – Nazarbaev'.
33 'Den' nezavisimosti prazdnuet Kazakhstan'.
34 'Tri milliarda tenge vydeliat na prazdnovanie 550–letiia Kazakhskogo khansta i 20–letiia ANK'.
35 'Serial o Kazakhskom khanstve snimut v Kazakhstane'.
36 'Tri seriala k 550–letiiu Kazakhskom khanstve snimut v Kazakhstane'.
37 Gidda, 'No More Borat, Kazakhstan Makes its Own "Game of Thrones"-Style TV Show'.
38 About 15 series are available on YouTube.
39 See Lymer, 'Rags and Rock Art'.
40 See Bigozhin, 'State, Shrine, and Sacred Lineage in Post-Soviet Kazakhstan'.
41 DeWeese, 'Sacred Places and "Public" Narratives'.
42 On the question of legitimacy around the shrine, see Kehl-Bodrogi, 'Who Owns the Shrine?'.
43 See Jessa, '*Aq jol* Soul Healers'.
44 See Louw, 'Pursuing "Muslimness"'.
45 On the notion of *arbak* in the Kyrgyz case, see Jacquesson, 'Power Play among the Kyrgyz'.
46 See Menzel, 'Occult and Esoteric Movements in Russia from the 1960s to the 1980s'.
47 Koch and White, 'Cowboys, Gangsters, and Rural Bumpkins'.
48 On Astana, see Köppen, 'The Production of a New Eurasian Capital on the Kazakh Steppe'; Koch, 'The "Heart" of Eurasia?'; Koch, 'The Monumental and the Miniature'.
49 On Kazakh miniseries, see Rollberg, 'Birth of a Nation on Television'.
50 Rancier, 'Resurrecting the Nomads'.
51 On historiographical debates in Kazakhstan, see, among others, Malikov, 'The Kenesary Kasymov Rebellion (1837–1847)'. More broadly, and for the Soviet period, see Kudaibergenova, '"Imagining Community" in Soviet Kazakhstan'.

9

Language and ethnicity: the landscape of Kazakh nationalism

In this chapter, I set aside the state narrative on Kazakhness and focus instead on groups of activists in Kazakhstan that can be defined as nationalists or national-patriots. These activists contend that state policies do too little to defend the Kazakhness of the country.

During perestroika, Kazakh nationalist motifs flourished within intellectual circles before taking on a more political cast at the start of the 1990s thanks to the Azat and Alash movements, though these were quickly liquidated by the authorities. Nationalist dissidence thus vanished from the political scene, though it remained visible (if discreet) in the academic world, especially around the promotion of Kazakh literature and the production of a national history alternative to the state-sponsored one.

Since the early 2010s, however, Kazakh nationalism has re-emerged on a different social basis, among a younger generation that interacts mostly on social media. So far, very few scholars have studied this re-emergence, with the notable exception of Diana T. Kudaibergenova and Serik Beisembayev.[1] My own research is based on print and online sources in Russian as well as semi-structured interviews conducted with the late Aldan Aimbetov, the chief editor of *Kazakhskaia pravda*, in May 2002, March 2003, and June 2004, and with five young leading nationalist activists – Zhanbolat Mamay, Mukhtar Taizhan, Aidos Sarym, Dauren Babamurat and Valikhan Tuleshov – in June 2015 in Almaty and in January 2016 in Washington, DC.[2]

Terminological debates

In the Soviet tradition, 'nationalism' (*natsionalizm*) is defined as a negative feature typical of capitalist societies and/or a 'remnant' (*perezhitki*) of pre-Soviet society noticeable among Soviet people that should be eradicated. Patriotism and internationalism, by contrast, are presented as the genuine way of expressing feelings of belonging to a national community. In the post-Soviet world, the negative load of the term nationalism is still very present and broadly shared by most populations, but multiple borrowings from Western literature and changes in mindset have led some in Kazakhstan to question this. Indeed, some groups now actively define themselves as nationalist and see this as a positive feature.

In the Kazakh language, 'nationalism' can be translated in two ways: *ultzhandylyq* and *ultshyldyq*. The first translation carries positive connotations, while the second is more ambiguous; it is sometimes negative, sometimes positive. Nationalism in the sense of *ultzhandylyq* supports emic expression, used by the subject, not perspectives applied by outside observers. During the perestroika years, the three main movements representing this nationalist trend – Alash, Azat and Zheltoksan – defined themselves as 'national-democrats' (*natsional-demokraty* in Russian, *ultshyl-demokratialyk* in Kazakh), a positioning common among those who called for the Soviet regime to democratize and for Soviet nationalities policy to give more autonomy to national cultures. In the second half of the 1990s, the terminology evolved, with groups starting to identify themselves as 'national-patriots' (*natsional-patrioty* in Russian, *ult-patriottary* in Kazakh), a term that was also, at that time, widespread in Russia and used to identify opponents of the Yeltsin regime. This term remains in use in Kazakhstan, and a whole group of *natspat*, or national-patriots, has emerged.

In today's Kazakhstan, state organs still draw the Soviet-era distinction between 'good' patriotism and 'bad' nationalism. As such, all those who add *national* to their definition of patriotism position themselves in opposition to the state on matters of national identity. However, terminological debates among Kazakh nationalists are numerous. The majority believe that patriotism only refers to state loyalty while nationalism refers to the ethnic nation and should be promoted among ethnic Kazakhs. Some, such as Dos Koshim (see below), self-identify as nationalists (*ultshyl*), not as national-patriots. According to him, 'the so-called Kazakh nationalists are in fact Kazakh patriots. Without these "nationalists" it is possible that Kazakhstan as a state would not even exist'.[3] As Diana T. Kudaibergenova notes, Kazakh national-patriots have not been able to develop a coherent theoretical and terminological framework for the use of *ultshyldyq*.[4]

The process of self-definition within this nationalist trend is not, as we have seen, specific to Kazakhstan: it relates to nationalist-themed terms that are widespread all over the world. However, in Kazakhstan, part of the debate is specifically rooted in intra-Kazakh polemics about the supposed loss of Kazakh identity through Sovietization/Russification. The use of the adjective *nagyz* ('real' in Kazakh) to describe Kazakhs who have successfully preserved their identity (that is, 'real' Kazakhs) and the adjective *shala* to describe those who have 'lost' it has led to mutual accusations and become a way to privilege certain categories of citizens. The phrase *Shala Kazakh*, which literarily means 'half-Kazakh', is used to target Russophone and urban Kazakhs, who are considered too detached from their Kazakhophone and rural roots.[5] This dissociation is based on the notion that Kazakhs have been colonized by Russians and should now decolonize their national conscience. This idea was indirectly formulated in the word *mankurt*, an old Turkic term updated by Chingiz Aitmatov in *The Day Lasts More Than a Hundred Years* (*I dol'she veka dlitsia den'*, 1980), who described an enslaved people deprived of their memory and, therefore, of their identity. The term found tremendous resonance in the Kazakh and Kyrgyz societies at the time of publication and has encapsulated criticism of the Soviet nationalities policy ever since.[6]

A large number of *publitsitika* (popular essays) have been published in Kazakhstan on the issue of nationalism, but these often read more like a nationalist manifesto or, at least, an engaged discussion on the topic than a scholarly analysis. An example of the former type of work is *The Kazakh Mission*, the edited volume of which was coordinated by Berik Abdylgaliuly, a nationalist theoretician and member of the Kazakhstan Institute for Strategic Studies (KISI);[7] the latter category is represented by *Kazakhstan: National Idea and Tradition*[8] by Kanat Nurov, president of the Aspandau Fund, a think tank and publishing house that has the support of some important political figures.[9]

Mapping the Kazakh national-patriotic landscape

The national-patriotic landscape in Kazakhstan is not unified politically or ideologically. Several generations, social networks and ideological orientations compete with each other. Even if any effort to create a typology is by definition schematizing, it is still meaningful to sketch the main groups. I identify four: the first historical parties of the perestroika years (Zheltoksan, Alash and Azat); the intellectual figures at the forefront of the language and culture struggle; the more politically oriented figures who seek to capitalize on so-called patriotic values; and the younger, social-media-oriented generation.

The founding fathers

During the last years of perestroika, three Kazakh nationalist movements emerged, each exhibiting a different degree of radicalism.[10] The first one chronologically, Zheltoksan (literally, December), was established in 1988 to request the liberation of prisoners arrested after the anti-Soviet/anti-Russian riots of December 1986.[11] Led by anti-communist activist Khasen Kozhakhmetov and poet-activist Aron Atabek (who went on to found the national-patriotic society Zheruyuk in August 1989), the movement was officially registered in March 1990 after Moscow authorized a multi-party political system in the Soviet Union. Zheltoksan demanded that the government revisit its interpretation of the riots of December 1986, exhibiting special concern for Kazakhs abroad and calling for Islam to become a central political and ideological factor of the new Kazakh society. It adamantly opposed the possible privatization of the country's land or natural resources. It did not call for Russians to be expelled *en masse* but urged their voluntary migration and demanded that Cossack activities be restricted. Later, Zheltoksan attempted to present itself as an alternative to President Nursultan Nazarbayev in the 1993 elections, where it was supported by some members of Alash and Azat.

More virulent was Alash, a political party established in April 1990. Taking its name from the historical Alash Orda movement of the early twentieth century, it hoped to play on this strong symbolic link to obtain recognition as the major representative of national interests. Alash's followers rallied around the slogan 'Islam, Turkism and Democracy': the party wanted to create an independent Islamic state – Greater Turkestan – that would have included all the Turkic peoples of the CIS, as well as expel all Slavs from Kazakhstan.[12] After the mufti of Kazakhstan, Ryspek Nysambayev, was attacked in December 1991 by some Alash members, charges were brought against the party and it was banned.[13]

One of Alash's main leaders, Aron Atabek, went into exile in Moscow but was arrested by the Russian security services on behalf of Kazakhstan after publishing the newspaper *Khak*, which disseminated a virulently anti-Nazarbayev article written by the dissident Karishal Asanov.[14] Atabek then fled to Baku, where he ardently defended the Azeri view of the Nagorno-Karabakh conflict for years. He became a well-known pan-Turkist activist as part of the Turkestan Committee, which sought to rally opposition groups in the four Turkophone countries of Central Asia. He returned to Kazakhstan in 1996, publishing some poetry inspired by Abay and joining the self-defence militias operating in certain districts of Almaty. In 2009, he was convicted of hostage-taking and of killing a policeman in a riot and was sentenced to 18 years in prison.[15] Still incarcerated as of late 2020, he is considered a political prisoner by such organizations as Pen International.[16]

The most imposing political organization, however, was the Azat (Freedom) movement, founded in July 1990 by former foreign minister Mikhail Isinaliev, Dos Koshim and the late historian Sabetkazy Akatay (1938–2003). Very active in demanding the independence of Kazakhstan during perestroika, Azat was weakened after its core demands were met with the Soviet collapse and independence. In contrast to the other two parties, Azat stood firmly opposed to violent inter-ethnic relations and recruited members from among the Slavs and other ethnic groups as well as ethnic Kazakhs. Nonetheless, it called for the formation of a democratic Kazakhstani patriotism that would give priority to the Kazakh population and language.[17] (Note that this Azat should not be confused with the opposition party of the same name created by Bolat Abilov in 2005.)

In 1992, segments of each of these three parties decided to establish a coalition with a less virulent ideology. They gathered together as part of the Republican Party of Kazakhstan (*Respublikanskaia partiia Kazakhstana*), led by Sabetkazy Akatay. Although the new party toned down its rhetoric in order to obtain registration, it refused to use the term 'Kazakhstani' and endorsed the systematic usage of 'Kazakh' when speaking of the new state. On 16 May 1994, a group of 11 nationalists from different organizations launched a hunger strike in front of the parliament building in Almaty and demanded the resignation of the government.[18] Instead, the militants were arrested and imprisoned, leading the various nationalist parties united under the Republican Party of Kazakhstan to abandon for several years their plans for large-scale national demonstrations. In 1999, Alash, still led by Akatay, was the only nationalist party to succeed in getting re-registered, this time under the name of the National Party of Kazakhstan – Alash (*Natsional'naia partiia Kazakhstana – Alash*). However, it proceeded to receive only 2.76 per cent of the vote in the legislative elections that term, lost its registration in 2003 and disappeared from political life.[19]

The intellectual circles

As political expressions of Kazakh nationalism were repressed, the struggle moved to the cultural field. Several intellectual figures representing academic and artistic circles have since become the standard-bearers of the nationalist struggle to preserve and promote

Kazakh language and culture. Many of these figures come from the fields of history, literature and linguistics, which were already the most Kazakhified sectors of academic life during the Soviet era, for the obvious reason that mastery of the national language was necessary in order to access local sources. Many were moulded by the Zhas Tulpar movement, a Kazakh student organization that was active in promoting Kazakh culture in Moscow and Leningrad during the 1960s and was accused by the KGB of 'bourgeois nationalism'.[20]

Even if some intellectuals, such as the aforementioned Sabetkazy Akatay, became involved in politics, most tried to remain above political divisions and interests. This allowed them to navigate the grey zone between official institutions and the opposition, forging consensus with the Nazarbayev regime. The face of this group was the writer and poet Mukhtar Shakhanov, former ambassador to Kyrgyzstan, member of parliament, and editor-in-chief of the cultural and literary journal *Zhalyn*, which has been published since 1969. Shakhanov also actively participated in ecological groups calling for protection of the Aral Sea and led the state commission investigating the 1986 Zheltoksan events.[21]

Other members of this group included the linguist and historian of Kazakh literature Tursynbek Kakishev (1927–2015), a professor at the Al-Farabi National University and one of the authors of a multi-volume work on the *History of Kazakh Literature*;[22] another prominent Kazakh writer, Qabdesh Zhumadilov, born in Xinjiang to a Kazakh family who emigrated to the Soviet Union during the Sino-Soviet honeymoon of the 1950s; Sofy Smatayev; and Mukhtar Magauin. Like Shakhanov, Akatay, Kakishev and Zhumadilov were known for their defence of Kazakh culture even in Soviet times. They competed with the Zhas Tulpar movement, which united mostly Russian-speaking Kazakh writers such as Olzhas Suleimenov, Murat Auezov and Satimzhan Sanbayev.[23]

Many figures of this generation fed into the Mother Tongue Society (*Ana tili Qogami*) and the Kazakh State Language movement (*Memlekettik Til*), which constituted the core of Kazakh cultural activism during the perestroika era. They contributed to the creation of the *Qazaq Tili* (*Kazakh Language*), registered as both an association and a journal in early 1990 with the goal of ensuring the promotion of Kazakh as the state language.[24] Another important figure, the journalist Aldan Aimbetov (1931–2006), belonged to this generation but decided another fate for himself. A professor at the state medical university, he launched the journal *Kazakhskaia pravda* in 1993[25] and self-published it until his death. It was for years the only Kazakh national-patriot journal published entirely in Russian.[26] It has since been complemented by *SolDat* and, more recently,

Tribuna (*Ashyq Alan*), bilingual Kazakh/Russian publications that likewise promote a national-patriotic agenda.[27]

A younger generation of nationalist activists emerged from the foundations and associations promoting Kazakh history and educational issues. The leading foundation in this category is probably the Alash Orda Fund, which collects works about the Alash Orda founding fathers as well as about Kazakh historians who worked on the topic during Soviet times.[28] One of the Fund's main figures today, Sultan Khan Akkuly, trained at the Mukhtar Auezov Institute for Literature and Art and, after working for many years for Radio Free Europe/Radio Liberty, joined the Lev Gumilev Eurasian National University to lead a small foundation devoted to the study of Alash. Sultan Khan Akkuly has been visible in the media in recent years on the issue of identifying the skull of Kenesary Kasymov, the last Kazakh military leader to fight against Russia, with the hope of repatriating the remains to his homeland.[29]

The conservative patriots

A third group offers a more political reading of national-patriotism and tries to capitalize on its potential outreach in order to build political power. One organization within this group is Ult tagdyry (Fate of the Nation), which emerged in 2005 under the leadership of Dos Koshim, focusing mostly on language issues[30] and inviting Russians to 'take the opportunity' to go back to Russia under Putin's repatriation state programme, launched in 2006.[31] Unhappy with the lack of a national holiday celebrating Kazakh history, Ult tagdyry also lobbied unsuccessfully to make either the 1916 uprising or the 1986 Zheltoksan events a national holiday.[32]

Dos Koshim has had a long career in political activism, beginning during the perestroika years with the fight to recognize Kazakh as the republic's official language. In the 1990s, he worked closely with the social-democratic party Azat, part of a network that included former prime minister Akezhan Kazhegueldin as well as human rights activists Evgeny Zhotvis and Sergey Duvanov. Loyal to his friends, Dos Koshim supported the rise of Zhotvis and Duvanov as political opponents to Nazarbayev, despite their obvious disagreements on the national identity issue. Dos Koshim continues to participate in the public debate about issues such as the Kazakh language and history, *Oralmans*, and the need for public policies to support the rural population.[33]

At its launch in 2005, Ult tagdyry was briefly in competition with another movement of the same name, which then changed its name to Khalyk dabyly (The Tocsin of the Nation), led by Bolatkhan Taizhan (who subsequently passed away) and Sabyrzhan Makhmet.[34] Another small political party, Ruhaniyat (Spiritual Strength), tried without success to register to participate in the 2011 elections on a platform of nationalism and environmental concerns. Its leader, Serikzhan Mambetalin, was put on trial in 2015 for 'inciting inter-ethnic hate' after publishing on his Facebook page excerpts from the latest book by Murat Telibekov, the leader of the nongovernmental organization Union of Kazakhstan's Muslims, known for its provocative anti-Kazakh statements.[35] Yet the rising star of this patriotic trend is Bekbolat Tleukhan, an MP and singer of classic Kazakh music known for his very nationalist agenda with reactionary values such as polygamy, and his promotion of rigorist Sunni Islam.

Some of these patriotic groups focus on empowering youth alongside promoting their conservative-values agendas. This is the case, for instance, with the Almaty-based Bolashaq (Future) youth movement (not to be confused with the state-funded fellowship programme of the same name). Its leader, Dauren Babamurat, has been working with rural youth and *Oralmans* since the mid-2000s, especially by bringing books to rural libraries and screening films in order to increase national pride.[36] The Bolashaq movement is known for its strong opposition to Western values: in 2013, its members burned symbols of St. Valentine (of Valentine's Day fame), seeing the saint as part of a decadent Western tradition of forcing young girls into early sex; they promoted instead a more national commemoration, namely of the legendary Kazakh couple Bayan sulu and Kozy Korpesh, to be celebrated on 15 April.[37] Bolashaq was one of the most visible street movements supporting the replication of the Russian law against so-called homosexual propaganda in Kazakhstan, an effort that ultimately failed. On more than one occasion, Babamurat has violently expressed his hate for gay people, whom he sees as 'degenerate'.[38]

Another youth movement is Alash kyzdary (or Alash arulary), which emerged in 2009 as the women's counterpart of Bolashaq. It defends the same conservative values as Bolashaq: its young leader, Sandugash Dzhumagulova, fights against 'American ideology, [which pushes for] girls to smoke, drink alcohol, use slang and have sex with almost unknown men'. [39] The group, which claims a membership of about 1,500 activists, has organized anti-abortion campaigns and raids to confiscate Kazakh porn videos.

Social media activists

A fourth group is comprised of younger people who use new tools such as social media to reach their audience. Of these, the most famous is probably Zhanbolat Mamay, who began his career as a popular journalist for the Kazakh-language *Zhas Alash* newspaper and is now the editor of *Tribuna/Ashyq Alan*. He leads the Rukh pen Til (Spirit and Language) youth movement, a small structure devoted to promoting the Kazakh language that rapidly emerged, as early as 2011, as a political platform for this new generation of national-patriots.[40]

Mamay has been one of the most active critics of Kazakhstan's entry into the Customs Union and then the Eurasian Economic Union. The feeling that the Nazarbayev era was coming to an end and that the Eurasian Economic Union was a strategic mistake perpetrated by an aging leadership gave national-patriots their largest public platform to date. They organized an 'anti-Eurasian forum' that was tacitly permitted by the authorities – likely to counter-balance pressures from Russia: they were authorized to meet publicly and garnered support from recognized intellectual and literary figures such as Sofy Smatayev, Temirkhan Medetbek, and the poet and writer Qabdesh Zhumadilov.[41] The young national-patriots also tried to organize a referendum on the Eurasian Union[42] and staged several digital actions – for instance, inviting people to wear medical masks to protest Russia's 'imperial virus'.[43]

The authorities' attitudes toward this new generation of national-patriots is ambiguous: they are marginalized and sometimes repressed but never totally silenced. In early 2012, Mamay was charged with inciting social discord during the Zhanaozen workers riots,[44] a charge carrying a jail sentence of up to 12 years, but he was quickly released.[45] Mamay was back in court a few years later on trumped-up charges: in May 2014, as tensions around the Donbas war peaked, the Kazakhstani authorities arrested him and Russian white-power nationalist Alexander Belov-Potkin, the former leader of the powerful Movement Against Illegal Immigration, for inciting inter-ethnic hatred.[46] Belov-Potkin allegedly organized a training camp for young members of the Kazakh nationalist group Ult-Azattygy, including Mamay. This story shares many features of the conspiracy theories and counter-messaging that shapes the post-Soviet information space. The Kazakhstani authorities opened the case at a highly opportune moment, allowing them to kill two birds with one stone: they signalled to Russia that they were taking the risk of destabilization by Russian nationalists seriously and they neutralized the most visible Kazakh nationalist activists at a time of growing popular resentment of Kazakhstan's entry into the Eurasian Economic Union. The allegation that Russian and Kazakh nationalists were working hand-in-hand to destabilize Kazakhstan does not seem plausible, and no further evidence was produced in support of the accusation.

Several other social media activists can also be mentioned here. For example, Mukhtar Taizhan, an economist who has been very active in drawing attention to the negative impact of the Customs Union with Russia on Kazakhstan's economy, leads the small foundation named after his father, Bolatkhan Taizhan, who was a member of Zhas Tulpar during the Soviet era. Maksat Il'yasuly, one of the leaders of the Antigeptil group, which objects to Russia using the Baikonur Cosmodrome,[47] became very visible during the spring 2016 protests against land reforms. Aidos Sarym, a historian and archivist by training, now coordinates the online Kazakh cultural project Abai.kz and heads the Altynbek Sarsenbayuly Foundation. In the early 2000s, Sarym held a number of leading positions in the Ministry of Information of Kazakhstan as well as the Office of the President of Kazakhstan in the early 2000s. He edited *National Tragedy of February 11, 2006* (2006), about Altynbek Sarsenbayev's political assassination, and *Zheltoksan* (2011), a ten-volume collection of documents and materials about the December riots. Valikhan Tuleshov, a philosopher who founded and coordinates the European Club of Kazakhstan Public Fund, worked for several years at the Institute of World Economy and Politics under the Fund of the First President, and later led the School of State and Public Policy at Almaty Management University. To this list can also be added political scientist Serikzhan Mambetalin; social activist Rasul Zhumaly; renowned essayist Azimbay Gali; Makhambet Abzhan, the head of the Shanyrak public association and former leader of the Union of Patriotic Youth, which is close to the Kazakhstani Communist Party;[48] and Rysbek Sansenbayuli, brother of the assassinated Sarsenbayev and chief editor of the popular newspaper *Zhas Alash*.[49]

This group does not necessarily share entirely similar worldviews, but they all are united by a strong anti-Russian narrative that does not rely only on linguistic issues or historical memories. Instead, they argue that a pro-Russian position favours authoritarianism in Kazakhstan and call for a more democratic regime. One of the main products of this new social media activism is the Facebook page Qazaq Orda, which has about 30,000 followers.[50] The page fights for what it calls Kazakhstan's decolonization, posting anti-Russian news articles, graphs and memes. Qazaq Orda was particularly active during the Ukrainian crisis, republishing pro-Ukrainian (including pro-Bandera) flyers and memes, anti-Putin caricatures and jokes that analogized Putin to Hitler (*'Putler'*); drawing parallels between the crisis and the Soviet-era Kazakh and Ukrainian genocides; and developing posters and memes about Kazakh history and the need to decolonize the country from any Russian influence.

Shared worldviews and lines of divide

Groups that self-identify as national-patriots are heterogeneous. While they share a similar broad agenda of promoting the Kazakhness of Kazakhstan, they advance different viewpoints on several important questions. Consensus exists on some issues, but the lines of divide between them are also critical. This quote from *Kazakhskaia pravda* provides insight into the national-patriotic perceptions of present-day Kazakhstan:

> One can say Kazakhs have almost negated themselves. What civilized people, having officialized its national language, speaks in a foreign language? What people had to leave the soil of its ancestors, a territory that is the ninth largest in the world, while having one of the lowest population density in the world? Why does one in every three Kazakhs today live abroad, their place is occupied by 129 diasporic nationalities? What native people on the authentic soil of its ancestors – with the exception of Native Americans – lives on reserves, having given its best territories to a non-native population? What people does not have the right to create a national-patriotic party or at least a movement? What else [do] Kazakhs have to give up, in the second decade of their independence, to trample their language, culture and mentality?[51]

The most widespread topic of discussion between national-patriot groups is thus the saving and promotion of the Kazakh language. This language-centric agenda has its roots in the Soviet period, when fighting for the right to speak and be taught in Kazakh constituted the cornerstone of nationalities policy. As Kazakhs were among the federal titular nationalities with the smallest share of national language fluency and the highest level of Russian usage, it was deemed crucial during the perestroika years to fight to protect the Kazakh language from near-certain extinction.[52]

National-patriots are united in the belief that the Kazakh language should be given priority and be the only state-recognized language, with Russian losing its status as a 'language of inter-ethnic communication', a status that they believe protects Russian while allowing Russian-speakers to avoid learning Kazakh.[53] As proclaimed in *Kazakhskaia pravda*, 'The language of each people, with the physical appearance of its representatives, is the foundation, the particularity, the shield of each nation. If the language were to disappear, the people would disappear as well'.[54] The majority of national-patriots favour the shift to Latin script, an old debate that regularly re-emerged on the Kazakhstani public scene until it was announced as an official policy for 2025 by Nazarbayev himself. According to national-patriots, Latin script is the symbol of modernity and of a pan-Turkic identity – with Kemalist Turkey as a beacon lighting the path – and a symbolic way to confirm the end of the Russian colonial era.[55] Some, however, called for a shift to Arabic, as was proposed during perestroika, when the journal of the Young Communists, *Pioner*, launched a project to teach Arabic script.[56] Today, however, this suggestion is considered too Islamic, if not Islamist, to enjoy broad support.

National-patriots position themselves in opposition to the state-backed notion of a Kazakhstani nation that celebrates the country's multi-ethnicity. According to them, the multi-ethnic Kazakhstani nation is an illusion created by the Nazarbayev regime in order to avoid confronting Russia and Kazakhstan's own Russian population, and because the elites currently in power are themselves a product of the Soviet regime and its ideology. According to national-patriots, the Kazakhstani nation would negate the right of Kazakhs to claim their own nation-state and, by extension, the linguistic and cultural primacy they believe they deserve. Many national-patriots openly refer to European nation-states as a model, suggesting that an authentic civic nation should emerge as an historical process from the merging of all ethnic or regional groups into one nation shaped by the language and culture of the majority. All citizens of Kazakhstan should, therefore, be called Kazakhs, just as all citizens of France are called French, whatever their original ethnicity may be. Dos Koshim has asked, for instance, for Kazakhstan to be renamed the 'Kazakh State' or 'Kazakh Republic'.[57]

Once that declaration of intent has been made, however, many national-patriots disagree about what kind of relationship to build with the country's Russian and Slavic minorities. Very few promote a pure 'Kazakhstan for Kazakhs' that would entail expelling non-Kazakhs. The *Kazakhskaia pravda* editorial board did, however, fall into this minority in the early 2000s, when they asked for the expulsion of ethnic Russians to free up jobs and housing.[58] Today, the majority of national-patriots claim that minorities are welcome to stay, but that they should speak Kazakh and share Kazakh values and traditions. All national-patriots are enthusiastic proponents of the repatriation of ethnic Kazakhs from abroad; having been protected from Russification and Sovietization, *Oralmans* are said to contribute to the re-Kazakhification of Kazakhs, inculcating traditions long lost by their modernized brethren in the homeland.[59]

National-patriots also tend to share a similar reading of Kazakh history, especially of the nineteenth and twentieth centuries. They believe the tsarist empire played one Kazakh *juz* (tribal confederation) off against another, whipped up fear of the Dzhungars to conquer the Kazakh territory, and planned the agricultural and demographic colonization of the steppes by Russian peasants. They see Soviet history as a direct continuation of Russian colonial policy, with an assumed agenda of demographic domination.

Their victimization narrative is built on two foundations. First is the memory of the political repression of Alash Orda leaders and the mass repressions of the 1937–8 purges.[60] Small groups of activists commemorate these tragic events every 31 May, the Day of Victims of Political Repression.[61] For them, the December 1986 riots were another episode in the Russian/Soviet effort to repress everything Kazakh.

The second foundation is the bloody sedentarization and collectivization of the early 1930s and the subsequent famine that killed about one-third of Kazakhs and pushed another third into emigration.[62] Borrowing from the Ukrainian Holodomor narrative, national-patriots created a Kazakh term to describe the famine, *Asharshylyk*. They asked for the same status as victims of genocide and hoped for similar international recognition.[63] The documentary film *Asharshylyk* by Kalila Umarov, based on Valerii Mikhailov's book *The Chronicle of the Great Dzhut* (*Khronika Velikogo Dzhuta*), was produced in 1992 and restored in 2013.[64] In 2019, Zhambolat Mamay released a new documentary on the famine, *Zhulmat*, viewed by half a million people on YouTube, that created vivid polemics within Kazakhstan and sparked some negative reactions from Russia.[65]

The Kazakh national-patriotic worldview is largely based on a shared endorsement of an alternate history and a romanticized Kazakh past. This alternate history finds inspiration in multiple sources, including the nineteenth-century Orientalist fascination with the supposed authenticity of the cultures of the steppes; Olzhas Suleimenov's grand vision of the unity of the steppes and the critical role of the steppe world in founding the ancient cultures of the Mediterranean; Lev Gumilev's rehabilitation of Turkic ethnic groups in the history of the Russian state;[66] and Murad Adzhi's folk history of the 1990s around the notion that Turks are at the origin of all major civilizations and human inventions. This alternative culture is thus shaped both by the legacy of the cultural underground of the Soviet era and the contemporary popularity of folk history and conspiracy theories.

All national-patriots tend to call for a revival of the Turkic roots of Kazakhness, although with varying levels of pan-Turkism. For all of them, the historical continuum among the peoples of the steppes is critical, even if they recognize the Kazakh Khanate of the fifteenth century as the birth of the first Kazakh state. They also cultivate romanticized notions about the freedom of nomadic culture and the figure of the *batyr,* the noble knight. Some give preference to an assumed pan-Turkic ideology relatively similar to the one in place in Turkey and in early twentieth-century Jadid circles, thus linking national-patriotism to Islamic belonging. Others shift their focus to a more Kazakh-centric pan-Turkism that is detached from Turkey, more secular and sometimes combined with Aryan supremacist motives, such as the 'Kazakho-aryanism' theory of Aron Atabek.[67]

On more contemporary issues, national-patriots present a relatively unified front. They consider current-day Kazakhstan to be a Russian colony and denounce what they see as Nazarbayev's submission to the Kremlin. They ask for the closure of all Russian military bases on Kazakhstani territory, including the Baikonur Cosmodrome, and reacted violently to the rapprochement with Russia signified by the Customs Union and the Eurasian Economic Union.

They have also denounced Kazakhs' cultural infeudation to Russia. In 2014, the Kazakh-language journal *Zhuldyzdar otbarsy – Anyz Adam* (*The Celebrity Family – The Most Famous Man*), known for popularizing world history, came under the media spotlight for publishing an issue devoted to Adolf Hitler and *Mein Kampf.*[68] A Russia-based veteran group accused the journal of propagating inter-ethnic hate, while the chief editor, Zharylkap Kalybay, defended himself by saying the journal had merely explained who Hitler was to the wider public, without supporting Nazi ideology.[69] The Kazakhstani justice system ordered Kalybay to pay a significant fine to the veterans' group, but the scandal resonated among Kazakh nationalists, who tried to use the case to demonstrate the subordination of Kazakhstani institutions to Russian public opinion and its 'obsession' with fighting fascism.[70]

On Kazakhstan's relationship with China, national-patriots have not forgiven Nazarbayev for abandoning some disputed border territories to Beijing in 1996, and they criticize China's exploitation of Kazakhstani raw resources. Like many nationalist groups in the post-Soviet space, Kazakh national-patriots share strong environmental concerns – a legacy of the Soviet ecological movement of the 1960s – and this provides another impetus for their denunciation of China's poor environmental standards and workers' rights. They also warn that Kazakhstan might become a Chinese agricultural colony and were vocal participants in the 2009 protests against the proposed transfer of over one million hectares of arable land to Chinese farmers. These protests forced the government to retract its plans and to recognize the illegality of transferring land to foreign nationals.[71] In spring 2016, the protests against land reform and the ability of foreigners to rent lands for up to 25 years again raised the public profile of national-patriots, especially in some provincial cities.

But beyond this façade of consensus, national-patriots are divided on many other important questions. Some, such as Murat Taizhan, Aidos Sarym and Valikhan Tuleshov, call for classic liberal values and a European model of development (though they do not stand for a pro-US foreign policy and many of them are proponents of a kind of pan-Turkic identity).[72] Others are much more critical of both the West's foreign policy – denouncing, for example, US firms operating in the Caspian Sea that help consolidate the Nazarbayev regime without enriching the country – and values. Indeed, many who call for conservative values in Kazakhstan are careful to differentiate the liberal West from the conservative West. They support the rise of far-right parties in Europe, the shared agenda of strong nation-state sovereignty, the rejection of any supranational construction and the promotion of so-called traditional family values. To a lesser extent, national-patriots are also divided on whether they see Russia or China as Kazakhstan's main enemy, a decision that depends on whether they look toward recent history and a medium-term future (in which case Russia is the problematic neighbour) or to ancient history and the long-term future (in which case emphasis is put on China).

Another dividing question among national-patriots in Kazakhstan relates to their conceptions of national identity. Atabek is the only figure to insist openly on the notion of national socialism: 'National-Socialism is not [the] fascism of Mussolini or Hitler!' he writes. 'National-Socialism is a political and economic term which scientifically underpins the state construction, with the interest of the Nation and of Social Justice at its core'.[73] His radical worldview remains in the minority, even if many national-patriots believe in some kind of genetic or biological definition of the nation. For instance, Dos Koshim has stated that 'Turkic unity, it seems to me, is in the blood'. [74] Similarly, some believe that Kazakh society should value *juz* (clan) lines as a constitutive element of the national identity. Others, however, see this as a 'backward' element cultivated by Russians and Soviets that should be rejected in order to become a unified, modern nation-state.

However, national-patriots' main disagreement relates to religion. Here, at least three schools can be identified: those who promote liberal values and a secular nationalism, those who call for the rehabilitation of Tengrism and those who link Kazakh national identity to Islam. The third trend appears to be the rising one. In the early 1990s, the group Alash called for a theocratic regime; since then, however, it has rapidly shifted toward a more secular narrative.[75] One of its past leaders, Aron Atabek, has since became a fervent proponent of Tengrism. He considers Islam to be a universalistic religion that negates the specific national features of each country and denounces Wahhabism as a new internationalism. Atabek's views also contain an underlying subtext of conspiracy regarding the links between Islam and 'Masonic' culture, an indirect way to consider both Arabs and Jews as Semites.[76] However, a growing trend among national-patriots is to link national identity and Islam, as Bekbolat Tleukhan does in calling for Kazakhs to adhere to strict Hanafi traditions.[77]

Potential for social mobilization

What will happen if this national-patriotism is fully mobilized? What audience supports it, and what topics may crystallize public opinion in favour of national-patriots? On the other side, where do they lack credibility?

The first priority for national-patriots is to secure their political legitimacy in the face of a regime that has successfully captured the narrative of the nation. The ethnic and linguistic Kazakhization of the state administration has been underway since the mid-1990s, and the regime has, at least thus far, been a source of upward social mobility for a large proportion of urban Kazakh youth.[78] National-patriots may claim that the Nazarbayev regime is a-national or anti-national (dominated by ethnic minority oligarchs, selling its resources to foreign firms and so on) but this discourse is too radical to gain broad public support. National-patriots must, therefore, recognize the success of the regime in nationalizing Kazakhstan and work in its shadow.

Many *natspat* acknowledge that they are both repressed and used by the regime against Moscow as involuntary puppets of the president's administration, AkOrda, though this does not undermine their ability to continue to act autonomously as well. One good example of this paradoxical status is Askar Nursha, a young scholar who was dismissed from the Kazakhstan Institute for Strategic Studies under the President after expressing concerns about the benefits of the Eurasian Economic Union but who quickly found a new niche at the no-less-official Institute for World Economy and Politics under the Fund of the First President.[79]

National-patriots themselves disagree on the extent to which their movements are political. Some see the cause as an intellectual trend that will progressively become mainstream with the rise of a post-Nazarbayev generation, while others would like to be politically engaged already and denounce the repression visited on them by the current authorities. Any attempt to organize national-patriotism as a political force has thus far failed. Any claim, for instance, that ethnic Kazakh oligarchs should be preferred over non-Kazakh ones (such as Alexander Mashkevich and Vladimir Kim), a claim that was quietly made by businessmen Nurzhan Subkhanberdin and Mukhtar Ablyazov at the peak of their influence, has been considered a direct attack on Nazarbayev's legitimacy.[80] Aidos Sarym summarizes this dual strategy:

> First possibility: the political landscape will soon be nationalized and all parties will then speak in the state language and define their ideology based on Kazakh culture, traditions and historical background. In that case the creation of a Kazakh political party is not necessary. Why create a Kazakh party if all other parties are Kazakh in spirit and essence? Second possibility: the political system will not modernize and will stay the same. In that case, for sure, the question of creating such a party will emerge. But in that case the debate should be about creating not a party that will advance some questions and topics, but a party that will ask for structural change in the whole political landscape of Kazakhstan.[81]

This quote aptly captures the internal contradiction of nationalism as political activism: once the goal of nationalizing the society and the state is obtained, the existence of a political party calling for nationalism no longer makes sense. Although Kazakhs now represent more than 60 per cent of the population, national-patriots continue to see them as a cultural minority in their own state.

A second issue for the movement to mobilize its potential is that national-patriots have not been able to bridge the gap between rural and urban populations, a schism that remains the main social and cultural divide in the country. National-patriotic literature reproduces the classic topics of the romanticized national awakening of the nineteenth century in Europe and Russia. It mourns the lost authenticity of Kazakh culture, exalts the Kazakh *aul* (village), tries to recreate genuine national values from scratch and complains about the degenerated and Russified 'asphalt Kazakhs'. But while *natspats* dream of reaching a rural audience, they themselves tend to be educated urbanites shaped in the late Soviet and early post-Soviet mould whose lives are largely disconnected from the countryside. Moreover, in order to mobilize rural youth, the issue of Islam and its place in national identity would have to be addressed openly.

Moreover, national-patriotism is still very much centred on the language issue. But once the Kazakh language is rescued from disappearance, which it arguably has been at this point, its symbolic defence will not be enough to support a political project per se. This is the conclusion of the WikiBilim group, a group of young activists that seeks to develop online educational content in the Kazakh language for Wikipedia in order to show the potential of an audience that not only consumes Kazakh-language content but is also capable of producing it.[82]

On the opposite side from these weaknesses, national-patriotism can rely on several strengths. First, Kazakhstan is demographically 'Kazakhifiying' rapidly, a trend projected to accelerate in the next two decades. The demographic gap between Kazakhs and non-Kazakhs is widening fast. In 2013, the natural growth rate of the Kazakh population was 2.3 per cent (though still lower than the 2.6 per cent growth in the Uzbek minority), while that of Russians and Ukrainians was negative at –0.51 and –1.96 per cent, respectively.[83] These demographic trends also impact the average age of each group. In 2013, the average age of Kazakhs was 28.9, compared with 38.5 for Russians, 43 for Ukrainians and 26 for the Uzbek minority.[84] This age gap of about a decade between ethnic groups means than the aging of Russian and Slavic minorities will accelerate, as the majority of them are already past reproductive age. In 20 to 30 years, the number of Russians will decline abruptly because of natural factors; the northern regions will be largely populated by pensioners. This already unbalanced equation tilts further in favour of Kazakhs with the repatriation of more than one million *Oralmans*.

New generations, especially among middle-class and provincial notables, will probably be the ones bearing the flag of Kazakh nationalism, becoming a more significant niche for politicians to capture with more nationalist policy decisions. Already today, some elites do not hide their support for a more pro-Kazakh policy in terms of language, culture and memory, among them Imangali Tasmagambetov, former mayor of Almaty, Astana, and then defence minister; Marat Tazhin, former foreign affairs minister, secretary of the National Security Committee, secretary of Kazakhstan's Security Council, and then ambassador to Russia; Akhmetzhan Yessimov, former mayor of Almaty; Mukhtar Kul Mukhammed, former minister of culture; and Berik Abdylgaliuly, who worked as *akim* (governor) and deputy *akim* in Kostanay and Karaganda. To this list could potentially be added, even if their stances on national-patriotism are less straightforward, Oraz Zhandosov, former deputy prime minister, former minister of finance and economy and the director of the Rakurs Center for Economic Analysis; and Bulat Utemuratov, said to be the richest man in Kazakhstan, who occupies several positions in the presidential administration and served as the president's special advisor on several issues. Moreover, a younger generation is already involved in the presidential party Nur-Otan and the current administration, pushing for a more assertive policy in terms of national identity (see Chapter 10).

The *natspat* movement is thus becoming increasingly visible. In 2009–10, it was mostly intellectual figures, led by Mukhtar Shakhanov, who protested against the Doctrine of National Unity and its mention of a Kazakhstani nation. In 2011, 138 public figures addressed an open letter to President Nazarbayev, the prime minister and the heads of the two chambers of parliament asking them to strip the Russian language of the special status granted to it by the constitution.[85] Since then, the topic of Kazakhstan's relationship with Russia has become the main channel for *natspats* to reach a broader public. This outreach began with public protests outside Russia's embassy and consulates in Astana, Almaty and Uralsk demanding the suspension of Russian rocket launches from Baikonur after a proton rocket crashed in Kzyl-Orda province in 2013. That same year, some 500 people gathered in Almaty to protest against the decision to join the Eurasian Economic Union and to ask for a referendum on the matter.

One of the probable but yet-to-be-explored strengths of national-patriotism in Kazakhstan is its likely ability to capture the current wave of conservative values that is apparent all over the post-Soviet space as well as in Europe. Sociological surveys conducted by the Almaty-based Strategy Centre for Social and Political Research revealed that only 18 per cent of respondents consider Western countries to be a good model for development (European countries received 13 per cent and the United States 5 per cent). Russia collected 22 per cent of said preferences, probably mostly among Russians and Russia-oriented Kazakhstani populations, while the notion that Kazakhstan should build its own path was selected by 43 per cent of respondents.[86] Another survey, conducted in 2014, shows that only 17 per cent of respondents believe that Western values are becoming more and more prevalent in Kazakhstan society, while 69 per cent feel that the culture of Kazakhstan should stay distinctive and resist outside influences and intrusions. One-third suggest that future cultural developments should be based on Kazakh national customs, values and traditions.[87] The current cultural zeitgeist in Kazakhstan therefore appears favourable to stronger nationalist claims.

When Nazarbayev stepped down from the presidency in March 2019, *natspats* hoped to conquer a reactivated public space. With the help of some patrons inside the system, a group led by Amirzhan Kosanov launched Jana Qazaqstan (New Kazakhstan), a new movement with a nationalist agenda. Key figures in the movement include Nazira Darimbet, Aidos Sarym and Rasul Zhumaly. Kosanov has a long history of political opposition, having worked with former prime minister Akezhan Kazhegeldin and then for the more nationalist Azat party. On 9 June 2019, during the presidential elections set up to elect Nazarbayev's successor, Kassym-Jomart Tokayev, Kosanov secured the highest vote share of any opposition candidate in the history of independent Kazakhstan: 16 per cent. However, he undermined his legitimacy by recognizing Tokayev's victory without even trying to leverage the votes he had won to secure a voice in the new government.

This disappointing post-electoral performance confirmed that the nationalist movement does not yet constitute a genuine opposition but remains more of a lobby within the current political system. Indeed, such a reality is hardly unique to Kazakhstan; in neighbouring Russia, nationalists have likewise experienced a 'managed' relationship with the authorities that sometimes allows them to be vocally critical but more often leaves them as part of the rank-and-file supporting the government. Jana Qazaqstan's announcement that they might transform the movement into an official political party would likewise follow the pattern established in Russia by the likes of Dmitri Rogozin's Rodina party.

Jana Qazaqstan's posture thus highlights the limits of the national-patriotic opposition: beyond defending ethnic Kazakhs' rights, its ability to advance a credible political agenda seems quite modest so far. The movement's political programme limits itself to principled statements about democracy, ethnocentric Turkic solidarity, leaving the Eurasian Economic Union, and criticizing Russia and China, but remaining vague on concrete economic and political reforms (except regarding private land ownership) and sound foreign policy measures. Moreover, while nationalist sentiments are on the rise among youth, the very limited social media presence of Jana Qazaqstan has called into question its ability to develop broader strategies for securing support among urban youth and to reach out to the rural population by other means.

The landscape of Kazakh nationalism or national-patriotism remains only loosely structured. Compared to the structures that exist in Russia, Ukraine or the Baltic states, it seems to still be in its infancy. But when viewed in the context of neighbouring Central Asian states, this national-patriotic trend has become an active part of society in a relatively similar manner as it has in Kyrgyzstan, although with a critical difference:

Kazakhstan has been able to avoid mass inter-ethnic riots (skirmishes between ethnic groups do happen regularly but on a very localized basis, mostly in rural areas between Kazakhs and Uzbeks, Dungans, Uyghurs, Chechens or Turks), while Kyrgyzstan's political life has been shaped to a not insignificant degree by the tensions between the Kyrgyz majority and the Uzbek minority.

Kazakh national-patriots occupy small niches: they dominate some cultural institutions, often state-sponsored but with limited outreach, and now use social media to spread their message and overcome their lack of political organization. Many groups recognize that before even trying a Gramscian strategy of penetrating the state and energizing the official political and intellectual life, national-patriots should focus on cultural enlightenment (*prosveshchenie*) in order to raise awareness among the population about what they consider to be critical issues for the future of the nation.

Kazakh national-patriots also display classic identity anxieties and post-colonial narratives. They feel alienated in their own country and have difficulties moulding an autonomous space for self-expression. They find themselves either co-opted by the authorities (if they agree to rally behind official institutions that promote Kazakh language and culture) or marginalized and sometimes penalized by a heavily developed bureaucracy. But their main difficulty has been more structural: given the success of the Nazarbayev regime in capturing the national identity narrative, the national-patriots have little room to attract an audience. To enjoy the new space opened by Nazarbayev's departure from the presidency, *natspats* will have to demonstrate that they have a structured political project to offer: fighting for the symbols of the nation does not say anything about the nature of the regime they would promote (democratic, hybrid, authoritarian), nor about its values and ideological orientations (pro-Western or not, with Islam as one of its main values or not), nor about the economic policies it would implement to keep citizens' standards of living on their upward trajectory.

National-patriots will also have to prove that a cosmopolitan nationalist elite can legitimately represents a rural Kazakh society that is mostly interested in upward social mobility and economic prospects. Valuing the *aul* as the place of authenticity of Kazakh values does not illuminate any clear economic development strategy. Integrating the *Oralmans* has shown obvious limits and anti-*Oralman* xenophobia has developed among ethnic Kazakhs themselves. To the despair of national-patriots, many ordinary Kazakhs find it easier to coexist with Russians than with *Oralmans*: Soviet and post-Soviet shared values remain a more efficient 'glue' for building a civic identity than a reconstructed and artificial pan-Kazakh identity. Feelings of belonging are much more embedded in 'banal nationalism' than in the existence of a theoretical nation. To be successful, therefore, national-patriots will have to come to terms with the Russian and Soviet past of the Kazakh nation and integrate it in a more positive way into their ideological construct.

Notes

1 See Beisembayev, *Fenomen kazakhskogo natsionalizma*.
2 To protect the activists, I will not attribute any of the quotations to any one individual.
3 Koshim, 'Kazakhskii natsionalizm – positivnyi natsionalizm'. See also Koshim, 'Natsional'nye problemy nevozmozhno reshit' bez politicheskikh reform'.
4 Kudaibergenova, 'O natsii i ee nositeliakh'.
5 See, for instance, the book by Zhakupov, *Shala Kazakh*.
6 Kudaibergenova, 'Mankurts, Kazakh "Russians" and "Shala" Kazakhs'.
7 Abdylgaliuly (ed.), *Kazakhskaia missiia*.
8 Nurov, *Kazakhstan*.
9 See their website, http://www.aspandau.kz.
10 See Ayaganov, *Politicheskie partii i obshchestvennye dvizheniia sovremennogo Kazakhstana*, 62–6, 77–80.
11 Kuzio, 'Nationalist Riots in Kazakhstan', 79–100. See also, for later events, Ro'i, 'Central Asian Riots and Disturbances', 21–54. During the *Zheltoksan* (Kaz.: December) riots in Almaty, the student crowds protested against the nomination of a Russian for a position that had been traditionally given to a Kazakh, seeing this as an unacceptable act of humiliation on Moscow's part.
12 Kusherbaev, *Etnopolitika Kazakhstana*, 130.
13 'Oppozitsionnaia partiia obviniatsia v izbienii muftiia'.
14 'Oskorbili prezidenta Kazakhstana'.
15 Akkuly, 'Kogda kazakhskii dissident saditsia v tiur'mu'.
16 Pen International, 'Take Action for Aron Atabek'.
17 Consulter Programma grazhdanskogo dvizheniia Azat.
18 On the general political situation of Kazakhstan in the 1990s, see Brill Olcott, *Kazakhstan*. On the hunger strike, see Kagarlitski, 'Kazakhstan's Parliament is Dissolved'.
19 On these three parties, see Babak et al. (eds), *Political Organization in Central Asia and Azerbaijan*, 99–104, 107–13, and 175–8.
20 Kudaibergenova, *Re-Writing the Nation*.
21 Shakhanov, 'A Report on Commission Proceedings'.
22 'Honored Figure of Kazakhstan, Doctor of Philology Tursynbek Kakishev'.
23 See more in Kudaibergenova, *Re-Writing the Nation*.
24 Landau and Kellner-Heinkele, *Politics of Language in the Ex-Soviet Muslim States,* 87.
25 Not to be confused with the official *Kazakhstanskaia pravda*.
26 'Umer Aldan Aimbetov'.
27 See, respectively, Yuritsyn, '"Taszhardan" ("Dat") okonchil desiatiletku' and Yuritsyn, 'Ezhenedel'nik "Ashyq Alan" ("Tribuna")'.
28 See the website http://rus.alash-orda.kz.
29 'Gde nakhoditsia cherep poslednego kazakhskogo khana Kenesary?'. See also Akkuly, 'Bez golovy Kenesary khana prazdnovanie 550-letiia Kazakhskogo khanstva budet nepolnym'.
30 'Dvizhenie Ult tagdyry predstavilo svoi proekt zakona o gosudarstvennom iazyke'.
31 'Kazakh National Patriots Urge Ethnic Russians to Go Home'.
32 Mavlonii, 'V Kazakhstane khotiat prazdnovat'z'.

33 'Novye trebovaniia registratsii protivorechat Konstitutsii i ne reshaiut problem – Dos Koshim'.
34 'Dvizhenie Ult Tagdyry-el tagdyry pereimenovalos' v Khalyk dabyly'.
35 Human Rights Watch, 'Kazakhstan: Two Activists Detained. Vague Criminal Charge Used to Target Critics'.
36 Dauren Babamurat, interviewed by the author, Almaty, 20 June 2015. See also 'Dauren Babamuratov, rukovoditel' molodezhnogo dvizheniia Bolashaq'.
37 Kovalev, 'V Kazakhstane Den' Koza Korpesh i Bayan-Suly pochti nikto ne prazdnuet'.
38 'Kazakhstan Looks to Ban Gay 'Propaganda''.
39 Tat'iana Alad'ina, 'Destvennitsy atakuiut'.
40 See, as early as 2011, the very critical article by Sagatova, 'Novaia politicheskaia zvezda Kazakhstana, ili Mal'chik dlia provokatsii Zhanbolat Mamay?'.
41 Mamashuly, 'Protivniki soiuza govoriat o roli Nazarbaeva'.
42 'Aktivisty boiatsia "evraziiskogo razmyvaniia RK"'.
43 'V Kazakhstane protivniki sozdaniia soiuza s Rossiei nadeli meditsinskie maski'.
44 On the riots, see Satpayev and Umbetaliyeva, 'The Protests in Zhanaozen and the Kazakh Oil Sector'. More broadly, see Howie and Atakhanova, 'Resource Boom and Inequality'.
45 'Zhanbolat Released from Arrest'.
46 'V RK rassleduiut delo po faktu razzhiganiia mezhnatsional'noi rozni'.
47 See https://www.facebook.com/Antigeptil.
48 'Prigovo molodomu oppozitsioneru Makhambetu Abzhanu ostalsia bez izmenenii'.
49 See the newspaper's website, http://zhasalash.kz.
50 See the group's Facebook page, https://www.facebook.com/QazaqOrda.
51 'Kazakhskaia Pravda vykhodit na tropu voiny?'.
52 See Fierman (ed.) 'Implementing Language Laws'.
53 'Dvizhenie Ult tagdyry predstavilo svoi proekt zakona o gosudarstvennom iazyke'.
54 *Kazakhskaia pravda* 6, 4.
55 Young nationalist activists, interviewed by the author, Almaty, June 2015.
56 Svanberg, 'Kazakhs'.
57 Koshim, 'Za kazakhov ia umru. Ia natsionalist'.
58 Aldan Aimbetov, interviewed by the author, Almaty, March 2002.
59 Young nationalist activists, interviewed by the author, Almaty, June 2015.
60 The purges resulted in about 100,000 people being arrested and 25,000 executed in the Kazakh SSR alone.
61 'V Kazakhstane otmechaiut den' pamiati zhertv politicheskikh repressii'.
62 Cameron, *The Hungry Steppe*.
63 'Genotsid kazakhov (Makash Tatimov, chast' 1)'.
64 '"Asharshylyk" Kalila Umarov Film – KALILAFILM.kz'.
65 'Smotret' vsem! Zulmat. Zulmat. Genotsid v. Kazakhstane. Asharshylyk turaly derekti fil'm!'.
66 See Bassin, *The Gumilev Mystique*.
67 Atabek, 'Serdtse Evrazii ili Velikii Ariiskii Kaganat Altyn-Orda'.
68 'Znaete, kakim on parnem byl?'.
69 'Zharylkap Kalybay: Propaganda Gitlera ne bylo, vy khotia by prochitaite!'.
70 'Zharylkap Kaylbay: ia ne opravdyvaiu fashizm / 1612'.
71 Lillis, 'Kazakhstan: China Looking to Lease Land for Agricultural Purposes'.
72 Sarym, 'Kazakhstan vybyraet tiurko-evropeiskii vektor'.
73 Atabek, 'Odin bog, odna religiia, odna ideologiia, odin narod'.
74 Koshim, 'Za kazakhov ia umru. Ia natsionalist'.
75 Kusherbaev, *Etnopolitika Kazakhstana: sostoianie i perspektivy*, 130.
76 Atabek, 'Odin bog, odna religiia, odna ideologiia, odin narod'.
77 'Deputat Bekbolat Tleukhan proshel proverku na detektore lzhi'.
78 Fierman, 'Changing Urban Demography'.
79 He signed a collective petition against Kazakhstan's entry into the Union. See 'Kazakhstanskie politologi protiv vkhozhdeniia Kazakhstana v Evraziiskii soiuz'.
80 See Peyrouse, 'The Kazakh Neopatrimonial Regime'.
81 Sarym, 'Edinym kazakhskim frontom'.

82 Rauan Kenzhekhanuly, interviewed by the author at the International Conference 'Youth in Kazakhstan: Societal Changes, Challenges and Opportunities', George Washington University, Washington, DC, 21 April 2014.

83 *Etnodemograficheskii ezhegodnik Kazakhstana*. I thank Aitolkyn Kourmanova for providing me with these figures.

84 *Etnodemograficheskii ezhegodnik Kazakhstana*.

85 'Pis'mo 138–mi: vzryvoopasnoe obrashechenie i kto stoit za nim?'.

86 Beisembayev, 'Tendentsii sotsial'no-demograficheskogo razvitiia kazakhstanskogo obshchestva'.

87 Institute of Eurasian Integration, 'Sovremennoe sostoianie i tendentsii vsekazakhstanskoi kul'tury'. See also, even if from 2009, *Ideologicheskie ustanovki i osobennosti identifikatsii naseleniia RK*.

10
Generational changes: the Nazarbayev Generation

In March 2019, Nursultan Nazarbayev stepped down from the presidency, a post that he had held since Kazakhstan's independence. This was not intended to be a departure from politics altogether: indeed, Nazarbayev had planned to remain in power through tailor-made institutions. Yet this strategy has not been playing out quite as intended. Although Nazarbayev's official successor, then-speaker of the upper house of parliament Kassym-Jomart Tokayev, was indeed elected and received 71 per cent of the vote, there were serious protests criticizing the handpicking of a successor and the non-transparency of the vote. The first protests began just after Tokayev proposed renaming Astana Nur-Sultan in honour of the president. Shocked by the lack of public consultation on a gesture that so clearly smacked of a cult of personality, protesters took to the streets under the slogan 'Nur-Sultan is not my city'. In the weeks that followed, protest sentiment grew steadily, with several thousand protesters turning out in both Almaty and Nur-Sultan, chanting slogans such as 'Old man out' (*shal ket*). The authorities decided to react with repression: several prosecutions and arrests of leaders took place, a clear sign that the change in president was in no way a change in regime, a transition toward democracy, or any kind of liberalizing perestroika.

Even if the protests have seen a large number of retired people, especially mothers, taking advantage of the current unstable context to express resentment, most of the protesters have been young people. These young people were all born under Nazarbayev's reign – those aged under 29 comprise 9 million people, or 51 per cent of the population of Kazakhstan – and hence represent what can be called the Nazarbayev Generation. They have no direct memory of the Soviet regime, only family recollections, though many of them do recall their parents' struggles in the difficult first decade of the country's independence. Since the early

2000s, they have lived in a world of political stability and relative material affluence, developing a strong consumerist culture. Even with growing government restrictions on media, religion and formal public expression, they have been raised in a comparatively free country. Who are they? What do they think and wish for? What are their social and cultural practices and behaviours? How do they see the world and Kazakhstan's place therein?

Sociological research on Kazakhstani society

Research on Kazakhstan to date has focused primarily on state construction, elite-level discourses, foreign policy, security issues and economic strategies. Studies of social and societal transformations, meanwhile, have remained peripheral. For a long time, there was no tradition of sociological surveys in the country – except those commissioned by state institutions, which are classified, often of mediocre quality and deploy doubtful methodologies – and few cultural anthropologists looking at the micro-level. However, things have changed in the past decade: we now have a whole generation of scholars, both Kazakhstani and foreign, who have been collecting sociological data and conducting interviews to gather local voices, offering both quantitative and qualitative insights into the evolutions of Kazakhstani society.

Youth – the most rapidly changing and receptive segment of Kazakhstani society – has been one of the main objects of this new wave of research that is transforming our knowledge of the country and helping us move beyond the usual clichés about 'Nazarbayev-stan'. It is not that the natural change of generations was heretofore ignored by scholars and the policy community; the expectation of a presidential transition has always been accompanied by discourses about the long-awaited arrival in power of new generations. But the view of these generations was oversimplified, focusing on their political and geopolitical orientations almost to the exclusion of their social and cultural practices. A black-and-white narrative cast the Bolashak generation – those trained abroad under the Kazakhstani state programme, who supposedly represented the liberal, Western-oriented youth of their day – in stark contrast with the desperate provincial youth, who were seen as being motivated by jihadism and as going to volunteer in the Syrian war theatre.

We now have at our disposal several categories of surveys. Among the biggest data sets comparing several tens of countries, Kazakhstan was surveyed by Asia Barometer in 2005,[1] World Values Survey in 2011,[2]

Life in Transition in 2006 and 2010,[3] the Pew Research Center in 2012 and 2013[4] and Gallup every year since 2006.[5] Several UN institutions have included Kazakhstan in their surveys, among them the United Nations Population Fund (UNFPA), the International Organization for Migration (IOM) and the International Labour Organization (ILO). Some foreign organizations have likewise conducted public opinion polls in Kazakhstan, such as the International Republican Institute between 2008 and 2011[6] and Friedrich Ebert Stiftung on youth in four Central Asian countries in 2015.[7] At the regional level, several institutions have also carried out surveys, often but not always focusing on questions relating to regional integration. Examples include Central Asia Barometer,[8] Eurasian Integration Monitor[9] and the Eurasian Development Bank.[10] In 2015, the Broadcasting Board of Governors (BBG) and Gallup published a series of surveys, conducted across the whole post-Soviet region, looking at Russian media influence.[11] In 2007 and 2012, Barbara and Azamat Junisbai conducted, with the Kazakhstan-based BRIF Research Group, two large surveys of between 2,000 and 3,000 interviewees, funded by the National Council for Eurasian and East European Research (NCEEER) and the National Science Foundation (NSF), comparing Kazakhstan and Kyrgyzstan.

To these should be added a long list of smaller nationwide surveys conducted by teams of local and/or foreign researchers. The government-funded research centre Molodezh' (meaning 'Youth') publishes a national report every year.[12] In 2010, Kazakhstan's Department for Youth Policy and the Centre for Analysis and Prognosis conducted a survey designed to gauge patriotism among young people. Data was collected in all fourteen oblasts, as well as the two cities of Almaty and Astana.[13] In 2017, the Institute of World Economy and Politics (IWEP) conducted a survey offering rare insight into Kazakhstani citizens' perceptions of the media.[14] The 'Strategiya' Center for Social and Political Research has implemented several surveys and polls commissioned by different institutions on topics ranging from youth to the media market.[15]

At a more individual level, Ro'i and Wainer conducted 700 interviews on religious identity in 2006;[16] Al-Farabi Kazakh National University surveyed young people on the 'Formation of Civic and Patriotic Education among Youth in Kazakhstan';[17] and the private Narxoz University, which teaches primarily economics to a student body of roughly 8,000 millennials and post-millennials, surveyed 1,500 schoolchildren (from ninth to eleventh grade) from Atyrau, Pavlodar, Shymkent, Kyzylorda and Semey in 2017.[18] Nazgul Mingisheva conducted a survey with 94 students at Karaganda State Medical University in 2015–17, and

Galym Zhussipbek and Zhanar Nagayeva distributed questionnaires to students of the private Suleyman Demirel atindagi Universitet in Almaty and the state medical university in Semey, as well as to working youth in Almaty and Atyrau.[19]

Needless to say, surveys geared toward generalizability may overlook context-specific understandings and local interpretations of terminology. Yet when taken together and complemented by cultural anthropological studies based on qualitative interviews, they shed light on the new directions taken by this Nazarbayev Generation.

Value-realm of a conformist generation

Based on this new wealth of data, what can we say about the Nazarbayev Generation? First, that 'generation' should probably be plural: there are in fact already two generations, Generation Y (born in the late 1980s and 90s, and also known as millennials) and Generation Z (those born in the 2000s). In many ways, Kazakhstani members of generations Y and Z are not so different from youth elsewhere in the world; they are in fact far more similar to each other than were their counterparts in previous generations. They are, for instance, all 'digital natives', living in a visual culture where one often communicates with images rather than with text;[20] they are obsessed with immediacy and community feedback; and they do not like planning for the future.[21] They are environmentally aware, think globally, favour blending cultures, embrace DIY (do-it-yourself) and are politically indifferent but believe in co-creative mechanisms.

The Nazarbayev Generation is quite conformist in its life goals: it believes in family values, marriage, having children, healthy living and material comfort. Young Kazakhstanis are not, on the whole, attracted to a quest for knowledge and see higher education only as a tool for getting a good job; they trust that having the right social connections will help them build their lives and careers.[22] They are far from a revolutionary generation: they do not challenge their parents' values and ways of life, trust family more than any other institution and, overwhelmingly (more than 90 per cent) view their relationships with their parents positively.[23]

They still differ from older cohorts in some respects: they are more individualistic and believe in their uniqueness; they are better disposed toward elements of a market economy, such as a private sector, entrepreneurship and a banking system; they display greater respect for individual success; and they are less troubled by social inequality and, therefore, less supportive of the state addressing this inequality.[24] In essence, they are the children of the economic liberalism that has shaped independent Kazakhstan. Consequently, the feeling of being affected by a class divide is mentioned by only one-third of young ethnic Kazakhs – with the Atyrau region showing the highest levels. Social inequality appears to be a very serious concern for some ethnic minorities, such as Ukrainians and Chechens, but not for Russians.[25]

Kazakhstani youths' support for economic liberalism does not translate into them being specifically favourable toward a democratic regime or liberal values. The 2011 World Values Survey found that all generations broadly supported the vague principles of a 'democratic system' (while also desiring a 'strong leader'), but that 18- to 29-year-olds were, if anything, somewhat less supportive (84 per cent compared to 90 per cent among those over 50, for example).[26] Similarly, research conducted by Barbara Junisbai, Azamat Junisbai and Christopher Whitsel demonstrates that 18- to 29-year-old Kazakhstanis are significantly *less* likely to express support for democracy than previous generations – or even their generational counterparts in Kyrgyzstan. Less than a quarter of them believe that 'citizens should be more active in questioning the actions of leaders', compared to 87 per cent of the population as a whole.[27] While two-thirds of youths declare that they are occasionally interested in politics, less than 10 per cent of them discuss politics with family and friends or participate in any form of civic activism.[28] As Junisbai, Junisbai and Whitsel conclude, 'In Kazakhstan, young people appear to be socialized in accordance with both aspects of the political context under consideration ...: presidential authoritarianism, which in Kazakhstan has a distinctly paternalistic flavor, and patronage politics'.[29] The 2015 Friedrich Ebert Stiftung survey confirms how low altruism and participation in citizens' initiatives fall on youths' lists of priorities. They are quite happy with society as it is, considering women, ethnic minorities and the religious to have sufficient rights.[30]

Just as they are not actively pro-democracy, Kazakh youths are not especially attracted to so-called Western values. A survey conducted in 2015 by Friedrich Ebert Stiftung found that 47 per cent of youth identified Russia as the country to which Kazakhstan should look for its development, while only 19 per cent felt that Europe should be the foremost model, 10 per cent China and 8 per cent the US.[31] However, there are several definitions of liberal values. A more refined perception of these values helps dissociate the rejection of liberalism in the sense of neoliberalism and identity politics – laissez-faire capitalism and the promotion of individual sexual and ethnic differences – from the backing of a more traditional liberalism – a responsible social democracy that provides good public services and protects basic individual rights.[32]

Changing benchmarks in national identity and language

In terms of national identity, Kazakhstan's youth population displays a complex combination of civic and ethnic identities. This reflects Kazakhstan's ambivalent conception of nationhood as a whole, which is torn between the promotion of an inclusive Kazakhstani identity focused on prosperity and a Kazakh-centric identity that celebrates Kazakhstan as the homeland of ethnic Kazakhs. Raised with this ambivalence, Kazakhstani youth echo its main features: ethnic identity continues to be most authoritative, but references to Kazakhstani identity are also on the rise. Even if youth do not spontaneously identify as Kazakhstani, they show strong patriotism, believing in the country, seeing their future in it, and supporting an inclusive definition of the nation based on territorial identity.[33] However, this Kazakhstani identity does not take the form of the kind of Kazakh-Russian/Slavic compromise expressed by the Eurasianist state identity. The non-ethnic identity that emerges is a result of globalization and cosmopolitanism more than any specific position in Kazakhstani nationhood vis-à-vis Russia. The symbolic identity battle is thus waged between a closed, isolationist Kazakh identity and an open, globalized Kazakh identity, with the median Russian/Slavic/Eurasian level now only one of many elements of the latter.

This identity shift is supported by profound demographic evolutions. Among youth, ethnic Kazakhs' dominance is now secured: in 2013, ethnic Kazakhs represented 66 per cent of the 25- to 29-year-old cohort and 71–3 per cent of every younger age group.[34] The demographic rebalancing in favour of Kazakhs has also been reinforced by the government's repatriation policy. While it is difficult to collect detailed demographic data on *Oralmans*, it seems that more than half of them are of working age and 40 per cent are children,[35] meaning that *Oralman* youth represent at least half a million people, further tipping Kazakhstan's younger cohorts in the direction of Kazakh ethnicity.

The dominance of ethnic Kazakhs among younger age cohorts does not automatically translate into a decrease in knowledge of Russian, however. On the contrary, this knowledge has been growing over the years. At the last Soviet census of 1989, 64 per cent of Kazakhstan's ethnic Kazakhs reported having Russian as their first or second language, while by 1999, this number had risen to 75 per cent.[36] The level of Russian fluency had risen even further by 2009, when 79 per cent reported the ability to write fluently in Russian, 84 per cent the ability to read Russian fluently, and 92 per cent the ability to understand spoken Russian.[37] Kazakhstan's next census, to be conducted in late 2020, will provide an indication of whether this trend is continuing or reversing.

But if the Russian language is enduring or maybe even becoming more widespread in Kazakhstan, it is not at the expense of the Kazakh language. On the contrary, it currently appears that both Kazakh *and* Russian are strengthening (or, at the very least, maintaining) their positions, meaning that the government's ambition of making virtually its entire population fluent in both languages is not unrealistic.[38] The share of Kazakhstanis who fluently write, read and understand Kazakh rises sharply with the younger generations. In 2009, among those under the age of 29, at least 80 per cent indicated that they understood some Kazakh, meaning that Kazakh is gradually gaining legitimacy as a national language the knowledge of which is unavoidable even for non-Kazakhs. Indeed, 55 per cent of young ethnic Russians agreed that every citizen of Kazakhstan should know the Kazakh language.[39]

The authorities hoped to spread the Kazakh language far more rapidly than turned out to be possible and passed laws upon laws trying to make it an influential language in the public space. Where voluntarist policy failed, demography succeeded: members of new generations arriving at school and university now more often speak Kazakh than Russian. Language use in schools is thus progressively shifting. As seen in Figure 10.1, 55 per cent of Kazakhstani students were studying in Kazakh and 41 per cent in Russian in 2003.[40] 15 years later, between 2017 and 2018, 66 per cent were studying in Kazakh and just 31 per cent in Russian. This 10 per cent decrease in Russian-language education reflects ongoing demographic change: by 2013, 73 per cent of schoolchildren were Kazakh, while only 16 per cent were Russian. Yet as Figure 10.1 shows, the number of pupils studying in Russian has been gradually increasing again since 2015 – which, given that the number of ethnic Russians continues to decline, means that ethnic Kazakhs and some minorities continue to choose a Russian-language education over a Kazakh-language one.

The broad rebalancing of the language of education in favour of Kazakh supports the policy of boosting Kazakh at the official level and in the media and cultural realm. This is complemented by Kazakhstan's trilingual policy, which advocates English as the third language of education. Mentioned by Nursultan Nazarbayev in his address to the nation in 2007 and then codified in several official documents,[41] this trilingual policy has been piloted in a network of 33 schools for gifted children as well

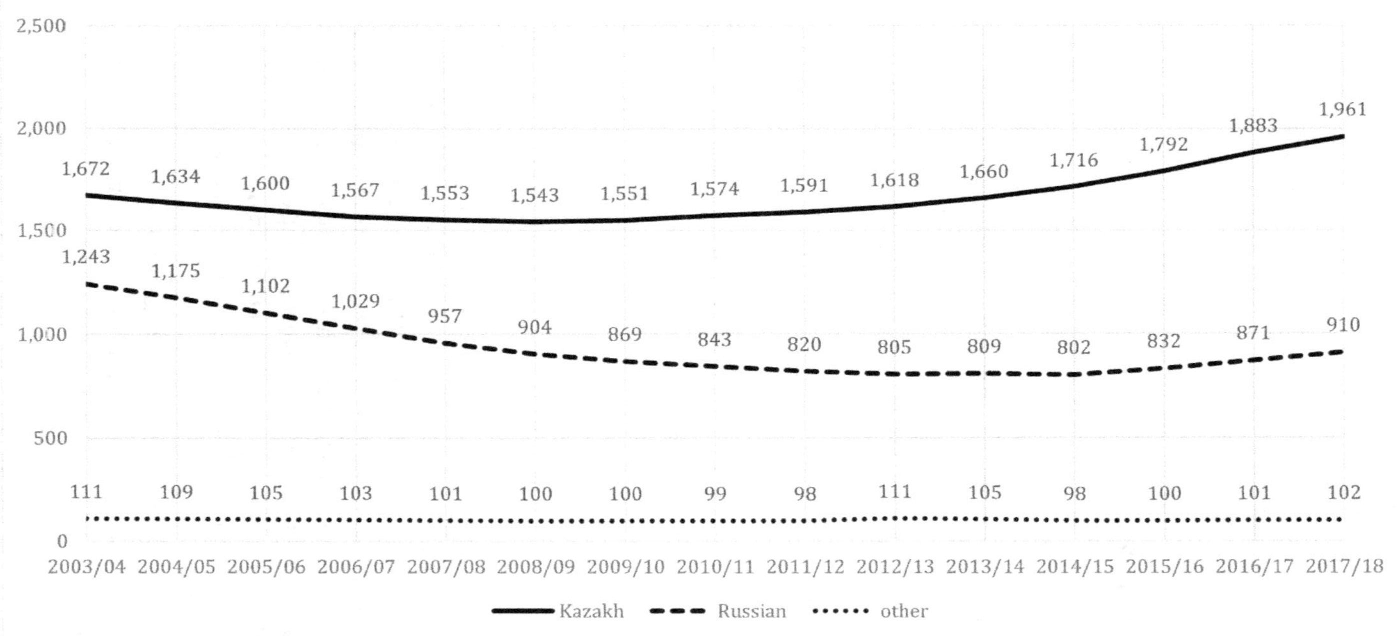

Figure 10.1 Grade school students in Kazakhstan by language of study, as a proportion of the total, 2003–18. Source: Statistical Agency of the Republic of Kazakhstan. 'Chislennost' uchashhikhsia obshheobrazovatel'nykh shkol po yazykam obucheniia, tysiach chelovek', 2018.

as in the Nazarbayev Intellectual Schools, with the (failed) hope of reaching 40 per cent of schools by 2020.[42] Not only was this roadmap obviously unrealistic in terms of time, but the push for trilingualism also dramatically weakens an already low-quality education. However, it does demonstrate how the Kazakhstani regime aims to artificially reduce the role of the Russian language by replacing it with English.

Norms and behaviours: a polarized generation

More than previous age cohorts, the Nazarbayev Generation is polarized in many of its norms, behaviours and values. This polarization is especially pronounced on issues related to so-called national traditions, especially those related to gender, which has become one of the fastest-evolving realms of identity worldwide. The relationship between genders is a central question for many youth, not only because they are at an age when gender identity takes a more 'definitive' form – in sexual orientation, marriage strategies and professional opportunities for women – but also because of the need to navigate contradictory cultural pressures. On the one hand, Kazakhstan has been re-traditionalizing gender roles: young people are expected to fulfil the roles conventionally associated with their genders and engage in the 'proper' behaviour for their cultural and social group.[43] On the other hand, youth have become accustomed to cultural products from abroad in which traditional gender identities are often challenged or transgressed.[44]

Additionally, the value codes espoused by youths depend on whether they are urban or rural, whether or not they are accustomed to travelling abroad and being in contact with foreigners, and the regional contexts from which they come. Indeed, regional differences are strong in today's Kazakhstan, with the western and southern regions remaining more traditional. Youth in Shymkent, for instance, are more conservative when it comes to issues associated with ethnicity – they position themselves less in favour of inter-ethnic marriages and of friendships with those from different ethnic groups, and prefer to associate with ethnic Kazakhs or Uzbeks over Russians – while youth in Astana and Almaty appear more cosmopolitan and more open to Russianness.[45] However, their everyday interactions with ethnic Russians or Slavs in the urban environment also make young Kazakh urbanites more likely to insist on their ethnic identity than their rural counterparts.[46]

Moral conservatism dominates Kazakhstani society. Homosexuality is understood as a deviance and is disapproved of by 60 per cent of ethnic

Kazakhs (45 per cent of ethnic Russians), with one-third neutral and only 3.4 per cent approving.[47] Two-thirds of youths oppose abortion and think it should be illegal or authorized only for medical reasons.[48] Preference is given to a traditional vision of family; women's chastity is valued even if pre-marital sex is globally accepted. Many young ethnic Kazakhs would like three to five children, but without any preference for boys over girls.[49] About 20 per cent of ethnic Kazakhs (less among ethnic Russians) favour polygamy. One-third of youth neither condemn nor accept bride kidnapping, often excusing it as a 'traditional' norm. Young people are quite equally divided between those who consider men and women to have equal social roles and those who see the man as the breadwinner and head of the family. Globally, ethnic Kazakhs are more conservative than ethnic Russians, as are rural dwellers over urbanites. Yet some segments of youth do criticize their traditional patriarchal society, including their parents' promotion of authoritarian behaviours at home, and challenge conservative norms by listening to music such as Q-pop band Ninety-One and hip-hop artist Scriptonite.

Religion is not directly associated with the re-traditionalization of gender norms, even if the two are often considered to be connected for those who link gender identity to Islamic values. On that matter, too, the Nazarbayev Generation is more polarized than their elders, with some groups advancing clear secular values and others promoting a more religious sensibility. A sizable majority of young people (80 per cent) consider themselves religious, would like to see religion play a bigger role in the country, and would welcome more religious education, but do not actively take part in any religious practices.[50] Among youths, one also notes the rise of practices such as not drinking alcohol, fasting during the month of Ramadan and performing *zakat* (giving alms to the poor and needy), but religious duties such as daily prayer are performed only by a tiny minority (about 6 per cent).[51]

Religious identity is growing faster than religious practice: halal food and Islamic fashion have become 'trendy' in some circles.[52] These new urban codes are particularly widespread among the middle classes involved in the private sector, for whom a bourgeois Islam goes hand-in-hand with advancing Islamic business ethics and copycatting patterns inspired by globalized Emirati-style entrepreneurs.[53] Social tensions within Muslim communities and in their interactions with secular segments of society are dominated by debates about female dress code, since the topic embodies issues of purity, morality, self-respect and the call for more control over a rapidly evolving society. References to Shari'a as religious orthodoxy, largely absent from Central Asian traditions, have emerged: the share of Kazakhstani people who felt that it would be 'very important' for good government to adopt laws in line with Shari'a more than doubled between 2007 (5.45 per cent) and 2012 (13.04 per cent),[54] independent of age cohort.

Another factor accentuating this polarization has been the socioeconomic opportunities (or lack thereof) offered to young people. Officially, more than 96 per cent of working-age youth do work, but of these, 16 per cent are self-employed, making them vulnerable in terms of job stability.[55] Moreover, about one-third of young Kazakhstanis of working age worked informally in 2017, without the protection of a labour contract, with lower wages and often in poor working conditions. Meanwhile, about 350,000 Kazakhstani youth have been found to be neither employed nor enrolled in any educational institution and are thus classified as NEET (not in employment, education, or training). This number has been growing since 2012, especially in the southern and western regions, indicating that many young people face the challenge of a skills mismatch: they lack the competencies that would make them attractive to employers.[56] Globally, the rural/urban gap is even more pronounced for the Nazarbayev Generation than for older generations: rural exodus and migration to cities constitutes one of the main social transformations since the country's independence, yet 43 per cent of youth still live in rural regions with noticeably less socioeconomic opportunities.

Some regions of Kazakhstan now constitute poverty pockets, in which prospects for youth are minimal. Petty crime thus presents itself as a path out of poverty for many youths (especially males) in search of a social role. As studied by Serik Beysembayev, cultural codes of masculinity and group solidarity among criminal networks and Islamic militant groups are quite similar, creating some capillarity between the two worlds.[57] Research done by Noah Tucker and his team on Rudnik, Satpayev and Kengir, near Zhezkazgan, for instance, has shown how deteriorated local conditions have been a push factor for jihadist radicalization.[58]

On the other side of the spectrum, among the upper and middle classes, many young people have had a chance to study abroad. In 2018, almost 90,000 Kazakhstan students studied abroad, mostly in Russia (69,000), followed by Kyrgyzstan (almost 5,000), and then Turkey, the US, the UK and the Czech Republic, at between 1,500 and 1,900 apiece.[59] While in the minority, 13,000 were able to get Bolashak state scholarships for this study abroad, and these young people now constitute the country's rising elite in state administration and big public and private firms.[60]

Wherever young people study abroad, a stay away from home often leads to a change in the components of their self-identification, obscuring some while reinforcing others. The repertoires of normalcy, in terms of both values and social practices related to gender issues, body language and family and community ties, may undergo important shifts. This negotiation is sometimes successful, leading to individual empowerment, but may fail if people believe cultural borrowings will be rejected by their native environment.[61]

Youth cultural ecosystems

Kazakhstani youth live in a highly connected world dominated by second-generation social media such as Instagram, Telegram and WhatsApp.[62] Internet penetration has been growing rapidly: as of 2018, 80 per cent of the Kazakhstani population had access to the internet, and the country leads Central Asia for the number of mobile internet users (more than 6 million active users via notebooks and smartphones) and for access to 3G and 4G.[63] Of the approximately 125,000 Facebook users in Kazakhstan in 2016, 45 per cent were aged 26 to 34 and 20 per cent were aged 18 to 24.[64]

YouTube plays a key role in shaping youth culture. In Kazakhstan, the most popular channel is the private music channel Gakku, which has 1.4 million subscribers and 892 million views, followed by Seventh Channel, known for its Kazakh-speaking sitcoms, and Yuframe, which presents small video sketches, social videos and pranks, watched 141 million times with over 635,000 subscribers.[65] But Kazakhstani youth are also globalized through cultural consumption: US and European channels, movies and bands dominate, but Turkish, South Korean and Indian productions have been growing in popularity in recent years, especially among female viewers.[66] Russian culture remains important, but it is no more than one of a plurality of both foreign and domestic products being consumed.

For the Nazarbayev Generation, finding the right balance between cultural authenticity and globalization is a central question. Indeed, Kazakhstani youth find themselves quite divided on critical components of identity. The norms of Kazakhness are still in the process of being defined and several contradictory trends create points of contention. We can observe this in the growing labelling of those who remain too close to Soviet/Russian references as *sovki* and the even more pronounced divisions between supposed *nagyz* and *shala* (see Chapter 9). Complementing this binary vision, young people have also developed an interest in genealogical identifications as a way to discuss cultural differences within the Kazakh nation. References to the *juz* have always been present in everyday discourse and social interactions in Kazakhstan, but youth are now divided on the issue: half of them think that *juz* connections matter, while the other half do not.[67] Youth interest has been shifting, in fact, toward sub-ethnic clan identities (Naiman, Kipchak, Zhetyru and so on), cultivated by growing folk literature and social media debates.

Youth cultural ecosystems are quite vibrant in Kazakhstan. A small but active segment of young people is devoted to creating a modern Kazakh culture that would be detached from Soviet legacies and Russian cultural influences, in tune with global trends, and connected to and inspired by Asia – be that South Korea, Japan, Singapore or Malaysia. Music often acts as the main vector for these new voices.[68] Even Almaty's small hipster community is delving into creating new original meanings for a globalized Kazakhness,[69] and musical production excels at combining different cultural influences to produce a 'fusion-type of lyrics and rhythms.'[70] A whole range of artists are now using art, and especially street and performing arts, to create a new public space for the discussion of topics usually considered too sensitive, from historical memory and identity to gender and corruption.[71] While social activism and volunteering remain valued only by a small minority of young people, changes are on the way. Young people do not report interest in institutionalized politics, but may work horizontally with their peers: some young activists use social media to express political dissidence, criticize the everyday corruption of politicians and bureaucrats, promote urban activism and charitable activity, organize awareness campaigns about women's rights or environmental issues and so on.[72]

In this youth ecosystem, nationalism occupies a larger space than it does for older generations. Symptomatically, part of the Nazarbayev Generation can also be described as the 'Q-generation', where *Q* stands for *Qazaqstan*, the Latinization of *Kazakhstan*. Through this highly symbolic change of letters, the Q-generation is making a strong statement in support of Kazakhstan moving away from Russia, turning toward Asia, and embracing its allegedly unique features.

The Nazarbayev Generation, or the end of 'post-Sovietism'

The Nazarbayev Generation displays genuine cultural pluralism. The question is, how can this translate into pluralism at the political and institutional level? The Kazakhstani state administration is quite young on average, with more than 22,000 civil servants under the age of 30 in 2014, but these young workers populate the administrative side of administration, not the decision-making level.[73]

That being said, the long-awaited rejuvenation of elite circles seems to have begun in the past few years. Several new, more youthful figures have taken up ministerial and mayoral posts:[74] in 2019 Bauyrzhan Baibek (b. 1974) became mayor of Almaty, the first Bolashak to reach such a high level; Baglan Mailybayev (b. 1975) spent six years (2011–17) as vice-president of the presidential administration; Maulen Ashimbayev (b. 1971), trained at Tufts University's Fletcher School, was first deputy of the presidential party Nur Otan in 2018–19; and former mayor of Astana Aset Issekeshev (b. 1971), then head of the presidential administration.

The state-controlled media sector has been reinvigorated by the arrival of a team of young, nationalist-minded figures, such as Erlan Karin (b. 1976), who have dynamized media production, especially in Kazakh, and have reached out to the younger generation. Minister of Information and Communication Dauren Abayev (b. 1979) has become one of the government figures most active on social media. A rapper, ZAQ, even won a seat in Zhas Otan, the youth wing of Nur Otan. To complement that trend, former Press Secretary of Nur Otan Aleksandr Aksyutits has been appointed head of a new social media holding, Salem Social Media, indicating a recognition on the part of the state that it needs to learn to communicate with youth.

During the spring 2019 protests, a new generation of activists emerged, structured under the slogan 'Oyan, Qazaqstan' (Wake Up, Kazakhstan), a direct reference to Alash Orda and to one of its main poets and activists, Mirjaqip Dulatuli (1885–1935). Since then, Oyan, Qazaqstan has become a better-organized movement that has taken the lead on protests by myriad smaller, decentralized groups. Oyan, Qazaqstan checks all the boxes that would make it a classic example of urban liberalism among the middle and upper classes. It is most prevalent in the two capitals, Almaty and Astana/Nur-Sultan, with less representation in provincial cities and probably no footholds at all in rural Kazakhstan. It brings together several leading figures, each of whom act in their own way, through social media, flashmobs, street art and so on. It relies heavily on social media: rooted in an Instagram campaign, it has originated several popular hashtags, including #QazaqKoktemi (Kazakh spring) and #MenOyandim ('I woke up'), as well as the famous rallying cry 'You cannot run from the truth', displayed on the sidelines of a marathon in Almaty just after Nazarbayev's resignation. Among the movement's main figures are pro-democracy activist Dimash Alzhanov, the artist Saule Suleimenova and her daughter Suinbike Suleimenova, the pop producer Anuar Nurpeisov, and Beybarys Tolymbekov, who originated the 'You cannot run from the truth' slogan.

Around these leaders are a few hundred young activists involved in a vibrant hipster culture that has thus far mobilized mainly around issues of urban management – from waste and traffic jams to new buildings and heritage preservation – and environmental protection. Since the beginning of the protests, urban and environmental issues have been supplemented by more political slogans around the notion of fair elections, the right to free speech and demonstration, respect for the Constitution, stopping illegal arrests and so on. As Kassymkhan Kapparov, an economist and member of the movement, explained during an interview, Oyan 'has a focus on promoting universal democratic values and human rights. There is no political agenda other than changes to the current political system that would allow the exercise of such rights'.[75]

Contrary to the national-patriotic side of the spectrum, this trend is more liberal and cosmopolitan, seeking to articulate Kazakhness with globalization and ready to take from the West without 'becoming' the West. Even if it does focus on issues related to democratization and human rights, it would be premature or excessive to label Oyan, Qazaqstan a pro-Western movement, as it is mostly centred on domestic issues with no foreign policy strategy. But its political agenda is more or less clear: a parliamentary democracy, reform of the judicial system, the election of local *akims* to develop local governance, and the de-monopolization of the economy. Some of the Oyan, Qazaqstan leaders, such as Dimash Alzhanov, were trained in Europe and may thus be able to connect with the famous Bolashak generation. The values and worldviews of this generation remain to be studied in depth, but one might suspect that they will come up with an original combination of national and globalized features and leave their mark on the country in the years to come.

The spring 2019 protests have thus crystallized into two main trends: Jana Qazaqstan and Oyan, Qazaqstan. On one side, the national-patriots have been trying – and thus far failing – to become agenda-setters inside the system; on the other, the more cosmopolitan and liberal groups active in the streets and on social media have been trying to influence the system from the outside. The groups thus show two possible directions for post-Nazarbayevian Kazakhstan and challenge the current political setup, which does not allow for widespread public participation in decision-making. Both push for a more nationalist, Kazakh-centric agenda, although one is more isolationist and backward-looking and the other more cosmopolitan, globalized and forward-looking; one is focused on cultural rights and the other on more universal political rights.

Over the course of Nazarbayev's three-decade reign, Kazakhstan has evolved from a post-Soviet republic facing the dilemma of a late and sudden independence to a nation with a new paradigm wherein the legacy of the Soviet Union has gradually receded and made room for new realities. First, Kazakhstan has succeeded in its Kazakhization; it is now the country of Kazakhs, in which ethnic minorities represent a declining part of the population. The old divide between the Russified urban world and the Kazakh-speaking rural world has been transformed. Rural dwellers have been moving to cities and confronting old urbanites with different cultural habits, and cities are progressively becoming a Kazakh-dominated realm, both ethnically and linguistically. The issue of the 'Russianness' of Kazakhstan's northern regions is likewise gradually losing its political acuity, being replaced by points of contention within the Kazakh nation itself.

At stake for the Nazarbayev Generation will be not so much the defining of Kazakhness in opposition to the Soviet legacy, Russia, and Russian minorities, but the many internal nodes of tension inside Kazakhness. Many questions will have to be addressed by the younger generations: What will be the role of *Oralmans* as a 'yardstick' of a less Sovietized/Russified/cosmopolitan Kazakhness? How can a balance be found between western and southern Kazakhstan, on the one hand, and the rest of the country, on the other, given what seems to be a growing gap in values and rising economic disparities? What kind of legitimacy will Islam have in the public space? Will the mores and values of the country be based on 'reinvented traditions' and the search for cultural authenticity (especially in gender relations) or on more cosmopolitan worldviews and behaviours? Should Kazakhstan project itself as leading the Central Asian region or move toward the lonelier trajectory of Kazakh Eli, looking to Mongolia, South Korea or Singapore as its model? What political regime and political culture will this Nazarbayev Generation promote – a patronal regime with an improved, more efficient, technocratic culture or a more genuine plurality and institutional consolidation?

Notes

1 Asian Barometer, 'Surveys'.
2 'WVS-7 in Kazakhstan'.

3 'Life in Transition Survey (LITS)'.
4 'Pew-Templeton Global Religious Futures Project, 2016 – Kazakhstan'.
5 Gallup, 'Kazakhstan'.
6 International Republican Institute, 'Kazakhstan'.
7 Umbetaliyeva et al., 'Youth in Central Asia: Kazakhstan'.
8 See its website, http://www.centralasiabarometer.org.
9 See its website, http://eurasiamonitor.org.
10 Eurasian Development Bank, 'Doklady TsII'.
11 Esipova, 'Assessing Russia's Influence in Its Periphery'.
12 See its website, http://eljastary.kz/articles/research.
13 Shaukenova (ed.), *Sotsial'naia aktivnost' molodezhi Kazakhstana v sovremennykh sotsial'no-politicheskikh realiakh*.
14 Institute of World Economics and Politics (WEP), 'Opros "Diagnostika obshchestvennogo mneniia v Kazakhstane"'.
15 See, for instance, Ileuova et al., 'Obzor kazakhstanskogo rynka teleindustrii'.
16 Ro'i and Wainer, 'Muslim Identity and Islamic Practice in Post-Soviet Central Asia'.
17 Tolen et al., 'Formation of Civil and Patriotic Education of Youth in Kazakhstan'.
18 Kosnazarov, 'Pokolenie "Zanizhennykh ozhidanii"'.
19 See Zhussipbek and Nagayeva, '"Cognitive Unconscious", "Modern Conservatism", and "Core Liberal Values"'.
20 Valerio, 'Meet Generation Z: Forget Everything You Learned About Millennials'.
21 'Issledovanie Sberbanka'.
22 Junisbai and Junisbai, 'Are Youth Different?'.
23 Umbetaliyeva et al., 'Youth in Central Asia: Kazakhstan', 20.
24 See Junisbai, 'Understanding Economic Justice Attitudes in Two Countries'.
25 Umbetaliyeva et al., 'Youth in Central Asia: Kazakhstan', 105–6.
26 World Values Survey, 'WVS-7 in Kazakhstan'.
27 See Junisbai and Junisbai, 'Are Youth Different?'.
28 Beisembayev, *Politicheskie i ideologicheskie ustanovki kazakhstanskoi molodezhi*. See also Kilybayeva et al., 'The Kazakhstani Youth's Engagement in Politics'.
29 Junisbai et al., 'What Makes "Ardent Democrats" in Kazakhstan and Kyrgyzstan?'.
30 Umbetaliyeva et al., 'Youth in Central Asia: Kazakhstan', 22.
31 Umbetaliyeva et al., 'Youth in Central Asia: Kazakhstan', 155–70.
32 See Zhussipbek and Nagayeva, '"Cognitive Unconscious"'.
33 See Burkhanov, 'Youth and National Identity', and Sharipova, 'Youth and Civic National Identity'.
34 *Etnodemograficheskii ezhegodnik Kazakhstana*, calculated from all ethnicities by age group (p. 17), Kazakhs by age group (pp. 35–6), and Russians by age group (pp. 51–2).
35 'Za 25 let v Kazakhstan pribylo bolee 957 tysiach oralmanov'.
36 Statistical Agency of the Republic of Kazakhstan, *Natsional'nyi sostav naseleniia Respubliki Kazakhstan, Tom 2*, 9.
37 Statistical Agency of the Republic of Kazakhstan, *Itogi Natsional'noi perepisi naseleniia Respubliki Kazakhstan 2009 goda*, 24.
38 'Ukaz Prezidenta Respubliki Kazakhstan: O Gosudarstvennoi programme razvitiia i funktsionirovaniia iazykov v Respublike Kazakhstan na 2011–2020 gody'. Specifically, the presidential decree calls for increasing command of Kazakh to 95 per cent of the adult population and command of Russian to 90 per cent of the adult population by 2020.
39 See Burkhanov, 'Youth and National Identity'. To read more on the titular and Russian perceptions of ethnicity, see Faranda and Nolle, 'Boundaries of Ethnic Identity in Central Asia'.
40 Suleimenova, 'Iazykovaia politika i russkii iazyk v shkolakh Kazakhstana', 102–7, 106.
41 See Agbo and Pak, 'Globalization and Educational Reform in Kazakhstan', 14; Karabassova, 'Teachers' Conceptualization of Content and Language Integrated Learning (CLIL)'. These documents are the state program of education development in the Republic of Kazakhstan for 2011–20, the state program of languages development and functioning for 2011–20, the roadmap of trilingual education for 2015–20, and the law 'On languages of the Republic of Kazakhstan'.
42 'Education Ministry: More Than 40 Per Cent of Schools Will Switch to Trilingual Education in 2018'.
43 Bigozhin, '"We Love Our Country in Our Own Way"'.

44 Kudaibergenova, 'Between the State and the Artist'.
45 See Hanks, 'Contours of Ethnonational Landscapes in Three Cities'.
46 See Sharipova, 'Youth and Civic National Identity'.
47 Umbetaliyeva et al., 'Youth in Central Asia: Kazakhstan', 103–4.
48 Umbetaliyeva et al., 'Youth in Central Asia: Kazakhstan', 117–18.
49 Umbetaliyeva et al., 'Youth in Central Asia: Kazakhstan', 20.
50 Umbetaliyeva et al., 'Youth in Central Asia: Kazakhstan', 109–55.
51 Umbetaliyeva et al., 'Youth in Central Asia: Kazakhstan', 110.
52 See Bissenova, *Learning to Be Bourgeois*.
53 Central Asia Program, '"Bourgeois" Islam, Prosperity Theology and Ethics in Muslim Eurasia'.
54 Junisbai et al., 'Two Countries, Five Years'.
55 International Labour Organization, 'Transitioning from the Informal to the Formal Economy'.
56 Alimkhanova, 'Understanding the Rising NEET Phenomenon in Southern Kazakhstan'.
57 Beisembayev, 'Religious Extremism in Kazakhstan'.
58 See Radio Free Europe, 'Not in Our Name'.
59 UNESCO, 'Global Flow of Tertiary-Level Students'.
60 See Bolashak International Scholarship of the President of the Republic of Kazakhstan, accessed 29 August 2020, https://www.bolashak.gov.kz/ru/o-stipendii/istoriya-razvitiya.html.
61 See Blum, 'Return Migration from the United States'.
62 Zhabayeva, 'Itogi oprosa: socsetiami pol'zuiutsia 70 per cent kazakhstantsev'.
63 'Tsifrovaia Tsentral'naia Aziia. Chast' pervaia: dostup k internetu'.
64 'Skol'ko liudei 'sidiat' v sotssetiakh v Kazakhstane'.
65 See Kosnazarov, '#Hashtag Activism'.
66 Mingisheva, 'Cultural Globalization and Youth Identity Construction'.
67 Umbetaliyeva et al., 'Youth in Central Asia: Kazakhstan', 107.
68 Insebayeva, 'Visions of Nationhood'.
69 Isaacs, 'The Kazakhstan Now! Hybridity and Hipsters in Almaty'.
70 Kudaibergenova, 'Punk Shamanism, Revolt and Break-Up of Traditional Linkage'.
71 Kudaibergenova, 'Contemporary Public Art and Nation'; Tsay, 'Contemporary Art as a Public Forum'.
72 Kosnazarov, '#Hashtag Activism'; Kabatova, 'Overcoming a Taboo'.
73 Bukanova and Masatova, *Obshchestvenno-politicheskoe uchastie kazakhstanskoi molodezhi*'.
74 Bazhkenova, 'Kazahstanskie "semidesiatniki" v politike'.
75 Kassymkhan Kapparov, interviewed by the author, online, 17 June 2019.

Conclusion: The missing pieces of Central Asia's nationhood puzzle

Post-colonialism and the issue of agency and victimhood

The main stumbling block of history-writing in independent Central Asia concerns the interpretation of Soviet rule as a form of colonialism. To date, although Central Asian official historiographies have engaged in surface criticism of the way in which the Soviets wrote national history, they have not undertaken any real revisionism: the methodological revolt of the former colony against the colonizer has not happened, and national historiographies remain deeply anchored within Russian and Soviet Orientalizing narratives.

The major moment of history to which Central Asian nation-builders could potentially refer as a historical alternative to the Soviet experience is the few decades stretching from the end of the nineteenth century to the 1930s. During that period, Central Asian national elites advanced well-articulated narratives about what they wanted for their nation and even proposed political projects that could serve as an alternative to incorporation into the Russian Empire/the Soviet Union, such as a union of Turkic nations. These initiatives, like the modernizing Alash movement among the Kazakhs and similar groups among the Uzbeks, Kyrgyz and Turkmens – as well as conservative efforts that had more religious-oriented agendas – were necessarily branded as enemies of Soviet power by Soviet historiography.

Paradoxically, however, these movements were *not* easily rehabilitated after independence. During perestroika and the early 1990s, references to them helped nationalist groups rally support for their efforts to denounce local Soviet elites.[1] Yet the majority of these nationalist circles expressed pan-Turkic (and sometimes pro-Turkey) solidarity and occasionally Islamic sensibilities that could not be accommodated by the young Central Asian states, all of which insisted on their national sovereignty, uniqueness and secularism. Such nationalist dissidence was therefore quickly shut down by the ruling regimes – not because of its critical stance vis-à-vis Russia, but because it accused the local authorities of representing continuity with Soviet domination and its bureaucratic structures.[2] But these dissident strands themselves failed to transform into genuine democratic movements, instead contributing to the rigidification of the identity markers on which post-communist elites built their legitimacy.[3]

Because of their political origins, then, the Central Asian regimes have largely disempowered their own historiographical efforts. For years, they have missed out on the opportunity to rehabilitate possible alternative histories, instead continuing to claim that the Soviet experience brought them an independence that they would not otherwise have secured. While this discursive line is entirely accepted in Kyrgyzstan and Tajikistan, where the Soviet regime is thanked for paving the way to independence, it is more controversial in the other three republics. The Turkmen, Uzbek and Kazakh regimes denounce Soviet colonialism, yet without openly promoting the few historical alternatives that existed – and without recognizing their own status as direct heirs of a Soviet regime they criticize for its colonialism.[4]

In recent years, however, the situation has been evolving, with the slow but progressive reintegration of some of the representatives of historic elites into the nation's pantheon. The first move was made in Uzbekistan, where national communist figures were gradually rehabilitated by official historiography – although 'cleansed' of their pan-Turkic and Islamist narratives.[5] In Kazakhstan, too, we can observe the hesitant reintroduction of figures associated with Alash into the state-validated pantheon through diverse commemoration performances, statuary and documentary films screened on national channels. The scholarly community, however, is still lacking a comprehensive study of the role of these national elites in developing alternatives to the Soviet project and on how their memory was transmitted during Soviet times before being instrumentalized to decolonize the national narratives.

The rehabilitation that these early twentieth-century national elites are enjoying today is indeed rooted in a broader phenomenon: the reformulation of local narratives of the Soviet experience through the prism of post-colonialism studies.[6] Whereas 30 years ago it was difficult for Central Asian elites to accept any comparison with the 'developing world', younger generations are more inclined to see their experiences reflected in other post-colonial situations – such as India's relationship with the United Kingdom or those of some West African countries with France – and to accept comparison to the 'Global South' without feeling humiliated. A new generation of local experts has been socialized in international organizations working on development aid or financial assistance, thereby discovering that Asian and African countries have far more advanced debates on these questions. The ability to integrate Central Asia into the wider discussion on post-colonial conditions and to engage in systemic comparative case studies may help encourage a discussion rooted less in emotional reactions and more in social science.[7]

Inside, but also outside the classroom: what reception for national biographies?

Whatever the content of contemporary history textbooks and their possible move toward a more post-colonial approach, we are still missing some key elements necessary to understand their full influence. For instance, we know a lot about the underlying logic of textbook production, but less about textbooks' reception by teachers and pupils. How are the texts taught? How much room for manoeuvre do teachers have in discussing the materials presented in textbooks? What really goes on inside the classroom? As each country has introduced one form or another of unified testing at the end of school/before entering university, teachers must follow a quite detailed calendar of how many hours must be devoted to each epoch and must train pupils to answer questions in a standardized way. Nevertheless, there is still some space for interpretation. Damira Umetbayeva's study of history teachers in Kyrgyzstan shows, for example, that many educators, especially those from the older generation of Soviet-educated personnel, try to transmit a more positive vision of the Soviet Union than is presented in today's textbooks.[8]

Not only do we lack data on the impact of history textbooks on Central Asian pupils, but we also know very little about the relationship between textbooks and other narrations of the nation with which citizens come face-to-face in their daily lives. Textbooks are not the only state-sponsored media: museums, statuary and toponymy are also deployed to display authorities' vision of the past. Each capital city has been enriched by at least one new history museum (either an entirely new construction or the transformation of a Soviet predecessor) exhibiting the new narrative. Local museums in provincial cities have followed the same trend of 'updating' their discursive line. Museums often display a slightly different narrative than the one presented in textbooks: written texts are more conservative and slower to evolve, while museology has greater opportunities to reshape itself. Perhaps, too, the room for innovation accorded by bureaucratic structures to museums is broader than that permitted to textbooks: traditionally, the censorship of texts has been more comprehensive than the censorship of visuals or artefacts, the interpretation of which is more malleable.

Urban landscapes have likewise been reshuffled, with massive changes to street and city names as well as the erection of statues aimed at erasing the Soviet past and promoting the new national pantheon. There are a few studies on these transformations, but they remain fragmented – focusing mostly on the changes of the 1990s or on a given city, especially Astana/Nur-Sultan[9] – and we still lack a comprehensive understanding of the non-written toolkit for developing the national biography. More importantly, we know very little about who the different agents behind these transformations are. Even in authoritarian countries, the authorities are not monolithic: they are comprised of several layers of powers, vested interest groups and patrons who may have their own preferences regarding history-writing. Decision-making processes surrounding the installation and removal of statues, for instance, are surprisingly diverse, with numerous competing actors and bureaucratic logics.[10]

Investigating this local level would make it possible to take into consideration the diversity of urban contexts. In Kazakhstan, for instance, under pressure from activists trying to preserve the memory of local figures repressed during Soviet times, municipalities may choose to invest in new statuary or commemorative plaques. A whole memory industry – with sculptors, artists and construction firms that specialize in memorial complexes – has developed. We have learned about the public reception of these new urban objects thanks to research inspired by Pierre Nora's notion of *lieux de mémoire* (sites of memory),[11] ethnography of the state,[12] and political geography works devoted to the subjective construction of space (including several studies on Akmola/Astana/Nur-Sultan).[13]

What seems to emerge from the different sets of data is a more positive vision of Russia and the Soviet past than history textbooks and official state historiography would lead one to expect. We have less detailed research on Soviet nostalgia in Central Asia than in Russia, but a body of corroborating evidence makes it possible to capture broad trends. Timur Dadabaev's research on memory of the Soviet Union in Central Asia, based on a series of unique interviews, highlights a nostalgia that textbooks usually ignore.[14] While sociological data remain sparse and insufficiently fine-grained, we can still elucidate that Russia enjoys a relatively positive image. For instance, the annual Gallup World Polls from 2006 to 2018, which surveyed four Central Asian countries – Kazakhstan, Kyrgyzstan, Tajikistan and Uzbekistan – found that Russia had the highest approval rate of any country, with 80 per cent of Central Asians, on average, expressing approval of the Russian government, an approval rate far higher than that accorded to any other external actor.[15]

A series of 10 focus groups conducted in 2019 in Kazakhstan by the Strategiya Centre for Sociological and Political Analysis[16] also confirm the persistence of Soviet-era narratives about history. For instance, when asked about the process by which the Kazakh Steppe joined the Russian Empire in the nineteenth century, the vast majority of participants reproduced the standard Soviet narrative of Kazakh hordes who were attacked by Dzhungars and therefore needed the protection of Russia, even if a plurality also held that the Russian tsars were engaged in a more cynical strategy of conquering the steppes. Yet all agreed that colonization had had complex results: the loss of national language, religion and independence, but also better access to education and technical knowledge.

When asked about the Soviet era, the majority of participants likewise reproduced the narrative that all Soviet nations were brothers and sisters under Russia's leadership, with only a few denouncing the destruction of the Kazakh nation, collectivization, the exploitation of natural resources, nuclear tests in Semipalatinsk and so on. Asked about the Soviet Union in general, participants gave predominantly positive responses: the Soviet Union offered order, discipline, ideology, humanity, spirituality, free education and medicine, high-quality products and so on. However, nostalgia does not mean wishing for going back in time: when asked if they would like to return to that state of affairs, almost all participants were explicitly against the idea and expressed satisfaction with Kazakhstan being an independent nation.

A more refined sociology of Central Asian sociocultural constituencies would probably capture some of the missing nuances and allow us to differentiate between the attitudes of different social groups. For instance, the fact that the teaching profession does not attract many young people (who see teaching as a last resort for those without any other job opportunities) and remains dominated by an older generation trained in the Soviet period probably causes teachers to be more 'pro-Soviet' than other sociocultural groups. Artemy Kalinovsky's research on massive developmental projects in Tajikistan similarly depicted a universe of engineers and technical professions who remain deeply committed to the Soviet modernizing project.[17] The largely Sovietized/Russified urban educated elites also tend to display a decisively positive vision of the Soviet decades, as they perceive the new, more ethnicized and nationalist environment to be inhospitable to them.[18] Perceptions of the past appear closely linked to one's personal situation and a nostalgic vision of a time when one's own profession or social identity was more highly valued.

Non-state-produced tools of narrating the nation

State-sponsored products related to the national biography must compete with non-state tools that belong more to the memory field than to the domain of history/historiography. Indeed, there are many forms of 'public history', defined here as any communication about the past crafted outside the traditional circles of academia and political elites – that is, with little or no input from professional historians. These imaginational registers may be just as powerful as history textbooks, if not more so, but they have remained largely overlooked in academic research.

Memory studies in Central Asia remain a largely underexplored field for research. We know that family memory remains the most efficient tool for transmitting the past – what parents and grandparents say at home may have a greater impact than what is taught at school because it is emotionally contextualized.[19] For instance, research conducted in Russia on family memories of Stalinist violence has confirmed that people who belong to families that were repressed during the Soviet era exhibit a more critical stance toward current politics and are more concerned about issues related to the politics of history than individuals who do not.[20] Both having a relative who was arrested unjustly and then executed, sent to a camp, or disappeared in the 1930s and having had discussions about the Stalinist repressions at home are strongly and consistently correlated with greater desire for historical knowledge, less cynicism about the knowability of history, and opposition to prioritizing national pride over historical objectivity.[21] As yet, there are no such studies of family memory in Central Asia, even at the elite level.

Interpretation of the past is also an intrinsic part of the imaginary world of art and fiction. How can we, for example, measure the role that Soviet-era films, regularly shown on Central Asian channels, play in shaping a vision of the past that may contradict what is written in the new textbooks? What about the impact of historical movies and series produced since independence, which are more fictional and romanticized than the official line taken by textbooks? Even less is known about the impact of video-game culture on younger generations' vision of the past. Research conducted in Europe and the United States has demonstrated the impact of personal identification with fictional characters in historically documented or more controversial settings.[22] The 'dryness' of history textbooks, which are dominated by boring texts heavy on dates and names, may mean that they are not an efficient tool for moulding new generations, who have grown up in a world of visuality, interactivity and immediate impressions.

Finally, while non-state actors cannot impact official history textbooks, they can invest in the field of public history. 'Popular history' or 'folk history' has been growing in Central Asia ever since the collapse of the Soviet Union, particularly in Kazakhstan and Kyrgyzstan, where the media market has historically been freer and where publications from Russia are distributed widely. Nationalist-oriented folk history has been quite successful in spreading an epic vision of the past not fully in line with more sober history textbooks. While it is difficult to gauge the impact of folk history, as we lack data on its circulation, anecdotal evidence confirms that it is widespread among the urban educated middle classes and student communities.

In Kazakhstan, for instance, the trilogy *Kochevniki* (*Nomads*) by the poet Ilias Esenberlin (1915–83) has shaped how generations of Kazakhs picture the nomadic Kazakh world of the fifteenth through nineteenth centuries. The same can be said of *Zhestokii vek* (*Cruel Century*) by the Buryat writer Isai Kalashnikov (1931–80), which describes Genghis Khan's rule and whose publication in 1979 struck a chord with the Turkic-speaking Soviet world. Lev Gumilev and Murad Adzhi also participated in this rehabilitation of Steppic history. In the 2000s, there emerged another form of folk history, related to traditional genealogical and clanic identities. This popular history, as well as popular philology, should not be dismissed as an object of study, as it allows individuals to construct a vision of Central Asia's agency in a way accessible to all.[23]

This popular public history gained new allies with the emergence of a more vocal national opposition that seeks to promote alternative biographies of the nation. As mentioned, alternative historical interpretations had existed in competition with those of the state during perestroika and the early years of independence, but they were rapidly marginalized and repressed, with the result that they did not reach a wider audience. Almost three decades later, the situation has evolved dramatically. While Central Asian governments remain strong proponents of bilateralism, it is now in good taste to express at least symbolic support for regional cooperation, especially since the onset of the 2016 Uzbek political thaw. Secularism remains the official discursive line, but reality has become much more complex: with the rise of Islamic identity and piety among Central Asians,[24] especially among the younger generations, the regimes realize that they must acknowledge cultural evolutions and embrace them rather than confront them.

A new generation of public intellectuals has also emerged. The use of social media allows them to reach a broader audience than the narrow literary circles of the perestroika years. They frequently defend ethnonationalist views that have a strong Turkic component, celebrating the greatness of Turkic civilization and the unique role of their own nation within it. But they do not profess pan-Turkism in the sense of calling for political unity among the Turkic peoples, and they are even less interested in espousing Erdoğan's Turkey as a model for emulation. Unlike their predecessors of the early post-independence years, these public intellectuals have been able to find a middle ground in their relations with the authorities. They position themselves as a kind of 'constructive opposition', just as Russian nationalists orient themselves toward the Putin regime: depending on the situation, they may either support the regime as the protector of the nation or else criticize it. In the latter case, they may face administrative difficulties or even arrest, but even when they come into conflict with the regime, these nationalist intellectuals usually receive gentler treatment by the authorities than do pro-Western human rights defenders. They all benefit from the presence of patrons inside the system who share their nationalist vision, while their middle-of-the-road position allows them to continue to exist even in a relatively restrictive political environment.

One example of the difficulty of reconciling official historiography with nationalist alternatives was the 2016 centenary of the 1916 Steppe Revolt. The celebration mobilized nationalist groups and all those who wanted to have an open and frank discussion about the uprising. The Kazakh and Kyrgyz authorities struggled to decide whether to meet these demands in order to satisfy this segment of their constituencies – as well as, in the case of Kazakhstan, to demonstrate autonomy from Moscow – or to repress them as a threat to relations with Russia.

The new generation of nationalist public intellectuals have also succeeded in blending old-fashioned perestroika-era claims about the destruction of the national languages and the supposed genocidal policies of the Soviet regime with more modern debates about globalization as a threat to sovereignty and the hidden hands manipulating world affairs – a narrative usually underpinned by anti-Semitism and claims that the 'national gene pool' is being destroyed by Western pro-LGBT+ policies. These narratives thus target not only Russia, as the former imperial centre, but also – and sometimes even to a greater degree – China and the West, whose presence in the region is seen as a new form of imperialism. These narratives are perfectly adapted to the 'confrontainment' social media environment in which the average citizen consumes news and accesses broader debates: they focus on conflict rather than compromise; they rely on emotions, polarization and stereotyping for storytelling; and they deploy negative content, incivility, conspiratorial explanations and character attacks. These intellectuals leave a powerful mark on public perceptions of the national biography that partly contradicts the official discursive line.

Last but not least, one of the key drivers of official nationhood in Central Asia has been the marginalization, if not sometimes the silencing, of Islam. Like nation, religion is not a given but a construct, one that articulates itself along with other aspects of life. It can take on multiple forms and identities, from being a purely transcendental faith in God to being an ideological ferment for political action, including diverse cultural, community and history-based phenomena that help people to situate themselves in the world. Understood both as universalist religion and as national tradition, Islam can both compete with and reinforce nationhood, projecting different Selves and Others. The interaction between religion and the nation can therefore go from symbiosis (the nation is defined by its majority religion and religion can be only a national tradition), through mutual indifference (secularism as state ideology and Islam as apolitical religion), to open or hidden conflict (Islam as a threat to the nation, or political Islam as alternative to the current logic of nationhood and as expressing a preference for a globalized Ummah). In Central Asia's nationhood, Islam has historically been the main ignored identity marker, but that situation is currently in flux. The need to fully reintegrate Islam into efforts to craft nationhood will become increasingly apparent in the coming years and decades.

All these elements lead to Central Asian societies becoming increasingly plural and their citizens having increasingly heterogeneous perceptions of what should constitute the national biography. Whereas they were previously state-centric, hegemonic and consensual, Central Asian nationhoods are now gradually coming to be shaped by plurality and heterogeneity in terms of ideological content, actors, and forms of co-creation.

Notes

1 On Uzbekistan, see, for instance, Fierman, 'Cultural Nationalism in Soviet Uzbekistan', and Critchlow, *Nationalism in Uzbekistan*.
2 Dudoignon, 'Changements politiques et historiographie en Asie Centrale'.
3 Kudaibergenova and Shin, 'Authors and Authoritarianism in Central Asia'.
4 Beissinger and Young (eds), *Beyond State Crisis*.
5 Kozgambaeva, 'Museum of Victims of Political Repression of South Kazakhstan Region'.
6 Khalid, 'Locating the (Post-)Colonial in Soviety History'; Kudaibergenova, 'The Use and Abuse of Postcolonial Discourses in Post-Independent Kazakhstan'.
7 For some promising examples, see, for instance, the Esimde project (http://esimde.org) in Bishkek, which is devoted to studying the 'blank pages' of national history through memory studies; the research of Bissenova and Medeuova, 'Davlenie metropolii i tikhii natsionalizm akademicheskikh praktik'; and the work of Suyarkulova, 'Becoming Sovereign in Post-Soviet Central Asia'.
8 Umetbayeva, 'Official Rhetoric and Individual Perceptions'.
9 Bell, 'Redefining National Identity in Uzbekistan'; Cummings, 'Leaving Lenin'; Kopack, 'Monuments and Memory in the Landscapes of Kazakhstan'; Cummings, 'Inscapes, Landscapes and Greyscapes'.
10 Moira O'Shea, 'The Symbolic Landscape of Bishkek'.
11 Medeuova, *Praktiki i mesta pam'iati v Kazakhstane*.
12 Reeves et al. (eds), *Ethnographies of the State in Central Asia*. See also Kudaibergenova, '"My Silk Road to You"'.
13 Bissenova, 'The Master Plan of Astana'; Fauve, 'A Tale of Two Statues in Astana'; Koch, *The Geopolitics of Spectacle*; Laszczkowski, *'City of the Future'*.
14 Dadabaev, *Identity and Memory*.
15 Laruelle and Royce, 'Kazakhstani Public Opinion of the United States and Russia'.
16 The focus groups had 10 participants each. Those in Almaty and Astana were conducted in Russian and Kazakh; those in Shymkent, Kzylorda, and Aktau only in Kazakh; and those in Karaganda, Petropavlovsk, and Ust-Kamenogorsk only in Russian. The questions were drafted by the author and Serik Beisembayev in Russian and translated by the latter into Kazakh; the data from all of the Kazakh-language focus groups were subsequently transcribed into Russian.
17 Kalinovsky, *Laboratory of Socialist Development*.
18 Cummings, 'Leaving Lenin'; Dadabaev, 'Recollections of Emerging Hybrid Ethnic Identities'; Dadabaev, 'Post-Soviet Realities of Society in Uzbekistan'.
19 Nikolayenko, 'Contextual Effects on Historical Memory'; Labanyi, 'The Languages of Silence'; Jockusch and Lewinsky, 'Paradise Lost?'.
20 Rozenas and Zhukov, 'Mass Repression and Political Loyalty'.
21 Gerber and Van Landingham, 'Ties that Remind'.
22 See Chapman, *Digital Games as History*; Lupu and Peisakhin, 'The Legacy of Political Violence'; McCall, 'Playing with the Past'.
23 Jacquesson (ed.), *History Making*.
24 Jones, *Islam, Society, and Politics in Central Asia*.

References

'147 Thousand Pilgrims Visit Manas Ordo National Complex in 2014'. *CA-News*, 5 February 2015, http://dem.kg/en/article/12284/147-thousand-pilgrims-visit-manas-ordo-national-complex-in-2014, accessed 18 October 2018.

'A Summary of Cultural Objects of Astana'. *Astana Times*, 3 July 2014, accessed 5 March 2021.

Abashin, Sergei. '*Mustakillik* i pamiat' ob imperskom proshlom: prokhodia po zalam tashkentskogo Muzeia pamiati zhertv repressii'. *Neprikosnovennyy zapas*, 66 (4) (2009), http://magazines.russ.ru/nz/2009/4/ab6.html, accessed 26 August 2020.

Abashin, Sergei. 'Reviews of Uzbek History Textbooks: The View from Russia'. *Eckert.Beiträge*, 8 (2010), https://d-nb.info/1002292948/34, accessed 5 March 2021.

Abdylgaliuly, Berik (ed.). *Kazakhskaia missiia*. Almaty: Daik-Press, 2007.

Abikeeva, Gul'nara. 'Uzbekistan: "Chopping Board" or Serious Cinema?'. *Studies in Russian & Soviet Cinema*, 4 (2) (2010): 221–6.

Abramzon, Saul Matvei. *Kirgizy i ikh etnogeneticheskie i istoriko-kul'turnye sviazi*. Leningrad: Nauka, 1971. Repr. Kyrgyzstan: Frunze, 1990.

Adams, Laura. *The Spectacular State: Culture and National Identity in Uzbekistan*. Durham, NC: Duke University Press, 2010.

Adams, Mark B. (ed.). *The Wellborn Science: Eugenics in Germany, France, Brazil and Russia*. Oxford: Oxford University Press, 1990.

Adzhi, Murad. *My – iz roda polovetskogo*. Rybinsk: Rybinskii dom pechati, 1992.

Adzhi, Murad. *Polyn' polovetskogo polia*. Moscow: PIK-kontekst, 1994.

Adzhi, Murad. *Evropa. Turki. Velikaia step'*. Moscow: Mysl', 1998.

Adzhi, Murad. 'Tengrianstvo v kontekste mirovoi kul'tury'. *Evraziiskoe soobshchestvo*, 1 (1998): 78–92.

Agbo, Seth A. and Natalya Pak. 'Globalization and Educational Reform in Kazakhstan: English as the Language of Instruction in Graduate Programs'. *International Journal of Educational Reform*, 26 (1) (2017): 1–30.

Agenstvo Respubliki Kazakhstana po statistike. *Chislennost' naseleniia Respubliki Kazakhstan po otdel'nym etnosam na nachalo 2018 goda*, http://stat.gov.kz/getImg?id=ESTAT260594, accessed 18 March 2019.

Aitmatov, Chingiz. 'Drevnetiurkskaia tsivilizatsiia: pamiatniki pis'mennosti'. *Kazakhstan: XXI vek*, 3 (2001).

Aitzhanova, Aktoty, Johannes F. Linn, Shigeo Katsu and Vladislav Yezhov (eds). *Kazakhstan 2050: Toward a Modern Society for All*. Oxford: Oxford University Press, 2014.

Akatai, Sabetkazy. 'Evraziistvo v kontekste kul'turnoi obshchnosti'. In *Kul'tura Kazakhstana: traditsii, real'nosti, poiski*, edited by E.B. Mambekov. Almaty: RNTsPK, 1998.

Akayev, Askar. *Kyrgyzskaia gosudarstvennost' i narodnyi epos "Manas"*. Bishkek: Uchkun, 2002.

Akbarzadeh, Shahram. 'Nation-Building in Uzbekistan'. *Central Asian Survey*, 15 (1) (1996): 23–32.

Akbarzadeh, Sharam. 'Why Did Nationalism Fail in Tajikistan?'. *Europe-Asia Studies*, 48 (7) (1996): 1105–29.

Akçali, Pinar and Cennet Engin-Demir (eds). *Politics, Identity, and Education in Central Asia: Post-Soviet Kyrgyzstan*. London: Routledge, 2013.

Akhmedov, Sharif A. 'Vozvrachshaias' k istorii "ariitsev" (k polemike mezhdu R. Masovym i A. Askarovym)'. *CentrAsia*, 20 January 2006.

Akhmedov, Sharif A. 'Echshe raz ob ariiskoi probleme'. *CentrAsia*, 23 March 2006.

Akkula, Sultan-Khan. 'Kogda kazakhskii dissident saditsia v tiur'mu, eto vygliadit ego lichnoi problemoi'. *Azattyq*, 17 December 2009, http://rus.azattyq.org/content/aron_atabek/1905440.html, accessed 5 March 2021.

Akkuly, Sultan Khan. 'Bez golovy Kenesary khana prazdnovanie 550–letiia Kazakhskogo khanstva budet nepolnym'. *7news.kz*, 15 May 2015, http://7news.kz/politika/sultan-han-akkuly-prazdnovanie-550–letiya-kazahskogo-hanstva-budet-nepolnym-bez-golovy, accessed 18 October 2018.

'Aktivisty boiatsia "evraziiskogo razmyvaniia RK"'. *Azattyq*, 17 January 2014, http://rus.azattyq.org/content/article/1180775.html, accessed 5 March 2021.

Alad'ina, Tat'iana. 'Destvennitsy atakuiut'. *Express Kz*, 13 November 2009, http://old.express-k.kz/show_article.php?art_id=34526&start=20, accessed 12 March 2014.

Alimkhanova, Dinara. 'Understanding the Rising NEET Phenomenon in Southern Kazakhstan'. *CAP Paper*, 206 (June 2018), https://centralasiaprogram.org/archives/12460, accessed 5 March 2021.

Alimova, Dilorom. *Dzhadidizm v Srednei Azii: puti obnovleniia, reformy, borba za nezavisimost*. Tashkent, 2000.

Alimova, Dilorom, Zoia Arifkhanovas and Shamsiddin Kamoliddin. 'Ob"ektivnost' i otvetstvennost': kakim ne dolzhen byt' etnicheskii atlas Uzbekistana'. *Pravda Vostoka*, January 14–15 2004. Republished in *O"zbekiston Tarihi*, 1 (2004): 72–85.

Anacker, Shonin. 'Geographies of Power in Nazarbayev's Astana'. *Eurasian Geography and Economics*, 45 (7) (2004): 515–33.

Anceschi, Luca. *Analysing Kazakhstan's Foreign Policy Regime: Neo-Eurasianism in the Nazarbayev Era*. London: Routledge, 2020.

Anderson, Benedict. *Imagined Communities: Reflections on the Origin and Spread of Nationalism*. New York: Verso, 1983.

Anderson, Lukas. 'Iran's New Cultural Nationalism: Iranian Cultural Diplomacy in Tajikistan'. *Central Asian Affairs*, 6 (1) (February 2019): 21–46.

Anholt, Simon. *Competitive Identity: The New Brand Management for Nations, Cities and Regions*. New York: Palgrave Macmillan, 2007.

'Anvar Mamraimo: Ia – mnogostanochnik'. *Antenna*, n.d., http://antennakz.com/znay-nashich/anvar-mamraimov-ya-per centE2 per cent80 per cent94–mnogostanochnik.html, accessed 12 March 2014.

Arii: istoriia i sovremennost'. Dushanbe: Sharki Ozod, 2006.

Arslonzoda, Rakhmatzhon. 'Istina rozhdaetsya v spore'. *CentrAsia*, 2 February 2006.

Asad, Talal. 'Afterword: From the History of Colonial Anthropology to the Anthropology of Western Hegemony'. In *Colonial Situations: Essays on the Contextualization of Ethnographic Knowledge*, edited by George Stocking. Madison: University of Wisconsin Press, 1991.

'"Asharshylyk" Kalila Umarov Film – KALILAFILM.kz', YouTube video, 26:56, uploaded by 'KALILAFILM / Derekti kino elemi', 24 July 2013, https://www.youtube.com/watch?v=Ag6PalmQ7g4&nohtml5=False, accessed 29 August 2020.

Ashurov, G. 'Ideinaia bor'ba vokrug knigi Akademika B. G. Gafurova *Tadzhiki*'. *Merosi niegon-Nasledie predkov*, 6 (2003): 72–8.

Askarov, Ahmadali. 'Ariiskaia problema: novye podkhody i vzgliady'. In *Istoriia Uzbekistana v arkheologicheskikh i pis'mennykh istochnikakh*, edited by A.A. Anarbaev, 81–91. Tashkent: FAN, 2005.

Assembleia narodov Kazakhstana. *Natsional'noe soglasie – osnova stabil'nosti i razvitiia Kazakhstan*. Astana: Assembleia narodov Kazakhstana, 1999.

Assembleia narodov Kazakhstana. *Dukhovno-kul'turnoe razvitie naroda – osnova ukrepleniia gosudarstvennoi nezavisimosti Kazakhstana*. Astana: Assembleia narodov Kazakhstana, 2001.

Assembleia narodov Kazakhstana. *Ob osnovnykh napravleniiakj deiatel'nosti Assamblei po realizatsii gosudarstvennoi natsional'noi politiki v svete trebovanii 'Strategii Assamblei narodov Kazakhstana'*. Pavlodar: Pavlodarskaia Assembleia narodov Kazakhstana, 2002.

Assmann, Jan and John Czaplicka. 'Collective Memory and Cultural Identity'. *New German Critique*, 65 (Spring–Summer 1995): 125–33.

Atabek, Aron. 'Liudi i bogi ili kak vybirat' religiiu'. *Beznen-Yul*, 2 (2005).

Atabek, Aron. 'Tengrianstvo – osnova natsional'nogo samosoznaniia kazakhov'. *Beznen-Yul*, 1 (2006), http://www.beznen-yul.narod.ru/arhiv/2006/1san/tengri.htm, accessed 12 March 2014.

Atabek, Aron. 'Odin bog, odna religiia, odna ideologiia, odin narod'. 26 June 2006, http://aronatabek.com/odin-bog-odna-religiya-odna-ideologiya-odin-narod.html, accessed 29 August 2020.

Atabek, Aron. 'Serdtse Evrazii ili Velikii Ariiskii Kaganat Altyn-Orda'. November 2012, http://www.aronatabek.ru/, accessed 29 August 2020.

Avesta i mirovaia tsivilizatsiia. Dushanbe: Akademiia Nauk Respubliki Tadzhikistan, 2001.

Ayaganov, B.G. *Politicheskie partii i obshchestvennye dvizheniia sovremennogo Kazakhstana*. Almaty: Ministerstvo pechati i massovoi informatsii respubliki Kazahstan, 1994.

Aydingün, Ayşegül and Ismail Aydingün. 'The Role of Language in the Formation of Turkish National Identity and Turkishness'. *Nationalism and Ethnic Politics*, 10 (3) (2004): 415–32.

Aytürk, İlker. 'Turkish Linguists against the West: The Origins of Linguistic Nationalism in Atatürk's Turkey'. *Middle Eastern Studies*, 40 (6) (2004): 1–25.

Ayupov, Nigmet G. *Tengrianstvo kak religioznaia sistema drevnykh tiurkov*. Almaty: n.p., 1998.

Ayupov, Nigmet G. 'Tengrianstvo'. *Izvestiia Akademii nauk respubliki Tadzhikistan*, 3–4 (2002).

Ayupov, Nigmet G. 'Naturfilosofiia tengrianstva'. *Evraziia: Obshchestvenno-politicheskii i literaturno-khudozhestvennyi zhurnal*, 6 (2004): 66–71.

Azat. *Programma grazhdanskogo dvizheniia Azat*. Alma-Ata: n.p., 1992.

B. G. Gafurov: dialog kul'tur i tsivilizatsii. Moscow: Institut vostokovedeniia RAN, 2000.

Babak, Vladimir, Demian Vaisman and Aryeh Wasserman (eds). *Political Organization in Central Asia and Azerbaijan: Sources and Documents*. London and Portland: Frank Cass, 2004.

Babakov, Orazmukhammed. *Antropologicheskii sostav turkmenskogo naroda v sviazi s problemoi etnogeneza*. Ashkhabad: Ylym, 1977.

Babamuratov, Dauren. 'Ia solidaren s Al-Farabi'. *Tribuna Kommunist Kazakhstana*, 14 October 2014, http://vmeste.com.kz/?p=2654, accessed 3 October 2017.

Baker, Christopher. 'The Power and Significance of the Ethnic Past'. In *History Making in Central and Northern Eurasia: Contemporary Actors and Practices*, edited by Svetlana Jacquesson, 21–40. Wiesbaden: Reichert Verlag, 2016.

Balibar, Etienne. *Race, Nation, Class: Ambiguous Identities*. New York: Verso, 2011.

Banks, Marcus. *Ethnicity: Anthropological Constructions*. London: Routledge, 1996.

Barbankulov, M. *Zolotaia baba (evraziistvo vo vsem i vsegda)*. Almaty: Rauan, 1998.

Barthold, V.V. *Zadachi russkogo vostokovedeniia v Turkestane*. Republished in *Polnoe sobranie sochinenii*, vol. IX. Moscow: Nauka, 1974.

Bassin, Mark. *The Gumilev Mystique: Biopolitics, Eurasianism, and the Construction of Community in Modern Russia*. Ithaca, NY: Cornell University Press, 2016.

Battis, Matthias. 'The Aryan Myth and Tajikistan: From a Myth of Empire to One National Identity'. *Ab Imperio*, 4 (2016): 155–83.

Bazhkenova, Gul'nara. 'Kazahstanskie "semidesiatniki" v politike'. *Radio Azattyq*, 13 August 2015, https://rus.azattyq.org/a/semidesyatniki-blog-bazhkenovoy/27186368.html, accessed 5 March 2021.

Beisembayev, Serik. 'Tendentsii sotsial'no-demograficheskogo razvitiia kazakhstanskogo obshchestva (na baze sotsiologicheskikh issledovanii)'. *Tsentral'naia Aziia i Kavkaz*, 14 (2) (2011): 83–100.

Beisembayev, Serik. *Politicheskie i ideologicheskie ustanovki kazakhstanskoi molodezhis*. Almaty: Strategiia Center for Social and Political Studies, 2013.

Beisembayev, Serik. *Fenomen kazakhskogo natsionalizma v kontektste segodniashnei politiki: ot otritsaniia k ponimaiiu*. Almaty: Open Society Public Policy Program, 2015, http://caa-network.org/cassions/wp-content/uploads/2015/07/nationalism_final.pdf, accessed 3 October 2017.

Beisembayev, Serik. 'Religious Extremism in Kazakhstan: From Criminal Networks to Jihad'. *Central Asia Fellowship Papers*, 15 (February 2016).

Beissinger, Mark and Crawford Young (eds). *Beyond State Crisis: Postcolonial Africa and Post-Soviet Eurasia in Comparative Perspective*. Washington, DC: Woodrow Wilson Center Press, 2002.

Bell, James. 'Redefining National Identity in Uzbekistan: Symbolic Tensions in Tashkent's Official Public Landscape'. *Ecumene*, 6 (2) (1999): 183–213.

Berdenova, K.A (ed.). *Evraziistvo v ekonomicheskoi i etnopoliticheskoi istorii Kazakhstana*. Almaty: Ekonomica, 1997.

Bergne, Paul. *The Birth of Tajikistan: National Identity and the Origins of the Republic*. London: I.B. Tauris, 2018.

Bertrand, Frédéric. 'Une science sans objet? L'ethnographie soviétique des années 20–30 et les enjeux de la catégorisation ethnique'. *Cahiers du monde russe*, 44 (1) (2003): 93–110.

Bezertinov, Raphael N. *Tengrianstvo – religiia tiurkov i mongolov*. Kazan: Slovo, 2004.

Bigozhin, Ulan. 'State, Shrine, and Sacred Lineage in Post-Soviet Kazakhstan'. *Central Asian Affairs*, 5 (3) (2018): 233–52.

Bigozhin, Ulan. '"We Love Our Country in Our Own Way": Youth, Gender, and Nationalism'. In *The Nazarbayev Generation: Youth in Kazakhstan*, edited by Marlene Laruelle, 115–32. Lanham, MD: Lexington, 2019.

Billig, Michael. *Banal Nationalism*. London: SAGE Publications, 1995.

Birdib, R. 'Globalizm – politika kolonizatorov'. *Beznen-Yul*, 1 (2006). http://www.beznen-yul.narod.ru/arhiv/2006/1san/global.htm, accessed 12 March 2014.

Bissenova, Alima. 'The Master Plan of Astana: Between the "Art of Government" and "the Art of Being Global"'. In *Ethnographies of the State in Central Asia: Performing Politics,* edited by Madeleine Reeves, Johan Rasanayagam and Judith Beyer, 127–48. Bloomington: Indiana University Press, 2014.

Bissenova, Alima. *Learning to be Bourgeois: The Rise of the Middle Classes in Post-Soviet Kazakhstan*. Publication forthcoming.

Bissenova, Alima and Kul'shat Medeuova. 'Davlenie metropolii i tikhii natsionalizm akademicheskikh praktik'. *Ab Imperio*, 4 (2016): 207–55.

Blakkisrud, Helge and Faruh Kuziev. 'Museums, Memory and Meaning-Creation: (Re)constructing the Tajik Nation'. *Nations and Nationalism*, 25 (3) (2019): 997–1017.

Blakkisrud, Helge and Shahnoza Nozimova. 'History Writing and Nation Building in Post-Independence Tajikistan'. *Nationalities Papers*, 38 (2) (2010): 173–89.

Blum, Alain and Martine Mespoulet. *L'Anarchie bureaucratique: Statistique et pouvoir sous Staline*. Paris: La Découverte, 2003.

Blum, Douglas. 'Return Migration from the United States: Exploring the Dynamics of Cultural Change'. In *The Nazarbayev Generation: Youth in Kazakhstan*, edited by Marlene Laruelle, 213–26. Lanham, MD: Lexington, 2019.

Bogaards, Matthijs. 'How to Classify Hybrid Regimes? Defective Democracy and Electoral Authoritarianism'. *Democratization*, 16 (2) (2009): 399–423.

Bohr, Annette. 'The Central Asian States as Nationalising Regimes'. In *Nation-Building in Post-Soviet Borderlands: The Politics of National Identities*, edited by Graham Smith, 139–66. Cambridge: Cambridge University Press, 1998.

'Bolashak International Scholarship of the President of the Republic of Kazakhstan', https://www.bolashak.gov.kz/ru/o-stipendii/istoriya-razvitiya.html, accessed 29 August 2020.

Bond, Andrew R. and Natalie R. Koch. 'Interethnic Tensions in Kyrgyzstan: A Political Geographic Perspective'. *Eurasian Geography and Economics*, 51 (4) (2010): 531–62.

Brandenberger, David. *National Bolshevism: Stalinist Mass Culture and the Formation of Modern Russian National Identity, 1931–1956*. Cambridge, MA: Harvard University Press, 2002.

Breen, Keith and Shane O'Neill (eds). *After the Nation? Critical Reflections on Nationalism and Postnationalism*. Basingstoke: Palgrave Macmillan, 2010.

Brill Olcott, Martha. *Kazakhstan: Unfulfilled Promise*. Washington, DC: Carnegie Endowment for International Peace, 2002.

Bromlei, Iulian. 'Etnos i endogamiia'. *Sovetskaia etnografiia*, 6 (1969): 84–91.

Bromley, Yulian. *Soviet Ethnology and Anthropology Today*. La Hague: Mouton, 1974.

Brubaker, Rogers. *Nationalism Reframed: Nationhood and the National Question in the New Europe*. Cambridge: Cambridge University Press, 1996.

Bukanova, Z. and B. Masatova. *Obshchestvenno-politicheskoe uchastie kazakhstanskoi molodezhi v kontekste modernizatsii gosudarstvennoi molodezhnoi politiki*. Astana: Nauchno-issledovatel'skii tsentr 'Molodezh', 2014.

Bulekbaev, S. and E. Unnarbaev. 'Evraziistvo kak ideologiia gosudarstvennosti'. *Evraziiskoe soobshchestvo*, 3 (2001): 5–12.

Burkhanov, Aziz. 'Kazakhstan's National Identity-Building Policy: Soviet Legacy, State Efforts, and Societal Reactions'. *Cornell International Law Journal*, 50 (1) (2017): 1–14.

Burkhanov, Aziz. 'Youth and National Identity: Then and Now'. In *The Nazarbayev Generation: Youth in Kazakhstan*, edited by Marlene Laruelle, 49–68. Lanham, MD: Lexington, 2019.

Burkhanov, Aziz and Dina Sharipova. 'Kazakhstan's Civic Identity: Ambiguous Policies and Points of Resistance'. In *Nationalism and Identity Construction in Central Asia: Dimensions, Dynamics, and Directions*, edited by Mariya Omelicheva. Lanham, MD: Lexington, 2016.

Cadiot, Juliette. *Le Laboratoire imperial*. Paris: CNRS Éditions, 2007.
Cameron, Sarah. *The Hungry Steppe: Famine, Violence, and the Making of Soviet Kazakhstan*. Ithaca, NY: Cornell University Press, 2018.
Carrère d'Encausse, Hélène. *Le Grand Défi: Bolcheviks et Nations 1917–1930*. Paris: Flammarion, 1987.
Central Asia Program. '"Bourgeois" Islam, Prosperity Theology and Ethics in Muslim Eurasia', *CAP Paper*, 198 (January 2018), http://centralasiaprogram.org/wp-content/uploads/2018/01/CAP-Paper-198-January-2018.pdf, accessed 5 March 2021.
Chapman, Adam. *Digital Games as History: How Videogames Represent the Past and Offer Access to Historical Practice*. London: Routledge, 2016.
Chirokogoroff, S.M. 'La théorie de l'ethnos et sa place dans le système des sciences anthropologiques'. *L'Ethnographie*, 32 (1936): 85–115.
Clarke, Michael. 'The "Centrality" of Central Asia in World History, 1700–2006: From Pivot to Periphery and Back Again?'. In *China, Xinjiang and Central Asia: History, Transition and Crossborder Interaction into the 21st Century,* edited by Michael E. Clarke and Colin Mackerras, 21–54. London: Routledge, 2009.
Collins, Kathleen. *Clan Politics and Regime Transition in Central Asia*. Cambridge: Cambridge University Press, 2006.
Consulter Programma. Grazhdanskogo dvizheniia Azat. Alma-Ata: n.p., 1992.
Cooley, Alexander and John Heathershaw. *Dictators without Borders: Power and Money in Central Asia*. New Haven, CT: Yale University Press, 2017.
Cooley, Alexander and John Snyder (eds). *Ranking the World: Grading States as a Tool of Global Governance*. Cambridge: Cambridge University Press, 2015.
Critchlow, James. *Nationalism in Uzbekistan*. Boulder, CO: Westview Press, 1991.
Cucciolla, Riccardo Mario. 'Sharaf Rashidov and the International Dimensions of Soviet Uzbekistan'. *Central Asian Survey*, 39 (2) (2020): 1–17.
Cull, Nicholas J. 'Soft Power's Next Steppe: National Projection at the Astana EXPO 2017'. *Place Branding and Public Diplomacy*, 13 (2017): 269–72.
Cummings, Sally N. 'The Kazakhs: Demographics, Diasporas, and "Return"'. In *Nations Abroad*, edited by Charles King and Neil Melvin, 133–52. Boulder, CO: Westview Press, 1998.
Cummings, Sally N. 'Inscapes, Landscapes and Greyscapes: The Politics of Signification in Central Asia'. *Europe-Asia Studies*, 61 (7) (2009): 1083–93.
Cummings, Sally N. (ed.). *Symbolism and Power in Central Asia: Politics of the Spectacular.* London: Routledge, 2010.
Cummings, Sally N. 'Leaving Lenin: Elites, Official Ideology and Monuments in the Kyrgyz Republic'. *Nationalities Papers*, 41 (4) (2013): 606–21.
'D. Sarygulov perechislil prichiny nyneshnogo krizisa v Kyrgyzstane'. *AkiPress*, 14 April 2007, http://fergana.akipress.org/news:23175/, accessed 5 March 2021.
Dadabaev, Timur. 'Post-Soviet Realities of Society in Uzbekistan'. *Central Asian Survey*, 23 (2) (2004): 141–66.
Dadabaev, Timur. 'Recollections of Emerging Hybrid Ethnic Identities in Soviet Central Asia: The Case of Uzbekistan'. *Nationalities Papers*, 41 (6) (2013): 1026–48.
Dadabaev, Timur. *Identity and Memory in Post-Soviet Central Asia*. London: Routledge, 2015.
'Dauren Babamuratov, rukovoditel' molodezhnogo dvizheniia Bolashaq', YouTube video, 1:32, uploaded by 'Sotsial'naia Platforma SDG-MEDIA', 5 November 2014, https://www.youtube.com/watch?v=k07Z5HCVWjU, accessed 29 August 2020.
Dave, Bhavna. 'National Revival in Kazakhstan: Language Shift and Identity Change'. *Post-Soviet Affairs*, 12 (1) (1996): 51–72.
Dave, Bhavna. 'Entitlement through Numbers: Nationality and Language Categories in the First Post-Soviet Census in Kazakhstan'. *Nations and Nationalism*, 10 (4) (2004): 439–59.
Dave, Bhavna. *Kazakhstan: Ethnicity, Language and Power.* London: Routledge, 2007.
De Cillia, Rudolf, Martin Reisigl and Ruth Wodak. 'The Discursive Construction of National Identities'. *Discourse & Society*, 10 (2) (1999): 149–73.
Debets, Georgii F. (ed.). *Trudy kyrgyzskoi arkheologo-etnograficheskoi ekspeditsii*. Frunze: Akademiia nauk, 1959.
Debets, Georgii F., Maksim G. Levin and Tatiana A. Trofimova. 'Antropologicheskii material kak istochnik izucheniia voprosov etnogeneza'. *Sovetskaia ethnografiia*, 1 (1952).
Decret no. 315 'O sovershenstvovanii deyatel'nosti Instituta istorii ANRU'. *Pravda Vostoka* (27 July 1998), 2–3.

'Den' nezavisimosti prazdnuet Kazakhstan'. *Tengri News*, 16 December 2014, http://tengrinews.kz/kazakhstan_news/den-nezavisimosti-prazdnuet-kazahstan-266983, accessed 5 March 2021.

Denison, Michael. 'The Art of the Impossible: Political Symbolism and the Creation of National Identity and Collective Memory in Post-Soviet Turkmenistan'. *Europe-Asia Studies*, 61 (7) (2009): 1167–87.

'Deputat Bekbolat Tleukhan proshel na detektore lzhi'. *Tengri News*, 16 October 2011, https://tengrinews.kz/kazakhstan_news/deputat-bekbolat-tleuhan-proshel-proverku-na-detektore-lji-199283, accessed 5 March 2021.

Deutsch, Karl Wolfgang. *Nationalism and Its Alternatives*. New York: Random House, 1969.

DeWeese, Devin. 'Sacred Places and "Public" Narratives: The Shrine of Ahmad Yasavi in Hagiographical Traditions of the Yasavi Sufi Order, 16th–17th Centuries'. *The Muslim World*, 90 (3–4) (2000): 353–76.

DeYoung, Alan J. (ed.). *Lost in Transition: Redefining Students and Universities in the Contemporary Kyrgyz Republic*. Charlotte, NC: Information Age Publishing, 2011.

Diat, Frédérique. 'Olzhas Sulejmenov: *Az i Ya*'. *Central Asian Survey*, 1 (1984): 101–21.

Diener, Alexander. 'National Territory and the Reconstruction of History in Kazakhstan'. *Eurasian Geography and Economics*, 43 (7) (2002): 565–83.

Diener, Alexander. 'Kazakhstan's Kin State Diaspora: Settlement Planning and the Oralman Dilemma'. *Europe Asia Studies*, 57 (2) (2005): 327–48.

Diener, Alexander. 'Problematic Integration of Mongolian Kazakh Return Migrants in Kazakhstan'. *Eurasian Geography and Economics*, 46 (6) (2005): 465–78.

Diener, Alexander. *One Homeland or Two? Nationalization and Transnationalization of Mongolia's Kazakhs*. Palo Alto, CA and Washington, DC: Stanford University Press and Woodrow Wilson Center Press, 2009.

Diener, Alexander. 'Imagining Kazakhstani-stan: Considerations of Nationalizing Social Space and Socializing National Space'. Paper presented at the 'Kazakhstan beyond Economic Success: Exploring Social and Cultural Changes in Eurasia' conference, Uppsala University, Sweden, 13–14 June 2014.

'Doktrina natsional'nogo edinstva Kazakhstana'. *Inform.kz*, 29 April 2010, http://www.inform.kz/rus/article/2263364, accessed 5 March 2021.

Dor, Rémy. 'L'épopée centrasiatique: Manas, le fils de la montagne'. In *Clats d'empires: Asie Centrale, Caucase, Afghanistan*, edited by Marlene Laruelle and Sebastien Peyrouse, 379–84. Paris: Fayard-CERI, 2013.

Drevniaia tsivilizatsiia i ee rol' v slozhenii i razvitii kul'tury Tsentral'noi Azii epokhi samanidov. Dushanbe: Mezhdunarodnyi nauchnyi centr, 1999.

Driscoll, Jesse. 'Hobbesian Neopatrimonialism'. In *Tajikistan on the Move: Statebuilding and Societal Transformations*, edited by Marlene Laruelle, 3–32. Lanham, MD: Lexington, 2018.

Dudoignon, Stéphane A. 'Changements politiques et historiographiques en Asie centrale (Tadjikistan et Uzbékistan, 1987–1993)'. *Cahiers d'Études sur la Méditerranée Orientale et le monde Turco-Iranien*, 16 (1993): 83–135.

Dugin, Aleksandr G. *Evraziiskaia missiia Nursultana Nazarbaeva*. St. Petersburg: Evraziia, 2004.

Dunn, John. 'The Paper Nation: Nationalist Iconography on Uzbek Currency'. Journal of Central Asian Studies, 3 (2) (1999): 32–66.

'Dvizhenie Ult Tagdyry-el tagdyry pereimenovalos' v Khalyk dabyly'. *Zonakz.net*, 25 November 2005, https://zonakz.net:8443/articles/10250?mode=reply.

Dymov, Oleg. *Teplo kazakhstanskoi zemli*. Almaty: Arys, 1999.

Dzhikiev, Ata. *Ocherk etnicheskoi istorii i formirovaniia naseleniia iuzhnogo Turkmenistana*. Ashkhabad: Ylym, 1977.

Dzhumakadyrov, Samat. '"Kyrk-choro" – provlastnyi proekt?'. *Radio Azattyk*, 17 July 2015, https://rus.azattyk.org/a/27133965.html, accessed 5 March 2021.

'Economic Eurasian Union Bears No Resemblance to USSR: President Nazarbayev'. *Tengri News*, 22 December 2014, http://en.tengrinews.kz/politics_sub/Economic-Eurasian-Union-bears-no-resemblance-to-USSR-President-Nazarbayev-258039, accessed 5 March 2021.

'Education Ministry: More Than 40 Per Cent of Schools Will Switch to Trilingual Education in 2018'. *Government of the Republic of Kazakhstan*, 14 June 2018, http://www.government.kz/en/novosti/1014976–education-ministry-more-than-40–of-schools-will-switch-to-trilingual-education-in-2018.html, accessed 18 October 2018.

Eleukenov, Sheriazdan R. (ed.). *Evraziiskii talisman*. Almaty: Bilim, 1996.

Epkenhans, Tim. *The Origins of the Civil War in Tajikistan: Nationalism, Islamism, and Violent Conflict in Post-Soviet Space*. Lanham, MD: Lexington, 2016.

Epkenhans, Tim. 'Oblivion, Ambivalence and Historical Erasure: Remembering the Civil War in Tajikistan'. In *Tajikistan on the Move: Statebuilding and Societal Transformations*, edited by Marlene Laruelle, 195–222. Lanham, MD: Lexington, 2018.

Ermatov, Gulzhigit. 'Understanding Illiberal Sentiments of Kyrgyz Youth'. *CAP Papers*, 173 (September 2016), https://centralasiaprogram.org/archives/9958, accessed 5 March 2021.

Esenova, Saulesh. 'Soviet Nationality, Identity, and Ethnicity in Central Asia: Historic Narratives and Kazakh Ethnic Identity'. *Journal of Muslim Minority Affairs*, 22 (1) (2002): 11–38.

Esipova, Neli. 'Assessing Russia's Influence in Its Periphery'. *BBG Research Series*, 2015. http://www.bbg.gov/wp-content/media/2016/02/Presentation-for-Posting-Russia-Research-Series-Final-_FMN-v6.pdf, accessed 29 August 2020.

Etnodemograficheskii ezhegodnik Kazakhstana. Astana: Kazakhstan State Agency of Statistics, 2013, http://www.demoscope.ru/weekly/2014/0583/biblio05.php, accessed 5 March 2021.

Eurasian Development Bank. 'Doklady TsII', https://eabr.org/analytics/integration-research/cii-reports/, accessed 21 February 2019.

European Bank for Reconstruction and Development. 'Life in Transition Survey (LITS)', https://www.ebrd.com/what-we-do/economic-research-and-data/data/lits.html, accessed 21 February 2019.

Faranda, Regina and David B. Nolle. 'Boundaries of Ethnic Identity in Central Asia: Titular and Russian Perceptions of Ethnic Commonalities in Kazakhstan and Kyrgyzstan'. *Ethnic and Racial Studies*, 34 (4) (2011): 620–42.

Fauve, Adrien. 'A Tale of Two Statues in Astana: The Fuzzy Process of Nationalistic City Making'. *Nationalities Papers*, 43 (3) (2015): 383–98.

Féaux de la Croix, Jeanne and Mohira Suyarkulova. 'The Rogun Complex: Public Roles and Historic Experiences of Dam-Building in Tajikistan and Kyrgyzstan'. *Cahiers d'Asie centrale*, 25 (2015): 103–32.

Ferrando, Olivier. 'Manipulating the Census: Ethnic Minorities in the Nationalizing States of Central Asia'. *Nationalities Papers*, 36 (3) (2008): 489–520.

Ferrando, Olivier. 'Policies and Practices of Language Education in Post-Soviet Central Asia: Between Ethnic Identity and Civic Consciousness'. In *Soviet and Post-Soviet Identities*, edited by Catriona Kelly and Mark Bassin, 254–77. Cambridge: Cambridge University Press, 2011.

Ferrando, Olivier. 'The Central Asian States and Their Co-Ethnics from Abroad: Diaspora Policies and Repatriation Programs'. In *Migration and Social Upheaval as the Face of Globalization in Central Asia*, edited by Marlene Laruelle, 239–62. London: Brill, 2013.

Fierman, William. 'Cultural Nationalism in Soviet Uzbekistan'. *Soviet Union/Union Soviétique*, 12 (1) (1985): 1–41.

Fierman, William (ed.). 'Implementing Language Laws: Perestroika and its Legacy in Five Republics'. *Nationalities Papers*, 23 (3) (1995): 505–659.

Fierman, William. 'Language and Identity in Kazakhstan: Formulations in Policy Documents 1987–1997'. *Communist and Post-Communist Studies*, 31 (2) (1998): 171–86.

Fierman, William. 'Changing Urban Demography and the Prospects of Nationalism in Kazakhstan'. *Canadian Review of Studies in Nationalism*, 27 (2000): 7–19.

Fierman, William. 'Kazakh Language and Prospects for its Role in Kazakh "Groupness"'. *Ab Imperio*, 2 (2005): 393–423.

Fierman, William. 'Language and Education in Post-Soviet Kazakhstan: Kazakh-Medium Instruction in Urban Schools'. *Russian Review*, 65 (2006): 98–116.

Fierman, William. 'Identity, Symbolism and the Politics of Identity in Central Asia'. *Europe-Asia Studies*, 61 (7) (2009): 1207–28.

Fierman, William. 'Reversing Language Shift in Kazakhstan'. In *Language Policy and Language Conflict in Afghanistan and Its Neighbors: The Changing Politics of Language Choice*, edited by Harold F. Schiffman and Brian Spooner, 140–1. Leiden: Brill, 2012.

Figueira, Dorothy. *Aryans, Jews, Brahmins: Theorizing Authority Through Myths of Identity*. New York: New York University Press, 2002.

Finke, Peter. *Variations on Uzbek Identity: Strategic Choices, Cognitive Schemas and Political Constraints in Identification Processes*. New York: Berghahn Books, 2014.

Foltz, Richard. 'The Tajiks of Uzbekistan'. *Central Asian Survey*, 15 (2) (1996): 213–16.

Forbes Manz, Beatrice. 'Tamerlane's Career and Its Uses'. *Journal of World History*, 13 (1) (2002): 1–25.
Fumagalli, Matteo. 'Ethnicity, State Formation and Foreign Policy: Uzbekistan and "Uzbeks Abroad"'. *Central Asian Survey*, 26 (1) (2007): 105–22.
Fumagalli, Matteo. 'Framing Ethnic Minority Mobilisation in Central Asia: The Cases of Uzbeks in Kyrgyzstan and Tajikistan'. *Europe-Asia Studies*, 59 (4) (2007): 567–90.
Fumagalli, Matteo. *Ethnic Conflict in Post-Soviet Central Asia: Exit, Voice, and Loyalty among Uzbek Minorities*. London: Routledge, 2019.
Gabdulhakov, Rashid. 'The Highly Securitized Insecurities of State Borders in the Fergana Valley'. *Central Asia Fellowship Papers*, 9 (March 2015).
Gafurov, A. 'Kto zhe obostriaet situatsiiu? K voprosu o diskussii istorikov Tadzhikistana i Uzbekistana'. *CentrAsia*, 8 February 2006, https://centrasia.org/newsA.php?st=1139391780.
Gafurov, Bobodzhan G. *Istoriia tadzhikskogo naroda v kratkom izlozhenii*. Moscow: Politizdat, 1949.
Gafurov, Bobodzhan G. *Tadzhiki: drevneishaia, drevniaia i srednevekovaia istoriia*, vol. 2. Dushanbe: Irfon, 1989.
Gafurov, Bobodzhan G. and Boris A. Litvinskii. *Uzlovye problemy etnogeneza i etnicheskoi istorii narodov Srednei Azii i Kazakhstana (teoreticheskii aspekt)*. Moscow: Nauka, 1976.
Gallup. 'Kazakhstan'. https://news.gallup.com/topic/country_kaz.aspx, accessed 21 February 2019.
'Gde nakhoditsia cherep poslednego kazakhskogo khana Kenesary?'. *Kaztube.kz*, 3 November 2014, https://kaztube.kz/video/154957, accessed 5 March 2021.
Gellner, Ernest. 'Ethnicity and Anthropology in the Soviet Union'. *European Journal of Sociology*, 18 (2) (December 1977): 201–20.
Gellner, Ernest. *Nations and Nationalism*. Ithaca, NY: Cornell University Press, 2009.
'Genotsid kazakhov (Makash Tatimov, chast' 1)', YouTube video, 8:34, uploaded by 'debashir', 17 August 2008, https://www.youtube.com/watch?v=SdpePACdkpY&nohtml5=False, accessed 29 August 2020.
Gerber, Theodore P. and Michael Van Landingham. 'Ties that Remind: Known Family Connections to Past Events as Salience Cues and Collective Memory of Stalin's Repressions of the 1930s in Contemporary Russia'. *American Sociological Review*, forthcoming.
Germanov, Valerii. 'S. P. Tolstov: maître, docteur, commandeur, ou l'histoire à travers l'archéologie et l'ethnographie'. *Cahiers d'Asie centrale*, 10 (2002): 193–216.
Gershenzon. 'Ariiskaia mifologiia i Tsentral'naia Aziia'. *CentrAsia*, 17 and 20 September 2003.
Gessat-Anstett, Élisabeth. 'Les mots/maux de l'etnografiâ: à propos d'une discipline et de ses attendus, l'ethnologie russe post-soviétique'. *Journal des anthropologues*, 87 (2001): 65–78.
Gidda, Mirren. 'No More Borat, Kazakhstan Makes its Own "Game of Thrones"-Style TV Show'. *Newsweek*, 28 January 2016, https://www.newsweek.com/kazakhstan-game-thrones-borat-kazakh-khanate-420437, accessed 5 March 2021.
Goodrick-Clarke, Nicholas. *Hitler's Priestess: Svitri Devi, the Hindu-Aryan Myth, and Neo-Nazism*. New York: New York University Press, 1998.
Gorshenina, Svetlana. *L'invention de l'Asie centrale: Histoire du concept de la Tartarie à l'Eurasie*. Geneve: Droz, 2014.
'Gossekretar' KP D. Sarygulov: 'Nam nado stat' nastoiashchimi, gordymi, chestnymi, prostymi… kyrgyzami" (interv'iu)'. *Vechernyi Bishkek*, 21 February 2006, www.centrasia.org/newsA.php4?st=1140514860.
Gullette, David. *The Genealogical Construction of the Kyrgyz Republic: Kinship, State, and 'Tribalism'*. Leiden: Brill, 2010.
Gullette, David and John Heathershaw. 'The Affective Politics of Sovereignty: Reflecting on the 2010 Conflict in Kyrgyzstan'. *Nationalities Papers*, 43 (1) (2015): 122–39.
Hamayon, Roberte N. 'Shamanism, Buddhism and Epic Heroism: Which Supports the Identity of the Post-Soviet Buryats?'. *Central Asian Survey*, 17 (1) (1998): 51–67.
Hamayon, Roberte. 'Construction of a National Emblem, Recomposition of Identities and "Heroic" Millenarianism in Post-Soviet Buryatia: A Reappraisal'. In *Circumpolar Ethnicity and Identity*, edited by Takashi Irimoto and Takako Yamada, 293–305. Osaka: National Museum of Ethnology, 2004.
Hanks, Reuel. 'Contours of Ethnonational Landscapes in Three Cities: Youths' Perspectives on Ethnic and Social Integration'. In *The Nazarbayev Generation: Youth in Kazakhstan*, edited by Marlene Laruelle, 153–65. Lanham, MD: Lexington, 2019.

Hardenberg, Roland. 'Collective, Communicative, and Cultural Memories: Examples of Local Historiography from Northern Kyrgyzstan'. *Central Asian Survey*, 31 (3) (2012): 265–76.

Haugen, Arne. *The Establishment of National Republics in Soviet Central Asia*. Basingstoke: Palgrave Macmillan, 2004.

Haupt, Georges, Michaël Löwy and Claudie Weill. *Les Marxistes et la question nationale, 1848–1914*. Paris: L'Harmattan, 1997.

Heathershaw, John. *Post-Conflict Tajikistan: The Politics of Peacebuilding and the Emergence of Legitimate Order*. London: Routledge, 2011.

Heathershaw, John and Parviz Mullojonov. 'Rebels Without a Cause? Authoritarian Conflict Management in Tajikistan, 2008–2015'. In *Tajikistan on the Move: Statebuilding and Societal Transformations*, edited by Marlene Laruelle, 33–62. Lanham, MD: Lexington, 2018.

Heathershaw, John. 'Tajikistan'. In *Post-Soviet Nations*, edited by Peter Rutland. *Central Asian Survey* (in press).

Hierman, Brent. 'Central Asian Ethnicity Compared: Evaluating the Contemporary Social Salience of Uzbek Identity in Kyrgyzstan and Tajikistan'. *Europe-Asia Studies*, 67 (4) (June 2015): 519–39.

Hirsch, Francine. 'Race without the Practice of Racial Politics'. *Slavic Review*, 61 (1) (2002): 30–43.

Hirsch, Francine. *Empire of Nations: Ethnographic Knowledge and the Making of the Soviet Union*. Ithaca, NY: Cornell University Press, 2005.

Hobsbawm, Eric. *Nations and Nationalism since 1780: Programme, Myth, Reality*. Cambridge: Cambridge University Press, 1991.

Hobsbawm, Eric J. and Terence Ranger. *The Invention of Tradition*. Cambridge: Cambridge University Press, 1995 [1983].

Hojiev, Khushbakht. 'Nation-Building and Nation-State Formation in Tajik School History Textbooks: A Comparative Perspective'. In *Writing History in Central Asia*, edited by Helge Blakkisrud. Publication forthcoming.

'Honored Figure of Kazakhstan, Doctor of Philology Tursynbek Kakishev Passed Away at the Age of 88'. *Inform.kz*, 7 September 2015, http://www.inform.kz/eng/article/2815227, accessed 5 March 2021.

Houtsma, Martijn Theodoor et al. (eds). *Encyclopédie de l'Islam*, vol. IV. Paris: Picard, 1934.

Howie, Peter and Zauresh Atakhanova. 'Resource Boom and Inequality: Kazakhstan as a Case Study'. *Resources Policy*, 39 (March 2014): 71–9.

Human Rights Watch. 'Kazakhstan: Two Activists Detained. Vague Criminal Charge Used to Target Critics', 16 October 2015, https://www.hrw.org/news/2015/10/16/kazakhstan-two-activists-detained, accessed 3 September 2020.

Hutchinson, John. *Nations as Zones of Conflict*. London: SAGE Publications, 2005.

Iakubovskii, Aleksandr Iu. *K voprosu ob etnogeneze uzbekskogo naroda*. Tashkent: UZFAN, 1941.

Iakubovskii, Aleksandr Iu. *Istoriia narodov Uzbekistana*. Tashkent: Akademiia Nauk Uz. SSR, 1947.

Iakubovskii, Aleksandr Iu. 'Voprosy etnogeneza turkmen v VIII-X vv'. *Sovetskaia etnografiia*, 3 (1947).

Ileulova, Gul'mira (ed.). 'Obzor kazakhstanskogo rynka teleindustrii na primere sravnitel'nogo analiza videokontenta telekanalov KTK, 31 kanal, Khabar'. *spik.kz*, 28 June 2015, http://www.spik.kz/articles/kult-tur/2015-05-28/issledovatelskiy-proekt-obzor-kazahstanskogo-rynka-teleindustrii-na, accessed 26 January 2017.

Ilkhamov, Alisher (ed.). *Etnicheskii atlas Uzbekistana*. Tashkent: Open Society Institute Assistance Foundation Uzbekistan, 2002.

Ilkhamov, Alisher. 'Arkheologiia uzbekskoi identichnosti'. *Etnograficheskoe obozrenie*, 1 (2005): 25–47.

Ilkhamov, Alisher. 'National Ideologies and Historical Mythology Construction in Post-Soviet Central Asia'. In *Patterns of Transformation in and Around Uzbekistan*, edited by Paolo Sartori and Tommaso Trevisani, 91–120. Reggio Emilia: Diabasis, 2007.

Ilkhamov, Alisher. 'Neopatrimonialism, Patronage and Factionalism in Post-Soviet Uzbekistan'. In *Neopatrimonialism in Africa and Beyond*, edited by Daniel Bach and Mamoudou Gazibo, 186–96. London: Routledge: 2012.

Ilolov, Mamadcho. 'Nasledie nashikh predkov. 2006-oi – God ariiskoi tsivilizatsii'. *CentrAsia*, 26 June 2005, https://centrasia.org/newsA.php?st=1119785220, accessed 8 March 2021.

'Informatsionnaia bezopasnost' Kazakhstana – v poiskakh ob"ektivnoi istiny'. Aspandau Club, 2014, https://aspandau.kz/index.php?route=news/news&npath=75, accessed 29 August 2020.

Ingham, Norman W. 'The Igor' Tale and the Origins of Conspiracy Theory'. *Russian History*, 44 (2–3) (2017): 135–49.

Insebayeva, Sabina. 'Visions of Nationhood: Youth, Identity, and Kazakh Popular Music'. In *The Nazarbayev Generation: Youth in Kazakhstan*, edited by Marlene Laruelle, 177–90. Lanham, MD: Lexington, 2019.

Institute of Eurasian Integration. 'Sovremennoe sostoianie i tendentsii vsekazakhstanskoi kul'tury'. Astana: Institute of Eurasian Integration, 2014.

Institute of World Economics and Politics (IWEP). 'Opros "Diagnostika obshchestvennogo mneniia v Kazakhstane"'. Astana: IWEP, 2017.

International Labour Organization. 'Transitioning from the Informal to the Formal Economy'. Report V (1), International Labour Conference, 103rd Session, 2014, https://www.ilo.org/wcmsp5/groups/public/@ed_dialogue/@actrav/documents/publication/wcms_545928.pdf, accessed 25 February 2021.

International Republican Institute. 'Kazakhstan'. https://www.iri.org/country/Kazakhstan, accessed 21 February 2019.

Introvigne, Massimo. *Le New Age des origines à nos jours: Courants, mouvements, personnalités*. Paris: Dervy, 2005.

Isaacs, Rico. '"Papa" – Nursultan Nazarbayev and the Discourse of Charismatic Leadership and Nation-Building in Post-Soviet Kazakhstan'. *Studies in Ethnicity and Nationalism*, 10 (3) (2010): 435–52.

Isaacs, Rico. 'Nomads, Warriors and Bureaucrats: Nation-Building and Film in Post-Soviet Kazakhstan'. *Nationalities Papers*, 43 (3) (2015): 399–416.

Isaacs, Rico. 'The Kazakhstan Now! Hybridity and Hipsters in Almaty: Negotiating Global and Local Lives'. In *The Nazarbayev Generation: Youth in Kazakhstan*, edited by Marlene Laruelle, 227–46. Lanham, MD: Lexington, 2019.

Isaacs, Rico and Abel Polese. 'Between "Imagined" and "Real" Nation-Building: Identities and Nationhood in Post-Soviet Central Asia'. *Nationalities Papers*, 43 (3) (2015): 371–82.

Isaacs, Rico and Abel Polese. *Nation Building in Post-Soviet Spaces: New Tools and Approaches*. Farnham: Ashgate, 2015.

Isliamieva, S. 'Gosudarstvennaia teoriia etnogeneza kazakhov v istorigrafii XX veka'. *Otan tarixy*, 4 (2003).

Ismagulov, Orazak. *Etnicheskaia antropologiia Kazakhstana*. Alma-Ata: Nauka, 1982.

Ismailova, Baktygul. 'Curriculum Reform in Post-Soviet Kyrgyzstan: Indigenization of the History Curriculum'. *Curriculum Journal*, 15 (3) (November 2004): 247–64.

'Issledovanie Sberbanka: 30 faktov o sovremennoi molodezhi'. *Adindex*, 10 March 2017, https://adindex.ru/news/researches/2017/03/10/158487.phtml, accessed 5 March 2021.

Istoricheskaia pamiat', natsional'noe soglasie i demokraticheskie reformy – grazhdanskii vybor naroda Kazakhstana. Almaty: Zhazushi, 1997.

Jacquesson, Svetlana (ed.). 'Karakalpaks et autres gens de l'Aral: entre rivages et déserts'. *Cahiers d'Asie centrale*, 10 (2002).

Jacquesson, Svetlana. 'Power Play among the Kyrgyz: State versus Descent'. In *Representing Power in Ancient Inner Asia: Legitimacy, Transmission and the Sacred*, edited by Isabelle Charleux, Grégory Delaplace, Roberte Hamayon and Scott Pearce, 221–44. Bellingham, WA: Center for East Asian Studies, Western Washington University, 2010.

Jacquesson, Svetlana. 'From Clan Narratives to Clan Politics'. *Central Asian Survey*, 31 (3) (2012): 277–92.

Jacquesson, Svetlana. 'Genealogies as a Craft: The Search for "Truth" and Authority in Contemporary Kyrgyzstan'. In *History Making in Central and Northern Eurasia*, edited by Svetlana Jacquesson, 100–21. Wiesbaden: Reichert Verlag, 2016.

Jacquesson, Svetlana (ed.). *History Making in Central and Northern Eurasia: Contemporary Actors and Practices*. Wiesbaden: Reichert Verlag, 2016.

Jacquesson, Svetlana. 'Claiming Heritage: The Manas Epic between China and Kyrgyzstan'. *Central Asian Survey*, May 2020: 324–39.

Jašina-Schäfer, Alina. 'Where Do I Belong? Narratives of *Rodina* among Russian-Speaking Youth in Kazakhstan'. *Europe-Asia Studies*, 71 (1) (2019): 97–116.

Jessa, Pawel. '*Aq jol* Soul Healers: Religious Pluralism and a Contemporary Muslim Movement in Kazakhstan'. *Central Asian Survey*, 25 (3) (2006): 359–71.

Jockusch, Laura and Tamar Lewinsky. 'Paradise Lost? Postwar Memory of Polish Jewish Survival in the Soviet Union'. *Holocaust and Genocide Studies*, 24 (3) (2010): 373–99.

Jones, Pauline. *Islam, Society, and Politics in Central Asia*. Pittsburgh, PA: University of Pittsburgh Press, 2017.

J'son & Partners Consulting, 'Obzor rynka televizionnogo kontenta v respublike Kazakhstan'. 27 June 2015, http://json.tv/ict_telecom_analytics_view/obzor-rynka-televizionnogo-kontenta-v-respublike-kazahstan, accessed 3 September 2020.

Junisbai, Azamat K. 'Understanding Economic Justice Attitudes in Two Countries: Kazakhstan and Kyrgyzstan'. *Social Forces*, 88 (4) (June 2010): 1677–702.

Junisbai, Barbara and Azamat Junisbai. 'Are Youth Different? The Nazarbayev Generation and Public Opinion'. In *The Nazarbayev Generation: Youth in Kazakhstan*, edited by Marlene Laruelle, 25–48. Lanham, MD: Lexington, 2019.

Junisbai, Barbara, Azamat Junisbai and Christopher Whitsel. 'What Makes "Ardent Democrats" in Kazakhstan and Kyrgyzstan?'. *PONARS Eurasia Policy Memo*, 489 (October 2017), http://www.ponarseurasia.org/memo/what-makes-ardent-democrats-kazakhstan-and-kyrgyzstan, accessed 5 March 2021.

Junisbai, Barbara, Azamat Junisbai and Nicola Ying Fry. 'Mass Media Consumption in Post-Soviet Kyrgyzstan and Kazakhstan: The View from Below'. In *Mass Media in the Post-Soviet World: Market Forces, State Actors, and Political Manipulation in the Informational Environment after Communism*, edited by Peter Rollberg and Marlene Laruelle, 139–58. Stuttgart: Ibidem-Verlag, 2018.

Junisbai, Barbara, Azamat Junisbai and Baurzhan Zhussupov. 'Two Countries, Five Years: Islam in Kazakhstan and Kyrgyzstan Through the Lens of Public Opinion Surveys'. In *Being Muslim in Central Asia: Practices, Politics, and Identities*, edited by Marlene Laruelle, 38–60. London and Leiden: Brill, 2018.

Juraev, Shairbek. 'The Evolving Role of Political Parties in Kyrgyz Politics'. In *Kyrgyzstan beyond 'Democracy Island' and 'Failing State': Social and Political Changes*, 2015.

Kabatova, Karlygash. 'Overcoming a Taboo: Normalizing Sexuality Education'. In *The Nazarbayev Generation: Youth in Kazakhstan*, edited by Marlene Laruelle, 289–303. Lanham, MD: Lexington, 2019.

Kagarlitski, Boris. 'Kazakhstan's Parliament is Dissolved'. *Greenleft.org*, 12 April 1995, https://www.greenleft.org.au/node/9524, accessed 5 March 2021.

Kakeyev, A. and V. Ploskikh. *Istoriia Kyrgyzov Kyrgyzstana*. Bishkek: Kyrgyzstan Academy of Sciences, 2003.

Kalinovsky, Artemy M. *Laboratory of Socialist Development: Cold War Politics and Decolonization in Soviet Tajikistan*. Ithaca, NY: Cornell University Press, 2018.

Kamoliddin, Shamsiddin. 'Neskol'ko zamechanii ob *Etnicheskom Atlase Uzbekistana*'. *Etnozhurnal*, October–November 2003 (no longer available online).

Kamoliddin, Shamsiddin. 'Eshche raz ob *Etnicheskom Atlase Uzbekistana*'. *Etnozhurnal*, February 2004, http://www.ethnonet.ru (no longer available online).

Kantar. 'Survey of Kazakhstan TV Audience'. *Kanar.kz*, http://kantar.kz/research/television, accessed 29 August 2020.

Karabassova, Laura. 'Teachers' Conceptualization of Content and Language Integrated Learning (CLIL): Evidence from a Trilingual Context'. *International Journal of Bilingual Education and Bilingualism* (November 2018): 1–13.

Karamanova, Minsar. 'State Program "Cultural Heritage" of Kazakhstan: Stages of Implementation and Value'. *Qazaqstan Tarihy*, 1 October 2013, https://e-history.kz/en/contents/view/1568, accessed 5 March 2021.

Karimov, Islam. 'Natsional'naia ideologiia – dlia nas istochnik dukhovno-nravstvennoi sily v stroitel'stve gosudarstva i obshchestva'. In Islam Karimov, *Nasha vysshaia tsel' – nezavisimost' i protsvetanie rodiny, svoboda i blagopoluchie naroda*, vol. 8, 419–62. Tashkent: Uzbekiston, 2000.

Kassenova, Togzhan. 'Kazakhstan and the Global Nuclear Order'. *Central Asian Affairs* 1 (2) (2014): 273–86.

Katargin, V. 'Kirgizia dlia kirgizov? V respublike poiavilas' pervaia partiia natsionaliticheskogo tolka'. *Gazeta.kg*, 29 August 2005, http://gazeta.kg/article/2005-08-29, accessed 12 March 2014.

'Katekhizis dlia nerusskikh'. *Beznen-Yul*, 1 (2006). http://www.beznen-yul.narod.ru/arhiv/2006/1san/KATEHIZIS.htm, accessed 12 March 2014.

Kayumova, Marina. 'Emigration of the "Crème de la Crème" in Uzbekistan: A Gender Perspective'. *Central Asia Fellowship Papers*, 8 (March 2015). https://centralasiaprogram.org/archives/7461, accessed 5 March 2021.

'Kazakh Head of the State Unveiled a Monument in Almaty'. *Trend.az*, 18 September 2006, https://en.trend.az/casia/kazakhstan/862247.html, accessed 5 March 2021.

'Kazakh National Patriots Urge Ethnic Russians to Go Home'. *Zonakz.net*, 16 August 2006, http://enews.fergananews.com/articles/1555, accessed 12 March 2014.

'Kazakh President Nazarbayev Granted "Leader of Nation" Title'. *Trend.Az*, 15 June 2010, https://en.trend.az/casia/kazakhstan/1704795.html, accessed 5 March 2021.

'Kazakhskaia Pravda vykhodit na tropu voiny?'. *Zonakz.net*, 19 February 2003, https://zonakz.net/8443/articles/2663, accessed 12 March 2014.

'Kazakhskoi gosudarstvennosti v 2015 ispolnitsia 55 let – Nazarbaev'. *Tengri News*, 22 October 2014, http://tengrinews.kz/kazakhstan_news/kazahskoy-gosudarstvennosti-v-2015–godu-ispolnitsya-550–let---nazarbaev-263876, accessed 5 March 2021.

'Kazakhstan', *Pew-Templeton Global Religious Futures Project, 2016*, http://www.globalreligiousfutures.org/countries/kazakhstan#/?affiliations_religion_id=0&affiliations_year=2010&region_name=All per cent20Countries&restrictions_year=2016, accessed 21 February 2019.

'Kazakhstan Looks to Ban Gay 'Propaganda' and Identify Gays by Searching for Degeneratism in their DNA'. *Tengri News*, 13 September 2014, https://en.tengrinews.kz/laws_initiatives/Kazakhstan-looks-to-ban-gay-propaganda-and-identify-gays-by-256105, accessed 5 March 2021.

'Kazakhstan Will Not Change Its Name to Get Rid of the 'Stan' Ending: Foreign Minister'. *Tengri News*, 13 June 2014, http://en.tengrinews.kz/politics_sub/Kazakhstan-will-not-change-its-name-to-get-rid-of-the-stan-ending-Foreign-254165, accessed 5 March 2021.

'Kazakhstanskie politologi protiv vkhozhdeniia Kazakhstana v Evraziiskii soiuz'. *Nur.kz*, 9 May 2012, https://www.nur.kz/217304–kazahstanskie-politologi-protiv-vhozhdeniya-kazahstana-v-evrazijskij-soyuz.html, accessed 12 March 2014.

Kehl-Bodrogi, Krisztina. 'Who Owns the Shrine? Competing Meanings and Authorities at a Pilgrimage Site in Khorezm'. *Central Asian Survey*, 25 (3) (2006): 235–50.

Keller, Shoshana. 'Story, Time, and Dependent Nationhood in the Uzbek History Curriculum'. *Slavic Review*, 66 (2) (2007): 257–77.

Kendzior, Sarah. 'Reclaiming *Ma'naviyat*: Morality, Criminality, and Dissent Politics in Uzbekistan'. In *Ethnographies of the State in Central Asia: Performing Politics*, edited by Madeleine Reeves, Johan Rasanayagam and Judith Beyer, 223–42. Bloomington: Indiana University Press, 2014.

Kesici, Özgecan. 'The Dilemma in the Nation-Building Process: The Kazakh or Kazakhstani Nation?'. *Journal on Ethnopolitics and Minority Issues in Europe*, 10 (1) (2011): 31–58.

Khalid, Adeeb. *Islam after Communism*. Berkeley: University of California Press, 2007.

Khalid, Adeeb. 'Locating the (Post-)Colonial in Soviet History'. *Central Asian Survey*, 26 (4) (2007): 465–73.

Khalid, Adeeb. *Making Uzbekistan: Nation, Empire, and Revolution in the Early USSR*. London: Cornell University Press, 2015.

Khamidov, Alisher. 'Propishetsiia li kurultai "patriotov" v Kirgizskoi konstitutsii?'. *Centrasia*, 18 April 2007, http://www.centrasia.ru/newsA.php?st=1176871380 (no longer available).

Kılavuz, İdil Tunçer. 'Political and Social Networks in Tajikistan and Uzbekistan: "Clan", "Region", and Beyond'. *Central Asian Survey*, 28 (3) (2009): 323–34.

Kilner, James. 'Kazakh State TV Station Ditches Russian Language Broadcasts'. *Daily Telegraph*, 8 September 2011, http://www.telegraph.co.uk/news/worldnews/asia/kazakhstan/8750245/Kazakh-state-TV-station-ditches-Russian-language-broadcasts.html, accessed 5 March 2021.

Kilybayeva, Shugyla, Gulnar Nassimova and Aliya Massalimova. 'The Kazakhstani Youth's Engagement in Politics'. *Studies of Transition States and Societies*, 9 (1) (2017): 53–71.

Kirby, Alan. 'The Death of Postmodernism and Beyond'. *Philosophy Now*, 58 (2006), https://philosophynow.org/issues/58/The_Death_of_Postmodernism_And_Beyond, accessed 26 August 2020.

Kirby, Alan. *Digimodernism: How New Technologies Dismantle the Postmodern and Reconfigure Our Culture*. London and New York: Continuum, 2009.

Koch, Natalie. 'The Monumental and the Miniature: Imagining "Modernity" in Astana'. *Social and Cultural Geography*, 11 (8) (2010): 769–87.

Koch, Natalie. 'Sport and Soft Authoritarian Nation-Building'. *Political Geography*, 32 (2013): 41–52.

Koch, Natalie. 'The "Heart" of Eurasia? Kazakhstan's Centrally-Located Capital City'. *Central Asian Survey*, 32 (2) (2013): 134–47.

Koch, Natalie. *The Geopolitics of Spectacle: Space, Synecdoche, and the New Capitals of Asia*. Ithaca, NY: Cornell University Press, 2018.

Koch, Natalie and Kristopher D. White. 'Cowboys, Gangsters, and Rural Bumpkins: Constructing the "Other" in Kazakhstan's "Texas"'. In *Kazakhstan in the Making: Legitimacy, Symbols, and Social Changes*, edited by Marlene Laruelle, 181–207. Lanham, MD: Lexington, 2015.

Kolstø, Pål. 'Anticipating Demographic Superiority: Kazakh Thinking on Integration and Nation Building'. *Europe-Asia Studies*, 50 (1) (1998): 51–69.

Kolstø, Pål. *Political Construction Sites: Nation-Building in Russia and the Post-Soviet States*. Boulder, CO: Westview Press, 2000.

'Konstitutsiia Respubliki Kazakhstana', http://www.akorda.kz/en/official_documents/constitution, accessed 5 March 2021.

Kopack, Robert. 'Monuments and Memory in the Landscapes of Kazakhstan'. Master's thesis, Michigan State University, 2013.

Köppen, Bernhard. 'The Production of a New Eurasian Capital on the Kazakh Steppe: Architecture, Urban Design, and Identity in Astana'. *Nationalities Papers*, 41 (4) (2013): 590–605.

Korchevskii, Mikhail. 'Seriia sotsial'nykh rolikov zapuskaetsia na kazakhstanskikh kanalakh'. *KTK.kz*, 26 March 2015, http://www.ktk.kz/ru/news/video/2015/03/26/58499, accessed 5 March 2021.

Koshim, Dos. 'Za kazakhov ia umru. Ia natsionalist'. Zonakz.net, 31 January 2008, https://zonakz.net:8443/articles/20831, accessed 17 October 2018.

Koshim, Dos. 'Natsional'nye problemy nevozmozhno reshit' bez politicheskikh reform', YouTube video, 16:47, uploaded by 'Informatsionnyi kanal "16/12"', 10 October 2014, https://www.youtube.com/watch?v=zTvm19_OPyw, accessed 5 March 2021.

Koshim, Dos. 'Kazakhskii natsionalizm – positivnyi natsionalizm'. *Altyn-Orda*, 27 January 2015, http://www.altyn-orda.kz/dos-koshim-kazaxskij-nacionalizm-pozitivnyj-nacionalizm, accessed 5 March 2021.

Kosmarskaya, Natalya. 'Russians in Post-Soviet Central Asia: More 'Cold' than the Others? Exploring (Ethnic) Identity under Different Sociopolitical Settings'. *Journal of Multilingual and Multicultural Development*, 35 (1) (2014): 9–26.

Kosnazarov, Daniyar. 'Pokolenie "Zanizhennykh ozhidanii"'. *Narxoz Business Review*, 2 (August 2017): 10–17.

Kosnazarov, Daniyar. '#Hashtag Activism: Youth, Social Media, and Politics'. In *The Nazarbayev Generation: Youth in Kazakhstan*, edited by Marlene Laruelle, 247–68. Lanham, MD: Lexington, 2019.

Kovalev, Vitalii. 'V Kazakhstane Den' Koza Korpesh i Bayan-Suly pochti nikto ne prazdnuet'. *KTK*, 15 April 2013, http://www.ktk.kz/ru/news/video/2013/4/15/22144, accessed 5 March 2021.

Kozgambaeva, Gul'nar. 'Museum of Victims of Political Repression of South Kazakhstan Region'. *KazNU Bulletin. History Series*, 84 (1) (2017): 248–52, https://bulletin-history.kaznu.kz/index.php/1-history/article/view/97/100, accessed 3 September 2019.

Kozybaev, Manash K. 'Uroki otechestvennoi istorii i vozrozhdenie kazakhstanskogo obshchestva'. *Stolichnoe obozrenie*, 10 July 1998, 3.

'Kto v Kirgizii khoziain'. Easttime.ru, 30 June 2008, http://www.easttime.ru/news/1/4/599.html, accessed 17 October 2018.

Kucera, Joshua. 'Tajikistan's Dream'. *The Wilson Quarterly* (Summer 2013): 8, https://www.wilsonquarterly.com/quarterly/summer-2014-where-have-all-the-jobs-gone/tajikistans-dream, accessed 5 March 2021.

Kucera, Joshua. 'Can a Homegrown University in Authoritarian Kazakhstan Incubate Reform?'. *Al Jazeera*, 20 June 2014.

Kudaibergenova, Diana T. '"Imagining Community" in Soviet Kazakhstan: An Historical Analysis of Narrative on Nationalism in Kazakh-Soviet Literature'. *Nationalities Papers*, 41 (5) (2013): 839–54.

Kudaibergenova, Diana. 'O natsii i ee nositeliakh'. *Ekspert Kazakhstan*, 5 (August 2013), http://expertonline.kz/a11460/, accessed 5 March 2021.

Kudaibergenova, Diana T. 'National Identity Formation in Post-Soviet Central Asia: The Soviet Legacy, Primordialism, and Patterns of Ideological Development since 1991'. In *Social and Cultural Change in Central Asia: The Soviet Legacy*, edited by Sevket Akyildiz and Richard Carlson, 160–73. London: Routledge, 2013.

Kudaibergenova, Diana T. 'The Ideology of Development and Legitimation: Beyond Kazakhstan 2030'. *Central Asian Survey*, 34 (4) (2015): 440–55.

Kudaibergenova, Diana T. 'Between the State and the Artist: Representations of Femininity and Masculinity in the Formation of Ideas of the Nation in Central Asia'. *Nationalities Papers*, 44 (2) (2016): 225–46.

Kudaibergenova, Diana T. 'Eurasian Economic Union Integration in Kazakhstan and Kyrgyzstan'. *European Politics and Society*, 17 (1) (2016): 97–112.

Kudaibergenova, Diana T. 'Nationalizing Elites and Regimes: Nation-Building in Post-Soviet Authoritarian and Democratic Contexts'. In *Kazakhstan in the Making: Legitimacy, Symbols and Social Changes*, edited by Marlene Laruelle, 113–30. Lanham, MD: Lexington, 2016.

Kudaibergenova, Diana T. *Re-Writing the Nation: Elites, Networks and Narratives in Modern Kazakh Literature*. Lanham, MD: Lexington, 2016.

Kudaibergenova, Diana T. 'The Use and Abuse of Postcolonial Discourses in Post-Independent Kazakhstan'. *Europe-Asia Studies*, 68 (5) (2016): 917–35.

Kudaibergenova, Diana T. 'Contemporary Public Art and Nation: Contesting "Tradition" in Post-Socialist Cultures and Societies'. *Central Asian Affairs*, 4 (4) (2017): 305–30.

Kudaibergenova, Diana T. '"My Silk Road to You": Re-Imagining Routes, Roads, and Geography in Contemporary Art of "Central Asia"'. *Journal of Eurasian Studies*, 1 (2017): 31–43.

Kudaibergenova, Diana T. 'The Archaeology of Nationalizing Regimes in the Post-Soviet Space: Narratives, Elites, and Minorities'. *Problems of Post-Communism*, 64 (6) (2017): 342–55.

Kudaibergenova, Diana T. 'Punk Shamanism, Revolt and Break-Up of Traditional Linkage: The Waves of Cultural Production in Post-Soviet Kazakhstan'. *European Journal of Cultural Studies*, 21 (4) (2018): 435–51.

Kudaibergenova, Diana T. 'Compartmentalized Ideology: Presidential Addresses and Legitimation in Kazakhstan'. In *Theorizing Central Asian Politics*, edited by Rico Isaacs and Alessandro Frigerio, 145–66. New York: Palgrave Macmillan, 2019.

Kudaibergenova, Diana T. 'Mankurts, Kazakh "Russians" and "Shala" Kazakhs: Language, National Identity, and Ethnicity Revisited'. In *The Nazarbayev Generation: Youth in Kazakhstan*, edited by Marlene Laruelle, 89–113. Lanham, MD: Lexington, 2019.

Kudaibergenova, Diana T. *Toward Nationalizing Regimes: Conceptualizing Power and Identity in the Post-Soviet Realm*. Pittsburgh, PA: University of Pittsburgh Press, 2019.

Kudaibergenova, Diana and Boram Shin. 'Authors and Authoritarianism in Central Asia: Failed Agency and Nationalizing Authoritarianism in Uzbekistan and Kazakhstan'. *Asian Studies Review*, 42 (2) (2018): 304–22.

Kurzman, Charles. 'Uzbekistan: The Invention of Nationalism in an Invented Nation'. *Critique: Journal of Critical Studies of the Middle East*, 15 (1999): 77–98.

Kusherbaev, Krymbek Eleuuly. *Etnopolitika Kazakhstana: sostoianie i perspektivy*. Almaty: Institut razvitiia Kazakhstana, 1996.

Kuzio, Taras. 'Nationalist Riots in Kazakhstan'. *Central Asian Survey*, 7 (4) (1988): 79–100.

Kuzio, Taras. '"Nationalising States" or Nation-Building? A Critical Review of the Theoretical Literature and Empirical Evidence'. *Nations and Nationalism*, 7 (2) (2001): 135–54.

Labanyi, Jo. 'The Languages of Silence: Historical Memory, Generational Transmission and Witnessing in Contemporary Spain'. *Journal of Romance Studies*, 9 (3) (2009): 23–35.

Landau, Jacob M. and Barbara Kellner-Heinkele. *Politics of Language in the Ex-Soviet Muslim States*. London: Hurst, 2001.

Laqueur, Walter. *The Struggle for the Middle East: The Soviet Union and the Middle East, 1958–68*. London: Routledge, 1969.

Laruelle, Marlene. 'Etnologiia, natsional'noe stanovlenie i politika v Uzbekistane'. *Ab Imperio*, 4 (2005): 279–92.

Laruelle, Marlene. 'L'appartenance à l'islam comme critère politique? La politisation des Directions spirituelles et la constitution de partis musulmans en Russie'. In *Islam et politique en ex-URSS, Russie d'Europe et Asie Centrale*, edited by Marlene Laruelle and Sébastien Peyrouse, 85–115. Paris: L'Harmattan and IFEAC, 2005.

Laruelle, Marlene. *Russian Eurasianism: An Ideology of Empire*. Washington, DC: Woodrow Wilson Press/Johns Hopkins University Press, 2008.

Laruelle, Marlene. 'Russia and Central Asia'. In *The New Central Asia: The Regional Impact of International Actors*, edited by Emilian Kavalski, 149–76. Hackensack, NJ and London: World Scientific, 2010.

Laruelle, Marlene. 'Conspiracy and Alternate History in Russia: A Nationalist Equation for Success?'. *Russian Review*, 71 (4) (2012): 565–80.

Laruelle, Marlene. 'The Paradigm of Nationalism in Kyrgyzstan: Evolving Narrative, the Sovereignty Issue, and Political Agenda'. *Communist and Post-Communist Studies*, 45 (1–2) (2012): 39–49.
Laruelle, Marlene (ed.). *Migration and Social Upheaval as the Face of Globalization in Central Asia*. London: Brill, 2013.
Laruelle, Marlene. 'The "Russian Idea" on the Small Screen: Staging National Identity on Russia's TV'. *Demokratizatsiya: The Journal of Post-Soviet Democratization*, 22 (2) (2014): 313–33.
Laruelle, Marlene. *Being Muslim in Central Asia*. Leiden: Brill, 2018.
Laruelle, Marlene. *Russian Nationalism: Imaginaries, Doctrines and Political Battlefields*. London: Routledge, 2019.
Laruelle, Marlene and Aurélie Biard. '"Tengrism" in Kyrgyzstan: In Search of New Religious and Political Legitimacy'. In *Representing Power in Ancient Inner Asia: Legitimacy, Transmission and the Sacred*, edited by Isabelle Charleux, Gregory Delaplace and Roberte Hamayon, 55–96. Bellingham, WA: Center for East Asian Studies, Western Washington University, 2010.
Laruelle, Marlene and Sebastien Peyrouse. *Les Russes du Kazakhstan: Identités nationales et nouveaux Etats dans l'espace post-soviétique*. Paris: Maisonneuve & Larose/IFEAC, 2004.
Laruelle, Marlene and Sebastien Peyrouse. *Globalizing Central Asia: Geopolitics and the Challenges of Economic Development*. New York: M.E. Sharpe, 2013.
Laruelle, Marlene and Dylan Royce. 'Kazakhstani Public Opinion of the United States and Russia: Testing Variables of (Un)favorability'. *Central Asian Survey*, 38 (2) (2019): 197–216.
Laszczkowski, Mateusz. 'Shrek Meets the President: Magical Authoritarianism in a Fairy-Tale City'. In *Kazakhstan in the Making: Legitimacy, Symbols and Social Changes*, edited by Marlene Laruelle, 63–88. Lanham, MD: Lexington, 2016.
Laszczkowski, Mateusz. *'City of the Future': Built Space, Modernity, and Urban Change in Astana*. New York: Berghahn Books, 2018.
Law of the Republic of Kazakhstan 13 December 1997 No. 204–1 on Population Migration, http://www.refworld.org/docid/3ae6b5740.html, accessed 5 March 2021.
Lewis, David. 'Illiberal Spaces: Uzbekistan's Extraterritorial Security Practices and the Spatial Politics of Contemporary Authoritarianism'. *Nationalities Papers*, 43 (1) (2015): 140–59.
Light, Nathan. 'History, Experience, and Narration: Novel Accounts and Multiplex Stories'. In *History Making in Central and Northern Eurasia: Contemporary Actors and Practices*, edited by Svetlana Jacquesson, 138–62. Wiesbaden: Reichert Verlag, 2016.
Lillis, Joanna. 'Kazakhstan: China Looking to Lease Land for Agricultural Purposes'. *Eurasianet*, 3 February 2010, https://eurasianet.org/kazakhstan-china-looking-to-lease-land-for-agricultural-purposes, accessed 5 March 2021.
Lillis, Joanna. 'Astana Follows Thorny Path toward National Unity'. *Eurasianet*, 29 April 2010, http://www.eurasianet.org/node/60952, accessed 5 March 2021.
Lillis, Joanna. 'Uzbekistan's First Daughter Gulnara Karimova Troubled by "Corruption Links"'. *The Guardian*, 1 November 2013, http://www.theguardian.com/world/2013/nov/01/uzbekistan-first-daughter-gulnara-karimova-troubled, accessed 5 March 2021.
Lillis, Joanna. 'Kazakhstan: Landmark Eurasian Union Treaty Signed Amid Protests and Arrests'. *Eurasianet*, 29 May 2014, http://www.eurasianet.org/node/68416, accessed 5 March 2021.
Liu, Morgan Y. *Under Solomon's Throne: Uzbek Visions of Renewal in Osh*. Pittsburgh, PA: University of Pittsburgh Press, 2012.
Louw, Maria Elisabeth. 'Pursuing "Muslimness": Shrines as Sites for Moralities in the Making in Post-Soviet Bukhara'. *Central Asian Survey*, 25 (3) (2006): 319–39.
Louw, Maria Elisabeth. *Everyday Islam in Post-Soviet Central Asia*. New York: Routledge, 2007.
Luhn, Alec, 'Uzbek President Bans Teaching of Political Science'. *The Guardian*, 5 September 2015, https://www.theguardian.com/world/2015/sep/05/uzbekistan-islam-karimov-bans-political-science, accessed 25 July 2017.
Lupu, Noam and Leonid Peisakhin. 'The Legacy of Political Violence across Generations'. *American Journal of Political Science*, 61 (4) (2017): 836–51.
Lymer, Kenneth. 'Rags and Rock Art: The Landscapes of Holy Site Pilgrimage in the Republic of Kazakhstan'. *World Archaeology*, 36 (1) (2004): 158–72.
Malikov, Yuriy. 'The Kenesary Kasymov Rebellion (1837–1847): A National-Liberation Movement or "a Protest of Restoration"?'. *Nationalities Papers*, 33 (4) (2005): 569–97, https://www.tandfonline.com/doi/abs/10.1080/00905990500354137, accessed 5 March 2021.
Mamashuly, Asylkhan. 'Protivniki soiuza govoriat o roli Nazarbaeva'. *Azattyq*, 22 May 2014, http://rus.azattyq.org/content/antievraziyskiye-slushaniya-v-almaty/25394060.html, accessed 5 March 2021.

Marat, Erica. 'National Ideology and Statebuilding in Kyrgyzstan and Tajikistan'. *Silk Road Papers*. Washington, DC: Central Asia-Caucasus Institute, January 2008, https://www.silkroadstudies.org/resources/pdf/SilkRoadPapers/2008_01_SRP_Marat_National-Ideology.pdf, accessed 5 March 2021.

Marat, Erica. 'Nation Branding in Central Asia: A New Campaign to Present Ideas about the State and the Nation'. *Europe-Asia Studies*, 61 (7) (2009): 1123–36.

Marat, Erica. '"We Disputed Every Word": The Plight of Moderates in Post-Violence Kyrgyzstan'. In *Kyrgyzstan beyond 'Democracy Island' and 'Failing State': Social and Political Changes in a Post-Soviet Society,* edited by Marlene Laruelle and Johan Engvall, 213–30. Lanham, MD: Lexington, 2015.

March, Andrew F. 'The Use and Abuse of History: "National Ideology" as Transcendental Object in Islam Karimov's "Ideology of National Independence"'. *Central Asian Survey*, 21 (4) (2002): 371–84.

March, Andrew F. 'From Leninism to Karimovism: Hegemony, Ideology, and Authoritarian Legitimation'. *Post-Soviet Affairs*, 19 (4) (2003): 307–36.

March, Andrew F. 'State Ideology and the Legitimation of Authoritarianism: The Case of Post-Soviet Uzbekistan'. *Journal of Political Ideologies*, 8 (2) (2003): 209–32.

Markowitz, Lawrence P. *State Erosion: Unlootable Resources and Unruly Elites in Central Asia*. Ithaca, NY: Cornell University Press, 2013.

Markowitz, Lawrence P. 'Explaining Political Order in Uzbekistan'. *Uzbekistan Initiative Papers*, 3 (February 2014), https://centralasiaprogram.org/archives/7843, accessed 25 February 2021.

Martin, Terry. *The Affirmative Action Empire: Nations and Nationalism in the Soviet Union, 1923–1939*. Ithaca, NY: Cornell University Press, 2001.

Masaru, Suda. 'The Politics of Civil Society, *Mahalla* and NGOs: Uzbekistan'. In *Reconstruction and Interaction of Slavic Eurasia and Its Neighboring Worlds*, edited by Ieda Osamu and Uyama Tomohiko, 335–70. Sapporo: Slavic Research Center, 2006.

Ma-Shan, 'Nursultan Nazarbayev, Kazakh "Leader of Nation", Hatches Succession Scheme'. *Daily Telegraph*, 13 May 2010, http://www.telegraph.co.uk/expat/expatnews/7718896/Nursultan-Nazarbayev-Kazakh-leader-of-nation-hatches-succession-scheme.html, accessed 5 March 2021.

Masov, Rakhim. *Tadzhiki: istoriia s grifom 'sovershenno sekretno'*. Dushanbe: Paivand, 1995.

Masov, Rakhim. 'Rol' Rossii v istoricheskikh sud'bakh tadzhikskogo naroda i ego natsional'no-gosudarstvennoi stroitel'stve'. *Nasledie predkov*, 5 (2001).

Masov, Rakhim. 'Turan – eto ne Turkestan'. In *Avesta v istorii i kul'ture Tsentral'noi Azii*, edited by A. Radzhabov. Dushanbe: Akademiia Nauk Respubliki Tadzhikistan, 2001.

Masov, Rakhim. 'Nash obshchii dom v Sodruzhestve Nezavisimykh Gosudarstv'. *Merosi niëgon – Nasledie predkov*, 6 (2003): 7–12.

Masov, Rakhim. *Arii: Istoriia i sovremennost'*. Dushanbe: Sharki Ozod, 2006.

Masov, Rakhim 'Tiurkizatsiia ariitsev: chush' ili nedomyslie? Otvet na stat'iu A. Askarova 'Ariiskaia problema: novye podkhody i vzglyady'. *CentrAsia*, 6 January 2006, https://centrasia.org/newsA.php?st=1136562180, accessed 8 March 2021.

Masov, Rakhim, 'Fal'sifitsirovat' i prisvaivat' chuzhuiu natsitoriiu nel'zia (otvet pantukistam)'. *CentrAsia*, 9 March 2006, https://centrasia.org/newsA.php?st=1136562180, https://centrasia.org/newsA.php?st=1141856700, accessed 8 March 2021.

Matveeva, Anna. 'Legitimizing Central Asian Authoritarianism: Political Manipulation and Symbolic Power'. *Europe-Asia Studies*, 61 (7) (2009): 1095–121.

Mavlonii, Dilbegim. 'V Kazakhstane khotiat prazdnovat' Nauryz v tri raza dolshe, nesmotria na krizis'. *Azattyq*, 12 March 2009, http://rus.azattyq.mobi/a/1508127.html, accessed 5 March 2021.

McCall, Jeremiah. 'Playing with the Past: History and Video Games (and Why it Might Matter)'. *Journal of Geek Studies*, 6 (1) (2019): 29–48.

McGlinchey, Eric M. 'Searching for *Kamalot*: Political Patronage and Youth Politics in Uzbekistan'. *Europe-Asia Studies*, 61 (7) (September 2009): 53–66.

Medeuova, Kulshat (ed.). *Praktiki i mesta pam'iati v Kazakhstane*. Astana: Evraziiskii natsional'nyi universitet im. L.N. Gumileva, 2017.

Megoran, Nick. 'Framing Andijon, Narrating the Nation: Islam Karimov's Account of the Events of 13 May 2005'. *Central Asian Survey*, 27 (1) (2008): 15–31.

Megoran, Nick. 'Shared Space, Divided Space: Narrating Ethnic Histories of Osh'. *Environment and Planning A*, 45 (4) (2013): 892–907.

Megoran, Nick. *Nationalism in Central Asia: A Biography of the Uzbekistan-Kyrgyzstan Boundary*. Pittsburgh, PA: University of Pittsburgh Press, 2017.

Menga, Filippo. 'Building a Nation through a Dam: The Case of Rogun in Tajikistan'. *Nationalities Papers*, 43 (3) (2015): 479–94.

Menzel, Birgit. 'Occult and Esoteric Movements in Russia from the 1960s to the 1980s'. In *The New Age of Russia: Occult and Esoteric Dimensions*, edited by Birgit Menzel, Michael Hagemeister and Bernice Glatzer Rosenthal, 151–85. Munich: Peter Lang, 2012.

Merchant, Tanya. 'Popping Tradition: Performing Maqom and Uzbek 'National' Estrada in the 21st Century'. *Popular Music & Society*, 32 (3) (2009): 371–86.

Mingisheva, Nazgul. 'Cultural Globalization and Youth Identity Construction'. In *The Nazarbayev Generation: Youth in Kazakhstan*, edited by Marlene Laruelle, 167–76. Lanham, MD: Lexington, 2019.

Mogilner, Marina. *Homo Imperii: A History of Physical Anthropology in Russia*. Lincoln, NE: University of Nebraska Press, 2013.

Moine, Nathalie. 'Passeportisation, statistique des migrations et contrôle de l'identité sociale'. *Cahiers du Monde Russe*, 38 (4) (1997): 587–99.

Moroz, Evgenii. 'Ot iudaizma k tengrianstvu: Eshche raz o dukhovnykh poiskakh sovremennykh krymchakov i krymskikh karaitov'. *Narod Knigi v mire knig*, 52 (2004): 1–6.

Morrison, Alexander. *Russian Rule in Samarkand 1868–1910: A Comparison with British India*. Oxford: Oxford University Press, 2008.

Motadel, David. 'Iran and the Aryan Myth'. In *Perceptions of Iran: History, Myths and Nationalism from Medieval Persia to the Islamic Republic*, edited by Ali M. Ansari, 119–45. London: I.B. Tauris, 2014.

Mukanov, T. 'Svetlaia vera rodiny tiurkov. K 100-letiiu restavratsii tengrianskoi very na Altae'. *Rukh-Miras*, 2 (2004): 73–80.

Mukhambetova, Asiia A. 'Tengrianskii kalendar' i vremia kazakhskoi kul'tury'. *Evraziia: Obshchestvenno-politicheskii i literaturno-khudozhestvennyi zhurnal* 2 (2001).

Mukhametchin, Rafiq. 'Les composants islamiques de la politique confessionnelle en république du Tatarstan'. In *Islam et politique en ex-URSS: Russie d'Europe et Asie centrale*, edited by Marlene Laruelle and Sebastién Peyrouse, 41–59. Paris: L'Harmattan, IFEAC, 2005.

Mukhtarov, Akhror and Shavkat Sharipov. *Akademik Bobodzhan Gafurov*. Dushanbe: Irfon, 1983.

Mumidzhanov, Kh. 'Avesta ob etnogeneze tadzhikov'. *Izvestiia Akademii Nauk Respubliki Tadzhikistan, seriia filosofiia i pravovedenie*, 1–2 (2002): 89–97.

Murzakulova, Asel and John Schoeberlein. 'The Invention of Legitimacy: Struggles in Kyrgyzstan to Craft an Effective Nation-State Ideology'. *Europe-Asia Studies*, 61 (7) (2009): 1229–48.

Mustafina, Mira. 'Voenno-patrioticheskie aktsii v den' rozhdeniia Talgata Begel'dinova stanut ezhegodnym'. *Old.Liter.Kz*, 7 August 2015, https://old.liter.kz/ru/articles/show/11283-voenno-patrioticheskie_akcii_v_den_rozhdeniya_talgata_begeldinova_stanut_ezhegodnymi, accessed 5 March 2021.

Nasirova, F. 'Chtrikhi k prarodine ariev (gorizonty molekulyarnoi genetiki cheloveka)'. In *Zoroastrizm i ego znachenie v razvitii tsivilizatsii narodov Blizhnego i Srednego Vostoka*, edited by A. Radzhabov. Dushanbe: Tojikiston, 2003.

National Society of Philosophers of Uzbekistan. *Ideia natsional'noi nezavisimosti: osnovnye poniatiia i printsipy*. Tashkent: Uzbekiston, 2001.

Natsional'nyi Sostav Naseleniia SSSR po Dannym Vsesoiuznoi Perepisi Naseleniia 1989 g. Moscow: Goskomstat SSSR, 1991, http://demoscope.ru/weekly/ssp/sng_nac_89.php, accessed 5 March 2021.

Nazarbayev, Nursultan. *Evraziiskii soiuz: idei, praktika, perspektivy*. Moscow: Fond sodeistviia razvitiiu sotsial'nykh i politicheskikh nauk, 1997.

Nazarbayev, Nursultan. *V potoke istorii*. Almaty: Amatura, 1999.

'Nazarbayev: Kazakhstan mozhet byt' pereimenovan v "Kazakh Eli"'. *Moskovskii komsomolets*, 6 February 2014, http://www.mk.ru/politics/article/2014/02/06/981453–Nazarbayev-kazahstan-mozhet-byit-pereimenovan-v-kazah-eli.html, accessed 5 March 2021.

'Nazarbayev zaiavil o vozmozhnom vykhode Kazakhstana iz Evraziiskogo soiuza'. *Newsru.com*, 31 August 2014, https://www.newsru.com/world/31aug2014/Nazarbayev.html, accessed 5 March 2021.

Nazarbayeva, Dariga. 'Spetsifika i perspektivy politicheskogo razvitiia Kazakhstana'. *Biulleten' Mezhdunarodnogo instituta sovremennoi politiki*, 3 (2003), http://www.iimp.kz/default.aspx?article_id=766, accessed 3 June 2014.

Nazarov, Erden. *Kazakhstan posle....* Almaty: Vektor, 2013.

Negmatov, Nugmon N. *Gosudarstvo samanidov (Mavarannakhr i Khorasan v ix–x vv.)*. Dushanbe: Donish, 1989 [1977].

Negmatov, Nugmon N. *Tadzhiki: Istoricheskii Tadzhikistan, sovremennyi Tadzhikistan*. Gissar: n.p., 1992.

Negmatov, Nugmon N. *Tadzhikskii fenomen: teoriia i istoriia*. Dushanbe: n.p., 1997.

Negmatov, Nugmon N. 'Istoki etnogeneza i kul'turogeneza ariev ariany'. *Narodnaia gazeta*, 24 March 2004.

Nikolayenko, Olena. 'Contextual Effects on Historical Memory: Soviet Nostalgia among Post-Soviet Adolescents'. *Communist and Post-Communist Studies*, 41 (2) (2008): 243–59.

Nikolayenko, Olena. 'Youth Media Consumption and Perceptions of Electoral Integrity in Kazakhstan and Kyrgyzstan'. *Demokratizatsiya*, 23 (3) (Summer 2015): 399–424.

Nikolayenko, Olena. 'Youth Media Consumption and Perceptions of Electoral Integrity in Kazakhstan and Kyrgyzstan'. In *Mass Media in the Post-Soviet World: Market Forces, State Actors, and Political Manipulation in the Informational Environment after Communism*, edited by Peter Rollberg and Marlene Laruelle, 399–424. Stuttgart: Ibidem-Verlag, 2018.

Niyazova, Makhinur. '"Kyrk choro." Raskachat' mezhnatsional'nuiu lodku?'. *24.kg*, 30 January 2015, https://24.kg/obschestvo/6014_kyirk_choro_raskachat_mejnatsionalnuyu_lodku, accessed 3 October 2017.

Nourzhanov, Kirill. 'Nation-Building and Political Islam in Post-Soviet Tajikistan'. In *Nationalism and Identity Construction in Central Asia: Dimensions, Dynamics, and Directions*, edited by Mariya Y. Omelicheva, 71–90. Lanham, MD: Lexington, 2015.

'Novye trebovaniia registratsii protivorechat Konstitutsii i ne reshaiut problem – Dos Koshim'. *365info.kz*, 4 February 2015, http://365info.kz/2015/02/novye-trebovaniya-registracii-protivorechat-konstitucii-i-ne-reshayut-problem-dos-koshim, accessed 5 March 2021.

Nurov, Kanat. *Kazakhstan: natsional'naia ideia i traditsii*. Almaty: Aspandau, 2011.

Ó Beachain, Donnacha and Rob Kevlihan. 'State-Building, Identity and Nationalism in Kazakhstan: Some Preliminary Thoughts'. *Dublin City University Working Papers in International Studies*, 1 (2011): 1–18.

Ó Beacháin, Donnacha and Rob Kevlihan. 'Threading the Needle: Kazakhstan between Civic and Ethno-Nationalist State-Building'. *Nations and Nationalism*, 19 (2) (2013): 337–56.

Ó Beacháin, Donnacha and Robert Kevlihan '"Imagined Democracy"? Nation-Building and Elections in Central Asia'. *Nationalities Papers*, 43 (3) (2015): 495–513.

'O Deklaratsii o Gosudarstvennom Suverenitete Respubliki Kazakhstan: Postanovlenie Verkhovnogo Soveta Kazakhskoi SSR ot 25ogo oktiabria 1990', http://adilet.zan.kz/rus/docs/B900001700_, accessed 5 March 2021.

O'Shea, Moira. 'The Symbolic Landscape of Bishkek: Visual Nationalism and Collective Memory in Public Art'. Paper presented at the American University of Central Asia, Bishkek, 1 November 2017, https://www.auca.kg/en/auca_news/3227/, accessed 29 November 2019.

'O smeshannikh brakakh'. *Beznen-Yul*, 3 (2005), http://beznen-yul.narod.ru/arhiv/2005/3san/smeshan.htm, accessed 3 June 2014.

'O strategicheskom plane Agenstva Respubliki Kazakhstan po sviazi i informatsii na 2014–2018'. *Tengri News*, 6 June 2014, http://tengrinews.kz/zakon/docs?ngr=P1400000621.

'O telekanale', Qazaqstan.tv, http://kaztv.kaztrk.kz/ru/view/channel/page_1221_pervyi-natsionalnyi-telekanal-kazakstan, accessed 18 October 2018.

Oka, Natsuko. 'Nationalities Policy in Kazakhstan: Interviewing Political and Cultural Elites'. In *The Nationalities Question in Post-Soviet Kazakhstan*, edited by Natsuko Oka, 109–45. Chiba: Institute of Developing Economies, 2000.

Oka, Natsuko. 'The "Triadic Nexus" in Kazakhstan: A Comparative Study of Russians, Uighurs, and Koreans'. In *Beyond Sovereignty: From Status Law to Transnational Citizenship?*, edited by Osamu Ieda, 359–80. Sapporo: Slavic Research Center, Hokkaido University, 2006.

Oka, Natsuko. 'Ethnicity and Elections under Authoritarianism: The Case of Kazakhstan'. *IDE Discussion Papers*, 194 (March 2009).

Omelicheva, Mariya. 'Islam in Kazakhstan: A Survey of Trends and Conditions for Securitization'. *Central Asia Survey*, 30 (2) (2011): 243–56.

'Oppozitsionnaia partiia obviniatsia v izbienii muftiia'. *Kommersant*, 23 December 1991, http://www.kommersant.ru/doc/2072, accessed 5 March 2021.

Orange, Mia and Bo Petersson. '"There Can Be No Other Sun in the Sky": Political Myth, Spirituality and Legitimacy in Contemporary Kazakhstan'. In *Contested Memories and the Demands of the*

Past: History Cultures in the Modern Muslim World, edited by Catharina Raudvere, 25–47. Cham: Palgrave Macmillan, 2017.

Ordabayev, Samat. 'Building Eurasian Economic Union on Consensus, Mutual Respect and Benefit'. *The Astana Times*, 20 May 2014, http://www.astanatimes.com/2014/05/building-eurasian-economic-union-consensus-mutual-respect-benefit, accessed 5 March 2021.

Orospakova, Zhyldys. '"Kyrgyz chororolu" – eshche odna peshka v politicheskikh igrakh'. *Radio Azattyk*, 16 February 2015, https://rus.azattyk.org/a/26852140.html, accessed 5 March 2021.

'Oskorbili prezidenta Kazakhstana', *Kommersant*, 14 November 1992, http://www.kommersant.ru/doc/29998, accessed 5 March 2021.

Ospanuly, N. 'Tiurkskaia ontologiia: metafizicheskie osnovaniia tengrianstva'. *Evraziiskoe soobshchestvo*, 1 (1998): 180–6.

Oushakine, Serguei Alex. *The Patriotism of Despair: Nation, War, and Loss in Russia*. Ithaca, NY: Cornell University Press, 2009.

Paskaleva, Elena. 'Ideology in Brick and Tile: Timurid Architecture of the 21st Century'. *Central Asian Survey*, 34 (4) (2015): 418–39.

Pen International. 'Take Action for Aron Atabek'. https://pen-international.org/news/on-world-poetry-day-help-free-imprisoned-kazakh-poet-aron-atabek, accessed 29 August 2020.

Peyrouse, Sebastien. 'Nationhood and the Minority Question in Central Asia: The Russians in Kazakhstan'. *Europe-Asia Studies*, 59 (3) (2007): 481–501.

Peyrouse, Sebastien. 'The Kazakh Neopatrimonial Regime: Balancing Uncertainties among the "Family", Oligarchs, and Technocrats'. In *Kazakhstan in the Making: Legitimacy, Symbols and Social Changes*, edited by Marlene Laruelle, 29–62. Lanham, MD: Lexington, 2016.

P'iankov, I.V. 'Ariana po svidetel'stvam antichnykh avtorov'. *Vostok*, 1 (1995): 35–44.

'Pis'mo 138–mi: vzryvoopasnoe obrashechenie i kto stoit za nim?'. *Altyn-Orda*, 28 October 2011, http://www.altyn-orda.kz/pismo-138–mi-vzryvoopasnoe-obrashhenie-i-kto-stoit-za-nim, accessed 3 June 2014.

Polese, Abel and Slavomir Horák. 'A Tale of Two Presidents: Personality Cult and Symbolic Nation-Building in Turkmenistan'. *Nationalities Papers*, 43 (3) (2015): 457–78.

Poliakov, Leeon. *The Aryan Myth: A History of Racist and Nationalist Ideas in Europe*. New York: Basic Books, 1974.

'Populiarnye onlain tv v kategorii "Kazakhstan"'. *vefire.ru*, https://vefire.ru/category/kazakhstan/, accessed 29 August 2020.

'Poseshchenie Intellektual'noi shkoly goroda Atyrau i vstrecha s predstaviteliami obshchestvennosti oblasti'. *Akorda*, 6 February 2014, http://www.akorda.kz/ru/events/astana_kazakhstan/working_trips/poseshchenie-intellektualnoi-shkoly-goroda-atyrau-i-vstrecha-s-predstavitelyami-obshchestvennosti-oblasti, accessed 5 March 2021.

'Posol'stvo Kazakhstan Obzor kazakhstanskogo rynka a na Ukraine prezentovalo fil'm "V ogon' za rodinu"'. *Tengri News*, 22 October 2014, http://tengrinews.kz/sng/posolstvo-kazahstana-ukraine-prezentovalo-film-v-ogon-rodinu-263890.

'Prezident Uzbekistana raskritikoval televizionnyi '"ura-patriotizm"'. *Regnum.ru*, 2 April 2017, https://regnum.ru/news/2257551.html, accessed 5 March 2021.

'Prigovo molodomu oppozitsioneru Makhambetu Abzhanu ostalsia bez izmenenii'. *Azattyq*, 10 February 2007, http://rus.azattyq.org/a/1180775.html, accessed 5 March 2021.

'Privyz k priverzhentsam etnicheskikh religii ural'skikh narodov'. *Beznen-Yul*, 12 (2002), http://www.beznen-yul.narod.ru/arhiv/2002/12san/prizyv.htm, accessed 3 June 2014.

'Putin poblagodaril Nazarbaeva za vklad v integratsiiu is sozdanie EAES'. *RIA Novosti*, 28 May 2019, https://ria.ru/20190528/1555041235.html, accessed 5 March 2021.

Radio Free Europe. 'Not in Our Name'. *Radio Free Europe/Radio Liberty*, https://pressroom.rferl.org/not-in-our-name, accessed 5 March 2021.

Radnitz, Scott. 'Paranoia with a Purpose: Conspiracy Theory and Political Coalitions in Kyrgyzstan'. *Post-Soviet Affairs*, 32 (5) (2015): 474–89.

Radzhabov, A. (ed.). *Zoroastrizm i ego znachenie v razvitii tsivilizatsii narodov Blizhnego i Srednego Vostoka*. Dushanbe: n.p., 2003.

Rainbow, David (ed.). *Ideologies of Race: Imperial Russia and the Soviet Union in Global Context*. Montréal: McGill-Queens University Press, 2019.

Rakhimov, Mirzokhid. 'Post-Soviet Transformations and the Contemporary History of Uzbekistan'. *Uzbekistan Initiative Papers*, 14 (March 2014), https://centralasiaprogram.org/archives/7863, accessed 25 February 2021.

Rakhmonov, Emo Masov. *Tadzhiki v zerkale istorii*, vol. 1, *Ot ariitsev do samanidov*. London: Flint River, 1999.

Rakhmonov, Emomali P. 'Opening Speech at the Conference for the Samanid State 1100 Years'. *Narodnaia gazeta*, 13 May 1999.

Rakhmonov, Emomali P. 'Tadzhikskaia gosudarstvennost': ot samadinov do rubezha XXI veka'. *Narodnaia gazeta*, 10 September 1999.

Rakhmonov, Emomali P. 'Tysiacha let v odnu zhizn''. *Narodnaia gazeta*, 23 September 1999.

Rakhmonov, Emomali P. 'O gode ariiskoi tsivilizatsii'. *Narodnaia gazeta*, 12 September 2003.

'Rakhmonov velel tadzhikam vspomnit' a svoem ariiskom proiskhozhdenii'. *Lenta*, 9 December 2005, http://www.lenta.ru/news/2005/12/09/rahmonov, accessed 5 March 2021.

Ram, Harsha. 'Imagining Eurasia: Olzhas Suleymenov's *AZ i IA*'. *Slavic Review*, 60 (2) (2001): 289–311.

Rancier, Megan. 'Resurrecting the Nomads: Historical Nostalgia and Modern Nationalism in Contemporary Kazakh Popular Music Videos'. *Popular Music and Society*, 32 (3) (2009): 387–405.

Rasanayagam, Johan. 'The Politics of Culture and the Space for Islam: Soviet and Post-Soviet Imaginaries in Uzbekistan'. *Central Asian Survey*, 33 (1) (2014): 1–14.

Rees, Kristoffer and Aziz Burkhanov. 'Constituting the Kazakhstani Nation: Rhetorical Transformation of National Belonging'. *Nationalism and Ethnic Politics*, 24 (4) (2018): 433–55.

Rees, Kristoffer Michael and Nora Webb Williams. 'Explaining Kazakhstani Identity: Supraethnic Identity, Ethnicity, Language, and Citizenship'. *Nationalities Papers*, 45 (5) (2017): 815–39.

Reeves, Madeleine. 'Migration, Masculinity, and Transformations of Social Space in the Sokh Valley, Uzbekistan'. In *Migration and Social Upheaval as the Face of Globalization in Central Asia*, edited by Marlene Laruelle, 307–32. London: Brill, 2013.

Reeves, Madeleine, Johan Rasanayagam and Judith Beyer (eds). *Ethnographies of the State in Central Asia: Performing Politics*. Bloomington: Indiana University Press, 2014.

Renan, Ernst. 'What is a Nation?'. Lecture delivered at the Sorbonne, 11 March 1882, https://web.archive.org/web/20110827065548/http:/www.cooper.edu/humanities/core/hss3/e_renan.html, accessed 26 August 2020.

Renfrew, Colin. *L'énigme indo-européenne: Archéologie et langage*. Paris: Flammarion, 1990.

Ro'i, Yaacov. 'Central Asian Riots and Disturbances, 1989–1990: Causes and Context'. *Central Asian Survey*, 10 (2) (1991): 21–54.

Ro'i, Yaacov and Alon Wainer. 'Muslim Identity and Islamic Practice in Post-Soviet Central Asia'. *Central Asian Survey*, 28 (3) (2009): 303–22.

Rollberg, Peter. 'Birth of a Nation on Television: *Astana – My Love*'. In *Mass Media in the Post-Soviet World: Market Forces, State Actors, and Political Manipulation in the Informational Environment after Communism*, edited by Peter Rollberg and Marlene Laruelle, 301–23. Stuttgart: Ibidem-Verlag, 2018.

Rollberg, Peter. 'Rascals, Misfits, Patriots: Youth in Kazakhstani Cinema'. In *The Nazarbayev Generation: Youth in Kazakhstan*, edited by Marlene Laruelle, 191–212. Lanham, MD: Lexington, 2019.

Rosenberger, Nancy. 'Patriotic Appetites and Gnawing Hungers: Food and the Paradox of Nation-Building in Uzbekistan'. *Ethnos*, 73 (2) (2007): 339–60.

Rozenas, Arturas and Yuri M. Zhukov. 'Mass Repression and Political Loyalty: Evidence from Stalin's "Terror by Hunger"'. *American Political Science Review*, 113 (2) (2019): 569–83.

Sabol, Stephen. 'The Creation of Central Asia: The 1924 National Delimitation'. *Central Asian Survey*, 14 (2) (1995): 225–41.

Sagatova, Elmira. 'Novaia politicheskaia zvezda Kazakhstana, ili Mal'chik dlia provokatsii Zhanbolat Mamay?'. *CentrAsia*, 19 June 2011, http://www.centrasia.ru/newsA.php?st=1308464520, accessed 18 September 2018.

Samubaldin, S.S. *Drakony i tigry Azii: Smozhet li kazakhstanskii "bars" proidti ikh tropami?* Almaty: Gylym, 1998.

Sarsembayev, Azamat. 'Imagined Communities: Kazakh Nationalism and Kazakhification in the 1990s'. *Central Asian Survey*, 18 (3) (1999): 319–46.

Sarygulov, Dastan. *XXI vek v sud'be kochevnikov*. Bishkek: Fond Tengir-Ordo, 2001.

Sarygulov, Dastan. *Tengrianstvo i global'nye problemy sovremennosti*. Bishkek: Fond Tengir-Ordo, 2002.

Sarygulov, Dastan. *XXI vek: chelovek i obshchestvo*. Bishkek: Fond Tengir-Ordo, 2003.

Sarygulov, Dastan. *Kyrgyzy: proshloe, nastoiashchee i budushchee*. Bishkek: n.p., 2005.
Sarym, Aidos. 'Kazakhstan vybyraet tiurko-evropeiskii vektor'. *Kazakhi Rossii*, n.d., http://kazakh.orgfree.com/index.php?dn=article&to=art&id=230&p=2, accessed 18 September 2018.
Sarym, Aidos. 'Edinym kazakhskim frontom: V prodolzhenii diskussii o natsionalizme'. *MGU Laboratory of the Political and Social Development of Near-Abroad Countries*, 13 July 2013, http://ia-centr.ru/expert/16138, accessed 18 September 2018.
Satpayev, Dossym and Tolganay Umbetaliyeva. 'The Protests in Zhanaozen and the Kazakh Oil Sector: Conflicting Interests in a Rentier State'. *Journal of Eurasian Studies*, 6 (2) (2015): 122–9.
Sattarov, Rafael. 'Is the Uzbek Development Model a Path towards True Modernization?'. *CABAR*, 25 November 2016, http://cabar.asia/en/rafael-sattarov-is-the-uzbek-development-model-a-path-towards-true-modernization/, accessed 26 August 2020.
Sattarov, Rafael. 'Spirituality and Enlightenment: Uzbekistan's State-Sponsored Ideology'. *Central Asia Papers* (July 2017), https://centralasiaprogram.org/archives/11408, accessed 25 February 2021.
Saudanbekova, E. 'Evraziistvo Gumileva i klassicheskoe russkoe evraziistvo'. *Mysl'*, 8 (1997): 30–4.
Saunders, Robert A. 'In Defence of *Kazakshilik*: Kazakhstan's War on Sacha Baron Cohen'. *Identities*, 14 (3) (2007): 225–55.
Scarborough, Isaac. 'From February to February and From Ru ba Ru to Rastokhez: Political Mobilisation in Late Soviet Tajikistan (1989–1990)'. *Cahiers d'Asie centrale*, 26 (2016): 143–71.
Scarborough, Isaac. '(Over)Determining Social Disorder: Tajikistan and the Economic Collapse of Perestroika'. *Central Asian Survey*, 35 (3) (2016): 439–63.
Schatz, Edward. *Modern Clan Politics and Beyond: The Power of "Blood" in Kazakhstan*. Seattle: University of Washington Press, 2004.
Schatz, Edward. 'The Soft Authoritarian Tool Kit: Agenda-Setting Power in Kazakhstan and Kyrgyzstan'. *Comparative Politics*, 41 (2) (January 2009): 203–22.
Schweitzer, Ryan Michael. 'Alphabet Transition in Uzbekistan: Political Implications and Influences on Uzbek Identity'. Central Asia Program, 14 May 2020, https://centralasiaprogram.org/archives/15780, accessed 26 August 2020.
Sedgwick, Mark. *Against the Modern World: Traditionalism and the Secret Intellectual History of the Twentieth Century*. New York: Oxford University Press, 2004.
'Seliger 2014 National Youth Forum', 29 August 2014, http://eng.kremlin.ru/news/22864, accessed 29 August 2020.
Seliverstov, Sergey V. *Kazakhstan, Rossiia, Turtsiia: po stranitsam evraziiskikh idei XIX- vekov*. Almaty: Baspalar uii, 2009.
'Serial o Kazakhskom khanstve snimut v Kazakhstane'. *Tengri News*, 4 November 2014, http://tengrinews.kz/cinema/serial-o-kazahskom-hanstve-snimut-v-kazahstane-264593, accessed 5 March 2021.
'Serial o Kazakhskom khanstve sokrashchen s 20 do 10 serii'. *Nomad*, 23 January 2015, https://nomad.su/?a=14-201501230009, accessed 5 March 2021.
Sériot, Patrick (ed.). *Un paradigme perdu: La linguistique marriste*. Cahiers de l'ILSL, Lausanne: Institut de Linguistique et des Sciences du Langage de l'Universite de Lausanne, 2005.
'Sessiia po etnogenezu Srednei Azii'. *Sovetskaia etnografiia* VI–VII. Moscow: Akademiia Nauk SSSR, 1947.
Shaikhutdinov, M. 'A. Dugin i imperskaia modifikatsiia evraziiskoi idei'. *Evraziiskoe soobshchestvo*, 2 (2002): 26–32.
Shaikhutdinov, M. 'Imperskie proekty geopoliticheskoi identichnosti Rossii'. *Evraziiskoe soobshchestvo*, 2 (2003): 5–14.
Shakhanov, Mukhtar. 'A Report on Commission Proceedings and on Further Clarification of the Circumstances of the December 1986 Events in Alma-Ata'. In *Conflict in the Soviet Union: The Untold Story of the Clashes in Kazakhstan*, edited by Cathy Cosman, Appendix A. New York: Helsinki Watch, 1990.
Shakhmatov, V.F. 'K voprosu ob etnogeneze kazakhskogo naroda'. *Izvestiia Akademii nauk Kazakhskoi SSR*, 6 (1950): 78–89.
Shaniiazov, Karim Sh. *Kanf davlati va kanglilar*. Tashkent: FAN, 1990.
Shaniiazov, Karim Sh. 'Üzbek halkining etnogeseziga oid ba'zi nazarij masalalar". *Obshchestvennye nauki v Uzbekistane*, 6 (1998).
Shaniiazov, Karim Sh. *Üzbek halkining šakllaniš žaraëni*. Tashkent: Shark, 2001.

Sharipova, Dina. 'Youth and Civic National Identity'. In *The Nazarbayev Generation: Youth in Kazakhstan*, edited by Marlene Laruelle, 69–88. Lanham, MD: Lexington, 2019.

Sharipova, Dina, Aziz Burkhanov and Alma Alpeissova. 'The Determinants of Civic and Ethnic Nationalisms in Kazakhstan: Evidence from the Grass-Roots Level'. *Nationalism and Ethnic Politics*, 23 (2) (2017): 203–26.

Shaukenova, Zarema K. (ed.). *Sotsial'naia aktivnost' molodezhi Kazakhstana v sovremennykh sotsial'no-politicheskikh realiakh*. Almaty: Ministerstvo obrazovaniia i nauki, 2014.

Shchuplov, Aleksandr. 'Olzhas Suleimenov: "Kazhdyi poet sozdaet svoi globus"'. *Rossiiskaia gazeta* 233, 22 September 2005, http://www.rg.ru/2005/09/22/suleymenov.html, accessed 5 March 2021.

Sheiko, Konstantin and Stephen Brown. *Nationalist Imaginings on the Russian Past: Anatolii Fomenko and the Rise of Alternative History in Post-Communist Russia*. Stuttgart: Ibidem Verlag, 2009.

Shin, Boram. 'Inventing a National Writer: The Soviet Celebration of 1948 Alisher Navoi Jubilee and Rewriting of Uzbek History'. *International Journal of Asian Studies*, 14 (2) (July 2017): 117–42.

Shirinov, T. Sh., A.A. Anarbaev and Yu. F. Buriakov. 'Arkheologicheskie issledovaniia v ANRU'. *Obshchestvennye nauki v Uzbekistane*, 8 (1993): 57.

Shnirelman, Viktor A. 'Zlokliucheniia odnoi nauki: etnogeneticheskie issledovaniia i stalinskaia natsional'naia politika'. *Etnograficheskoe obozrenie*, 3 (1993): 52–68.

Shnirelman, Viktor A. *Who Gets the Past? Competition for Ancestors among Non-Russian Intellectuals in Russia*. Washington, DC: Woodrow Wilson Center Press and Johns Hopkins University Press, 1996.

Shnirelman, Viktor A. 'Ot konfessional'nogo k etnicheskomu: bulgarskaia ideia v natsional'nom samosoznanii kazanskikh tatar v XX veke'. *Vestnik Evrazii*, 1–2 (1999): 137–59.

Shnirelman, Viktor A. 'Nazad k iazychestvu? Triumfal'noe shestvie neoiazychestva po prostoram Evrazii'. In *Neoiazychestvo na prostorakh Evrazii*, edited by Viktor A. Shnirelman, 162–4. Moscow: Bibleisko-bogoslovskii Institut, 2001.

Shnirelman, Viktor A. 'Aryans or Proto-Turks? Contested Ancestors in Contemporary Central Asia'. *Nationalities Papers*, 37 (5) (2009): 557–87.

Shozimov, Pulat D. *Tadzhikskaia identichnost' i gosudarstvennoe stroitel'stvo v Tadzhikistane*. Dushanbe: Irfon, 2003.

Shuraev, Arman. '90 protsentov otechestvennykh serialov nel'zia pokazyvat". *meta.kz*, 2 March 2012, quoted in Ileulova, 'Obzor kazakhstanskogo rynka teleindustrii'.

Sidikov and Kjuka, 'Karimov: Uzbek Migrants Are "Lazy" "Beggars" "Don't Exist"'. *RFE/RL*, 26 June 2013, https://www.rferl.org/a/uzbekistan-karimov-beggars-migrants-remittances/25028531.html, accessed 5 March 2021.

Skalnik, Peter. 'Towards an Understanding of Soviet Etnos Theory'. *South African Journal of Ethnology*, 9 (4) (1986): 157–66.

Skalnik, Peter. 'N. Ia. Marr and the National Origins of Soviet Ethnogenetics'. *Slavic Review*, 55 (4) (1996): 826–62.

'Skol'ko liudei 'sidiat' v sotssetiakh v Kazakhstane'. *Tengri News*, 8 February 2016, https://tengrinews.kz/internet/skolko-lyudey-sidyat-v-sotssetyah-v-kazahstane-288639, accessed 5 March 2021.

Slezkine, Yuri. 'The USSR as a Communal Apartment, or How a Socialist State Promoted Ethnic Particularism'. *Slavic Review*, 53 (2) (1994): 414–52.

Smagulova, Juldyz. 'Language Policies of Kazakhization and Their Influence on Language Attitudes and Use'. *International Journal of Bilingual Education and Bilingualism*, 11 (3–4) (2008): 440–75.

Smith, Anthony. *National Identity*. London: Penguin, 1991.

Smith, Anthony. *Nations and Nationalism in a Global Era*. Cambridge: Polity Press, 1995.

'Smotret' vsem! Zulmat. Zulmat. Genotsid v. Kazakhstane. Asharshylyk turaly derekti fil'm!', YouTube video, 1:25:35, uploaded by 'Demokratiialy Kazakstan \ Demokraticheskii Kazakhstan', 30 January 2019, https://www.youtube.com/watch?v=-QZdrtPVOuU&t=45s, accessed 29 August 2020.

Solomon, Susan Gross. *Health and Society in Revolutionary Russia*. Bloomington: Indiana University Press, 1990.

Spechler, Dina Rome and Martin C. Spechler. 'The Foreign Policy of Uzbekistan: Sources, Objectives and Outcomes: 1991–2009'. *Central Asian Survey*, 29 (2) (2010): 159–70.

Spechler, Martin C. *The Political Economy of Reform in Central Asia: Uzbekistan under Authoritarianism*. London: Routledge, 2008.

Spehr, Scott and Nargis Kassenova. 'Kazakhstan: Constructing Identity in a Post-Soviet Society'. *Asian Ethnicity*, 13 (2) (2012): 135–51.

Stalin, *Le Marxisme et la question nationale et colonial*. Moscow: Editions sociales, 1949 [1913].

Statistical Agency of the Republic of Kazakhstan. 'Natsional'nyi sostav, veroispovedanie i vladeniia yazykami v Respublike Kazakhstan—itogi Natsional'noi perepisi naseleniia 2009 goda v Respubliki Kazakhstan'. 2010, https://web.archive.org/web/20180809112751/http://stat.gov.kz/getImg?id=WC16200032705, accessed 18 September 2018.

Statistical Agency of the Republic of Kazakhstan. *Itogi Natsional'noi perepisi naseleniia Respubliki Kazakhstan 2009 goda: Analiticheskii otchet*. Astana: n.p., 2011, 24, https://web.archive.org/web/20180814232734/http://stat.gov.kz/getImg?id=WC16200032648, accessed 18 September 2018.

Statistical Agency of the Republic of Kazakhstan. 'Chislennost' uchashhikhsia obshheobrazovatel'nykh shol po yazykam obucheniia, tysiach chelovek'. 2018, https://web.archive.org/web/20180503223048/http://stat.gov.kz/getImg?id=ESTAT094527, accessed 19 March 2019.

Stephens, Holly DeNio. 'The occult in Russia today'. In *The Occult in Russian and Soviet Culture*, edited by Bernice Glatzer Rosenthal, 357–76. Ithaca, NY: Cornell University Press, 1997.

Suleimenov, Olzhas. *Az i Ya*. Alma-Ata: Zhazushy, 1975.

Suleimenova, Eleonora D. 'Iazykovaia politika i russkii iazyk v shkolakh Kazakhstana'. *Vestnik TsMO MGU*, 1 (2010): 102–7.

Suny, Ronald G. *Intellectuals and the Articulation of the Nation*. Ann Arbor, MI: University of Michigan Press, 1999.

Suny, Ronald G. 'Provisional Stabilities: The Politics of Identities in Post-Soviet Eurasia'. *International Security*, 24 (3) (1999–2000): 139–78.

Suny, Ronald G. 'Constructing Primordialism: Old Histories for New Nations'. *Journal of Modern History*, 73 (4) (2001): 862–96.

Suny, Ronald G. and Terry Martin (eds). *A State of Nations: Empire and Nation-Making in the Age of Lenin and Stalin*. Oxford: Oxford University Press, 2001.

'Survey Timetable'. *Asian Barometer*, 2005, http://www.asianbarometer.org/survey/survey-timetable, accessed 29 August 2020.

Suyarkulova, Mohira. 'Becoming Sovereign in Post-Soviet Central Asia: "Discursive Encounters" between Tajikistan and Uzbekistan'. PhD thesis, University of St. Andrews, 2011.

Svanberg, Ingvar. 'Kazakhs'. In *The Nationalities Question in the Soviet Union*, edited by Graham Smith, 318–30. London: Longman, 1990.

Tadzhiev, Habibulla. *Teoreticheskie i metodologicheskie voprosy natsional'noi ideologii*. Tashkent: Uzbekiston, 1999.

'Talgat Tadzhuddin: "Russian Muslims already have their Caliphate: It's called Holy Russia"'. *Islam Review*, 11 November 2015.

Tashenov, Bolebai. *Evraziistvo v etnokul'turnoi istorii Kazakhstana*. Almaty: Arys, 2000.

Tchoroev, Tyntchtykbek. 'Historiography of Post-Soviet Kyrgyzstan'. *International Journal of Middle East Studies*, 34 (2) (2002): 351–74.

'Televizionnyi rynok Kazakhstana'. *tvmedia.kz*, 2014, http://www.tvmedia.kz/tv, accessed 18 September 2018.

The Echo of Central Asia. 'The Naked Truth about Censorship in Uzbekistan'. *Global Voices*, 10 April 2016, https://globalvoices.org/2016/04/10/the-naked-truth-about-censorship-in-uzbekistan/, accessed 25 July 2017.

'The Strategy for Development of the Republic of Kazakhstan until the Year 2030'. *Akorda.kz*, 1997, https://www.akorda.kz/en/official_documents/strategies_and_programs, accessed 5 March 2021.

Thibault, Helene. *Transforming Tajikistan: State-Building and Islam in Post-Soviet Central Asia*. London: I.B. Tauris, 2018.

Tillet, Lowell. *The Great Friendship: Soviet Historians on the Non-Russian Nationalities*. Chapel Hill, NC: University of North Carolina Press, 1969.

Tishkov, Valery. 'The Phenomenon of Ethnicity in Russian Context'. n.d., http://www.valerytishkov.ru/cntnt/publikacii3/knigi/the_mind_a1/the_phenom.html, accessed 26 August 2020.

Tishkov, Valerii. *Rekviem po etnosu: Issledovaniia po sotsial'no-kul'turnoi antropologii*. Moscow: Nauka, 2003.

Tolen, Zhengisbek, Slushash Tulenova, Elnura Assyltaeva and Nurken Aitymbetov. 'Formation of Civil and Patriotic Education of Youth in Kazakhstan'. *Procedia: Social and Behavioral Sciences*, 116 (2014): 4859–63.

Tolipov, Farkhod. 'Tsentral'naia Azia – eto piat' "stanov': Polemika s kazakhskimi evraziitsami'. *Tsentral'naia Azia i Kavkaz*, 44 (2) (2006): 18–29.

Tolipov, Farkhod. 'Flexibility or Strategic Confusion? Foreign Policy of Uzbekistan'. *Uzbekistan Initiative Papers*, 2 (February 2014), https://centralasiaprogram.org/archives/7841, accessed 25 February 2021.

Tolstov, Sergei P. *Drevnii Khorezm*. Moscow: MGU, 1948.

Tolstov, Sergei P., R.N. Nabiev, Ia. G. Guliamov and V.A. Shishkin (eds). *Istoriia uzbekskoi SSR*, vol. 1, book 1. Tashkent: Akademiia nauk, 1956.

Tolz, Vera. *Russia's Own Orient: The Politics of Identity and Oriental Studies in the Late Imperial and Early Soviet Periods*. Oxford: Oxford University Press, 2011.

'Tri milliarda tenge vydeliat na prazdnovanie 550–letiia Kazakhskogo khansta i 20–letiia ANK'. *Tengri News*, 19 November 2014, http://tengrinews.kz/kazakhstan_news/milliarda-tenge-vyidelyat-prazdnovanie-550–letiya-kazahskogo-hanstva-20–letiya-265489, accessed 5 March 2021.

'Tri seriala k 550–letiiu Kazakhskom khanstve snimut v Kazakhstane'. *Times.kz*, 16 February 2015, http://timeskz.kz/6219–tri-seriala-k-550–letiyu-kazahskogo-hanstva-snimayut-v-kazahstane.html, accessed 18 September 2018.

Tsay, Alexandra. 'Contemporary Art as a Public Forum'. In *The Nazarbayev Generation: Youth in Kazakhstan*, edited by Marlene Laruelle, 269–87. Lanham, MD: Lexington, 2019.

'Tsifrovaia Tsentral'naia Aziia. Chast' pervaia: dostup k internetu'. Central Asian Analytical Network, 3 June 2018, https://caa-network.org/archives/12646, accessed 3 September 2020.

Tsyryapkina, Yulia. 'Evolution of the Russian Language in the Tashkent Region's Urban Spaces'. *Uzbekistan Initiative Papers*, 19 (October 2014), https://centralasiaprogram.org/wp-content/uploads/2015/05/UI-papers-19-Yulia-Tsyryapkina.pdf, accessed 25 February 2021.

'Ukaz "O dal'neishei sovershenstvovanii sistemy gosudarstvennogo upravleniia respubliki Kazakhstan"'. 7 March 2014, https://online.zakon.kz/Document/?doc_id=1050588, accessed 3 September 2020.

'Ukaz Prezidenta Respubliki Kazakhstan: O Gosudarstvennoi programme razvitiia i funktsionirovaniia iazykov v Respublike Kazakhstan na 2011–2020 gody'. *Online Zakon*, 2011, https://online.zakon.kz/document/?doc_id=31024348, accessed 29 August 2020.

Umbetaliyeva, Tolganay, Botagoz Rakisheva and Peer Teschendorf. *Youth in Central Asia: Kazakhstan*. Almaty: Friedrich Ebert Foundation Kazakhstan, 2016, https://library.fes.de/pdf-files/bueros/kasachstan/13343.pdf, accessed 29 August 2020.

'Umer Aldan Aimbetov'. *Zonakz.net*, 21 April 2006, http://zonakz.net/articles/15338, accessed 5 March 2021.

Umetbayeva, Damira. 'Official Rhetoric and Individual Perceptions of the Soviet Past: Implications for Nation Building in Kyrgyzstan'. *Central Asian Affairs*, 2 (3) (2015): 287–306.

UN Development Program. *Status of Oralmans in Kazakhstan: Overview*. Almaty: UNDP, 2006.

UNESCO. 'Global Flow of Tertiary-Level Students'. http://uis.unesco.org/en/uis-student-flow, accessed 21 February 2019.

Urinboyev, Rustamjon. 'Law, Social Norms and Welfare as Means of Public Administration: Case Study of Mahalla Institutions in Uzbekistan'. *NISPAcee Journal of Public Administration and Policy*, 4 (1) (2011): 33–57.

Urinboyev, Rustamjon. 'Smartphone Transnationalism in Non-Western Migration Regimes: Transnational Ethnography of Uzbek Migrant Workers in Russia'. In *Labour, Mobility and Informal Practices in Russia, Central Asia and Eastern Europe*, edited by Rano Turaeva and Rustamjon Urinboyev, 89–113. London: Routledge, 2021.

U.S. Commission on International Religious Freedom. 'Annual Report 2014: 15th Anniversary Retrospective: Renewing the Commitment'. 2014, https://www.uscirf.gov/sites/default/files/USCIRF%202014%20Annual%20Report%20PDF.pdf, accessed 29 August 2020.

'V Kazakhstane otmechaiut den' pamiati zhertv politicheskikh repressii'. *Tengri News*, 31 May 2014, https://tengrinews.kz/kazakhstan_news/kazahstane-otmechayut-den-pamyati-jertv-politicheskih-256238, accessed 5 March 2021.

'V Kazakhstane protivniki sozdaniia soiuza s Rossiei nadeli meditsinskie maski'. *Uralskweek.kz*, 29 May 2014, http://www.uralskweek.kz/2014/05/29/v-kazaxstane-protivniki-sozdaniya-soyuza-s-rossiej-nadevayut-medicinskie-maski, accessed 5 March 2021.

'V Kazakhstane sniat ria istoricheskikh fil'mov'. *Kaztag.kz*, 25 September 2013, https://kaztag.kz/ru/news/v-kazakhstane-snyat-ryad-istoricheskikh-filmov, accessed 18 September 2018.

'V Kyrgyzstane zavershili rabotu nad akademicheskim izdaniem eposa Manasa, kotoroe dlilos' 20 let'. *Kabar.kg*, 28 August 2014, http://www.kabar.kg/rus/science-and-culture/full/81700, accessed 5 March 2021.

'V Oshe namechaetsia provedenie respublikanskogo kurultaia natsional'no-patrioticheskikh sil'. *AkiPress*, 13 April 2007, http://fergana.akipress.org/news:23167, accessed 5 March 2021.

'V RK rassleduiut delo po faktu razzhiganiia mezhnatsional'noi rozni'. *Zakon.kz*, 21 May 2014, http://www.zakon.kz/4625687–v-rk-rassledujut-delo-po-faktu.html, accessed 18 September 2018.

Valerio, Anita. 'Meet Generation Z: Forget Everything You Learned About Millennials'. SlideShare, 6 January 2015, https://fr.slideshare.net/aniuxbombiux/meet-generation-z-forget-everything-you-learned-about-millennials, accessed 29 August 2020.

Van der Nienke, Heide. *Spirited Performance: The Manas Epic and Society in Kyrgyzstan*. Amsterdam: Rozenberg, 2008.

Vasil'eva, G.P. *Etnograficheskie dannye o proiskhozhdenii turkmenskogo naroda*. Moscow: Nauka, 1964.

Verkhovskii, Aleksandr, Galina Kozhevnikova and Anton Shekhovtsov (eds). *Radikal'nyi russkii natsionalizm: struktury, idei, litsa*. Moscow: SOVA-Center, 2009.

Vinokurov, Evgeni. 'Eurasian Economic Union: Current State and Preliminary Results'. *Russian Journal of Economics*, 3 (1) (2017): 54–70.

Vklad iranskikh narodov v razvitie mirovoi tsivilizatsii: Istoriia i sovremennost'. Dushanbe: Donish, 2002.

Volkov, Volkov, Nigora Bukhari-zade and Yuri Chernogaev. 'Storony "ariiskoi" medali'. *Nemetskaia volna*, 8 January 2005, http://www.materik.ru/print.php?section=analitics&bulsectionid=13049, accessed 18 September 2018.

Vrevskii, Aleksandr V. 'Otkrytie Kruzhka,' in *Protokoly Kruzhka liubitelei arkheologii Turkestana* (Tashkent), 11 December 1895, 2.

Vsesoiuznoe soveshchanie po etnogenezu turkmenskogo naroda: Tezisy dokladov i nauchnykh soobshchenii. Ashkhabad: Akademiia nauk Turkmenskoi SSR, 1967.

Walker, Shaun. 'Gulnara Karimova Speaks Out over Infighting in Uzbekistan's First Family'. *The Guardian*, 20 December 2013, http://www.theguardian.com/world/2013/dec/20/gulnara-karimova-uzbekistan-first-family, accessed 5 March 2021.

Weitz, Richard. 'Kazakhstan's National Development Strategies: An Assessment'. *Central Asia Policy Brief*, 14 (December 2013), https://centralasiaprogram.org/archives/7518, accessed 8 March 2021.

Weitz, Richard. 'Uzbekistan's National Security Strategy: Threat and Response'. *Uzbekistan Initiative Papers*, 12 (March 2014), https://centralasiaprogram.org/archives/7858, accessed 25 February 2021.

Weller, R. Charles. *Rethinking Kazakh and Central Asian Nationhood: A Challenge to Prevailing Western Views*. Newton, MA: Asia Research Associates, 2006.

Wilkinson, Cai. 'Imagining Kyrgyzstan's Nationhood and Statehood: Reactions to the 2010 Osh Violence'. *Nationalities Papers*, 43 (3) (2015): 417–36.

Witte, Michelle. 'Proposed Changes to Oralman Legislation to Relax Some Settlement Rules'. *Astana Times*, 28 July 2014, http://www.astanatimes.com/2014/07/proposed-changes-oralman-legislation-relax-settlement-rules, accessed 5 March 2021.

Wolfel, Richard L. 'North to Astana: Nationalistic Motives for the Movement of the Kazakh(stani) Capital'. *Nationalities Papers*, 30 (3) (2002): 485–506.

World Values Survey. 'WVS-7 in Kazakhstan: Working Meeting with the WVSA Secretariat'. World Values Survey, 6 June 2018, https://www.worldvaluessurvey.org/WVSNewsShow.jsp?ID=370, accessed 29 August 2020.

Young, George M. *The Russian Cosmists: The Esoteric Futurism of Nikolai Fedorov and His Followers*. Oxford: Oxford University Press, 2012.

Yuritsyn, Vladislav. 'Ezhenedel'nik "Ashyq Alan" ("Tribuna") – novoe nezavisimoe izdanie'. *Zonakz.net*, 10 September 2012, http://zonakz.net/articles/54339?mode=reply, accessed 5 March 2021.

'Za 25 let v Kazakhstan pribylo bolee 957 tysiach oralmanov'. *Zakon.kz*, 9 February 2016, https://www.zakon.kz/4773927–za-25–let-v-kazakhstan-pribylo-bolee.html, accessed 6 October 2019.

'Zakon Respubliki Kazakhstan ot 23ogo iulia 1999 goda no. 451–1: O sredstvakh massovoi informatsii'. *Online.zakon.kz*, http://online.zakon.kz/Document/?doc_id=1013966, accessed 29 August 2020.

Zhabayeva, Sholpan. 'Itogi oprosa: socsetiami pol'zuiutsia 70 per cent kazakhstantsev'. *Informburo*, 21 April 2017, https://informburo.kz/novosti/itogi-oprosa-socsetyami-polzuyutsya-70–kazahstancev.html, accessed 6 October 2019.

Zhakupov, Zhumabay. *Shala Kazakh: Proshloe, nastoiashchee, budushchee*. Almaty: Aspandau, 2008.

'Zhanbolat Mamay Released from Arrest'. *Open Dialogue Foundation*, 13 July 2012, http://en.odfoundation.eu/a/793,zhanbolat-mamay-released-from-arrest, accessed 5 March 2021.

'Zharylkap Kalybay: Propaganda Gitlera ne bylo, vy khotia by prochitaite!'. *Tengri News*, 21 April 2014, https://tengrinews.kz/tv/novosti/obschestvo/1533, accessed 5 March 2021.

'Zharylkap Kaylbay: ia ne opravdyvaiu fashizm / 1612', YouTube video, 5:38, uploaded by 'Informatisionnyi kanal "16/12"', 9 July 2014, https://www.youtube.com/watch?v=S0nCEOddlZQ, accessed 29 August 2020.

Zhumaev, Rustam Z. *Politicheskaia sistema Respubliki Uzbekistan: stanovlenie i razvitie*. Tashkent: Akademia nauk RU, 1996.

Zhussipbek, Galym and Zhanar Nagayeva. '"Cognitive Unconscious", "Modern Conservatism", and "Core Liberal Values" in the Context of Youth's National Identity'. In *The Nazarbayev Generation: Youth in Kazakhstan*, edited by Marlene Laruelle, 133–52. Lanham, MD: Lexington, 2019.

'Znaete, kakim on parnem byl? V Kazakhstane vyshel zhurnal posviashchennyi 125–letiiu Adolfa Gitlera'. *Russiankz.info*, 18 April 2014, http://russianskz.info/economy/5568-znaete-kakim-on-parnem-byl-v-kazahstane-vyshel-zhurnal-posvyaschennyy-125-letiyu-adolfa-gitlera.html, accessed 5 March 2021.

Zuijderduijn. '"Traitors of the Tajik Nation": The Regime's Framing and Persecution of the Islamic Opposition'. BA thesis, Leiden University, 2016, https://openaccess.leidenuniv.nl/handle/1887/41328, accessed 26 August 2020.

Index

www.ingramcontent.com/pod-product-compliance
Lightning Source LLC
LaVergne TN
LVHW010731020926
846742LV00029B/40
* 9 7 8 1 8 0 0 0 8 0 1 4 0 *